COLLISION COURSE

COLLISION COURSE

Carlos Ghosn and the Culture Wars

That Upended an Auto Empire

HANS GREIMEL

WILLIAM SPOSATO

HARVARD BUSINESS REVIEW PRESS

BOSTON, MASSACHUSETTS

Copyright 2021 Hans Greimel and William Sposato
All rights reserved
Printed in the United States of America

10 9 8 7 6 5 4 3 2 1

No part of this publication may be reproduced, stored in or introduced into a retrieval system, or transmitted, in any form, or by any means (electronic, mechanical, photocopying, recording, or otherwise), without the prior permission of the publisher. Requests for permission should be directed to permissions@harvardbusiness.org, or mailed to Permissions, Harvard Business School Publishing, 60 Harvard Way, Boston, Massachusetts 02163.

The web addresses referenced in this book were live and correct at the time of the book's publication but may be subject to change.

Editorial production by Christine Marra, *Marra*thon Production Services. www.marrathoneditorial.org

Library of Congress Cataloging-in-Publication Data
Names: Greimel, Hans, author. | Sposato, William, author.
Title: Collision course : Carlos Ghosn and the culture wars that upended an auto empire / Hans
    Greimel and William Sposato.
Description: Boston, MA : Harvard Business Review Press, [2021] | Includes index. |
Identifiers: LCCN 2021009356 (print) | LCCN 2021009357 (ebook) | ISBN 9781647820473 (hardcover)
    | ISBN 9781647820480 (ebook)
Subjects: LCSH: Ghosn, Carlos, 1954– | Nissan Jidōsha Kabushiki Kaisha. | Régie nationale des
    usines Renault. | Mitsubishi Jidōsha Enjiniaringu Kabushiki Kaisha. | Strategic alliances
    (Business)—Japan. | Chief executive officers—Japan. | Automobile industry and trade—Japan. |
    Automobile industry and trade—Corrupt practices—Japan. | Commercial crimes—Japan.
Classification: LCC HD9710.J32 G74 2021 (print) | LCC HD9710.J32 (ebook) |
    DDC 338.7/6292220952—dc23
LC record available at https://lccn.loc.gov/2021009356
LC ebook record available at https://lccn.loc.gov/2021009357

ISBN: 978-1-64782-047-3
eISBN: 978-1-64782-048-0

The paper used in this publication meets the requirements of the American National Standard for Permanence of Paper for Publications and Documents in Libraries and Archives Z39.48-1992.

To my daughters, Nozomi and Miyuki,

who inspire, motivate, and make life worth living.

—Hans Greimel

To my mother and father for their commitment that made my career

in journalism possible, and to my wife, Pei-chi Tung, for all her support

and endless patience throughout the writing of this book.

—William Sposato

CONTENTS

PREFACE

Like many of life's most interesting partnerships, ours was something of a chance event. Even as we individually covered the events surrounding Carlos Ghosn and Nissan through its many dramatic moments and implausible twists, neither of us was thinking of writing a book.

Helping drive us forward was the good fortune of being ringside witnesses for many of the story strands weaving this saga together. Based in Tokyo, we have a combined forty years of journalism experience in Japan.

Hans is a veteran automotive reporter, Detroit-bred and deeply immersed in the Japanese car business for nearly fifteen years. He had direct access to Carlos Ghosn during the writing of this book. Many of the quotes from Ghosn in the book come from those conversations and from interviews and other interactions Hans had with Ghosn for more than a decade as part of his reporting for *Automotive News*, the news source of record for the global car industry. William has spent two-plus decades reporting and writing about Japan Inc., its economy and financial markets, while also integrating a deep understanding of Japan's complex, two-century history of opening up to the West and how it impacts the country even today.

From the machinations of the corporate executives to the behind-the-scenes intrigue of government officials who can, in reality, ill-afford to see their national brands wither away, we have talked with the key players involved in the Nissan-Renault story, at every level. We spoke to more than fifty auto executives, business leaders, policy makers, legal experts, academics, and other sources, both foreign and Japanese. This came on top of the daily reporting we did for spot news of the scandal since the night it erupted, November 19, 2018. Some of these people have requested to be quoted on background to protect themselves and we have honored that. To everyone who took the time to speak with us, we are most grateful.

Through those conversations, it became clear that there is one truth most agree on: Carlos Ghosn didn't just leave an indelible mark on the Renault-Nissan-Mitsubishi Alliance that he helped create and then ruled over for nearly two decades. He left a lasting impact on the industry and on Japan. He is arguably one of the most influential foreigners ever to set foot in this country.

His transformation of Nissan remade the auto industry and ripples throughout global economies to this day. He pioneered a new kind of globalized business for an era in which companies from different nations and radically different business cultures might dare to work as a team toward a shared vision, while somehow preserving their own identities, even as they scale to massive size—in the Alliance's case into the largest auto group in the world.

Yet, Ghosn's scandal cast a harsh spotlight on Japanese corporate governance, the judicial system, and even its jails. From this may come change, as often happens in a country always concerned about its international image. It also raised questions about the role of government as a shareholder and string-puller in the world of private industry. In the end, the upheaval upended Ghosn's once-sterling legacy as an innovative business leader and left observers asking if his vision for a truly transnational Franco-Japanese auto alliance was a model for future industry consolidation, or if it was just a fleeting mirage.

And then there was the bombshell question the world was left asking: Did the man long lauded as a global management guru improperly hide his own compensation and siphon funds from the company he was lionized for saving? Ghosn (like his co-defendant, former Nissan director Greg Kelly) denies any wrongdoing. But Ghosn's legacy will always bear the stain of that suspicion—after being indicted four times in Japan and drummed out of the industry.

In tackling this subject, the challenge for us was not what to include, but what could be left out. The various stories span two decades, three continents, several countries, and dozens of key players. Many aspects were complex, convoluted, and sometimes unimaginable, if not outright bizarre. One of the world's most celebrated and esteemed auto executives is arrested with no prior signs to the world that any potential misconduct had been afoot. He is thrown in jail for 130 days and at first denied access to lawyers and family in a justice system that in many ways is antithetical to Western norms. Then, after pledging to clear his name in court, the famed executive packs himself into a trunk and is smuggled out of the country by a team of operatives led by a former Green Beret. He then resumes his life in Lebanon as an international fugitive. Even today, we find the entire odyssey almost impossible to believe.

There is a misleadingly simple narrative in the Ghosn story, centered on good guys, bad guys, individual greed, and a made-for-Hollywood getaway. Our approach, and a primary motivation to take on a book, was to offer an account that chronicles a more complex tale with more nuanced characters, not to mention ramifications that will continue for years. At stake in the Alliance and its future are hundreds of thousands of jobs on five continents—from car dealers in India to factory workers in Tennessee to design engineers in the Paris suburbs, plus thousands more at suppliers and business partners around the world.

Beyond explaining the extraordinary and fast-changing maneuverings, we also wanted to place the events in a broader cultural, political, and historical perspective and to try to answer the many questions that these events have raised. Is Japan's judicial system unjust? Was Ghosn a victim of that system or a schemer who ran afoul of the law in virtue of his own avarice and ego? Can big companies with their own national identities truly work together? Is nationalism supplanting globalism? How can the auto industry adapt to an onslaught of change? These are just some of the threads that we have tried to pull together.

It was US author and literary agent John Butman who initially gave us the idea to become partners, and then provided steady encouragement to cajole two journalists into writing something longer than a thousand words, something that would stand the test of time rather than just recount a day's or a week's events. John saw that the Ghosn story was one that went beyond the sensational headlines. He saw something that would captivate people beyond the narrow universes of the auto industry and corporate Japan. And he saw in our pairing that putting together an auto geek and policy wonk could yield something neither of us could do on our own, and we are grateful for all of that.

Sadly, John passed away, suddenly, before he could see the finished product. But his spirit and his inspiration can be found in our pages.

Most of all we want *Collision Course* to be a compelling read. What we uncovered in our reporting was in turns enlightening, surprising, amusing, and disturbing. We hope the book inspires many conversations among its readers, not just about Carlos Ghosn and his legacy, but about the ideals of justice, the future of the auto industry, and the role of government in international business.

—Hans Greimel and William Sposato
Tokyo, Japan
April 2021

COLLISION
COURSE

1

GHOSN SHOCK

AS NISSAN'S CORPORATE JET BEGAN ITS DESCENT INTO Tokyo, Carlos Ghosn buckled up, brought his comfy bucket seat out of its recline, and maybe stretched his arms and legs as he peered out the oval window at the metropolis sprawling to the horizon below him.

Even though the plane had a rear cabin where he liked to slumber on long-haul flights like this one from Beirut, he often complained about that ever-present foe, jet lag.

"There is no medicine, there is no trick. I've tried everything. Nothing works," he once confided about the strain of constantly crisscrossing the world's time zones. "The first day, no matter what, there is a moment where you are not very clear."[1]

• • •

Indeed, red-eye and all, this trip to Japan started like any other for Ghosn, then still the storied and sterling chairman of the Renault-Nissan-Mitsubishi automotive empire known as the Alliance. It was a journey Ghosn had made countless times before in the nineteen years since he first landed in Japan back in 1999 to revive a then near-bankrupt Nissan Motor Co. that had become a national embarrassment to the Asian economic power.

Platinum prestige frequent-flier miles come with the territory for any CEO. But globe-trotting Ghosn took it to a whole new level. He routinely leapfrogged from the suburbs of Tokyo and Paris, where the partners were headquartered, to all points in between as, over the course of nearly two decades as one of the car industry's most visible and admired leaders, he built the Franco-Japanese Alliance into the rare shining example of an international car consortium that actually worked.

His three-way partnership—an audacious gambit in its ambition, scope, and cross-cultural sensitivity—seemed to *thrive*, even as countless other attempted tie-ups—Daimler-Chrysler, VW-Suzuki, Ford-Mazda—littered a graveyard of broken unions.

Ghosn's march of progress was remarkable. The former tire executive from Michelin had been with Renault as its No. 2 executive for less than four years when the French automaker sent him to rescue Nissan as part of its $5.4 billion bailout of the troubled Japanese carmaker. Ghosn parachuted in as the chief operating officer of Japan's No. 2 automaker at the age of just forty-five. Yet, by 2000 he was promoted to president, and in 2001 he was CEO. In the process, he became a celebrity executive feted for his voodoo-like conjuring of the Japanese zombie carmaker back to life.

The French company gambled big in taking a controlling stake in foundering Nissan. But Renault was so impressed with Ghosn's handiwork in rebuilding Nissan—today known for its popular Altima sedan, Rogue crossover, and GT-R sports car—that it made him its own CEO in 2005. That gave Ghosn unprecedented sway over two global companies on two continents. He was the first person to serve simultaneously as CEO of two *Fortune* 500 companies—and not just any companies, but a team of preeminent carmakers that were standard-bearers for the industrial might of France and Japan, two of the world's leading economic heavyweights. It was a juggling act attempted by only the brashest of business titans.

In some ways, Ghosn himself was the epitome of the global economy. He wielded fluent command of four languages—English, French, Portuguese, and Arabic—and he carried passports from three countries—France, Brazil, and Lebanon. Later in life, he had residences in no less than four—including pads in Paris, Beirut, Rio de Janeiro's beachside Copacabana district, and a luxurious apartment in a Tokyo high-rise with a stunning skyline view.[2] Born in Brazil in 1954 to a family with Lebanese roots, he moved to Lebanon at the age of six. Later, it was on to France to complete his education and launch the career that would first make him famous. Then infamous.

As the head of Renault and Nissan, Ghosn methodically knitted the companies closer together. And he was always on the lookout to add new ones to their sphere of influence. Tie-ups with Germany's Daimler AG, the maker of Mercedes-Benz luxury cars, and with Russia's biggest automaker AvtoVAZ extended the Alliance's reach. And a crowning deal in 2016 gave the Alliance control of Mitsubishi Motors Corp., purveyor of the Pajero SUV, and with it, world-beating scale and bragging rights as Earth's biggest auto group.

What's more, Ghosn seemed to make it happen through finesse, not force. The Alliance was a new kind of corporate cooperation. For sure, it was held together by Renault's commanding 43.4 percent stake in Nissan. But the partnership was not a full merger, and Ghosn carefully managed it that way, as a slow integration that tried to respect Nissan's independence. Nissan held only a 15 percent stake in Renault, as the company initially in need of a bailout. But it was often given an outsize voice despite its smaller holding.

There were, at times, strained relations between anchor partners Nissan and Renault. But Ghosn was keenly aware that bonding them through a merger was playing with fire. As partners, they pooled their scale to leverage cheaper prices when buying everything from shock absorbers to brake pads, and they pooled their know-how in engineering engines, transmissions, and the mechanical guts of the cars that customers didn't see. But each company kept its own styling, marketing, brand name, and perhaps most important—its own executive suite. It was a delicate balance, to be sure. Messing with the equation could have broad ramifications.

But somehow, Ghosn pulled it off.

In not only saving Nissan from bankruptcy but building it into a profitable global innovator, Ghosn became a kind of adopted folk hero in Japan—where even regular people knew him as "Ghosn-san." Fans would stop him for autographs, and with his flared nose, dark hair, and arched eyebrows, he always stood out in the homogenous host country. It was joked that he looked like Mr. Bean. But there was no mistaking Ghosn—who was invariably attired in fine Italian wool, not dowdy English tweed.

Ghosn looked and acted every part the charismatic global CEO in a country where "salaryman" business leaders came from a humdrum cookie cutter. Ghosn was direct, fast-talking, energetic, and animated. He had little time for small talk and ran his daily schedule by the minute, as precisely as Japan's perfectly punctual bullet trains. In public discourse, he sometimes bumbled his usually articulate English—which was spoken in a thick French accent. But he wielded an innate gift of communication that still left listeners believing they nonetheless understood every word, no matter how broken. Ghosn was quick with an answer to any question, and never shirked the hard ones. His style was firing back streams of facts and figures, from memory, at a Gatling gun gait.

Ghosn became one of the highest-profile and most sought-after executives in the auto industry—nay, the world of international business—with observers likening him to such legends as Alfred Sloan, the luminary who cobbled together the brands of the early General Motors, or Lee Iacocca, the American comeback artist who saved Chrysler from oblivion in the 1980s and became a household name. Commensurate with that alpha dog persona, Ghosn was also one of the highest-paid executives in Japan, shattering the nation's remuneration norms despite its cultural discomfort with supersize salaries.

By now, it was late 2018, and Ghosn was riding high and gearing up for his final grand act as the Alliance's visionary founder. Thanks to his coup in adding Mitsubishi to the group in 2016, Ghosn had put himself at the pinnacle of the industry. His Alliance ballooned to become the world's top seller of light vehicles in 2017, moving 10.6 million units—nearly one of every eight vehicles sold globally.[3] It pipped German giant Volkswagen AG and left Japanese archrival Toyota Motor Corp. back in No. 3. By combining Nissan with global partners through a strength-in-numbers strategy, he transformed a company on death watch into a world leader.

Basking in this triumph, Ghosn had just signed a new four-year contract to continue leading Renault, and by extension, its entire orbit of affiliated companies. But the new mandate came with strings attached: His mission was to somehow make his Alliance "irreversible." That was Renault's flash-point term for cementing the three companies into a permanent partnership that wouldn't splinter when Ghosn finally left the scene. What exactly that meant to each partner was a matter of interpretation. The French side seemed to think it meant a holding company that guaranteed individual corporate identities. For the Japanese, it seemed like a code word for full takeover. But Ghosn was confident he could soothe any showdown—just as he had been doing for nearly two decades.

Ghosn was already sixty-four, an age at which most CEOs are already lounging at the beach house or hitting the links. He still sported his tailored attire, but his increasingly creased face belied his years, despite his immaculately coiffed, jet-black hair—rumored to keep its youthful sheen through a regime of regular coloring. He was also stepping back into a more big-picture, strategic role. Trips to Tokyo were rarer now. Befitting his revered stature as an automotive icon, Ghosn oversaw Renault, Nissan, and Mitsubishi as chairman of all three, and held the reins as CEO at Renault, to boot. But Nissan had its own CEO, Hiroto Saikawa, a man hand-picked by Ghosn as his most trusted deputy to handle day-to-day operations there.

A far bigger task weighed on Ghosn's mind. He had just three more years to permanently weld the companies together, under his "irreversible" mandate. To some, especially on the French side, this would be the Alliance's grand finale. But in Japan, there was more than a little trepidation about potentially losing autonomy through a full merger. Still, if he could pull it off, he could seal his reputation as one of the industry's greatest leaders and drive off into a golden sunset of retirement in 2022. Ghosn extended the four-year contract with Renault against his better judgment, and reportedly against the wishes of his family, but he couldn't resist completing this last chapter.

. . .

This time, his Gulfstream G650 touched down at Tokyo's Haneda International Airport just as the dim November sun was descending to the horizon. The plane's custom registration number—a black N155AN emblazoned on the tail engine—left little doubt about who was on board. It was a not-so-subtle nod to the Nissan nobility the jet shuttled around the globe.

Among the events on Ghosn's agenda for this visit was a soiree to celebrate his Alliance. Hosted by the governor of Tokyo, it was to unfold at the Mitsubishi Kaitokaku, a mammoth, century-old European-style villa built by an early industrialist in central Tokyo. It was typical of the galas where Chairman Ghosn was used to being celebrated as the center of attention. And separately on the agenda: thorny high-level discussions about the holding company Ghosn envisioned as binding the companies together, on which he hoped to have a decision as soon as the spring.

After Ghosn deboarded late afternoon on November 19, he snaked through Haneda airport's arrival halls as he had done so many trips before. But this time, when he reached the brightly lit Japanese immigration control where tidy agents take every visitor's fingerprints and photo, the routine visit suddenly deviated into a bewildering odyssey.

When the unsuspecting über-executive handed over his credentials, as Ghosn describes it, the officious border agent did a double take at his papers.

"We have a problem with your passport. Can we move please to another room to discuss something?" the man asked ominously. Ghosn agreed, and waiting for him there was an official from the Tokyo Public Prosecutors Special Investigation Unit—a hard-boiled squad of elite lawmen normally tasked with cracking organized crime and political corruption.

"Mr. Ghosn, I'm from the prosecutor's office. We'd like to talk to you," the man said. Ghosn protested that he was a little busy, but the officer wasn't taking no for an answer. "No, no, no, you have to come with us," the investigator insisted.

And thus, before the renowned executive had even cleared immigration, Ghosn was taken into custody and whisked away for interrogation.

By the end of the night, he was locked in a cell at the monolithic Tokyo Detention House in the Kosuge neighborhood, near the banks of the Arakawa River in an old northern quarter of the capital city.

Ghosn never saw it coming. They took away his mobile phone, and he wasn't even allowed to call his daughter Maya, then waiting for him at his corporate apartment in downtown Tokyo. Maya, one of his four adult children, including two other daughters and a son, would later say that first word of her father's arrest came courtesy of Twitter.

Prosecutors wouldn't immediately tell Ghosn precisely why he was being detained, he later said. Instead, the line of questioning went, "Why do you think you are being arrested?"

The dumbfounded Ghosn had no answer.

"I didn't even understand what was going on," Ghosn recounted in an interview. "You don't know if it's something serious or if it's a mistake. You don't know the reason for which you are arrested. I thought I had landed in North Korea, not in Japan."

Ghosn's "one phone call" was finally afforded him the next day.

After the shell-shocked Ghosn weathered his first night in jail, he was asked whom he would like to contact for an attorney. He instructed prosecutors to reach out to Nissan executive Hitoshi Kawaguchi. It seemed a natural choice.

As the carmaker's senior vice president for government relations, Kawaguchi had connections in the highest echelons of Japanese politics. What Ghosn didn't know was Kawaguchi also had been cooperating, for months, with prosecutors in the very probe that culminated in the previous night's takedown. Kawaguchi was in on the sting.

. . .

Word of Ghosn's arrest dropped like a bomb on Japan around dinnertime on November 19. And someone else in on the bust was the Asahi Shimbun Co., publisher of one of Japan's biggest broadsheet dailies. It had a digital reporter onsite at Haneda to chronicle the lurid affair. Its video footage shows the executive jet taxiing across the tarmac. Then, it cuts to a scene of dark-suited prosecutors marching aboard its lowered airstair. As the team rummages around, the plane's window shades are lowered to shield the proceedings from prying eyes. It became the searing symbolic snapshot of Ghosn's zero hour.

Nissan's global headquarters in Yokohama—just a twenty-minute drive from the scene of the snare—entered crisis mode as the headlines electrified and stupefied the nation. As the news flashes lit up smartphones, many assumed there must have been some kind of media mix-up. Surely, these headlines could not be correct. Carlos Ghosn? Arrested?

But Nissan, the company he saved from the scrap heap nearly two decades earlier, wasted no time in confirming the bizarre truth. Ghosn was indeed in custody, and Saikawa himself would be holding an emergency press conference later that night to explain why.

The media swarmed Nissan's gleaming high-rise HQ near the Yokohama waterfront long before Nissan even sent out invitations to the 10 P.M. news briefing there. The line of journalists vying for a seat streamed over the causeway suspended across the carmaker's airy showroom, down a concourse, and nearly out the front doors of the building. Hundreds crammed into the standing-room-only eighth-floor briefing room when a dour-looking Saikawa entered and TV cameras began broadcasting live nationwide.

Saikawa, then sixty-four, was an impassive Nissan lifer with a close-cropped brush cut and deliberate, deadpan demeanor. He had been one of Ghosn's trusted aides since Day One and Ghosn's go-to man during the Nissan revival. Back then, he had been entrusted to break up the company's cozy old-boy network of interlaced suppliers while hard-balling them to lower prices on parts and components. Ghosn himself had tapped Saikawa as co-CEO in October 2016, when engineering Nissan's controlling stake in Mitsubishi. In appointing Saikawa, he said, "There is no difference between what I think and what he thinks." Saikawa was even known inside the company as one of the "Ghosn Children" for his close ties to the boss.

Now, Saikawa was getting harsh and emotional as he stared down the Japanese and international press. Sometimes stumbling for the right words, he blasted his onetime mentor as being a "mastermind" of serious financial misconduct during his time at the helm.

Ghosn, Saikawa said, underreported his income in official financial filings, and the board of directors would vote later in the week to dismiss him as chairman. Saikawa also announced that Greg Kelly, an American director on the Nissan board, had been arrested the same evening and was charged as Ghosn's alleged accomplice in the scheme. Kelly, despite awaiting treatment for a serious neck ailment in the United States, says he was lured to Japan by a bogus request to attend an urgent high-level meeting. He landed the same afternoon at Tokyo's other international airport, and the two execs were nabbed in near simultaneous swoops.

Saikawa said Ghosn was able to carry out and conceal the misdeed for nearly a decade because he had concentrated so much power in himself as an unchallenged, unchecked overlord. "This is a negative impact of the long regime of Mr. Ghosn," he declared.

"This is an act that cannot be tolerated," Saikawa insisted. "It's very difficult for me to express it in words. Beyond being sorry, I feel big disappointment and frustration, despair and indignation or resentment." Saikawa professed that the arrest of his boss would not affect Nissan's longstanding partnership with Renault. But he also raised eyebrows by signaling it opened the door for change: "This is a good opportunity to revise the way we work."

. . .

Ghosn's arrest was nothing less than mind-boggling—almost akin to hearing that an icon like Iacocca or General Electric's Jack Welch had just been picked up by the police, let alone locked up in jail. Or, at least it was mind-boggling to everyone except a small cadre of Nissan insiders who had secretly been working with prosecutors for months.

In fact, the whole affair was so stunning, Japanese media quickly coined a special name for it: "Ghosn Shock." The tagline echoed an initial "Ghosn Shock" that the innovative executive triggered when he landed in Japan and began disrupting conventional business practices to bring the then-moribund Nissan back from the brink of bankruptcy.

But the term was also a partial nod to the local shorthand for the Great Recession. In Japanese, it is known as "Lehman Shock" because the global financial crisis was triggered partly by the 2008 Chapter 11 filing of Wall Street heavyweight Lehman Brothers. The investment bank's bankruptcy is still the largest in US history. Ghosn Shock didn't precipitate a global economic collapse. But in many ways, it hit the Alliance just as hard. All because the group's leader was suddenly cut out of the equation.

By lopping off the head of the Alliance, Ghosn's arrest immediately torpedoed share prices at Nissan and Renault. Nissan's stock dropped about 5 percent the following day. A year later, it had plunged 27 percent, and by early March 2020 had lost nearly half its value. Renault shed nearly 8 percent in the coming days and eventually tumbled by two-thirds. Sales and profits at both companies, and then Mitsubishi, soon imploded in turn. By early 2020, as the Alliance strained without its leader, all three automakers were booking losses.

Indeed, Ghosn Shock unleashed waves of chaos that ricocheted throughout the global auto industry and the halls of justice in Japan. At stake was not only the fate of the automakers and the hundreds of thousands of people who rely on the group for their work. Ghosn's arrest also spurred questions about Japan Inc.'s reputation for ethical management and fueled scrutiny of Japan's judicial system as fair and balanced.

Long simmering tensions broke to the surface, and like a cue ball cracking a racked billiard table, the Ghosn Shock triggered myriad collisions.

Collisions between companies, between people, legal systems, old and new technologies. More broadly there were collisions of culture, of nations, and the question of the internationalization of regional economies. The French and Japanese governments, each eager to protect "its companies," found themselves trying to manage a growing crisis. Indeed, as gradually became clear, it was a crisis partly of their own making, as government bureaucracies in Paris and Tokyo jousted over the direction of the Alliance.

Executives at Renault were completely blindsided. So were officials in the French government, which looked on with especial apprehension at the tumult that now engulfed Renault, an automaker founded in 1898 and a cornerstone of French industry. The French state had a 15 percent stake in Renault with near double voting rights, giving it iron-clad control of the French automaker—and by extension, over Nissan. Renault has a 43.4 percent stake in Nissan. But Nissan, under the Alliance agreement, has only a 15 percent stake in Renault with no voting rights.

Ghosn's arrest exposed conflict that long seethed under the surface of an Alliance that leaders had long painted as the perfect picture of cross-cultural cooperation. The friction point in this nonmerger merger was the matter of which company really had control, and what would happen under Ghosn's new marching orders to make the tie-up "irreversible."

Nissan was Renault's crown jewel. Over the years, the Japanese company that once teetered on the edge of bankruptcy grew to exceed its erstwhile white knight in sales and profits. It blossomed into a rich cash cow that routinely pumped up the balance sheet at government-backed Renault with healthy injections of regular dividends.

Saving the partnership with Nissan meant nothing less than saving jobs at Renault. And for a French state then under siege by weeks of populist "yellow vest" street protests against low pay and inequality, preserving employment was a top priority. President Emmanuel Macron pledged to be "extremely vigilant" about Alliance stability.

But even as executives on both sides publicly reaffirmed their commitment to the Alliance, distrust bubbled behind the scenes. Not privy to the details of Nissan's probe or evidence supporting the charges against Ghosn, the Renault side was loath to turn its back so quickly on its longtime leader. "This was an attack on Renault," recalled one Alliance executive. "People were like, 'He's our guy, and we didn't even know why.'"

To plenty, it all smelled rotten. Nissan described Ghosn's arrest as a stone-cold criminal case. But others said it smacked more of a backstabbing plot from *Game of Thrones*.

French headlines spelled it out: "Is the Ghosn affair a coup d'état fomented by Nissan?"; "Carlos Ghosn in prison: scandal or conspiracy?"[4]

The *Wall Street Journal* editorial board was soon dubbing the whole saga the "Ghosn Inquisition." "Communist China? No, capitalist Japan," the business daily protested. "The publicly available facts are murky, but the episode ought to trouble anyone concerned with due process and corporate governance in Japan."

Murky indeed. Nissan said Ghosn's arrest had its origins in a company whistle-blower who discovered financial irregularities. An internal probe was launched in late spring 2018. A small group that included the company auditor, a whistle-blower, and Kawaguchi began digging through financial records and untangling paper trails. They eventually worked with prosecutors, who set the trap for Ghosn and his accused accomplice Kelly.

It wasn't far-fetched, among the conspiracy-minded, to suppose Nissan had even engineered the takedown to stop Ghosn from completing his plan to integrate the companies and finish the final chapter of the Alliance. At Nissan's late-night news conference, just hours after Ghosn's arrest, one Japanese journalist asked Saikawa point-blank: Was this not a boardroom coup? "That is not how we see it," Saikawa flatly replied.

But Saikawa himself was among those most skeptical of plans to bring the companies closer. Ghosn's preferred solution—combining them under a holding company—was nothing short of a full merger, he believed. That would be the end of a strong, independent Nissan. Before the arrest, Saikawa and Ghosn sparred over this behind closed doors, amid speculation Ghosn planned to replace Saikawa over the dispute.

After Ghosn's arrest, relations between Nissan and Renault turned icy. Alliance communications that normally happen through face-to-face meetings, phone calls, or video links were rerouted through corporate lawyers in writing. Squabbling erupted over Nissan's internal investigation and its findings, over the appointment of new board members to replace Ghosn and Kelly, and over Nissan's new initiative to totally overhaul corporate governance to improve transparency and accountability. It seemed like the Alliance was on the same path to breakup followed by the litany of multinational partnerships that came before it.

Nissan moved swiftly to oust Ghosn. The board dismissed him as chairman three days after his arrest, and Mitsubishi followed the next week. Renault, however, appointed Ghosn deputy Thierry Bolloré as interim CEO, almost half-hoping Ghosn might return to work.

. . .

But Ghosn only continued to languish in the Tokyo jailhouse, without bail. By early January, he was indicted on three counts. Slowly, a picture of the charges came into focus. The first two counts alleged he violated Japanese financial laws by failing to report more than $80 million in deferred income between the 2010 and 2017 fiscal years, from April 1, 2010, through March 31, 2018, that was supposedly owed him after retirement. Nissan, as a corporate entity, was also indicted on the charges, for the alleged improper financial filings. So was Kelly, as Ghosn's alleged enabler.

A third charge in late December alleged breach of trust in the misappropriation of a separate sum of millions of dollars in Nissan funds for Ghosn's personal use by channeling that money to cover an investment loss of his during the Great Recession.

If Ghosn's two-month legal odyssey of being hit with successive charges and kept in solitary confinement without bail seemed drawn out and draconian, that was by design.

It is part of the Japanese playbook for anyone who runs afoul of the law, and it largely clashes with Western ways, especially in relation to white-collar criminals. The country's powerful prosecutors can keep suspects, without formally charging them, under a system that allows for their "rearrest" under different but tangential allegations.

In Japan, prosecutors can, with approval by a judge, lock away suspects for up to twenty-three days without formal charges. And during this lockup, suspects can be submitted to hours of daily interrogations in the absence of their defense attorneys. The arrangement has the added benefit, for prosecutors that is, of allowing investigators to pressure confessions from jailed suspects just desperate to get out. It also buys prosecutors time to fish for new evidence that can allow them to "rearrest" the suspect, and thereby start the cycle all over again.

Such legal devices, seemingly at odds with Western notions of civil liberties, form the foundation of the Japanese justice system's much-quoted 99 percent conviction rate. Americans and Europeans might wonder whether this foolproof sentencing machine is rigged. To Japanese, however, it is a source of pride and credited as the bedrock of the country's extremely low crime rates, violent or otherwise. In a country where arrest all but ensures time behind bars, critics say innocent until proven guilty is mostly a theoretical ideal.

Indeed, with restricted access to lawyers, Ghosn struggled to even answer the charges publicly. His first full-throated defense came when, during a brief administrative court appearance, he personally protested his innocence and read judges a point-by-point defense. After more than a month in lockup, his famously black hair was showing its gray roots and his face had gone gaunt, courtesy of a Spartan jail diet heavy in rice, pickled vegetables, and miso soup. The ousted chairman was in handcuffs, wearing a dark suit with no tie and green plastic slippers.

As Ghosn's case made international headlines, it cast a glaring spotlight on these vagaries of Japan's legal system. His struggle came to symbolize the clash between Japanese and Western justice, and it forced Japan's government into the embarrassing position of having to defend its legal system on the global stage. To Ghosn's supporters, he had now become a potent lightning rod for human rights advocacy in Japan. And the upheaval even emboldened voices inside Japan to speak up for legal reform.

The international face-off culminated in a stinging rebuke of Japan's approach to justice and jailing when a working group of the United Nations Human Rights Council called Ghosn the victim of an "arbitrary" arrest that denied him the right to a fair trial.

Japan, the body argued, owed Ghosn compensation or other reparations.[5]

. . .

On January 24, 2019, two months after Ghosn's first arrest, the fallen titan was forced to resign from Renault.

But that hardly resolved tensions between Nissan and Renault, amid mounting speculation among industry observers that the duo was headed for a breakup. Resentment rose on both sides. Many at Nissan, long tired of its second-class status, wanted more say in Alliance affairs, given its bigger size and profits. Yet rebalancing the stakes was a nonstarter for many at Renault. To them, Renault's grip was a matter of shareholder's rights. And Renault was master of Nissan through its 43.4 percent stake;

that was that. The old guard at Renault headquarters in the Paris suburb of Boulogne-Billancourt were loath to let the junior partner start dictating terms.

The acrimony and recriminations would mount throughout 2019 and reach a crescendo when Renault's new management again launched a bid to make the Alliance "irreversible." Tensions escalated when Renault was rebuffed and attempted a stunning end-run around Nissan to merge instead with Fiat Chrysler Automobiles (FCA), the Italian-American automotive giant. Renault's abrupt cold shoulder to Nissan and sudden courting of FCA gave many industry watchers, in Japan and around the world, whiplash. They began asking whether Renault and Nissan could ever salvage the nineteen-year Alliance, which once-upon-a-time seemed to pioneer a whole new approach to partnerships.

Indeed, the chaos called into question the very basis of Ghosn's legacy: that it was possible to partner two companies with vastly different corporate cultures—or even national identities—and induce them to cooperate through mutual respect and shared goals. That all seemed like so much happy talk now, an illusion that Ghosn had masterfully projected.

Was Ghosn's quest for ever-bigger scale really the answer to the pressures facing the global auto industry? And what is government's role in industry in an age of globalization? France's holding in Renault no doubt complicated relations with Nissan. But the Japanese government had its own long history of protecting its national champions. Japan's powerful Ministry of Economy, Trade, and Industry (METI) wasn't custodian of a government stake in Nissan, but as became clear, it had Nissan's back when times got tough.

In retrospect, Ghosn took a dim view of all the government intervention, on both sides.

"The largest automotive group has been practically dismantled because of the interference from political entities," he said in an interview for this book. "There is absolutely no doubt that you had Japanese government interference from one side and French government interference on the other side. Now, everybody's going to say the other guy started it. But without any doubt, they are ultimately responsible for the demise of the companies."

Even the initial charges against Ghosn laid bare a collision of international norms about executive pay. In Japan and France, CEOs are expected to accept salaries that are modest by US standards. But as an international high-flier who had his pick of any job, Ghosn played by a different set of calculations and expected higher scale for his skills.

For years, Ghosn's salary—extravagant by Japanese and French measures, at least—was a flash point at Nissan shareholders' meetings. The company spent considerable time and resources trying to deflect criticism by justifying the payouts as the price to pay for retaining his talent. Ghosn was also wary of attracting unwanted attention to his handsome remuneration in France, another country where more modest salaries are the norm and where the government, as a top shareholder, kept tight reins on executive compensation. Prosecutors, however, said he went too far when he illegally hid about half of his Nissan payout from public view in a scheme to compensate him after retirement.

Why? To spare himself the embarrassing scrutiny of pulling down such unseemly sums—and the possibility he might be fired because of it.

. . .

As 2019 dragged on, Ghosn's legal woes would only worsen, with a fourth charge against him, another breach of trust allegation—and the most serious allegation yet.

All combined, he faced up to fifteen years in prison, if convicted.

By now the showdown came increasingly under an international spotlight. With the deck stacked against him in Japan, Ghosn's wife, Carole, emerged as a chief crusader trying to win the court of international public opinion. She and her husband's high-powered legal team, replete with a former French ambassador and human rights lawyer, petitioned the United Nations to censure Japan's legal system and even pressured US president Donald Trump and other world leaders to champion Ghosn's cause at international summits. Ghosn's 130 days in jail before bail was Exhibit A in their litany of alleged abuses.

As his Alliance languished without him, Ghosn seemed bent on beating the rap and restoring his reputation in a Japanese court of law.

Ghosn even had a detailed narrative for how he was framed: He was no crook. Instead, he had been set up by a group of treacherous Japanese executives at Nissan and government bureaucrats in Tokyo who wanted to block a merger with Renault by taking out the plan's chief architect. His enemies were trying to protect Nissan's independence and their own jobs, colluding with Japanese prosecutors in a corporate conspiracy of epic proportions.

Nissan and prosecutors saw things differently. To them, Ghosn had been the unchecked epicenter of power so long that he had blurred the boundaries between company coffers and his personal pocketbook. His stunning fall from grace was directly triggered by his own misdeeds and entirely separate from any strategic differences between Renault and Nissan.

These battle lines hardened as both sides hunkered down to prepare for what promised to be one of the biggest, mostly closely scrutinized corporate trials in Japanese history. In late 2019, Ghosn was out on bail, living in a government-approved home in Tokyo, and—by all accounts—laser-focused on preparing with his lawyers for the fight of his life. After rescuing Nissan, he would now try to rescue himself. Expectations spiraled.

But then, the wily strategist shocked the world again. With a trial date pending, Ghosn brazenly jumped bail in Japan and fled to his ancestral homeland of Lebanon, aided by a team of operatives led by a former Green Beret. The thrilling dark-of-night escape involved secretly racing halfway across Japan, packing the then sixty-five-year-old captain of industry into an oversized audio equipment case and smuggling him through lax airport security.

Ghosn left behind a record-setting bail payment of ¥1.5 billion ($13.7 million).

Yet to Ghosn, the price was worth it. He was now essentially a free man, sheltering in a country that has no extradition treaty with Japan and which is loath to deport its own. Suddenly, it was unclear whether he would ever answer the charges in court. To his accusers, Ghosn's escape was nothing short of proof he was guilty all along. But he had a different explanation for not entrusting his fate to a Japanese judge.

"I have not fled justice—I have escaped injustice and political persecution," he said in a statement released on New Year's Eve 2019, after landing in Beirut. "I am now in Lebanon and will no longer be held hostage by a rigged Japanese justice system where guilt is presumed, discrimination is rampant, and basic human rights are denied."

Once an iconic international businessman, he was now an iconic international fugitive.

Looking back on the day of his arrest, Ghosn later conceded in an interview from Lebanon that he never imagined the wild ride ahead—for him, his family, or the auto empire he built. When the guard closed the cell door behind him that very first night, he felt the same as the rest of the world.

"You're shocked. You're not angry. You're just shocked," Ghosn said. "It doesn't just sound like a Kafka novel. It is a Kafka novel."

2

───

ROCK STAR CEO

THE FIRST TIME GHOSN LANDED IN JAPAN, TO FIX Nissan, was way back in May 1999. Within two months, a mostly hand-picked crew of thirty executives from Renault arrived, diagnosing the patient and preparing to prescribe some hard medicine.

On October 18, 1999, two days before the Tokyo Motor Show, a crowd gathered in the grand ballroom of the capital city's Royal Park Hotel. Anxiety was running high; Ghosn was about to outline the long-awaited—and, in some corners, especially among longtime Nissan managers, long dreaded—Nissan Revival Plan that his team had just spent the last three months preparing.

Most expected fireworks from a man who earned the nickname "Le Cost Cutter" for his ruthless efficiency in slashing overhead, and jobs, first at Michelin, then at Renault. Now, as Renault's fix-it man for Nissan, Ghosn held court in Tokyo, rattling off the failings of his Japanese predecessors at the country's flailing No. 2 carmaker—a blue chip company that traced its roots to the 1910s and whose very name is a contraction of the Japanese characters for "Japan" and "industry."

Ghosn was characteristically blunt and incisive. Nissan lacked profit orientation, it lacked customer focus, it lacked cross-functional work, it lacked a sense of urgency, and most critically, it lacked a shared vision for a long-term plan. Global market share had been in continuous decline, shrinking from 6.6 percent in 1991 to 4.9 percent in 1999. Production had plummeted by 600,000 vehicles a year in the period. The company's factories in Japan had the capacity to make 2.4 million vehicles a year, yet they were churning out a mere 1.28 million. Nissan had racked up losses in seven of the past eight fiscal years, including the one Ghosn just parachuted into.[1]

"The key facts and figures about Nissan point to a reality: Nissan is in bad shape," he said.

Throughout the harangue, one man sat impassively off to the side: Yoshikazu Hanawa, the Nissan president who had the ignoble distinction of being the man that sold the company to foreigners. Hanawa was nominally Ghosn's boss—and twenty years Ghosn's elder, which meant a lot in seniority-obsessed Japan. But it was clear to everyone who ran Nissan now.

The tension and contrasts were stunning, noted Richard Johnson, a former managing editor of *Automotive News* who attended the event. "During a question-and-answer session, Hanawa mostly deferred to his 'subordinate.' If there is no greater torment in Japanese culture than loss of face, then Hanawa must have been in excruciating pain," Johnson wrote at the time.

"Hanawa paled next to the astonishing Mr. Ghosn, whose performance that day is how we will remember the 1999 Tokyo auto show," Johnson's account continued. "Ghosn exuded energy and self-confidence. Hanawa appeared shamed and ready to quit."[2]

Onlookers didn't give Renault good odds for turning around Nissan, despite its $5.4 billion cash injection for an initial 36.8 percent stake in Nissan, which would increase over time.

In *Shift: Inside Nissan's Historical Revival*, his own 2005 memoir of the audacious rescue, Ghosn recalls that fellow industry bigwig Bob Lutz, who by then had cycled through executive positions at General Motors, BMW, Ford, and Chrysler, pooh-poohed the craziness of wasting money on Nissan. Lutz compared Renault's gambit to parking "$5 billion in a containership and sinking it in the middle of the ocean."[3] Ghosn also admits giving himself just a 50-50 chance of success at the time. But publicly, he said he would quit if he couldn't pull it off.

. . .

Nissan's problems were part of a wider miasma afflicting the entire nation. After decades of record-breaking growth that followed World War II, it had appeared that Japan was unstoppable. It wasn't. In 1990, what was later dubbed the "Bubble Economy" burst with almost no warning. By 1999, the talk was of the "Lost Decade." Overall economic growth was stalled near zero with no clear way out. Doubts about the future were everywhere.

. . .

Nissan was no exception. The go-slow approach favored by the government, which spanned a decade, was not going to work for Japan's second-largest automaker. Complicating any Nissan recovery built on slimming payrolls was the fact that by 1999, the Japanese labor market was showing worrying signs. The unemployment rate had risen to 4.7 percent, and while this was less than half of what the United States had seen in December 1982 at 10.8 percent, it was a shock for an economy that prided itself on lifetime employment, a system that had sent the jobless rate as low as 1 percent in the go-go years of the 1960s.

Indeed, lifetime employment was—and to a large extent still is—part of the broader social contract that bound the state, companies, and employees together. It was a system that led to broad prosperity with low income disparity, a solid infrastructure, nearly nonexistent violent crime, and, as most visitors note, immaculate streets free of litter. It was not a system to be challenged easily.

Even as Ghosn was preparing to arrive in Japan, Hiroshi Okuda, president of Toyota Motor Corp. and head of one of Japan's employer organizations, told reporters in a May 1999 briefing that "cutting jobs is the last thing management should do. If you do so only to raise profitability or the value of shares, that's wrong in the light of Japan's style of management."[4]

. . .

Ghosn's first collision was already in the making even before he settled in. Yet, when it came time to spell out Nissan's remedy, the interloping outsider hardly braked for impact. In announcing the Nissan Revival Plan at the Royal Park Hotel, Ghosn unabashedly pledged to be guided by just one rule:

"No sacred cows, no taboos, no constraints," he said. "Believe me, we don't have a choice."[5]

Ghosn's team canvassed thousands of people, from factory workers and dealers to customers and suppliers, to get a full picture of what was wrong. His appeal for input from the rank-and-file was a jarring departure in Japan and it helped earn the trust of Nissan's workforce and steel them for change. From this intel, he whipped up a whirlwind of numerical targets and financial metrics. The methodical attention to detail, cost, efficiency, and profits would become a hallmark of Ghosn's way of pushing the company forward in successive midterm business plans for the rest of his career there.

Under the revival plan, Nissan would slash debt by nearly half to $6.7 billion in four years. It would cut costs 20 percent over that period. It would shutter five factories in Japan. And, more controversially, it would shed twenty-one thousand jobs. The job cuts alone, which would largely befall Japanese workers, were a potential powder keg. But Ghosn hardly stopped there.

Still on tap were a host of reforms that made the Japanese establishment squirm. Ghosn promised to blow up traditional practices that long greased the wheels of Japanese business but often added little value, or sometimes may have detracted from performance.

In his sights were Japan Inc.'s distinctive *keiretsu* system of corporate tie-ups, its custom of binding companies through cross-shareholdings and its long-standing ritual of seniority-based job promotion. Ghosn threatened an entire tradition of relationship-based business culture.

Like many other big business groups in Japan, Nissan had long leaned on a network of suppliers and other affiliated companies as a kind of vertically integrated one-stop shop. Such clubs of companies, known as *keiretsu* in Japanese, have their benefits. They help stabilize one another's finances in times of trouble by holding cross-shareholding in partner companies.

They can lower transaction costs tied to such hassles as broken contracts and fielding bids, and they can borrow the expertise of partner companies with greater ease. Their secure ties also help keep all the businesses focused on long-term goals, rather than quick churn-and-burn gains.

But the keiretsu also carry heavy baggage. The cross-holdings tie up valuable capital that could otherwise fund expansion or new product development. And, over time, they run the risk of growing bloated and stale, as cozy connections supersede cost competitiveness.

Over the course of mere months, Ghosn relentlessly took an ax to all this. Cost and benefit would be the new ultimate arbiters.

For starters, he chopped down Nissan's cross-holdings. At the time, Nissan held stakes in some 1,394 keiretsu companies, and Nissan owned stakes of more than 20 percent in a majority of them. Indeed, he deemed that of all those tie-ups Nissan was part of, only *four* were absolutely essential to Nissan's core business. By breaking those bonds, Ghosn could free much-needed capital.

Next, Nissan would cut loose half of the 8,045 suppliers from which Nissan bought parts, services, and raw materials. Contracts would go to the most competitive bidder, connections be damned.

Nissan also implemented performance-based career advancement. And the new system would leverage bonuses and stock options to incentivize managers, foreshadowing future compensation showdowns that undergirded Ghosn's later legal troubles.

Finally, in a last slap to Japanese business tradition, Ghosn leapfrogged two generations of Nissan top brass to tap employees in their forties as members of the new revival teams that would reboot the company and determine its fate. Nissan would prize ability over age.

"The measures taken were not conventional in Japan. The harshness of the restructuring was something that is not so common in Japan," recalls one French executive on Ghosn's original thirty-member task force. "People were not expecting it to work that way.

"But somewhere, from the very beginning, there was a very good willingness to go through this pain in order to revive a company," the executive said. "I think they were, at the same time, relieved to be in an alliance and not in a takeover."

. . .

The invasive surgery not only worked, it rescued Nissan with incredible speed.

By 2002, a year ahead of schedule, Nissan had bounced out of the red, back into the black, and achieved a sturdy operating profit margin of 4.5 percent while cutting debt to under ¥700 billion ($5.3 billion). And in the fiscal year ending March 31, 2004, just two years after that and less than five years since his arrival, operating margin at a company once on death's doorstep swelled to an astounding 11.1 percent. Global sales surged, from 2.6 million vehicles when Ghosn took over to nearly 3.4 million in the fiscal year ended March 31, 2005.

Ghosn eliminated thousands of jobs from roughly 131,000 in early 1999. But Nissan survived to see its payroll grow to more than 183,000 people by early 2005. Ghosn closed five factories, but Nissan lived on to open ten more assembly plants, including several with partner companies, over the rest of his tenure. Most of those new factories were outside Japan, which is one reason the Japanese government and media might not have applauded so much. But the overseas footprint helped keep Nissan's domestic operations strong as well.

Among the new factories was a $930 million assembly plant in Canton, Mississippi, announced in late 2000, which would spearhead Nissan's recovery in the critical US market.

Nissan already had deep roots in the United States, winning early converts with such iconic offerings as the Datsun 240Z, the affordable, everyman's sports car that landed stateside in 1969. Nissan went native in 1983 with its first US assembly plant in Smyrna, Tennessee—a car-making factory that would become the biggest in all of North America.

But US sales plunged in the 1990s as American customers shunned Nissan vehicles that were essentially repackaged versions of smaller, narrower cars designed for the Japanese home market. Japanese rivals, such as Honda and Toyota, by contrast had learned to cater to US tastes with bigger and wider versions of their stalwart sedans, the Accord and Camry.[6]

By Ghosn's own reckoning, of the forty-three different nameplates that Nissan marketed in 1999, only four were profitable.

As Nissan repositioned itself, the new Canton plant would help Nissan fulfill American demand in two crucial segments that were really starting to take off. The plant, Ghosn determined, would make the brand's first full-size pickup and its first full-size SUV—two vehicle types absolutely needed to sate the US market's appetite for big, rugged workhorses.

Skeptics who had feared a radical strip down of the Japanese industrial flagship emerged as some of Ghosn's biggest backers. Ghosn's "Le Cost Cutter" moniker sometimes morphed into "Le Cost *Killer*" for added impact in some media reports. But Japan soon dumped those labels and feted him with new nicknames, such as "Mr. Fix-It" and "Seven-Eleven," the latter a tribute to his legendarily long working hours. He won over public opinion partly through a concerted media campaign that tried to humanize him and underscore his cultural sensitivity. Ghosn stood out as an individual in a country where CEOs are usually faceless, interchangeable men in ill-fitting charcoal suits.

"The *koho*, Nissan's communications department, had trouble keeping up with me," Ghosn recounts in *Shift*. "Readers learned about my typical day, about my factory visits, about my dinners with my family. Some people thought that I was, in fact, going too far in this direction."

. . .

As a turnaround story, it reads smoothly and pleasantly, but of course the ride was bumpy and sometimes painful, especially in the beginning.

At the 2000 annual shareholders meeting, Ghosn's first since taking charge, he was assailed for neglecting to bow before his speech. "You've got to teach him some manners," one attendee yelled at Hanawa, the *Financial Times* reported at the time. Ghosn's retort: "There are many Japanese habits I don't know, but that's because I have been working very hard, and I don't have time outside Nissan."[7]

Honoring Nissan's identity was an important part of his winning the hearts and minds of Japan. Ghosn played into Japanese pride by reviving some of the Nissan marque's most storied nameplates, cars that had been canned during the downturn due to cost cutting.

Chief among them was a reincarnated Z-Car, the 350Z. He singled that out in his 1999 Nissan Revival Plan as a symbol of the renaissance. Ghosn also gave rebirth to the high-performance GT-R, a legendary sports coupe affectionately known as "Godzilla" among its worldwide fan club.

Pampering Nissan's ego helped the employees absorb the stress of all the upheaval.

"Nissan became a profitable company, the Z was coming back, the GT-R was coming back, and people were excited because the company almost died, and his personality was very interesting," said a Japanese executive on Ghosn's turnaround team.

Indeed, Japanese observers had a hard time pigeonholing Ghosn as the stereotypical foreign expatriate, though many surely wanted to, especially early on. In fact, he's not a stereotype. Born in Brazil's upper Amazon basin, raised in Lebanon, and schooled in France, Ghosn was always a bit of square peg. He pursued his upper education in Paris, graduating with an engineering degree from the prestigious École Polytechnique. Ghosn was always something of an outsider among the business elite of France. As both a citizen of the world and perpetual outsider, he seemed more relatable to many Japanese. He wasn't their preconceived blond-haired, blue-eyed European. And the fact he stood just 170 cm (five feet, seven inches) also didn't hurt. "He's not tall. That's important," one longtime Japanese colleague said.

Ghosn's uniqueness allowed him first to upend traditions, abruptly, and to live outside the norm for the country's bland, buttoned-down Japanese executives. His turnaround soon made him something rare in Japan, a superstar CEO, a persona he did not back away from.

"I was told that the Japanese frequently go through periods of infatuation with people who are in the public eye," Ghosn wrote in *Shift*. "They seemed to succumb to 'Ghosn-mania.'"

People stopped him for autographs and were captivated by even the smallest details of his personal life. They wanted to know where he bought his eyeglasses or where he got his haircut. And perhaps most famously, there was even a 2001–2002 manga comic book lauding his exploits. It was titled *The True Story of Carlos Ghosn*. New copies sell for about $70 on Amazon's Japan site and used copies can still fetch more than $100.

Those around Ghosn noticed he seemed to like the attention.

"Yes, I never heard him complaining too much," one French executive close to him recalled. "I think he was quite proud to be recognized here and there. He was celebrated."

Ghosn had upturned Japanese business tradition and deftly averted a potentially explosive culture clash with the aplomb of a seasoned diplomat. He was treated like a rock star CEO.

"When it became clear that the Nissan Revival Plan was a full success, it happened as a kind of miracle and Ghosn was credited for it," the French executive said. "In Japan, it was simply a miracle. No one thought it was possible."

. . .

But even as he navigated the collision course, other clashes were set in motion in those early years.

Indeed, it wasn't long before Nissan's share price started outperforming Renault's and industry onlookers began speculating about a shift in power from the savior to the saved, from the French toward the Japanese partner.

Among the club of Nissan young Turks that Ghosn elevated to power despite lacking seniority was Hiroto Saikawa, the man sitting at the helm in 2018 when Ghosn was hauled off to jail. Just four months Ghosn's elder, Saikawa was tapped as the senior manager of a newly created purchasing strategy department. His task was to break up the keiretsu and drill down hard on cost. In a word, he was Ghosn's enforcer. And by all accounts, Saikawa excelled at it.

"When he was given a task or target, he achieved it," said one former Nissan executive who worked closely with Ghosn and Saikawa. "Saikawa always brought good results. But he was always pushing a target number and just pushing everybody. He was so task oriented."

Saikawa helped launch the Renault-Nissan Purchasing Organization (RNPO), a way to pool the buying power of the companies to extract lower prices for parts and services in exchange for higher order volumes. The outfit was one of earliest, most successful triumphs of the Alliance and also one of its most enduring. Indeed, the so-called RNPO continued to underpin profitability and product planning across the group two decades later, even amid myriad other troubles. Interlacing the companies also made it harder to pull them apart.

In fact, just seven years after its creation in 2001, RNPO was on pace to cover 90 percent of all Alliance purchasing to the tune of a whopping $94.7 billion. The keiretsu was no more.

Ghosn was so impressed by Saikawa's genius for squeezing every yen that he promoted him to be chairman of Nissan's management committee for the Americas, a job so important that Ghosn himself had personally handled it for three years. So, in 2007, he handed the wheel to Saikawa, putting him on the fast track to the top.

By then, Ghosn had already moved on to bigger things.

. . .

Ghosn's stunning Nissan turnaround earned him the chief executive job at Renault in 2005. He was now CEO of both automakers as well as cochairman of Nissan, to boot. At the Renault shareholder meeting in April 2005, he described the job of simultaneously leading Nissan and the French carmaker as difficult and different. "In the auto industry success doesn't last long and it is never guaranteed," he said. "We need to earn our success every day."[8]

In *Shift*, Ghosn portrayed it as pioneering new ground, not just for the automotive industry but for the entire international business community: "It's true that the operation scheduled to begin in 2005 will be something entirely new. But the Alliance itself is something new, and what we've accomplished at Nissan is new. There's a sort of continuity in all this newness," he wrote. "We're creating a new model and new references in management, but we're also going through an experience that will be valuable even beyond the world of the company."

The heroic triumph of saving Nissan—and the stratospheric status that came with it—also seemed to cultivate a deep-seated sense of entitlement in the miracle worker that foreshadowed looming conflicts. In the coming years, Ghosn demanded escalating compensation commensurate with his talents and achievements. And that, in turn, increasingly raised eyebrows in Japan, triggering showdowns with Nissan shareholders. It also began to raise hackles back in France, where social norms kept a tight lid on remuneration. Many saw the annual payouts as just too exorbitant. But in Ghosn's eyes, he always deserved at least as much as he demanded.

Indeed, after his arrest, Ghosn rarely bit back on his bitterness in being prosecuted, thrown in jail, and indicted, all after rescuing the nation's No. 2 automaker. Even while living in Lebanon as an international fugitive with his reputation in tatters, he insisted he would battle until the end to resuscitate his legacy of pulling off one of the auto industry's greatest comebacks.

"The Nissan of pre-1999 is a company which didn't deserve to live," he told *Automotive News* in a February 2020 interview from Lebanon. "That's what it was, a zombie."

"Even the Japanese banks didn't want to lend one yen to Nissan . . . My ambition for the company and my engagement with the company were at the base of the revival," he said. "I am preparing to defend myself, to defend my rights, defend my legacy, defend my name . . . The last thing I want is people who have cheated and lied to get away with it."

3

JAPAN IS DIFFERENT

THE CHALLENGES FACING CARLOS GHOSN AS HE FIRST sought to take on one of the world's most entrenched corporate cultures were far from unique. He knew early on that he needed to understand which rules should be flouted to bring about a painful but necessary change and which social norms remained inviolate. These differences between Japan and the rest of the industrialized world range from the smallest details of innocuous transactions to the fundamental questions of a company's role in society.

Senior foreign executives who have operated with ease around the world often come to Japan with a sudden look of fear, having heard about the complexities of Japanese business culture. Do you bow or shake hands? (Both are acceptable, but let the other side make the first move.) What do you do with the business card you are handed? (Look at it carefully and make a brief innocuous comment. Never just shove it in your pocket.) At the obligatory dinner, do you refill your glass of beer from the bottle in front of you? (Never. It suggests your hosts are not taking proper care of a guest.) Can you get drunk at dinner? (Only after your hosts do, and never mention it the next day. What happens at dinner, stays at dinner.)

Then, there are the bigger questions for which the answers in Japan are often different than in the rest of the world, such as: Why does a company exist? Do shareholders come first or last? Do workers represent just labor input or are they important stakeholders? Are companies and governments allies or natural enemies? Is taking a long-term perspective a smart strategy or just an excuse for failing to deliver results?

There is no shortage of foreigners willing (for a fee) to lecture Japanese companies on how they should operate. However, it's worth remembering that the Japanese have been in business as long as anyone else. The world's four oldest corporations all come from Japan. The oldest is Nishiyama Onsen hotel near Tokyo, which first opened shop back in the year 705. The former record holder, construction group Kongo Gumi of Osaka, was founded in 578, but was forced into liquidation in 2006 after taking on too much debt, a tribute to the old adage that past performance may not be indicative of future results. So, while many management gurus may look askance at Japan, these companies, and the major Japanese companies that followed, operated on a set of corporate values and principles that were created centuries before Six Sigma or Value Stream Mapping. In this world, owners and employees share a common vision that the company comes before the individual and that success comes from putting the needs of your customers first.

This traditional Japanese corporate perspective was summed up in a late 1990s interview with a senior editor at the Asahi newspaper company. Its flagship daily, *Asahi Shimbun*, is Japan's (and the world's) second-largest circulation newspaper at more than six million copies daily. From the perspective of management, the job of the company was to employ the best people at premium salaries. There were also hefty contributions to foundations, museums, and other recipients for the public good, with the shareholders getting whatever was left over.

This approach still guides many Japanese companies today where job cuts remain the exception, even in tough times. It is also a focal point for much of the criticism of Japanese companies from foreign investors, who contend that a company's purpose is to make as much money as possible, with the government responsible for all the societal issues.

But this "global" viewpoint is itself in transition today, in many respects moving closer to traditional Japanese concepts. Where hedge funds and corporate raiders have for decades pushed the concept of shareholder value (as seen in ever-rising stock prices), new voices have now emerged. Even the World Economic Forum (WEF), the quintessential talking shop for the rich and powerful, clearly noticed the winds changing in 2020, using its fiftieth anniversary to launch a new Davos Manifesto. As it was described by WEF founder Klaus Schwab, "companies should pay their fair share of taxes, show zero tolerance for corruption, uphold human rights throughout their global supply chains, and advocate for a competitive level playing field."[1] This is closer to the ethical underpinnings of 1,400-year-old Japanese companies than today's hedge funds.

The need to accept the American-led world of post–World War II global capitalism in itself reflects a key element of Japan, in which society has long demonstrated a history of being able to adapt without making fundamental change.

On balance, Japan has probably changed less in the postwar period than have the perceptions about the country from outside. In 1979, Asia expert and Harvard professor Ezra F. Vogel could convincingly lay out the strong points of Japan's economic system and suggest that America had much to learn. His book *Japan as Number One: Lessons for America* was meant to show how the Japanese approach to teamwork and careful decision making had turned the country into "the world's most competitive industrial power." Unfortunately, his book, and especially the title, were taken as some kind of warning that the Japanese were coming to take American jobs.

This fear was replaced in the 1990s by the equally one-sided notion that Japan's economy had fallen off a cliff. Ever since the sudden end of Japan's high growth with the collapse of the Bubble Economy in 1990, US officials would lecture their Japanese counterparts on the need to "get the economy back on track." Many of the same values that had been seen as virtues when Japan's economy was soaring in the 1960s and '70s (consensus building, thoroughness, detailed knowledge) became liabilities in the 1990s (risk averse, unimaginative, detail obsessed).

· · ·

Rather than being a pioneer, when he arrived in 1999 Ghosn was in some ways just the latest figure in history to head into the maze of doing business in Japan. Like those before him, he needed to demonstrate willfulness and stubbornness along with flexibility and compromise. Like Japan, he too needed to adapt without making fundamental change.

Ghosn could analyze a long history of foreign involvement in Japan, much of which had failed to meet the initial optimistic expectations. The first such foray, in modern times, was around 1570 when the Portuguese and later the Dutch, along with neighboring China and Korea, were allowed to have limited trade with Japan, which was then a nation that coveted its isolation. This was chiefly through the port of Nagasaki in the southern main island of Kyushu. It was hardly a warm welcome. Foreshadowing today's foreigners' complaints about excess regulation, there were myriad restrictions controlling the number of ships that could enter the port each year and the number of foreigners who could be based in the city. To ensure that "foreign ways" would not influence the populace, a special two-acre island was constructed in the harbor to house all of those from outside, with only one bridge into the central city. Aside from unwanted cultural mingling, this was meant to stop the spread of Christianity after missionaries had targeted Japan and other Asian countries as ripe areas to find new converts.

This mutually advantageous if limited relationship continued for more than 250 years until the rather noisy busting up of the party by American commodore Matthew Perry in 1853. His two expeditions, heavy on gunboat diplomacy, were meant to open up Japan. The Japanese response was straight from their traditional playbook. Outright opposition gave way to delaying tactics meant to put off the inevitable, then grudging acceptance of the new reality and finally a co-opting of the system. The whole transformation only took fifty years, and a similar scenario would play out in much the same way in the aftermath of World War II through the boom economy of the 1960s and 1970s.

Under threat of invasion (it would have been a fairly small one, given Perry's limited force) Japanese officials signed the Convention of Kanagawa in 1854 and the Harris Treaty of 1858. These opened the Japanese market to imports, curtailed tariffs, and allowed foreigners to set up residence. Following the US lead, Great Britain, France, and Russia all piled in with similar demands and subsequent treaties. Among the most irksome aspects for the Japanese was the introduction of "extraterritoriality," under which foreign nationals were shielded from the Japanese legal system (an approach Ghosn would no doubt endorse today).

The economic transformation that eventually resulted from Perry's expedition was little short of astounding. From their first glimpse of a steam engine in 1853,[2] Japanese officials embraced the new Western ways. By the early 1900s, government-promoted conglomerates, known as *zaibatsu*,[3] were transforming the country. Many of those are well-known names to this day, including various offshoots from today's corporate giants Mitsubishi, Mitsui, and Sumitomo. All three are still active players in banking/financial services, autos, real estate, import-export promotion, and natural resources. Another lesser-known zaibatsu was Nihon Sangyo Co. (Japan Industry). The group had wide-ranging interests in real estate, insurance, mining, and fisheries. In 1933, it purchased a small company called DAT Automobile Manufacturing Co. and the unit soon began using the parent company's shorter name: Nissan.[4]

Japan's industrial and economic success also paved the way for a military transformation, one that was to further bolster such industrial giants as Nissan. Far from the humiliation of seeing the unmatched power of American and other Western warships in the 1850s, Japan's navy was by 1904 able to take on the Russian force in the Russo-Japanese War. Japan's clear victory in 1905 was the first by an Asian nation over a European power and sent shock waves around the world when it was clear there was a new regional and potentially global power. All of this required modern industry, and Nissan was among the beneficiaries.

. . .

In some ways, Japan succeeded too well. Its subsequent militarization and expansionism through Korea and China was to create a brutal colonialism and sow the seeds of defeat in World War II. This total collapse would usher in the man who was arguably the most influential foreigner in the modern history of the country, General Douglas MacArthur, an autocratic figure who presided over one of the most unsettled periods in Japanese history and whose influence remains firmly entrenched today.

With the US military in charge, many of MacArthur's actions had a profound impact on the direction of the country, ranging from the legal system to an ongoing military alliance that keeps fifty thousand US military personnel on Japanese soil. The residents of Okinawa have long protested the large US military presence in their prefecture, while Tokyo residents complaining about low-flying planes in 2020 were told that the better routes could only be used by the US military.

More sweeping in nature is the very constitution that governs Japan, one that a group of American experts was given a week to create in 1947. The document renounces the use of military force, and despite opposition from some conservatives who note it was drafted by "foreigners," it remains in place today and has never been amended, itself a record among countries.

MacArthur's impact was nearly as strong in the corporate world. He took on the prewar zaibatsu conglomerates, ordering that they be broken up or turned into stockholding companies. Here, however, entrenched interests managed to again adapt to their new circumstances. Under a 1947 mandate, MacArthur's office came up with a list of 325 companies to be targeted under direction of the Deconcentration Board. But as a senior adviser to the State Department said in a 1949 report, the orders were quietly put aside for all but twenty-eight of the target companies. Utilities, finance, and insurance firms were all exempted. For one of the few that went ahead, Oji Paper Manufacturing, the adviser noted that "the successor companies continue to occupy office space in the same building and to maintain close liaison," a good example of Japan's adapting to new circumstances but keeping its principle goals intact.

In another case,[5] shares in subsidiaries of Nomura, Japan's biggest brokerage firm, were sold to employees to help appease the occupation authorities. What wasn't known was that they used money lent to them by the firm, and dutifully sold the shares back to the parent soon after MacArthur was wheels up from Tokyo's Haneda airport.

Still, many of the big names were eventually split up in some fashion. This did not mean the end of what could today be called "crony capitalism." The break-up of the zaibatsu structure led to the creation of the less hierarchical keiretsu system of interlocking relationships, in which companies across a broad range of sectors banded together in loose co-operatives and often took cross-shareholdings in one another. Most were built around a financial institution to help in meeting the capital needs of the various members. Nissan was part of the Fuyo Group, led by the now-defunct Fuji Bank. The Fuyo Group still exists, with Nissan as a member, but the alliance is a loose one with few concrete ties between the members.

A much tighter alliance has historically existed around the sprawling Mitsubishi Group, which today numbers around six hundred companies (even the Mitsubishi people claim they do not know the exact figure)[6] with independent shareholding structures. The group ties are technically restricted to areas of social responsibility and public-interest activities. In reality, the close ties remain, especially among the core group of companies that include the trading firm Mitsubishi Corp., banking giant Mitsubishi UFJ Financial Group, and Nissan partner Mitsubishi Motors. As of 2020, Mitsubishi Corp. remained the No. 2 shareholder in Mitsubishi Motors, at 20 percent, second only to Nissan's 34 percent stake. The two companies are also partners in the fast-growing markets of Southeast Asia, and according to executives within the trading firm, the health of Mitsubishi Motors remains a central concern for them. The long-term strategic approach of Japanese firms could mean there will be new maneuverings around the status of Mitsubishi Motors after the strains created in the Renault-Nissan Alliance by the Ghosn affair.

. . .

The keiretsu system was meant to create corporate cohesion through the cross-shareholding relationships, creating a vast web of corporate interests. The positive side of this was that companies had a clear interest in seeing that other firms also stayed healthy, a far cry from the Western capitalist model of trying to squeeze your suppliers, charge your customers as much as possible and drive your competitors into the ground. Its structure was an example of how corporate Japan, seeing one model disappear, shifted to another with the core goals unchanged. In his book on Japanese cultural tradition, *Fall Seven Times, Get Up Eight*, Kyoto University of Foreign Studies professor Satoshi Hara says that a free-market economy and democracy (together with individualism based on liberty and equality) were introduced to Japan after World War II by the United States. Japan accepted them, he contends, without much consciousness that it would lead to the loss of the traditional moral values they had nurtured for centuries, such as frugality, compassion, and respect for the elderly:

> [A]fter the defeat in WWII, the Japanese hastily rushed to pursue economic interests under the official flag of economic reconstruction. In doing so, they simply accepted the new western philosophy without paying serious consideration to its implications. . . .
>
> During the post-war period, the Japanese breathlessly pursued economic reconstruction and development and did not have time to reflect what values and virtues they truly needed to build a new life.[7]

In the world of business, this was reflected in the concept that a company should benefit its customers, suppliers, and the general public. Cross-shareholdings were a part of this balanced relationship. They provided a generally supportive set of owners who would not be especially interested in their own shareholder value for the simple reason that they were typically your business partners. Your higher profit could come at their cost through higher prices. It also guarded against any hostile corporate takeovers, which given Japan's focus on cooperation, not confrontation, were mainly a threat from overseas. The cross-shareholding ratio of listed companies, which had fallen to 20 percent in 1949 just as MacArthur had wanted, started to rise again as old alliances were reborn. The percentage would peak at more than 50 percent in 1990,[8] meaning that more than half of all shareholdings were in friendly hands.

This all worked well, until it didn't. The problem came with the stock market crash from 1990 onward, which saw shares fall more than 80 percent over a thirteen-year period. The losses were as interlocked as the companies in the keiretsu. So, at a time when companies were themselves struggling in terms of their business, they also had to pay the price of the problems of their close partners. This constituted a major drag on the economy, especially since the stock market decline did not hit bottom until nineteen years later, in 2009. There was a great deal of talk about the need to unwind these now burdensome shareholdings. Action was much slower. It was not until 2014 and many rounds of painful asset write-downs that the holdings fell to 16 percent of the total. In the end, it was a newly strengthened corporate governance code by the government and the Tokyo Stock Exchange in 2015 that would eventually force the recalcitrant companies to act.[9]

The process also demonstrates how the Japanese government and regulators will first try to work in cooperation with the corporate sector, with regulations from above the last step, not the first. This relationship would also feature in the Ghosn affair. The US perspective of perpetual conflict over taxation, regulation, and the rights of labor are largely alien to Japanese, and in fact to many other Asian countries. The concept of state capitalism reaches a peak in China where it is difficult to know where a company ends and the Communist Party begins. A 2010 survey by the McKinsey consulting group found that 67 percent of companies in Asia saw the government as advocates for their company, while only 38 percent of US companies and 40 percent of EU companies share this "win-win" view.

The government's central role in helping to guide the "invisible hand" of free enterprise has a long history in Japan. From the Meiji era that began in 1868 until the end of World War II, the zaibatsu were owned by powerful families that worked with the government and often lent money to fund public projects in exchange for monopoly power in various areas. When the age of the keiretsu came after World War II, the details were different, but the process was little changed. As noted by Ezra F. Vogel, front and center in this effort was the Ministry of International Trade and Industry (MITI), the forerunner to today's Ministry of Economy, Trade, and Industry (METI), which was active in practically every area of corporate Japan.[10] "MITI officials are so persistent in their efforts to look after the welfare of Japanese industry that they are dubbed by their countrymen as *kyōiku mama*, overanxious mothers who hover over their children and push them to study." These bureaucrats were active participants in restructuring industries, promoting mergers, helping companies or industries in trouble, and helping to create winners in strategically important sectors.

This support was in full view in the 1970s when Japan, which had become the world's second-largest economy, was also, from a foreigner perspective, the world's second-largest market opportunity. This was an unwanted distinction on the part of Japan, which liked being a powerhouse exporter that was largely closed to most imports. The wide range of trade barriers was dizzying and resulted in years of heated arguments with various US administrations.

Even more galling to American competitors was that their Japanese rivals often borrowed US ideas, most notably the quality control theories of W. Edwards Deming, who came to Japan in the 1950s to lecture corporations eager to learn how to focus on quality from the beginning of the manufacturing process and to build cooperation rather than production quotas. The Deming Prize, created in his name, remains one of the most coveted prizes within Japanese industry, one which Nissan took home in 1960 for excellence in industrial engineering.

At first, Japan, like China today, sheltered its domestic auto industry by handicapping import competition with hefty tariffs. This gave local champions, such as Toyota and Nissan, the shelter they needed to develop for the domestic market and then build an export base. Japan eliminated tariffs on auto imports by 1978.[11] But by then, they didn't need them. Japanese autos were well on their way to conquering overseas markets.

And it was too late for foreign brands to really gain a foothold in Japan's saturated local market, where they lacked a local retail network and could only offer giant gas guzzlers that didn't suit Japanese tastes or market needs. It didn't help that the steering wheels were on the wrong side. Government's guiding hand played a big role in making Japan a global automaking juggernaut.

Free trade was a part of capitalism that, until recently, Japan never really liked. Their main strategy to push back against imports was most often one of foot-dragging, hoping the problem would go away. The pressure from overseas did decline, but not for reasons Japanese companies would have wanted. Slow to change and hit by lower-cost competition, Sony and Panasonic lost their crowns as the electronics leaders and saw their export markets fade away. Japanese automakers, meanwhile, moved much of their production overseas, opening plants where they were selling their cars. And an aging and shrinking Japanese market was no longer as attractive a proposition for foreign companies looking to sell their products. The war effectively ended when nobody cared anymore and companies were left to fend for themselves.

In this new climate, officials at METI say that they no longer hold the hands of companies. "Unlike some decades ago, the Japanese government today is not overly concerned about protecting Japanese industries from capital participation by foreign entities," said one former METI official. "Although the government, especially its officials, might feel sympathetic to the management of a company like Nissan, it would be difficult for them to tread on the dangerous ground of overtly siding with them," said another former official.

For Ghosn, METI was not as reticent as it claimed. In his 2020 book written from Lebanon,[12] he charges that former and current figures within the Ministry were involved in a plot to bring him down. He describes former METI official and newly appointed Nissan board member Masakazu Toyoda as the mastermind behind the plot and says that the METI minister at the time, Hiroshige Seko, was in the background. He did not deliver proof, saying that disclosure of the documents could be legally problematic.

METI has not commented directly on the Ghosn allegations. One official dismissed the idea that the ministry would take part in a boardroom pie fight. At the same time, emails from Nissan show that the ministry was more than willing to engage with their French counterparts on Alliance issues and saw a clear need to stand up to protect Nissan as a Japanese company.

Both the Japanese and French governments said publicly through the crisis that they wanted to see a strong Renault-Nissan alliance, but where they differed sharply was what exactly that meant. When French president Emmanuel Macron pressed Japanese prime minister Shinzo Abe on the future of the two carmakers, Abe replied that it was up to the two companies. "What's most important is to keep a stable relationship," he was quoted as saying. "This is not something that the governments can determine." For Nissan, with the backing of the government, the alliance structure in place showed that the relationship was here to stay, and that there was no need for major changes. While Nissan was happy with the "status quo," in the words of one Nissan email, the French government wanted to move from cohabitation to marriage—to find some structure that would result in a merger in practice if not in name.

For METI, that was a line in the sand and there was no pretense of staying out of Nissan's corporate affairs if a full merger was being pushed from overseas. It would make Nissan *not Japanese.* The bureaucrats in Tokyo saw that this would require more than gentle nudging. "If, in part, the French government wanted a deal that was good only for them, we would not allow that to happen," said a METI official.

Another issue to emerge in the affair was the role played by the member of Parliament for the district that includes Nissan's headquarters in Yokohama, who just happened to be one of Japan's most powerful politicians. At the time, Yoshihide Suga was the chief cabinet secretary, the No. 2 figure to the prime minister and responsible for policy coordination across government ministries. Nissan CEO Saikawa said in a series of May 2018 email exchanges on the Renault relationship issue that Suga and Prime Minister Shinzo Abe had been "very discreet, but with very solid support." The exchange of emails also talked of asking Suga for help in dealing with METI. When Ghosn was arrested in November, Japanese media noted that Hitoshi Kawaguchi, the head of Nissan's government relations and a key player in the internal investigation that brought Ghosn down, visited Suga the next day. Despite media reports that Kawaguchi and Suga were close, little evidence emerged to suggest that Suga had played a more active role in the affair or in the decision to arrest Ghosn. In 2020, Suga moved from his enabler role to become Japan's prime minister following Abe.

On balance, the documentation, as well as interviews with government officials and company executives, pointed to a Japanese government approach that was, well, Japanese. It is clear that the government was keenly interested in the state of affairs at one of its most iconic brands and that there were concerns at what they saw as overt French efforts that could risk the future of Nissan as a Japanese company. At the same time, the bureaucrats were clearly skeptical of what they were hearing. One METI official said that with so many leaks it was difficult to trust what was coming from within the company. The problem for Nissan, the official said, was not "who was in charge," it was how the company could end its long history of infighting and "be a great company."

4

THE GLOBAL
STANDARD

GHOSN'S SUCCESS IN HOLDING THE REINS OF BOTH Renault and Nissan made him a kind of living legend in the auto world. And he perpetuated the mystique by routinely saying, in a humblebrag way, that any wannabe CEOs waiting in the wings would wisely think twice before attempting such a delicate, exhausting, cross-cultural balancing act.

"I would not recommend to anyone else that they do the job I've been doing. Being in charge of two companies and having to run between two countries is extremely taxing on people. I had to do it because I had no choice," the time-zone traveling dual CEO told *Automotive News* in 2014. "I was put in a position where I had to and there was a clear benefit to the Alliance."[1]

His ideal handoff, he said, would be separate successor CEOs, one for Renault, the other for Nissan. The implication, it seemed, was that no mere mortal could handle the load—that he was irreplaceable.

Plenty of pundits seemed to agree Ghosn had something special.

Fortune magazine named him one of the world's top 12 executives outside the United States.[2] A joint survey by PricewaterhouseCoopers and the *Financial Times* tapped him as the world's third-most-respected business leader, behind only such luminaries as Microsoft's Bill Gates and

General Electric's Jack Welch.[3] *Automotive News*, the Detroit-based bible of the global auto industry, named Ghosn the "Industry Leader of the Year" in its annual All-Star listing three times: in 2000, 2001, and 2003.

In a poll asking Japanese people which "celebrity" they would choose to lead the country after its deadly 2011 earthquake–tsunami–nuclear meltdown disaster, which killed over nineteen thousand people, Ghosn was one of only two non-Japanese on the list. The other: then US president Barack Obama, two slots below Ghosn.[4]

In 2006, Ghosn was appointed an honorary Knight Commander of the British Empire, an award bestowed upon those wielding transformational influence in a domain such as business, science, or the arts. In Ghosn's case, his contribution was saving Nissan, a company that then had 5,500 employees and two hundred dealers in the United Kingdom.[5]

Ghosn's corporate jujitsu became the subject of MBA seminars and good management tomes, all while attracting job overtures from rival carmakers—especially downtrodden American ones—hoping to harness his abilities for their own turnarounds.

"He was a tough CEO, a master, absolutely amazing in how prepared he was for every discussion," said one former executive who regularly briefed Ghosn on his visits to Japan. "It was pretty typical that you came in with a multiple-page PowerPoint deck. He'd be ten pages ahead as I'm trying to say something to him, and he'd be comprehending everything."

In business dealings, Ghosn came across as brusque and cold, perhaps arrogant—but matter-of-factly so, not maliciously so. Small talk was never his thing. Meetings were clocked out to the second, from start to finish. Those around him sometimes played a parlor game of calculating the value of his time. Estimates ranged from $150,000 to $250,000 an hour. In keeping with that time-is-money mindset, Ghosn was a very fast talker—usually clocking a speedy 160 words per minute, compared with the 130-word pace of most public speakers. To almost all his underlings—and he only had underlings—he was always "Mr." Ghosn. Few had the permission—or courage—to call him Carlos.

Among the books touting Ghosn's talents was *The Ghosn Factor*, a 2006 title promising readers twenty-four lessons from "the world's most dynamic CEO." Each chapter focuses on a purported maxim of Ghosn-style leadership, such as "break the mold," "focus on profitability," "empower your people," and "generate value."

The author, Miguel Rivas-Micoud, writes of Ghosn, "What makes Carlos Ghosn different from all the others is that he actually does what he says he will do . . . He believes in total transparency and in constant communication that flows in all directions within the company. He also believes in rewarding contribution wherever it occurs."

One of the last chapters, "Reward Performance," outlines the importance of rewarding those who do well. Indeed, Ghosn is hailed for introducing a merit-based advancement system to Nissan as well as incentive programs for managers, overhauls that injected fresh blood and new ideas into Nissan's ossified corporate ladder.[6]

. . .

Just as Ghosn believed in rewarding employees who excelled, he also firmly believed in being adequately rewarded himself for his performance as the visionary leader. And his calculus of his own market value was informed—or inflated, critics said—by a parade of suitors who knocked on his door over the years, trying to lure him away.

Among those enamored by Ghosn's abilities was Kirk Kerkorian, the Las Vegas casino tycoon and billionaire activist investor with a penchant for dabbling in the auto industry.

By 2006, Kerkorian had accumulated a 9.9 percent stake in General Motors, making him the company's largest shareholder. That year, he floored GM management by proposing they form a three-way alliance with Renault-Nissan. GM was in a downward spiral after slumping to a $10.5 billion loss in 2005, and Kerkorian's implicit strategy was to install Ghosn at the top and have him work his magic.[7] Talks to lure Ghosn into leading a GM turnaround dragged on for months. But in the end, GM CEO Rick Wagoner—who insisted all along that GM didn't need help—fended off the interloping Kerkorian by rallying a board vote against tie-up talks and saving his own skin in the process.

Even before the Kerkorian gambit, Ghosn was propositioned by rival Detroit automaker Ford Motor Co.[8] Not once, but twice. Bill Ford, the great-grandson of company founder Henry Ford, made the first approach in 2003, offering Ghosn the COO job along with a promise to eventually take over from Bill Ford as CEO. The overture was a nonstarter for Ghosn. He would be CEO *and* chairman, or nothing at all.[9]

In 2005, after all, Ghosn became top dog at Renault *and* kept his CEO role at Nissan. Renault was facing some struggles, but he had just taken command and was working on a revival plan for the French company as well. He saw huge potential in building both up together.

Ghosn's rebuff did little to dull Ford's enthusiasm. In fact, it may have even whetted Bill Ford's appetite, because the American auto mogul made another pass at Ghosn in 2006 while Kerkorian was kibitzing to install Ghosn at GM. Ford's message then: If things don't work out with GM, we'll be on standby. Ghosn—by then holding down the CEO jobs at both Renault and Nissan as well as the cochairman post at Nissan—demurred once again. Ford finally poached Alan Mulally from Boeing, and Mulally went on to deftly save the carmaker.

But things didn't work out for GM. In June 2009, just three years later, America's biggest carmaker filed for Chapter 11 bankruptcy protection after being broadsided by the global financial crisis. It was placed under government oversight as part of an $80 billion bailout of GM and Chrysler, the Detroit rival that also filed for Chapter 11.[10] Steering the rescues was Steve Rattner, the so-called car czar appointed by the Obama administration. When the White House finally dismissed Wagoner and sought a new CEO to dig GM out of bankruptcy, Rattner had a good idea of who could pull it off.

"Ghosn, in the minds of many, is the best automotive CEO to emerge since Alfred P. Sloan Jr., the father of General Motors," Rattner wrote in *Overhaul*, his 2010 book recounting the bailout.[11] To Rattner, Ghosn was "intense—almost like a coiled spring—earnest, and precise, all wrapped in a compact package of determination and drive."

It was during a 2009 dinner with Ghosn at the Four Seasons Hotel in Washington, DC, that Rattner sprang another offer to run GM and guide it out of the Great Recession. This time, too, Ghosn declined. The Renault-Nissan chief would later say he felt too much loyalty to his current employers to abandon ship and leave them without a captain in the middle of the worldwide financial hurricane.

. . .

Over the years, while he was being courted, Ghosn cultivated a public persona as a worldly captain of industry with a taste for the finer things in life: Multiple houses on different continents, globetrotting on private jets, rubbing shoulders with the political and financial elite at the Davos World Economic Forum—and crucially, many of those around him say, a need for ever-greater remuneration.

The world changed when Ghosn was made Renault CEO and keyholder of the whole Alliance, said one high-level French automotive executive who has known Ghosn for more than two decades. "He started traveling the world, and his life started to change, meeting a lot of people he never met before. On top of his generous ego, he has fantastic charisma. Maybe he felt there were no limits. But every human being has a limit."

Ghosn developed an interest in modern art and fashion. In fact, he requested meetings with some of Japan's biggest creative minds, including painter-sculptor Takashi Murakami, photographer Hiroshi Sugimoto, and designer Yohji Yamamoto. Ghosn's taste in clothes evolved from humdrum salaryman to CEO chic. Notably, he also dumped his fuddy-duddy eyeglasses and finally opted for laser eye surgery.[12]

In the early days, Ghosn often sought advice in selecting wardrobe for public appearances such as car debuts. Nissan even had a team of stylists to tailor him to every occasion. But he quickly graduated from such handholding and did things his own way.

"He probably wasn't so confident with selecting a suit and so on, but gradually he took an interest in learning," said one Japanese executive who worked closely with Ghosn for more than fifteen years. "He thought that to be a top-level business executive, you have to have an appreciation of art. He opened his eyes wider than just business."

Ghosn became the first auto bigwig to hobnob with heads of state and the global banking elite at the annual World Economic Forum at

the Davos ski resort in the Swiss Alps. On the first full day of the annual conclaves, he would hold court in a dozen back-to-back interviews
with the world's broadcast media. For Ghosn, it was a clever way to set
the public agenda for the global auto industry at the start of the year.
Other auto executives eventually followed him to Davos but could rarely
register the same impact. Toyota Motor Corp. president Akio Toyoda,
for instance, partook in 2010. But the Japanese press lambasted him for
what many perceived as a lavish exercise in self-indulgence. The cowed
Toyoda never went back.

"Ghosn became one of the prominent characters at Davos," said a
French executive who worked closely with Ghosn for nearly two decades. "At the time, I think we saw the positive side of it. Your boss was
being recognized internationally and bringing positive awareness to the
company. But as an individual, he was becoming more of a kind of show-
biz star."

In 2015, Ghosn was named "World's Most Influential French Person"
by *Vanity Fair France*.[13] Renault trumpeted the news on its corporate
website.

Back in Lebanon, where Nissan had secured Ghosn a company house,
he bought into a state-of-the-art winery called Ixsir on the country's
northern coast. And his family acquired a 121-foot Custom Line Navetta
37 yacht built by the Italian boat maker Ferretti.[14] The vessel, which the
company catalog lists as having seven bathrooms, five main cabins and
four cabins for crew, was christened *Shachou*, Japanese for "company
president," or more casually, "boss."

In the United States or Europe, such trappings would rarely raise eyebrows. And in Japan, they didn't either. At least not until 2010, when a
change in Japan's financial disclosure rules suddenly put Ghosn's pay
under an uncomfortable public spotlight. Before that year, Japanese
companies, in their public filings, could simply lump together the total
sum of compensation allotted for all directors. But in a push for greater
transparency after the global financial crisis, the Japan Financial Services
Agency required companies to detail individual compensation for any
director whose total payout exceeded ¥100 million (roughly $1.1 million
at the time).

Needless to say, Ghosn was pulling down much more than that. In fact, Nissan reported that he was paid ¥891 million ($9.6 million) in 2010, in cash and share rights.[15] By the standards of *Fortune* 500 companies, it may have been a bargain. But no other executive at Nissan made more than ¥200 million ($2.2 million) that year. And Ghosn's pay was the highest of any CEO at a listed Japanese company. Akio Toyoda, president of what was then the world's largest automaker and the crown jewel of Japan Inc., didn't even have to report pay that year. His total compensation simply didn't exceed the threshold. And when Toyoda finally got a raise in 2011, his compensation package climbed to only ¥136 million ($1.47 million), still only a fraction of Ghosn's.[16] Takanobu Ito, the president of Honda Motor Co., Japan's other Big Three automaker, took home even less in the first year of disclosure, just ¥115 million ($1.2 million).[17]

The salary issue was a blind spot in Ghosn's otherwise smooth handling of the numerous cross-cultural challenges. His parade of corporate suitors proved to him that he was a big catch for competitors. But the fact that Ghosn was making more than six times as much as his Japanese counterparts mystified and miffed a lot of Japanese observers, starting with Nissan's own investors. Many grumbled about having to pay Ghosn a full salary despite getting only half his time—Ghosn split his attention between two companies, Renault and Nissan, after all. Ghosn's pay—now out in the open for all to see—suddenly erupted as a flash point at annual shareholders' meetings. And the clash of sensibilities over Ghosn's pay—both in Japan and in France—proved to be one of the biggest collisions in the whole saga building toward the auto titan's downfall.

· · ·

To this day, the typical Japanese shareholders' meeting remains a quaint throwback to a simpler era when companies at least played lip service to small-time, individual investors. Staged with much pageantry, the gatherings usually convene in June at a hotel ballroom or conference center, attracting hundreds of shareholders from the far-flung corners of Japan.

The investors themselves are mostly mom-and-pop pensioners with their retirement funds wrapped up in their stake. The company's top brass turns out to field their questions, hear their gripes, and count their votes on the day's business. Finally, in traditional Japanese fashion, the shareholders are sent home with gifts of gratitude for their loyalty, such as boxed sweet bean treats or wrapped towel sets. They are mostly pro forma affairs wrapped up in a half-day or so.

Nissan's meetings during the Ghosn era were almost carnival-like affairs at the Pacifico Yokohama National Convention Hall, a sprawling complex attached to the InterContinental hotel on the Yokohama waterfront, not far from Nissan's twenty-two-story global headquarters. Nissan's latest vehicles would be on display in the lobby with engineers or salespeople on standby to explain their features. And the day was capped with everyone filing out of the cavernous auditorium to a banquet room for a curry-rice lunch. There, Nissan executives would mingle with the masses, although Ghosn typically excused himself at this juncture.

During the question-and-answer period, a young woman dubbed Miss Fairlady, in tribute to the brand's Fairlady Z sports coupe, as the Z-Car is known in Japan, would pick shareholders to ask whatever was on their mind, from the incisive to the inane. Dressed in a cutesy elevator girl ensemble, Miss Fairlady would randomly select the ticket numbers of lucky participants from a glass box on stage. Even in the best of times, these Q&A sessions could get heated. But when Ghosn's generous pay package came up, investors turned indignant and weren't afraid to show it.

"You are always talking about this: Mr. Ghosn's compensation is high. And I agree," barked one shareholder at the 2011 meeting. "The total full-year dividend is 22.4 billion yen, and your compensation is 1 billion out of that. It's about five percent. But operating profit is only point three percent compared with revenue. . . . Compared to the dividend you are delivering, your compensation is so much higher. . . . What do you think about these points?"

It is not surprising that Ghosn's salary would become a focal point in the growing dispute with Japanese shareholders and Nissan traditionalists. Across all industries, executive compensation is one of the clearest fault lines between Japan and other developed countries, particularly the United States.

In their annual survey for 2018, consulting group Willis Towers Watson put the average Japanese CEO annual compensation among major firms at a relatively modest ¥123 million ($1.1 million), including base pay and short-term incentives. That compares with $3.79 million for the average chief executive among top-listed US companies. The gap grows when long-term incentives are thrown in, often in the form of various stock option plans that shareholders often naively believe come at no cost to them. With that, Japanese CEO pay nudges up to ¥156 million ($1.4 million), while that of their US counterparts soars past $13.3 million. Japanese executives are notoriously proud of this state of affairs, lecturing about the evils of American greed and how their approach demonstrates the importance of the organization over the individual.

. . .

This is not merely sophistry on their part and is in many ways baked into Japanese culture, dating back to the "premarket" days of a feudal system. In the era of hereditary nobility that lasted until 1868, the hierarchy put samurai warriors, farmers (largely peasants on a subsistence income), and skilled craftspeople all above the merchant class, who were considered to be the bottom rung of society (except for outcasts). This did not, of course, prevent them from becoming hugely wealthy. One result of this split personality can be seen to this day in the form of traditional Japanese architecture, where the merchant houses of Kyoto and other ancient centers are finely crafted but bare of ornamentation, considering the wealth of the occupants.[18] This has religious roots in Zen Buddhism but also reflects the fact that the merchants needed to keep a low profile to avoid standing out and creating resentment. During Japan's feudal Edo period from 1603 to 1868, merchants were specifically banned from having a house of more than one or two stories. It was, and still is, considered bad form to flaunt wealth in Japan.

There are other historical reasons for downplaying wealth in Japan. Most of Japan's major companies were originally family affairs, rising first as zaibatsu conglomerates and morphing into less centralized coop-eratives in the keiretsu system after World War II. This trend continues today. Akio Toyoda would not likely have risen to the top of one of the world's most successful companies without having had the foresight to pick the right parents. His grandfather founded the company, and the family still owns an estimated 1 percent, worth around $2 billion. In addi-tion, the Toyoda family continues to hold sway thanks to a constellation of extended family members with leadership positions at Toyota Group companies. Similarly, Tadashi Yanai, founder of UNIQLO parent com-pany Fast Retailing, still owns 21.6 percent of the group, enough to make him Japan's richest man.

In the end, if you own the company, what does it matter what your paycheck looks like? As any entrepreneur will have calculated, you will have the money either as an employee or an owner, and it doesn't really matter which. In addition, salaries are typically the least tax-effective way to reward someone, especially when you control the corporate le-vers to make myriad tax avoidance schemes possible. It's only when you bring in "hired help"—professional managers like Ghosn—who realize that they may be short-termers that annual compensation becomes an issue.

This Japanese self-deference in public doesn't mean that you need to scrimp in private. The Japanese tax system helps to encourage an array of fringe benefits that augment income and grease the wheels of com-merce. Authorities are quite liberal in terms of what constitutes a "busi-ness expense" for companies. The Akasaka area of Tokyo, conveniently located near major corporate headquarters as well as the corridors of power for high-level government officials, is populated by exclusive and highly discreet restaurants that will charge thousands of dollars for a meal, bringing together major decision makers in private rooms out of the public view. Senior corporate figures will also enjoy dedicated cars and drivers on call at all hours, and their apartments in the central and pricey parts of town will be paid by the company as a business cost.

This is not as far-fetched as it seems. In their daily lives, senior execu-tives in Japan are never really off the job. The lavish entertaining at night is almost always with some kind of business partner or company executive. Dining with one's spouse is not a part of this equation and wives (gender equality remains a distant dream) will happily go about their own lives. Anyone who has sat through a dinner with the boss, or worse, your partner's boss, can appreciate the value in this approach.

This corporate largesse also extends to expensive gifts for business partners, an extension of an overall proclivity for gift giving. When asked out to dinner, expect that you will receive a gift, even if the other party is treating. Not having a gift of your own ready will be a major cultural faux pas.

· · ·

When the new rules for disclosure emerged in 2010, Ghosn understood his pay was a potential powder keg—not only in Japan but also in France, where cultural mores were arguably even more squeamish about big payouts.

This was underlined in the trial of Greg Kelly, the American Nissan director arrested with Ghosn and accused of scheming to help hide his boss's pay. During the 2020 court hearings, a senior Nissan manager in charge of executive compensation testified that Ghosn was alarmed that, when the rules changed in 2010, no other Japanese executive made enough to cross the threshold for disclosure.

Toshiaki Ohnuma, one of the plea bargainers serving witness for the prosecutors, said that in that year, the only top brass initially required to divulge remuneration were Ghosn and two other non-Japanese executives. At the time, Ohnuma said, Ghosn seemed less concerned by the fact that Japanese executives actually made much less money than by the fact the rest of the world would find out about it.

"How much the directors are receiving will be widely known to Japanese employees. There was concern that this may lead to complaints that only non-Japanese directors were receiving higher pay although every employee was working hard," Ohnuma testified.

Ghosn offered a novel solution, according to Ohnuma. The chairman, who earned his Le Cost Cutter reputation through unforgiving economizing, decided the best way to defuse resentment would be to award special bonuses to three Japanese executives, including Hiroto Saikawa, the man once considered his right-hand man. The extra pay bump was just enough to nudge these executives over the threshold so their respective income would have to be disclosed as well. Thus, with three non-Japanese *and* three Japanese on the public disclosure list, it seemed at least balanced.

Despite such creative accounting, Ghosn's package still soared high above the others'. So, before shareholders, he usually came armed with a clear, unapologetic message that the new Nissan played by different, international rules.

"It's true, we don't pay as a function of the Japanese standard. We pay as a function of the global standard because we want to be able to attract global talent," a calm and collected Ghosn countered during the 2011 showdown with investors. "When you compare Nissan compensation to Toyota compensation or to Honda compensation, well, we have differences. It's coming from the fact that some of our competitors pay only as a function of the Japanese standard. We don't. That's the big difference."

Before the shareholder meetings, Kelly would prepare data compiled for Nissan from Towers Watson, the global compensation consultancy that later became Willis Towers Watson. It showed Nissan's executive pay was modest by comparison with global benchmarks. In 2011, for example, Ghosn was paid $12.5 million. But the industry average for automotive CEOs was just under $18 million. And the highest-paid CEO was pulling down nearly $29 million at the time, nearly two and a half times Ghosn's haul.

Compared with the top pay at other companies that had been courting Ghosn, Nissan seemed to be shortchanging its savior. In 2010, for instance, as Ghosn was disclosing his pay for the first time, Alan Mulally—the man Ford settled on as CEO after being rebuffed by Ghosn and the hero executive credited with saving Ford from disaster during the Great Recession—was earning over $26 million.[19]

Dan Akerson, the chairman and CEO of General Motors in 2010, was taking home a seemingly more modest $2.5 million. But GM's executive pay was curbed as a condition of its government bailout.[20] A better measure of GM's traditionally more inflated standard would be the

sums doled out to Rick Wagoner, the man who blocked a Nissan tie-up
and then presided over GM's fall into bankruptcy. Even as GM staggered
toward its humiliating Chapter ii debacle, Wagoner banked almost $20
million in 2007 and more than $16 million in 2008. In 2009, the year GM
went bust, his salary portion was slashed to just $1—yes, one dollar—but
Wagoner still pocketed close to $3 million in other compensation before
being fired.[21]

"There was a very specific strategy employed at the meetings," said
one former executive who helped prepare Nissan's response to shareholder blowback over Ghosn's pay.

"The argument was that Nissan was not a Japanese company. It was a
global company, and more so than Toyota, Honda or any other Japanese
company. As such, the way in which the company structured its compensation and attracted overseas talent was to pay basically US standard
salaries for executives, particularly overseas executives."

Nissan had grounds to paint itself as a truly international player. Forty-
eight of the top hundred positions at the carmaker were non-Japanese in
2015. Some were French, coming from Renault. But the pool included
people from Brazil, Portugal, Britain, the Netherlands, the United States,
India, Germany, Italy, Spain, China, Canada, and South Africa. No other
Japanese carmaker—least of all Toyota or Honda—could boast such national diversity at its highest echelons. And executives at those rival automakers privately denigrated Nissan as no longer being a "real Japanese"
company.

"The difficulty was trying to judge Nissan as a Japanese company
when in fact it wasn't," one former Nissan executive said. "But because
it was listed on the Tokyo Stock Exchange, it was judged as a Japanese
company by the Japanese. Actually, outside Japan, Ghosn's salary was
nothing remarkable. It really wasn't. But inside Japan, obviously it was
quite sensational."

. . .

Over the years, the voyeuristic outrage over Ghosn's outsize compensation gradually faded, and even Nissan's mercurial investors grew weary

of fighting the point. But his reported remuneration kept climbing. It declined only two years during the remainder of his time with the company and peaked at just above ¥1 billion (about $9 million) in the fiscal year ending March 31, 2017.[22] Even then, however, Ghosn was still outearned by his contemporaries. GM CEO Mary Barra earned nearly $22 million that year, while Ford CEO Jim Hackett pulled in almost $17 million.

Many who worked with Ghosn at Nissan say he deserved every penny for saving the company. "Obviously he was getting paid a lot," said one former Alliance executive. "But you can objectively state, that if money were the thing that were most motivating for him, he would have left a long time ago."

Later, in 2020, at the trial of Greg Kelly, it became clear just how widespread the fear was inside Nissan that Ghosn would jump ship. Kelly—with the help of a cadre of other top executives—studied elaborate schemes to heap more compensation on Ghosn without having to publicly disclose the astonishingly high sum. Kelly himself stated that the company needed to do so to retain Ghosn's talent, though he insisted they only considered legal ways of doing so and only as compensation for Ghosn's postretirement services.

Ghosn's running concern wasn't just the public embarrassment of disclosing his compensation in Japan; he was apparently also intensely troubled about a potential backlash in France, where sensitivities about executive pay are even more prickly. During the Kelly trial, a key government witness testified Ghosn was afraid of being fired from Renault if the true scope of his pay package were known.

"Mr. Ghosn was concerned that the true level of his compensation was disclosed, the French state would fire him because the French state was sensitive to his compensation," said Nissan executive Hari Nada, who ran the CEO and chairman's office under Ghosn. For Nissan executives convinced they needed to keep Ghosn's talent in-house, it was important that he was also secure in his position at Renault. "Mr. Ghosn was a representative of Renault at Nissan," Nada said. "His power in Nissan rests on his nomination into Nissan from Renault, which depends on the French state."

Some around Ghosn say compensation remained a sore point for him until the end, partly because he wasn't earning as much as his global rivals. And partly because he resented having to constantly justify the amount, even though it was less than others in the industry.

"It was public that he was frustrated. Because for him, compensation was an evaluation of his own value," said one former Renault executive close to Ghosn. "When he was comparing his own compensation to that of the head of Ford, the head of General Motors, or people like this, he was of the belief that he was not at the right level, because he believed he had the same value or even more than some of these guys. And because France is France, and Japan is Japan, and the references in these countries are what they are, he could not get the same level of compensation. That's the fact."

What rarely got mentioned in Japan, however, was the fact Ghosn concurrently earned a salary as the chairman and CEO of Renault. But because of the French government's ownership stake in Renault, the payout wasn't nearly as generous as Nissan's, even though Renault was nominally the controlling partner in the Alliance. In May 2018, long before his arrest, Ghosn contracted for fixed base pay of just €1 million (about $1.2 million) from Renault, although the amount was amplified by variable compensation and long-term incentives, which could more than double that.[23]

Ghosn got another bump when Mitsubishi joined as the third leg of his Alliance. After bringing the smaller Japanese carmaker under his command, Ghosn earned ¥227 million (about $2 million) as its new chairman.[24]

Add all that together, and Ghosn's package came closer to Detroit levels, but it still fell short, despite his having to run three different companies on two continents.

But then in late 2018, seemingly out of nowhere, Japanese prosecutors said something different was happening all along. Ghosn, now under lock and key, wasn't just squeaking by with substandard pay packages in the shadow of his industry peers all those years, they said. He actually was secretly squirreling away huge sums to be paid after retirement in a deferred compensation scheme that ran afoul of the law. The concealed amount, according to prosecutors, exceeded an astronomical $80 million over eight years. In fact, in most of those years, the hidden sum was even higher than the pay disclosed to shareholders at the contentious annual meetings.

The upshot, prosecutors alleged, was that Ghosn's total compensation—salary, incentives, and the postponed payouts—over the period was virtually double what he and the company had been reporting. If true, he was playing both sides—complaining about not being on par with Ford and GM chiefs while actually earning at least as much, if not more, if you combined his public salary with this alleged secret stash, and throw in pay from Renault and Mitsubishi.

The bombshell allegations threw a critical new light on his preoccupation with pay and sent Ghosn and the auto empire he built and ruled into deep crisis.

Looking back after his escape to Lebanon, Ghosn insisted he might never have landed in such legal trouble if he hadn't been so steadfastly loyal to Renault and Nissan in the face of all the job offers. He could have packed up for Detroit and led Ford or GM instead. And at his Beirut news conference in January 2020, his first since his arrest, he made sure to bemoan the ill-fated overture from car czar Rattner to run GM a decade earlier.

"He was offering me a pay which was double my pay. I said, 'You know what? I understand your offer is very attractive. But a captain of the ship doesn't leave the ship in difficulty,'" Ghosn said. "I made a mistake. I should have accepted the offer."

5

MEMORIES ARE SHORT

THE JAPAN OF 1999 WAS A COUNTRY LARGELY DRAINED of its confidence.

Every year since 1957, the Bank of Japan (BOJ)—the country's central bank—has carried out the quarterly Tankan survey to gauge corporate sentiment in the country. The Tankan is so highly regarded by Japanese companies that 99 percent of those surveyed send back a response to the confidential questionnaire. The most closely watched element of the survey is a Diffusion Index on the state of business that compares the number of positive viewpoints minus negative ones, so that a score of zero means that businesses overall have a neutral view of where the economy is heading.

The headline figure for major companies announced in December 1998 was negative 56.

It was the lowest score since the mid-'70s oil crisis and a long, long way from the heady plus-53 reading that was seen at the height of the Bubble Economy in 1989. Japan's economy had moved back into recession in 1998, suffering its longest downturn in the post–World War II period.[1] "1998 was a year of distress, shock and pain," chief economist for Jardine Fleming Securities, Chris Calderwood, told Reuters at the time. Normally upbeat business leaders were already rattled by the state of affairs.[2]

"The Japanese economy is on the verge of collapsing," Sony chairman Norio Ohga had warned in the spring of 1998.[3]

What had been one of the industrialized world's fastest-growing economies throughout much of the postwar era had now suffered two major contractions in the decade since the collapse of the Bubble in 1990. The heart of the problem had been an unsustainable rise in asset prices, especially in real estate. This has been summed up in the aphorism that at the peak in 1989, the 350 acres of the Imperial Palace in central Tokyo were supposed to be worth more than all the property in Florida or California. Otherwise savvy economists talked about how the Japanese property market was "different," and that Japanese investors never sold, so prices would stay high forever. One analyst had the unfortunate timing to say in 1989, just before the crash, that "the prospect of a real land-price collapse strikes most analysts as remote."

In fact, property prices plummeted, taking billions of dollars out of the economy and sending the stock market into its own long slide. It took twenty years for both markets to hit bottom soon after the end of the global Great Recession in 2009. By this time, both land and shares were worth just 20 percent of their peak levels.

The incredibly long time to work through this market fall was due in part to cautious government measures and accounting rules that allowed companies to keep putting off the day of reckoning. It is easy to see this as bureaucratic inertia, but it was in many ways a purposeful and consistent policy approach. By unwinding the bad loans and deflationary pressures slowly, Japan avoided the social upheaval that can come from a sudden retrenchment. There were no fire sales of assets. There was no massive spate of store bankruptcies and boarding-up of shopping streets. For most people, little had changed, with 95 percent of the workforce continuing to have jobs. Some Japanese officials were even smug about the difference with downturns in the United States, arguing that since Japan was rich, it could take its own time. Foreign visitors used to the headlines about Japan's economic malaise were shocked when they came to a Tokyo that looked as neat and modern as ever. As more than one American executive commented when visiting Japan during this period, *If this is a recession, then I want one as well.*

The declines were real, however, and came despite record low interest rates and lavish government spending that tried to bring back the glory days of high growth. Instead, they gave Japan the distinction of having the largest government debt burden in the world.

Sony's Ohga was not alone in warning that Japan could be entering a deflationary trap, in which lower prices and continued economic contraction spiral downward together. Government officials tried to stay optimistic, saying that policy measures would head off the problem, but it was clear that the risks were growing. Minutes of the policy board meetings at the BOJ in February 1999 spoke of the need "to avoid possible intensification of deflationary pressure and to ensure that the economic downturn will come to a halt." While the wording was the cautious bureaucratic language favored by central banks, one board member was more direct. "Japan's economy was already caught in a vicious circle of deflation," the member said in a warning that was to prove prescient.[4] The BOJ would spend the next twenty years trying to break out of deflation, with only limited success. The ailment mutated and eventually proved to be contagious, with falling prices eventually spreading to the Eurozone economy and elsewhere.

•   •   •

While policy makers showed cautious concern, Japanese corporate boardrooms were in crisis mode. In November 1997, Yamaichi Securities, one of Japan's four biggest brokerage firms with a hundred-year legacy, announced that it was going out of business. Its collapse, a kind of mini precursor to the Great Recession that was to come a decade later, was due to the usual mixture of bad business decisions and the uncovering of a scheme to hide $1.6 billion in bad loans. Yamaichi's failure in strategy and the illegal steps to hide the truth were not much of a surprise to Japan's business leaders. What did shock them was the fact that no one came to save it. Major banks were themselves facing an avalanche of bad loans, making them unable, or unwilling, to step in. Even Fuji Bank, the partner firm for Yamaichi through its keiretsu corporate affiliation, declined to throw a lifeline. Fuji had its own problems and would disappear into a merger five years later, in 2002.

"In this case, the financial market hunted down a weak financial institution and cut it off," said one financial analyst at the time. The *Wall Street Journal*, in reporting on Yamaichi, said "Plagued by an enormous bad-loan problem, a sickly stock market, heavy government-budget deficits and an economy that once again looks to be sliding into stagnation, Japan has reluctantly turned to the only tonic it can: Deregulation and the untender mercies of the free market."[5]

One of the potential solutions to the deflation problem was to make the Japanese labor market function properly, a point raised mainly by foreign economists. Under Japan's lifetime employment model, employees remain loyal to the company they enter within a month of graduating from university. Since almost no one ever leaves, there is no retention problem and therefore no real reason to reward good performance, especially when prices at stores are mostly falling every year. Although creating a free-flowing labor market was a government goal to help raise productivity and end deflationary pressures, 1999 was a bad time to implement a policy that would raise unemployment in the short term. While unemployment was still low by global standards, 4.7 percent of workers in 1999 were out of work. (It would peak at a record high of 5.5 percent in October 2002.)

"In America, people are used to the idea they might lose their jobs and think they can find another one," one government official told Reuters at that time. "In Japan, once a salaried employee loses his job, he thinks his career is over." The official made clear that the government was concerned that "rising unemployment could result in political instability." A major concern was that the next group of the unemployed could be the lawmakers in the ruling party.[6]

. . .

Ghosn faced what seemed an intractable problem: how to make the cost savings necessary to rescue Nissan while avoiding a hostile reaction from workers and skittish government officials. Synergies with Renault would be an important step, but they would have to be done carefully. Given Nissan's dire straits, even Japanese government officials had to put on a brave face about foreign influence in the august Japanese company. At the same time, Ghosn had the freedom that would have been denied a domestically bred CEO.

"Ghosn was seen as something of a knight in shining armor on a white steed. He was completely unknown in Japan," said one investment banker active in European-Japan corporate mergers. "People were afraid, but I think they also recognized that something like this unknown foreigner was necessary because otherwise Nissan had nowhere else to go, it was really the last resort."

It didn't hurt that Ghosn was coming from France. Whereas the French tend to generate strong views in many countries, their image in Japan is one of unparalleled beauty, style, and culture. France is the top European tourist destination for Japanese travelers and there is even a purported medical condition, known as the Paris syndrome, for Japanese people who suddenly feel acutely depressed or even ill when they travel to the City of Light, due to their shock that the city is not as wonderful as they had dreamed. The condition appears to be the stuff of urban myth, but it does manage to warrant its own Wikipedia entry. The feeling is reciprocated. In France, *japonisme*, the influence of Japanese fine arts, fashion, and aesthetics, became a trend in the nineteenth century and remains popular.

In the corporate world, cultural similarities had likewise contributed to the success of a multinational alliance when so many others had failed in the past. Both countries share a certain attachment to bureaucracy and a concern for employees that make job layoffs in either country a rarity.

For Nissan, the positive results were clear. By 2007, the company's market value was up an impressive 820 percent from its near-bankruptcy state at Ghosn's arrival. In all, the Ghosn years added $60 billion in value to Nissan. "For the first six or seven years, all went well. The accolades were justified," said the investment banker.

Much of this came from strong gains in the critical overseas markets, particularly the United States and China. But Nissan had also made unprecedented inroads into dismantling the keiretsu system of corporate ties to cut its costs. In this, Japan's recovering economy played a role.

Overall economic growth averaged slightly above 1 percent. The numbers were hardly what they'd been in the go-go years of the 1960s and '70s, but they were sufficient for corporate Japan to help restock its coffers. Within this, Japan's total corporate profits rose steadily, climbing 85 percent from 1999, the year of Ghosn's arrival, to 2007.

Over that same time the Tankan survey of business confidence rose to plus 23, a vast improvement from December 1998's score of negative 56. This meant that suppliers and other business partners were in a much better position to accept the more severe negotiations that Ghosn brought to the table. As one partner executive put it, "Once a system is established, no one wants to change it. Ghosn triggered changes throughout the system." An improving labor market also meant less political heat on the twenty-one thousand job cuts Nissan initiated under Ghosn. The headline unemployment rate, which had been inching up near to the 6 percent level, had fallen back down to under 4 percent in 2007.

In terms of corporate value, 2007 would represent the high point for Ghosn and Nissan. The share price would soon fall sharply, along with the rest of corporate Japan, from the massive impact of two seismic events, the global financial crisis of 2008–2009 and the horrific March 2011 earthquake, tsunami, and nuclear plant disaster in northern Japan. The economy would later see a rebirth in 2013 under an aggressive growth strategy by Prime Minister Abe. This time, Nissan would not be so lucky as it fell into new troubles.

When the economy got going in 2013, Ghosn had been at Nissan for nearly fourteen years. It was a long time for any chief executive, especially one who focuses on corporate turnarounds. It was also Ghosn's longest tenure in any one position since starting his career back in 1978. By now, the rapt media attention over the auto industry legend had started to fade. The global accolades from *Time* and *Fortune* in the early 2000s had by 2017 become an honorary postage stamp in Lebanon. Whatever his performance, Ghosn was no longer the "new best thing."

While other foreign executives have avoided Ghosn's fate of being thrown in prison, some have faced their own difficult times and a hostile reaction. As one consultant who has worked with numerous foreign executives in Japan put it: "If you are a foreign CEO in Japan and you get it wrong, they tear you apart."

One such case was the ordeal faced by Sarah Casanova, a Canadian veteran executive with McDonald's who became CEO of McDonald's Japan in 2013. The chain has been a fixture in Japan since 1971, and by 2010 had grown to more than 3,300 outlets, with an especially strong appeal among families.

But within a year of her arrival, the chain was hit with scandals over a supplier that was allegedly using expired meat and another that had shipped processed chicken from outside Japan that contained foreign objects. Although McDonald's said the allegations were never proven, Casanova was attacked in the media for not apologizing "properly," a cardinal sin in a country where the deep bow of remorse is a required ritual for any company, domestic or foreign, that is facing a scandal.[7] Sales per outlet plunged by nearly 40 percent and the company started posting losses.[8] Casanova did manage to get a handle on the many problems (aside from the food safety issues, the company had also overexpanded) and sales started rising. But it took her three years to get the company out of the woods.[9]

Nippon Sheet Glass, with much of its business now overseas, has gone through two foreign CEOs in quick order, with neither lasting more than two years. More recently, pharmaceutical group Takeda took on French national Christophe Weber, who created initial worries in the boardroom with a landmark $62 billion purchase of Irish drug maker Shire in 2019, the largest-ever foreign purchase by a Japanese company.[10] Few other foreigners have tried to take the helm in Japan's corporate fleet. A 2012 study found that just 1 percent of Japanese company CEO appointments were foreigners, compared with 30 percent in Europe.

. . .

The first major Japanese company that saw a foreigner take the reins was automaker Mazda, and the decision came from overseas. In 1996, Ford increased its stake in the struggling Japanese automaker to 33.4 percent, enough to give it effective control over executive appointments. The first in a string of foreign CEOs was Henry Wallace, a British national.[11] It was not an enthusiastic welcome. His Japanese predecessor had strongly denied that he was stepping down, and was less than convivial at their joint news conference. For the Japanese public there was general shock, and the news media focused on how mass layoffs would soon begin. Wallace spoke no Japanese, and some financial analysts questioned how he could run a Japanese company where every document and meeting would need to be translated for him, issues that would challenge Ghosn three years later. "I can't tell you how many times I've been told, 'You don't understand Japanese business practices,'" Wallace said in a 1996 interview. "It just means they don't want to change."[12]

Wallace got the ball rolling on the needed turnaround of Mazda, but most of the credit has gone to American Mark Fields, who was just thirty-eight years old when he was sent over by Ford in 1999. Just as Ghosn was doing with Nissan, Fields took aim at Japan's seniority system, promoting younger people and creating a clear Mazda brand amid its myriad competitors. He stayed three years. "Ghosn is every inch as awe-inspiring as his media legend, but Fields did not pale by comparison," said John R. Harris, a former speechwriter for Fields, as well as for Ghosn in later years. But Fields, and Ford overall, got little credit for helping to put Mazda on a stronger footing before the two companies severed most ties in 2008. The "Zoom Zoom" tagline, one of Mazda's biggest marketing successes, came from the Ford side. In Harris's view, "Mazda taught Ford how to build cars, but Ford taught Mazda how to sell cars."

The highest-profile foreign import to follow was British-American executive Howard Stringer, the former CBS executive who had the unenviable job of turning around electronics behemoth Sony, a group that, like Nissan, was trying to recapture past glories. Even more than Japan's automakers, Sony had come to symbolize the country's image as an innovative leader ready to take on, or take over, the world. Whereas Japanese cars were successful due to quality and competitive pricing, Sony was all about innovation. The Sony Walkman portable music system, introduced in 1979, was itself a legendary story of individualism, and presaged the era of the Apple iPod. The development of the Walkman came at the personal request of Sony cofounder Masaru Ibuka, who wanted it for himself so that he could listen to opera while traveling. The Walkman became the classic case of a hugely successful product that no one had previously known they even needed or wanted. Over the next twenty years, the company would sell more than 230 million units, just one facet in a broad line of electronics products that were considered top of the line.

But by 2000, Sony—like Japan Inc. more generally—was bloated and directionless. The company had invested heavily, paying $3.4 billion for Hollywood icon Columbia Pictures Entertainment. The idea was a merging of hardware and software, a strategy that never bore fruit.

Stringer joined Sony in the United States in 1997, and became chairman of the group in 2005 at a time when the one-time brand leader had fallen into a morass of disconnected product lines with varying levels of quality. In a ranking of global brands that year, Korea's Samsung came above Sony for the first time ever, kicking it out of the No. 20 position.[13] The problems were easy to see in Tokyo's glamorous Ginza district, where many major brands have showrooms to build excitement for their products. Apple, which had opened up two years earlier, had massive crowds on a daily basis. Sony's showcase location nearby felt like a morgue.

Like Ghosn, Stringer saw that he needed to shake things up, saying that he wanted to make Sony "cool again," in his words. He began efforts to bring in younger engineers who could design products running on sophisticated software and better tied into the then-growing world of online. He launched a $2 billion restructuring that cut ten thousand jobs, closing eleven production facilities. In short, he started the company down what would be a long road.

Despite the efforts, immediate success proved elusive. When Stringer stepped down in 2012, the company's stock price was 60 percent lower than when he took control in 2005. It was still losing money, although some external factors, such as the devastating 2011 earthquake and tsunami, were partly to blame. Stringer's best move in many respects was his choice for a successor to continue the restructuring. At age fifty-one, Kazuo Hirai was young to be in charge of a major Japanese company and was in some ways another "foreigner." He had grown up in California and was said to be more fluent in English than in Japanese. By the time

Hirai retired in 2019, Sony was strongly profitable, if not the major global player that it had been in its heyday. In its story on Hirai's departure, the *Nikkei* financial daily wrote of how he had "remade Sony," that he had "breathed fresh air into a company often mired in internal power struggles." The piece discussed Sony's long history, its iconic founders, and the various leaders through the years. Stringer didn't get any of the credit.[14]

In some ways, this appearance of ingratitude could be forgiven. Few people, or organizations, want to talk about when they were at their most vulnerable. History has shown that turnaround specialists seldom get credit for what they've done after they leave the stage. Perhaps the most famous was British wartime prime minister Winston Churchill. Seen as a radical (and to some a racist) figure for much of his career, he would later be seen as the perfect leader to save Britain, and in many respects the free world, from Nazi Germany. His mistake, however, was overstaying. After being unceremoniously ejected by the British populace in an election just two months after the victory in Europe, he returned to leadership in 1951 in a postwar Britain that was losing its empire and global influence. Britain was by then much more focused on domestic issues and social reforms than in grand power plans, areas in which Churchill had little interest. He was to step down amid ill health in 1955 without much positive comment for his postwar record.

The corporate world is no less forgiving than the electorate. One of the greatest falling-from-grace episodes was the story of General Electric, the far-flung manufacturer of everything from railroad locomotives to household appliances that soared under the charismatic and uncompromising Jack Welch, only to nosedive soon after his departure. Welch transformed the company during his twenty-year tenure from 1981 to 2001, and was hailed in the business guru sector as the greatest executive of his time. In 1999, he would be named no less than the "Manager of the Century" by *Fortune* magazine. Welch was of like mind with Ghosn when it came to properly compensating high-performing senior executives, including himself. Upon retiring, Welch took home a severance package filled with benefits estimated by an external corporate governance firm to be worth $417 million, the largest such payment ever.[15]

Welch left on a high note (as his bonus suggests), but he also sowed the seeds of its eventual near-collapse. At the time of his departure, 43 percent of the company's business came from the GE Capital financial business. This was smart business—in the short term—given the over-sized profits from financial services.

But times change. Banking didn't look like such a great bet in 2008, when the global financial crisis took its toll of major companies around the world and threatened GE's very existence. Dealing with the mess fell to Welch's handpicked successor, Jeffrey Immelt, who has taken much of the blame for the downward spiral that was to follow. Even though the company still employed over 200,000 people in 2020, it was a shell of its former self. Total market capitalization was at just 10 percent of the peak under Welch and it suffered the ignominy of being removed from the corporate world's most exclusive club, the Dow Jones Industrial Average.

Was Welch to blame? Harvard Business School assistant professor Gautam Mukunda, an expert in organizational behavior, says that part of Welch's success was that he was well suited to what the market de-manded at the time.

"Think about the very best performing leaders. The highest level of performance comes when your approach and the underlying circum-stances are a perfect fit. You are perfectly optimized for that environment. The thing about being perfectly optimized for a certain environment is that the better optimized you are for a certain environment, the worse optimized you are for all other environments."

Did Ghosn, like Churchill, overstay? Did a change in the environment shift him from the perfect fit to the wrong fit, like GE? Fraud allegations aside, there had been concerns among some key stakeholders that he was pushing for ever-higher sales at any cost, without making the proper investments to keep the Nissan lineup fresh. As Mukunda notes, a turn-around expert such as Ghosn would be an unlikely choice for a more stable, consensus-dependent environment. In some ways, it is a tribute to Ghosn that he managed to stay on top for so long past the turnaround, given the fact that Western CEOs typically have much shorter reigns. The average US CEO is in office for less than seven years.[16]

Itaru Koeda, a forty-three-year veteran of Nissan who retired as a co-chairman of the company in 2008, said that Ghosn had, indeed, stayed too long. Testifying in the trial of Greg Kelly, Koeda said that after a decade, Ghosn had hand-picked all of those around him and therefore held too much power. Others agreed. When Ghosn was arrested, then nineteen years into the job, he was seen as more isolated from those around him, more disconnected from the business, and he didn't see the looming threats around him. "He was managing through a very small team, he had become more alone in his own company," said one consultant who worked with Ghosn. "Why couldn't he see what was happening? It was obvious."

6

PRESSURE COOKER

GHOSN COULD BARELY CONTAIN AN IMPISH SMILE AS he drove the daring, if funny-looking, new car onto the stage. It was a bulbous, sky-blue hatchback that ran solely on electricity and emitted no carbon dioxide or other noxious gases. Ghosn promised it would be the first affordable, mass-market electric vehicle (EV) for a world still addicted to gasoline. Its name: Nissan Leaf.

The date was August 2, 2009, a decade into Ghosn's reign and a year before his prodigious pay would raise the ire of shareholders at the annual meeting. It was also a time when electric cars were still seen as gimmicky science fair projects or derided as glorified golf carts. Few automakers were taking them seriously, let alone actually selling them. And hardly any customers seemed to want one.

But in Ghosn's eyes, the Leaf was so important that he timed its debut to the opening of the company's gleaming new twenty-two-story world headquarters building overlooking the Yokohama waterfront, just south of Japan's capital city on Tokyo Bay. The glassy high-rise, towering over a glitzy gallery that could showcase more than thirty vehicles, stood in dramatic contrast with Nissan's shabby old office between the elaborate Kabuki-za Theater, a monument to traditional Japanese culture, and the bustling, blue-collar Tsukiji Fish Market. Ghosn unveiled both to the world that day—the car and the building—each symbolizing Nissan's bright future and ambition for global leadership.

The Leaf was such a watershed product that former prime minister Junichiro Koizumi was not only on hand for the day's ceremonies but actually sitting in the Leaf's passenger seat as Ghosn carefully steered the car through the showroom of his beautiful new office tower and parked it before hundreds of journalists craning for a glimpse. The Leaf was as much a win for Japanese ingenuity and innovation as it was for Nissan itself. Ghosn seemed to be delivering the revolutionary car to the world on behalf of the entire country.

"This car represents a real breakthrough," proclaimed Ghosn, in a pale blue-gray suit alluding to the clear, clean skies of an all-electric tomorrow. "As its name suggests, the Leaf is totally neutral to the environment. There is no exhaust pipe, no gasoline-burning engine. There is only the quiet, efficient power provided by our own compact lithium-ion battery packs."

Not long after the Leaf's release, Ghosn made an equally bold prediction. The Renault-Nissan Alliance alone, he said, would sell a cumulative 1.5 million battery-powered electric vehicles by the end of March 2017. Nissan and Renault, he pledged, would have seven more all-electric nameplates by then.

· · ·

By any measure, Ghosn was a pioneer in trailblazing new frontiers in the auto industry. He saw a future for electric vehicles while rivals were still dabbling in gasoline-electric hybrids. He wanted to leapfrog that halfway technology, then championed by archrival Toyota, and land straight into what he saw as a radical new future of zero emissions cars.

And Ghosn stole a lead on the competitors again in 2013, when he declared that Nissan would develop self-driving cars and have them for sale in 2020. At the time, even high-end luxury brands such as Mercedes-Benz and BMW were offering just rudimentary driver-assist features that could only aid steering and braking at low speeds. Ghosn's pledge that mass-market Nissans, of all brands, would be a world leader in cars that could navigate intersections by themselves while drivers sit back and relax set the industry abuzz.

"There is no doubt he was a visionary. Nissan was a forerunner in many technologies," said a former top executive who worked under Ghosn for years. "Certainly, electric vehicles. Arguably too early, before the rest of the world was ready. We were ridiculed by other manufacturers saying electric vehicles would never take off. And again, with autonomous driving. Nissan socialized that before any other mass-market provider."

High ambition for EVs and self-driving cars was a trademark of Ghosn's leadership. So was his resolve in pursuing ever-bigger scale. He was one of the industry's earliest and most vocal proselytizers of consolidation and mass volume. High technology and grand scale—ideally approaching ten million vehicles a year globally—went hand in hand. Even a decade later, in 2020, only Toyota and Volkswagen were churning out vehicles at that stratospheric level. Conventional wisdom maintained that automakers needed to pool resources for the costly investment in the high-tech, next-generation batteries needed for EVs and the complex sensors of autonomous cars.

Strength in numbers was a founding principle of the Renault-Nissan partnership from Day One. But now, spiraling costs and cutthroat competition were creating a pressure cooker in the car business, and it seemed like the Alliance was perfectly positioned to leverage its scale to take on the challenge. The trick would be harnessing the resources of both to cope.

Cost pressure raised the stakes of battling Toyota, General Motors, and Volkswagen. Eking out each extra vehicle was key to driving down unit cost in an era when pundits routinely predicted that smaller players would either go bust or get gobbled up. Ghosn was among the prognosticators. "No three-million-unit carmaker can make it," he declared in 2010,[1] a year in which Nissan booked worldwide sales of just over four million vehicles.[2]

With Renault chipping in another 2.6 million, that put the global Alliance far past a healthy six million units.[3] The Franco-Japanese duo, however, was still playing catch up to the big boys. Toyota and GM both sold about 8.4 million vehicles in 2010, and Volkswagen AG delivered 7.3 million.

But the drive to boost volume and cut costs also put Renault and Nissan on a collision course with each other. The partners grappled with how to piggyback their product development to achieve scale while preserving their brand identities. More than ever, carmakers were forced to invest in costly new fuel economy and safety technologies that customers didn't necessarily want but regulators nonetheless demanded. Engineers at Renault and Nissan began to clash on the best way to meet these requirements as top brass nudged them to cooperate more, share designs, and worst of all, to prideful engineers enamored with their own genius, make compromises.

"More and more, you had to invest in areas that have no value to customers," said a former Nissan top executive involved with product planning. "The investment amount was getting higher and higher. And that means you have to reduce costs to maintain profits. It's big pressure. To get agreement between the two companies, it wasn't easy."

· · ·

Around that time, governments in the United States, Europe, China, and Japan began rapidly ratcheting up fuel economy standards. The United States uses a system known as the Corporate Average Fuel Economy (CAFE) standard to determine how far, on average, the country's vehicles should drive on a gallon of gasoline. In 2007, the US Congress made its first change to the country's CAFE rules in almost two decades. The new fuel economy goal was 35 miles per gallon (mpg) by 2020, an amazing 40 percent jump over efficiency levels of the day.

Then, President Barack Obama took office, and he declared that pace of improvement still wasn't fast enough. He called for a CAFE fleet average of 35.5 mpg by 2016.[4] Obama tightened the screws again in 2012 by setting a new goal that jacked up the fleet average for cars and light trucks to about 54.5 mpg by 2025.[5] That was later revised down to 46.7 mpg, but it was still a lofty goal.[6] Regulators didn't care how companies did it, so long as they made cleaner cars. Stunned automakers conceded the only way to get there was the costly road of reengineering their vehicles to run on electricity instead of gasoline. Even as President Donald Trump later relaxed these ambitious targets, most automakers had already accepted the long-term reality that eventually they would have to go electric.

The cost-impact of electrifying cars to comply with the new fuel economy rules was enormous: The modest 24-kilowatt-hour lithium-ion batteries in the first-generation Leaf—which could power the car for only one hundred miles—initially cost around $10,000 apiece to produce—accounting for a big chunk of the car's lofty $32,780 sticker price.[7]

Nissan invested a massive $2 billion to upgrade its factory complex in Smyrna, Tennessee, to manufacture 150,000 Leafs and 200,000 battery packs a year. And globally, that was just one of three similar outlays to build sister facilities in Japan and the United Kingdom to manufacture the newfangled car worldwide.[8] All told, Renault and Nissan planned to jointly invest €4 billion (about $5.7 billion) in electric vehicle projects to have enough factory firepower to churn out 500,000 of the zero-emissions cars a year.[9]

At the same time, increasingly stringent safety standards kept pushing up the cost of developing and manufacturing vehicles. And worse for all carmakers, the addition of new safety equipment and stronger auto bodies also kept adding weight to vehicles at a time when engineers wanted to slim cars down to save fuel. Then, the advent of self-driving cars, with lidar scanners that initially cost thousands of dollars a pop and expensive computer chips, compounded the dizzying cost calculation.

"You need more money, and because you don't have the money, you are forced to slow down, and because you cannot develop new vehicles, you can't pay for everything that you need," a former top-level Renault executive recalled of the product planning conundrum. "It was a topic that I had to discuss ten times a day. It was my nightmare: How to use in the best way the company's money for the development of the cars, not exceeding the budget."

On the surface, a juggernaut like the Renault-Nissan Alliance seemed primed to thrive in this new landscape. It had massive scale enveloping the globe and a joint CEO full of confidence in the coming technological revolution. Ghosn had a formula for how the Alliance could come out ahead. By developing joint platforms, sharing technologies, pooling purchasing, and jointly producing vehicles, the companies would generate so-called synergies. It was Ghosn's buzzword for savings from mass scale and avoided costs. In 2017, the year before his arrest, the Alliance targeted €10 billion ($11.30 billion) in savings and benefits by taking advantage of these synergies by 2022.

The strategy created some big successes, starting with the Alliance's creation of a so-called Common Module Family (CMF) system to underpin vehicles at both Nissan and Renault. An average car is made from about thirty thousand parts. The goal was to use the same part in as many vehicles for each brand as possible—the chassis, frame, underbody, engine bay, cockpit, and electrical systems—thereby creating a standardized setup used by both brands. Automakers call the approach "commonization." The vehicles would look different, have their own body shapes and styling cues. But underneath, in the areas customers don't see, the vehicles would be essentially the same. Some engineers likened it to dressing up the same mechanics with different "top hats."

The idea had been around for a long time, with GM rolling out Chevrolets, Pontiacs, and Buicks that had different names and different bodies but were nearly identical beneath the skin. The Chevrolet Citation, Pontiac Phoenix, Oldsmobile Omega, and Buick Skylark of the 1980s were essentially the same car underneath their lightly facelifted sheet metal. But Volkswagen leveraged the strategy with the greatest success in recent years—sharing underpinnings across the VW, Škoda, SEAT, and even Audi brands. Success there bred imitation, and the idea was coming into vogue throughout the industry.

The Alliance wanted 70 percent of Renault and Nissan vehicles to be riding on just three platforms, one each for minicars, compacts, and midsize vehicles, by 2020.

The Alliance's first commonized CMF system was a smash hit after it debuted in 2013. It was originally used for the Nissan Rogue, Qashqai, and X-Trail crossovers and in the Kadjar and Koleos crossovers from Renault, among other vehicles. The partners promised that the platform would cover 1.6 million vehicles a year and slash costs by as much as 30 percent. The Rogue became one of Nissan's bestselling nameplates in the world. And in 2019, a full six years after its launch, the aging Rogue remained Nissan's bestselling vehicle in the United States and was the sixth bestselling vehicle in the entire country.

But finding common ground for the common platform was never easy.

No detail was too small to spark disagreement among engineers at the companies, even parts as seemingly insignificant as the headlamp control stem jutting from the steering column. In developing the first CMF, each company came to the table pitching its traditional approach for this component, as was done with the hundreds of others tagged for commonization. But there was a problem.

The cycle order of Nissan's light switch was off-auto-parking lights-on, and Nissan's headlamp high beam was activated with a push-pull of the stem. But Renault's lights went off-parking lights-on-auto, and its high beams switched on and off with a pull-pull motion. This would have to be commonized, and it took six months to reach an agreement even on this innocuous matter. In the end, the Alliance used Nissan's high beams and Renault's light cycle.[10]

"Where things got difficult is when you approached technology and the product itself," said one former Renault engineering executive. "When you are an engineer, what sometimes happens is you believe your solution is the only one, especially when you worked hard on it. That generates a lot of fights."

. . .

As much as the Leaf was a symbol of the Alliance's promise in this bold new era, it also embodied the challenges of fully leveraging the Alliance. Amazingly, the Leaf was not part of the joint platform play, and it was clear in its development it would be a long time before it could be. As Nissan engineers raced to develop the car at the company's cloistered technical center surrounded by mountains south of Yokohama, their French counterparts at Renault were busy working on their own electric car, the Renault Zoe.

Despite being developed nearly in parallel, the Leaf and Zoe shared virtually no common components. One executive leading the Nissan program said the only joint part was a wire harness connected to their inverters, the gadget in an EV that generates electrical current for the motor. "It was a piece of plastic with wires that go through it, and it basically clamps together," the executive said.

The natural area for the two companies to cooperate would have been the car's most expensive components—the lithium-ion battery or the electric motor. But engineers are a stubborn, proud bunch, and the gear heads at both companies suffered from a not-invented-here syndrome when it came to outside technology. Batteries became a big battleground during development.

Nissan wanted to use its own batteries, which were produced in a joint venture the carmaker founded with Japanese electronics giant NEC Corp. Renault wasn't convinced that was a cost-effective strategy and wanted to buy batteries from South Korea's LG Chem. The sides also differed on the electric motor. Nissan wanted a traditional magnetic motor because it was cheaper. Renault wanted an induction motor, arguing that it didn't use rare earth metals that are mainly sourced from China, thereby alleviating supply chain worries. "Everybody in front of the other, said my system is the best in the world," recalled one former top-level Renault executive.

As executives from both sides came to loggerheads over the technologies at a joint management meeting, Ghosn was requested to make a final call—an amazing appeal to the CEO for a matter normally settled by underlings many rungs below.

But to the frustration of many involved, Ghosn didn't make one. He listened to both sides and simply let them pursue their separate strategies. In one view, this made sense. Electric vehicles were still using nascent and rapidly changing technologies. It might be prudent to avoid putting all the Alliance's eggs in one basket. On the other hand, it flew in the face of achieving joint savings through bigger scale—the whole reason for having an Alliance in the first place.

"It was a scandal," said the Nissan EV executive. "The cars were being developed in the same timescale against the same EV strategy, and the two companies couldn't agree on a common platform, and Ghosn wouldn't rule. So, the entire powertrain was done from two entirely different philosophical perspectives. The Renault one, which was very much lean on your suppliers, and the Nissan one which was entirely rely on your capability in-house."

When the Leaf finally went on sale in 2010, there were only a handful of competitors on the market for pluggable cars, such as the Chevrolet Volt, Mitsubishi i-MiEV, Tesla Roadster, and Toyota Prius PHV. But the Volt and Prius PHV weren't even true EVs. Technically, they were hybrid vehicles because they still included a gasoline-burning internal combustion engine.

By 2018, however, rivals were rushing to market with plans to roll out one hundred electrified models through 2022. The list of players grew to include Audi, Hyundai, Kia, Ford, Volkswagen, Porsche, Mazda, Honda, BMW—in a word, virtually every major player.

Despite being a first mover in the EV market, Nissan now looked like a laggard. It was still leaning almost exclusively on its Leaf nearly a decade later. Most of the other EV models once planned, including an all-electric car for the premium Infiniti brand, never materialized. And a common platform to underpin EVs at both Renault and Nissan still wasn't scheduled to enter production until 2020, at the earliest. What of Ghosn's goal to sell 1.5 million EVs across the Alliance by early 2017? He missed it by more than a million. By July of that year, the Alliance moved just 481,000 worldwide, although the Leaf accounted for more than half.[11] The Alliance had squandered its EV lead.

· · ·

More pressure was mounting from the times Ghosn did side with one company over the other. Even though he demurred on decisions, such as the EV architecture, he habitually turned to Nissan to spearhead key new technologies, including electric and autonomous cars. In the mind of Nissan engineers, this was only natural. Nissan had a much bigger and more rigorous engineering arm and was known as an innovator. Renault, by contrast, was more of a fast follower. Another company might be first to market with a new technology, and Renault would quickly try to match it. Renault often deferred to Nissan because the Japanese partner had deep roots and expertise in the critical US and China markets, important regions where Renault had little or no presence.

But engineers on each side had dim, if mostly unspoken, opinions about their counterparts at the other company, and resentment flowed both ways.

The Nissan folks tended to look at the Renault side as lackadaisical, if not lazy. The view was only underlined by the generous Christmas and summer vacations that were suddenly sanctioned at Nissan. Throughout hard-charging corporate Japan, paid vacation is a benefit on the books but one few employees actually avail themselves to. Taking time off borders on dereliction of duty and is seen as burdening one's colleagues.

In Japan, an entire ritual of workplace gift-giving evolved around assuaging one's guilt for taking time off. The vacationing party is obliged to bring back a souvenir treat—such as a box of chocolates or other sweets—for coworkers to share. It's a sign of appreciation for picking up the slack. After the tie-up with Renault, Nissan employees—mostly the international ones—were now checking out before Christmas or taking weeks off at a time in the summer, something unheard of at other Japanese companies.

The so-called Vacation Deprivation study, a regular survey conducted by the online travel-booking site Expedia, paints the stark contrast. In France, workers are allotted an average of thirty vacation days a year and make sure to burn through every one.

In Japan, they get just twenty, but bother to use only half.[12]

Nissan, like other Japanese manufacturers, takes meticulous care to keep factories maintained, organized, and sparkling clean. A key factory management principle is called 5S, which stands for the Japanese principles of *seiri, seiton, seiso, seiketsu,* and *shitsuke.* Translated into English, it means "sort, set in order, shine, standardize, and sustain discipline." The mindset is one reason visitors to a Japanese car plant are immediately astonished by the spotless floors. Renault factories left the opposite impression on Nissan's production engineers. Instead of cleaning its floors, Renault was said to sometimes simply paint over the dirt.

To this day, Nissan engineers complain they do the heavy lifting on product development and research, even though both companies are supposed to contribute 50-50 to each project, not only in terms of money but in personnel and other resources. At Nissan, many couldn't escape the nagging feeling that Renault was bloated and slow, partly as a legacy of being a state-owned industry for so long. Even though the French government's stake had been whittled down to 15 percent over the years, the impression was that old habits die hard.

"Renault looked at the Alliance as, 'How can Nissan fix my problems?'" said one former top tier Nissan executive. "I always thought that the Renault people were a touch lazy, not fixing their own problems and looking at Nissan to fix their problems rather than having a goal themselves. Whereas Nissan would say, 'This is my problem. I'll fix it myself.'"

But the scorn flowed both ways. The Renault side tended to see Nissan as arrogant and inflexible, hopelessly hemmed in by rules. Renault also resented having to chip in half the resources and funding when their payoffs would be smaller. Renault almost always reaped less revenue from the new technologies simply because it was only two-thirds the size of Nissan and could sell the systems in fewer cars.

"There was resentment. Nissan had the upper hand," said the former Nissan executive. "Some people in Renault would think, 'We own forty-three percent of Nissan, so why can't we have that for free.' There was always a lot of tension that technology was coming from Nissan."

At the same time, Renault executives felt that their Nissan counterparts were slavishly in thrall to the almighty engineers, so much so that they lost all track of what customers really wanted in a car or were willing to pay for. There was a lot of head shaking at what Westerners considered "unnecessary perfection." The result was stellar technology in cars that mostly sat on dealer lots for a lack of customer research or strategic marketing.

"At the end of the day, the car was genetically just too expensive," said one former Renault executive. "They would kind of just throw products out there in a haphazard way and hope to find the customer without any concern for profitability."

Some at Renault also feared being blotted out by Nissan's massive size. To the chagrin of French traditionalists, Renault began internalizing elements of Japanese corporate culture, and Japanese ways slowly infiltrated the company. Japanese loanwords, such as *gemba*, a reference to frontline operations, such as the factory floor, or *kaizen*, meaning the pursuit of continual improvement, became ingrained in Renault parlance.

"Japanese industrial culture was imported to Renault. That was quite difficult for some people in Renault," said a former adviser to Ghosn at the French company. "Nissan had historical superiority in engineering, and the Renault side caught up in recent years. But the Nissan side did not acknowledge the progress. That was very annoying for the Renault side."

Some at Renault also grumbled that Ghosn favored Nissan by picking its executives for the plum positions in Alliance leadership. In 2014, as Renault and Nissan prepared to celebrate the Alliance's fifteenth anniversary, Ghosn introduced the "next significant wave of integration." The Alliance moved toward an idea of "convergence," a new buzzword adopted to mean combining joint functions across the Alliance under a single executive. Until this point, with the exception of purchasing, important functions had been siloed within each company. Now, Nissan people were tapped to head the important and influential portfolios of engineering, manufacturing, and supply chains across both companies.

Convergence was supposed to knit operations together and streamline decision making. But in some corners, executives on both sides complained it had the reverse effect of creating just one more layer of bureaucracy between the top and the engineering studios. It also sowed fear at each company of losing autonomy. If a single executive was calling the shots for both companies, was a full merger really that far away? And if that happened, who would be in the driver's seat then?

Ghosn's end game was murky, even to his closest advisers. But the visionary leader kept boring down on two top priorities: more integration and bigger scale.

. . .

Industrywide, consolidation was a hot theme. Sergio Marchionne, then CEO of Fiat Chrysler Automobiles and Ghosn's alpha dog auto executive rival in Europe, was a global bandleader calling for more mergers as the only way carmakers could survive in the crucible of spiraling costs for new technologies. In April 2015, Marchionne made the case to industry analysts in a provocative presentation called "Confessions of a Capital Junkie."[13] He said automakers were wasting billions of dollars developing the same products and needed to team up. By his calculation, the world's top car manufacturers spent €100 billion ($132.83 billion) on product development in 2014 alone—to the tune of €2 billion ($2.66 billion) a week. By commonizing parts and development, in the way Renault and Nissan had been attempting, Marchionne reckoned automakers could average savings of 45 to 50 percent.

Convinced of his worldview, Marchionne even courted Ford and GM to tie up with Fiat Chrysler. But he was rebuffed by executives at those rivals who were leery that Marchionne predicated any partnership on his being the CEO of the combined entity, just as Ghosn had emerged on top at Renault and Nissan.

Adding to the urgency was an influx of high-tech companies and startup electric vehicle makers from Silicon Valley and China. These interlopers leveraged deep pockets and enthusiastic investors pumping them up with capital. The newcomers challenged old-school metal benders with new, faster ways of building cars. While established players struggled to invest in new electric vehicle and battery factories, for instance, they also needed to absorb the huge fixed costs they had already sunk into an industrial infrastructure geared toward yesterday's technology. Bright-eyed upstarts could invest in the latest, greatest production engineering without any of that overhead. Traditional carmakers were consumed by a real fear of being leapfrogged by wannabe automotive players like Tesla, Elon Musk's darling of Palo Alto, or newbie EV aspirants from China with names few Americans even recognized, such as NIO, Xpeng, and Byton.

Tesla alone would soon be giving the established players the heebie-jeebies. Old-guard automakers initially dismissed Tesla as a short-lived vanity project of its quixotic and erratic billionaire founder. Musk, after all, has a spaceship company, SpaceX, and talked about colonizing Mars. Initially, the quality of Tesla's cars was questionable at best, with glaring gaps between the sheet metal—an offense abhorrent to traditional players, which spent decades perfecting their production prowess.

But against all odds, Tesla struck a chord with a fanatic customer base, and its cars soon became the next must-have high-tech gadget, on par with the Apple iPhone. Tesla obtained the Holy Grail that eluded practically every other carmaker—customers looked past the cars' quirks and hungered to buy them simply because they were a Tesla. The name had that much brand power. After years of losses, Tesla refuted the naysayers and started churning out profits. Tesla stock became the toast of Wall Street, and its shares kept climbing. By 2020, even Toyota president Akio Toyoda bemoaned the fact that Tesla's market capitalization—soaring above $450 billion—exceeded the value of Toyota and Japan's six other automakers *combined*. And that was despite the fact that Toyota was selling nearly eleven million vehicles a year—and Tesla just 367,500, less than 5 percent of Toyota's total.

Electric natives disrupted the establishment with new ways of developing and manufacturing cars. Traditional automakers roll out redesigned vehicles at a leisurely pace of every four to seven years. The newcomers, by contrast, brought a Silicon Valley mindset for much faster product cycles. New smartphones, after all, are released almost every year. Some auto entrants could go from blank slate to prototype in as little as two years, thanks to the help of cloud computing. And with over-the-air updates, the software in their cars could be updated instantaneously. From Detroit and Stuttgart to Seoul and Yokohama, established automakers struggled to pick up the development pace and stay competitive.

Meanwhile, new automotive giants were rising from emerging markets, such as India and China. Traditional automakers at first laughed off these newcomers, believing their home countries could never produce true global rivals to the likes of Ford, Daimler, or Honda. The laughing stopped when those companies began buying up big-name brands. India's Tata Motors acquired Jaguar and Land Rover from Ford in 2008. And China's Geely, formally known as Zhejiang Geely Holding Group

Co., snapped up Sweden's premium Volvo brand and the erstwhile British sports car icon Lotus. Geely really stunned the industry in 2018, when it secretly amassed a 9.7 percent stake in Germany's Daimler AG, the parent company of Mercedes-Benz, to become its top shareholder.[14] These new global juggernauts threatened to subvert the long-established industrial hierarchy—one in which Renault and Nissan had prime standing.

If all this weren't enough, new modes of mobility, such as the ride-hailing boom ushered in by giants Uber in the United States and Didi Chuxing in China, changed the ways cars were being used. Car sharing threatened to undermine the business model of individual car ownership and transform conventional automakers into rote manufacturers of utilitarian people movers that modern mobility providers, such as Uber, would buy in mass and churn through, with little interest in trivialities like emotional design, handling, or variety. Other young Turks had wilder visions for a future of self-driving delivery vehicles that would bring your Amazon orders to your door. Ford even teamed with Domino's pizza chain on a pilot program that had autonomous vehicles deliver hot pies to hungry customers. Old-school automakers worldwide no longer saw a future in actually building cars and frantically tried to reposition themselves as "new mobility" companies.

Bob Lutz, the former General Motors vice chairman who pooh-poohed the idea of saving Nissan from bankruptcy, penned a provocative vision of the coming collision in an essay for *Automotive News* called "Kiss the Good Times Goodbye." Human-driven cars would be "legislated off the highways" as the safety of autonomous vehicles exceeded that of the traditional hand-piloted kind. Those highways would become an endless stream of commoditized canister cars zipping along at 120 mph. "These modules won't be branded Chevrolet, Ford or Toyota. They'll be branded Uber or Lyft or who-ever else is competing in the market," the auto industry legend wrote. People who still know how to drive would amaze their friends, just like people today who know how to saddle up and ride a horse.[15] Lutz's timeline for this to happen? The 2030s. Such was the Sturm und Drang convulsing the auto industry in the mid-2010s.

· · ·

If this future came to pass, automaker margins would be squeezed even further—if they managed to stay in business at all.

Consolidation, Fiat Chrysler's Marchionne conceded, wasn't easy. For starters, there would be culture clashes meshing different companies—Nissan and Renault were an early signal of this, even if others didn't realize it. There would be unprecedented complexity managing newly created mega-manufacturers. Inequality of the integrated parties and a lack of brand distinction further complicated the equation. Daimler's spectacularly failed merger with Chrysler—in the days before Fiat stepped in with its own lifeline—was the obvious red flag to any company attempting its own tie-up.

But like most auto leaders of the time, Marchionne saw no other way forward.

"Consolidation carries executional risks, but benefits are too large to ignore," his analysis concluded. "It is ultimately a matter of leadership style and capability."[16]

Renault and Nissan strained under these same pressures. And Ghosn kept adding to the strain. He bolted on more and more companies to the Alliance in the never-ending quest for the scale that was the foundation of the Alliance strategy. In a nod to his vision, Ghosn at one point even looked into trademarking the name Global Motors as a new moniker for the growing group.

In 2010, he brought Daimler into the mix as a junior partner, through a minority crossholding deal. The German company took a 3.1 percent stake each in Renault and Nissan, while Nissan and Renault reciprocated with their own 1.55 percent holdings in Daimler. Then, the Alliance expanded again in 2014 by taking a 67.1 percent stake in the holding company that controlled AvtoVAZ, Russia's biggest automaker.

Ghosn's most ambitious move to build scale came in 2016, when he orchestrated Nissan's purchase of a controlling 34 percent stake in then struggling Japanese rival Mitsubishi Motors Corp. By adding Mitsubishi's sales volume to his existing portfolio, he could finally claim to be selling the most cars in the world. At a press conference that October, Ghosn trumpeted the deal as a watershed and was appointed chairman of the newly acquired Mitsubishi.

"Today, our global alliance has reached an inflection point," he said. "With Mitsubishi, the alliance will have a scale advantage over most carmakers and a handicap to none."

He was right. The next year, 2017, the three-party Renault-Nissan-Mitsubishi Alliance booked global light vehicle sales of 10.61 million vehicles, just enough to pip Volkswagen and Toyota for the world title. Ghosn's achievement only helped solidify his reputation as a living legend of the automotive industry. And it seemed a natural justification for the handsome compensation package, by Japanese and French standards at any rate, that he demanded and received. He was a visionary, somehow juggling a trio of companies and guiding them into an uncertain future of new technologies, new markets. Certainly, he believed at least, that kind of leadership was worth every penny.

Even as tensions between Nissan and Renault simmered under the pressure cooker of an industry undergoing radical, rapid change, Ghosn was always confident, in public, of being able to coax the companies closer while protecting their independence.

"The consolidation of the industry for many people means A buys B, or B absorbs C," Ghosn told the *Automotive News* World Congress in 2016. The Alliance approach, he insisted, was different. "It's a very modern interpretation, where you don't have to choose between scale and freedom or autonomy. You can have both. You can have your own brand and benefit from a larger scale."[17]

But there was, he conceded, a slight catch: "You just have to make sure it works."

7

COLLISION COURSE

TO GHOSN, THE ALLIANCE WAS A NEW KIND OF TIE-UP that transcended nationalism to pool the best from all companies in a cooperative structure. It was neither French nor Japanese, and it was led by a man who was not Japanese and was never accepted as truly French. Despite all this, conservative forces on each side were fomenting tensions as the balance of power tilted far away from Renault, which had saved Nissan in the first place, and toward Nissan, which was driving sales and profits, and now pulling Renault along.

In the face of all the idealistic talk from the top about a pan-nationalist carmaker, many Ghosn underlings still saw business through a more parochial lens. It wasn't just parochial employees. The countries' respective governments, too, were pushing for more control for their own side. In France, traditionalists at Renault and in the government wanted Renault to wield its full weight as Nissan's controlling shareholder. Meanwhile, counterparts at Nissan and in the Japanese government not only feared a full takeover but began agitating behind the scenes for the Japanese partner to have a bigger say in Alliance affairs.

"There was dissatisfaction on both sides [of the Alliance]," said one top Nissan executive and longtime Ghosn lieutenant. "It was amazing to me that for such a long time the Alliance was painted by us as this perfect alternative to a merger and acquisition, but in fact there was an underlying tension the whole time. The relationship between [the] two companies was pretty negative right from the beginning."

. . .

Back in 2000, after Ghosn's first year at Nissan, both partners were on roughly even footing in terms of size. Thanks to his Nissan Revival Plan, the Japanese carmaker made more than double the profit of Renault, but their global sales were in the same ballpark. Nissan booked net income of about ¥331 billion (around $2.6 billion) in the fiscal year ended March 31, 2001,[1] compared with Renault's net income of just above €1 billion ($1 billion) in its fiscal year ended December 31, 2000.[2] But Nissan booked only about 200,000 more vehicle sales than Renault (2.6 million vs. 2.4 million).

By 2005, when Ghosn took the helm of both companies, the gulf between the two had dramatically widened. Renault was still selling about the same number of cars, while Nissan had added a million vehicles per year and was booking net income of ¥518 billion yen (near $4.4 billion). Renault's profit was up to €3.4 billion ($4 billion), but more than two-thirds of those earnings came from dividends from its stake in Nissan.[3] Nissan's market capitalization was now nearly twice as big as Renault's. In the course of just several years, Nissan completely eclipsed Renault.

From Nissan's point of view, especially the company's Japanese old guard, the carmaker's onetime rescuer was now the one being rescued. Particularly vexing was the complex and uneven cross-shareholdings that glued the Alliance together to Renault's advantage.

Renault owned about 43 percent of Nissan, and Nissan about 15 percent of Renault, but Nissan had no voting rights included in its stake. At the same time, the French government owned a 15 percent stake in Renault—itself a fact that worried many in Tokyo—and that stake was eventually endowed with *double* voting rights. That made a foreign government the biggest investor in Nissan's controlling shareholder.

As Nissan outgrew Renault, this imbalance put the companies on another collision course. In short, the deal was originally structured to Renault's benefit, because at the time Renault was doing the saving. Now, times had changed. Nissan was the clear market champion, but the deal still tilted toward Renault.

And this time, the conflicts stretched far beyond car batteries and wiper switches. The jousting was for control of the entire Alliance. Diverging national interests of France and Japan, long hidden behind a facade of a mutually sustainable partnership, burst into the open. Traditional notions of corporate mergers and acquisitions held by groups within Renault and Nissan clashed with Ghosn's vision of a postnational strategic partnership. And conflicting notions about government involvement in big business stirred bad blood and lingering suspicion that continue to taint the Franco-Japanese union today.

In many ways, Ghosn's vision for a new kind of transnational company, something that had yet to be truly achieved in the automotive sector, had pushed people too far from their comfort zones. A backlash was brewing.

"Ghosn is actually superradical," said one former adviser who reported directly to him in an Alliance role for several years during this period. "What he was trying to do was unprecedented in the history of the auto industry, which was combine strong companies that are truly nationally significant and keep them together in a way that was not just one economic cycle but was really permanent. That is something that is supercontroversial."

Ghosn said it survived so long because he mastered a fragile equilibrium. "It was a delicate balance between respecting identities and moving forward with synergies. You can't make an alliance just respecting identities, because then people are going to say, 'Why are we working together?' But you also cannot make an alliance by only moving with synergies because that means a merger, and mergers have a lot of traps in terms of who is the winner and who is the loser," he said in an interview for this book. "That's why it worked."

. . .

It was controversial because few industries are wrapped in as much prestige, power, and prosperity as the global automotive sector. Govern-

ments worldwide take keen interest in fostering their automotive industries and protecting them for several reasons.

First and foremost, auto manufacturing employs huge swaths of society, from the engineers designing the vehicles and workers assembling
them, to the suppliers making the parts and sales staff moving the finished cars off dealer lots. The US industry alone directly employs over
1.7 million people and has historically contributed 3 percent of the country's gross domestic product, according to the Center for Automotive
Research. It supports another eight million American jobs through its
purchase of goods and services.[4]

In Japan, the auto industry's influence is even weightier. Although
Japan's population is less than half the size of the United States', some
5.5 million people work in auto-related jobs—with 880,000 Japanese employed directly in automobile production. About 8.2 percent of the entire
country's workforce traces its livelihood back to automobiles and trucks.[5]

Even as automotive brands in the United States consolidated around
the Detroit Three of General Motors, Ford, and Chrysler, Japan sus-
tained a homegrown stable of stubbornly independent manufacturers
well into the twenty-first century. The short list includes brands that are
household names around the world: Toyota, Nissan, Honda, Mitsubishi,
Mazda, Subaru, and Suzuki.

France's auto industry directly employs about 205,000 people and supports 2.2 million jobs. Its national champions include Renault as well as
Peugeot-Citroën's parent company PSA Group, both top 10 global producers as recently as 2018.[6]

National auto industries also drive huge investment into innovation and advanced technologies, from high-performance batteries and
computer chips to laser sensors and artificial intelligence. The sector is
deemed so critical to national security and prosperity that China pri-
oritized electric and self-driving cars as part of the government's Made
in China 2025 strategic plan to dominate next-generation value-added
industries on the global stage. In the United States, the Trump administration imposed billions of dollars of tariffs on Chinese imports of assem-
bled vehicles and auto components to protect local automakers. And it

threatened the same against trade partners in Europe, Japan, and South Korea, arguing that the flow of imports from these auto powerhouses was so devastating to the domestic economy that it posed a threat to national security.

Finally, it's hard to overestimate the emotional attachment to a nation's auto brands. The cars represent a country's cultural aesthetic, technological achievement and affluence. Iconic nameplates, such as the Ford F-150 pickup, Toyota Prius hybrid, or Porsche 911 sports car, say as much about the people who drive them as they do about the countries that created them. Simply having a homegrown automaker is a source of national pride in many countries. It has resulted in such vanity projects as the unlikely creation of the Malaysian national auto brand Proton, back in the 1980s, even though Proton's cars were originally just rebadged versions of vehicles designed and engineered by Mitsubishi.

Customers meanwhile have deep attachments to their automobiles for financial reasons as much as for nationalistic ones. Purchasing a car is the second-biggest investment most people will ever make, after buying a home. They want to protect that investment for their pocket book and take pride in everything it symbolizes.

Both Nissan and Renault have outsize roles in their respective home country psyche. The circle in Nissan's brand logo represents the rising sun of the Japanese national flag. And Renault channels a national pride in scientific prowess stretching back to Nicholas-Joseph Cugnot, the French inventor credited with building the world's first self-propelled land vehicle in 1770, a three-wheeled steam-powered wagon with a massive kettle-like boiler dangling off the front.

Renault is perhaps best known in the United States as the purveyor of Le Car, a short-lived 1970s compact hatchback sold before the company quit the US market in the 1980s. But the French automaker has a storied history dating back more than 100 years.

Louis Renault, one of Renault's three founding brothers, debuted his fledgling company's first car, the pint-size, open-top Type A Voiturette, on Christmas Eve 1898 when he drove the one-cylinder contraption up Montmartre's rue Lepic, the steepest street in Paris. The stunt so wowed his countrymen that he booked twelve orders that night. More than a century later, his company was global, with 180,000 workers in thirty-nine countries.

To most governments, it is inconceivable to let these companies disappear, a point driven home by Washington's bailout of GM and Chrysler during the 2008–2009 Great Recession.

"These companies exist as wards of the state because they employ so many people," the former Ghosn aide said. "It's important to understand that Renault and Nissan are each very special companies to their home countries. This is the backdrop. There is feverish interest in both Japan and France for their own auto companies. It tends to be much more passionate than for, say, finance or pharmaceuticals or other industries. Big financial companies can merge all the time, and you don't even notice it. But in the auto industry, you really do."

. . .

As Nissan recovered its profitability and its sense of pride, executives there wanted a bigger say in Alliance decision-making. Some agitated for voting rights in Renault. Some wanted to rebalance the shareholdings to limit Renault's sway. Some wanted both.

Trepidation about the Alliance's built-in imbalance extended to the halls of government in Tokyo. Japan's powerful Ministry of Economy, Trade, and Industry (METI), which plays an active role in promoting and protecting the country's business interests, grudgingly backed Renault's bailout in 1999 as the only way to save Nissan and its thousands of Japanese jobs.

Yet looming over the relationship was an inconvenient truth for those at Nissan or in the Japanese government who longed for an equal seat at the table. Nissan signed away that right in the original Alliance master agreement handing Renault the keys to the company.

"Renault could unilaterally import and pick and choose Nissan board members. And Renault could also appoint, depose or anoint a Nissan CEO. And the opposite was not true. And this was all written into the articles of the Alliance way back in 1999," the Ghosn aide said. "Most people still to this day don't know that. They think, 'Oh, Nissan is a bigger company, it should have more power.' But the articles of the Alliance have Renault owning Nissan. That's the reality. It's just, lock, stock, and barrel, Renault owns Nissan."

Despite the contractual realities, the agitated Nissan forces triggered alarm at Renault. Some at Renault worried it might lose its grip on its prize possession and profit machine.

"All of a sudden there was a fear on the Renault side that Nissan could not only walk on its own two feet, it didn't need Renault anymore, and that it would just spin off and walk away from the Alliance because Renault was no longer needed," said one long-serving Renault executive who worked at both carmakers. "That provoked on the Renault side fear, saying, 'Whoa, time-out guys. Wait a bit. Don't forget who's the boss here. We bought you. We saved you. So, what's all this nonsense about trying to flex your muscles?'"

Ghosn never lorded it over Nissan, partly because he had made his name by reviving the company and took pride in its success. He also believed a takeover mentality would spell doom for the partnership, as it had for other auto mergers, most notably the one that joined Daimler and Chrysler. (And to his critics, he didn't want to kill the goose that lays the golden eggs—Nissan was still the biggest source of his income.)

"To Ghosn's credit, he always managed the two companies very separately and maintained that equilibrium between them and talked about them as equal partners," said another former executive who worked with Ghosn in France and Japan. "We were pushing it always as Alliance synergies happen because the two companies were motivated to work together, because they could achieve more by working together rather than working apart, and so on. He would rarely force either company to do something."

But now that Renault was the partner playing catch up, some at Nissan and in the Japanese government shuddered at the possibility of the French government, through its control over Renault, siphoning work from Nissan to pad out production and save jobs at underperforming factories in France. Pooling production was always pitched as a raison d'être for the Alliance and as a critical source of synergies. In reality, allocating vehicles from one company to be built at an assembly plant of the other was among the most politically charged decisions. Each side was loath to give up production, and potentially jobs, to fill the other's factories.

The issue of protecting production assumed primacy in Japan in the early 2010s, as the country's automakers began building more factories overseas. Japan—which built its economy in large part on exporting cars—was suddenly making more cars in the overseas markets where they were sold. Vehicle exports began to fall, stoking fears about a hollowing out of the domestic auto industry. The Japanese even had a buzz word for the phenomenon at the time: *kuudouka*, which means "hollowing out" in reference to the empty factories. In 2010, Nissan did what was once unthinkable. It began shipping Thailand-built vehicles back to Japan for sale there, an alarming reversal of the usual product flow. Reacting to political pressure to stem the home country decline, Toyota pledged to keep capacity to build three million vehicles a year in Japan.[7] Likewise, Nissan sought to assuage domestic concerns about lost jobs by promising to keep producing at least one million vehicles a year in Japan.[8]

But the same pressures applied to Renault. And in Japanese eyes, Nissan was given good reason to worry about Renault's intentions in 2013. At the time, European auto sales were in decline, and the market was awash in excess production capacity. Half of the region's 160 auto plants were operating at around only 70 percent capacity. That was a miserable, money-losing production pace for any manufacturer. Customers were simply buying far fewer cars than the companies were configured to churn out.[9]

The crisis was especially acute at Renault and its Flins assembly plant along the Seine River northwest of Paris. The company's biggest and oldest auto plant in France, Flins dates to 1952, ancient by industry standards. It employed 2,600 people and has churned out more than eighteen million vehicles over a half century. But in 2013, Renault's plants were shuffling along at just about 60 percent of total capacity. Workers at Flins were worried about their viability if they couldn't somehow find more work.[10]

"Le Cost Cutter" Ghosn had closed plants before, and he might do so again.

As labor tensions soared, Renault reached a deal that allowed the company to trim some workers in exchange for protecting job sites in France and boosting production in France by a third. Renault also pledged to keep annual output at Flins above 110,000 vehicles. That's where Nissan came in.[11] In a decision still derided at Nissan today, the Alliance decided to fill Flins with production of the Nissan Micra, the Japanese brand's popular subcompact hatchback. Pressuring Ghosn the entire time was the French government, then struggling to safeguard jobs amid soaring 10 percent unemployment.

Nissan had just moved production of the Micra out of its UK plant to a low-cost factory in India three years earlier. The plant in Chennai, then a 70-30 Nissan-Renault joint venture, capped costs by installing used presses from Renault and buying other machinery from low-cost South Korean makers for the first time.[12] Nissan believed local production of the small car was key to capping production costs and eventually cracking the massive, up-and-coming India market. Now, Nissan executives were incensed that Renault was asking it to send production back to France, where productivity and wages couldn't compete.

"It was perceived as a huge win for France. Nissan felt like this was a forced move," the Ghosn aide said. "That's how Nissan saw it, Ghosn in cahoots with the French government forcing Nissan to make cars in its home state. It was incredibly controversial internally."

Nissan acquiesced, but a bigger collision was fast approaching.

. . .

A year later, the French state triggered another crisis over control when it executed an end run around Renault to secure double voting rights in the company under the country's Florange law. The law passed in March 2014 under the government of Socialist president François Hollande and took effect in 2016. It granted double voting rights to long-term "loyalty" shareholders, such as the French government. Giving favored investors two votes for the price of one was designed to protect French companies from hostile takeover bids. At the Alliance, the new blowup became known as the Florange Crisis.

The law's name came from the French city of Florange, where the steelmaker ArcelorMittal tried to shut down two blast furnaces following a 2006 hostile takeover. In an aggressively protectionist move to save jobs, Hollande's government threatened to nationalize the steelworks and only backpedaled after ArcelorMittal agreed to invest in the site and abandon layoffs.[13]

Companies could opt out of the new Florange law through a shareholder vote, and Ghosn intended to do just that at a 2015 general meeting. If the French government's 15 percent stake in Renault already concerned some in Japan, the prospect of doubling those voting rights really rattled them. He wanted to assuage Nissan's concern about voting rights and forestall any government meddling in Renault's corporate affairs.

Even within Renault, there were two camps. Some old-guard conservatives were focused on ensuring Renault's leverage over Nissan. Others, including Ghosn and the more internationally minded, were more concerned about the government's leverage over their own company.

"Ghosn was always a great believer in keeping the two entities [Renault and Nissan] apart. But he was under enormous pressure from the French government, and particularly Renault internally to pull the two together," one top Nissan executive said of Ghosn's showdowns with the government in Paris.

Even though some at Nissan worried about Ghosn's true loyalties, he himself also didn't like what he saw as interference from the French government.

"I was not the most popular guy in the successive French governments because I was fundamentally against any intervention from governments, particularly in industry," Ghosn recalled in an interview with *Automotive News* after his escape to Lebanon. "One day I will write a book about the influence—the bad influence, in my opinion—of government in business, and particularly in the car industry. I have so much evidence of this. I think any intervention is negative, and they've proven it widely."

As Renault prepared for the 2015 general shareholders' meeting to opt out of the Florange provisions, France's economy ministry hatched a plan to foil the opt-out and ensure its hold on double voting rights. Just three weeks before the vote, without warning to Ghosn or Renault, France upped its 15 percent stake in Renault to 19.7 percent to ensure it held enough votes at the meeting to prevent an opt-out of the Florange law.[14] Then, after securing the enhanced voting rights, France shrewdly sold down its stake back to 15 percent, with its double voting rights now intact. The economy minister behind the scheme was Emmanuel Macron, the future president of France. It was the start of a fraught relationship with Macron that would come back to haunt Ghosn after he was arrested in Japan and needed the French government's help.

"It was a very powerful signal to Nissan and the Japanese government that the French are really out for blood on this," the Ghosn aide from Paris recounted. "They could do whatever it takes to take over the company, and they could do something like this again and strengthen the Alliance charter to make France even more in control. They [Nissan] didn't realize this devil was that big of a threat. Nissan said this devil can grow another head."

. . .

The French intervention sent shock waves through Nissan and triggered a swift pushback from Hiroto Saikawa, then vice chairman and Ghosn's No. 2. Saikawa, as one of Ghosn's earliest recruits during the Nissan Revival Plan, had been an Alliance true believer from the start. But this was more than he could bear. Saikawa later said he was not about to stand by while the French orchestrated what some at Nissan said would be an "invasion" of his company.

"Nissan's worry was any decision centered in Europe or France could be forced on Nissan, and that would destroy Nissan's future," Saikawa said. "At the end of the day, we have to protect Nissan."

Saikawa's first instinct was to reach for the "nuclear button," one of several strategies developed internally at Nissan as a way to push back on Renault or stop a merger. In this scenario, Saikawa—with a tacit go-ahead from Ghosn—told the French government Nissan wanted to rebalance the crossholdings and bring down Renault's stake in Nissan to around 33 percent. Another option would be to threaten that Nissan would raise its stake in Renault to 25 percent, a move that would void Renault's voting rights in Nissan under Japanese law. Saikawa was the front man, but Ghosn had his back behind the scenes, and Greg Kelly, the American Nissan director arrested with Ghosn, was a key player in negotiating Nissan's pushback.

Nissan's maneuvering spooked the French government, and by the end of 2015, Saikawa and Kelly brokered a compromise, through a Restated Alliance Master Agreement unveiled in December.

Under the agreement, France would keep its double voting rights on key decisions such as dividends, the appointment of French government representatives on the board, the disposal of large Renault assets, take-over bids and the matter of Nissan voting rights. But the government would limit its voting rights in Renault to between 17.9 and 20 percent on most other matters.[15]

Nissan still wouldn't get voting rights. But Renault agreed to a noninterference clause as part of an Alliance "Stability Covenant." Renault said it would not interfere with Nissan governance over issues such as appointing and dismissing board members, and it pledged not to oppose motions that are backed by the Nissan board. The end effect of the Florange Crisis was Renault actually losing leverage over Nissan and its board.

Nissan had parried the French government's power play, even though it did little to strengthen its own voice in Alliance affairs. But for now, the Alliance preserved its tenuous balance. Inside Nissan, even Saikawa's critics conceded that his victory in staving off the French was one of his finest hours.

Renault hardliners, however, saw the accord as a humiliating capitulation that surrendered some of carmaker's most important privileges as Nissan's controlling shareholder.

. . .

The Florange Crisis left lasting scars and deep distrust, especially at Nissan. Ghosn himself was keenly aware of the nuclear buttons because he needed them as leverage to tell the French government to back off. But factions inside Nissan were beginning to doubt his true intentions and wondered whether he was succumbing to merger pressure from the French state, the arbiter deciding whether Ghosn kept his job.

"It really rekindled the flame of the ones who were proponents of dissolving and disintegrating the Alliance," said a former top-level Renault executive who worked at both companies. "It set the stage for a much more difficult, and much more acrimonious relationship at the operating level."

Ghosn, looking back on the episode after fleeing Japan for Lebanon, called the Florange Crisis the tipping point that soured Alliance relations. "As for what really started the Japanese to become hostile and destructive, I think it was the Florange law," he said in an interview.

As the Alliance limped on, not everyone shared Ghosn's vision of the tie-up as a superior, radical new way to collaborate. Financial analysts and even company insiders sometimes wondered whether an outright merger made more sense.

The Alliance's loose setup promised cost-saving synergies to both companies, but a merger was often proposed as delivering faster, meatier results. Industry observers said synergies rarely translated directly into earnings because Nissan and Renault didn't share balance sheets. Synergies tracked savings from avoided costs, a nebulous calculus at best. Hard-headed number crunchers argued that only a full merger could truly unleash the profit potential of this unwieldy conglomerate.

"We fudged it," one former Alliance executive conceded. "How do you measure cost avoidance? You say, well, I was going to spend a billion dollars on this new platform, but now I'm doing it with Renault, so therefore, I've saved a half-billion dollars. The synergy numbers were always theoretical because you could never trace them to the bottom line."

And despite Ghosn's public image as the hard-nosed pragmatist calling the shots at both companies, he was limited in his ability to truly force a decision to the detriment of one company over the other. As the top representative of two independently traded companies, he was forced to constantly weigh the inherent conflict of interest in representing the two companies. Any decision that obviously benefited one at the expense of the other put Ghosn on thin ice. This meant it was difficult for him to coerce compromises from either Renault or Nissan, even if the result benefited the Alliance as a whole. In the end, the Alliance was not a listed entity and had no shareholders to whom Ghosn was beholden.

"There are a lot of people that speculate Ghosn was a kind of referee like you have in soccer or in rugby. No, he was not a referee," recalled one former top-level Renault executive who worked with Ghosn for years. "I attended hundreds of meetings under the chairmanship of Mr. Ghosn. I can swear in front of any judge that Mr. Ghosn could influence, but never decide to oppose the interest of one of the companies."

Nothing could happen unless it was a win-win, and as time went by, those propositions grew fewer and farther between. And while a merger might be able to squeeze more juice from the lemon, a merger would have also crossed a bright red line for Nissan.

"The Japanese were adamantly against a merger from the very beginning," said one former top-level Nissan executive. "There was plenty of good spirits about collaborating with Renault. But there was almost a hundred percent antimerger feeling."

. . .

It would have dismayed Nissan's Japanese executives to know that Ghosn had already been studying a merger. Dubbed "Project Caterpillar"—an allusion to the Alliance's hoped-for metamorphosis into a beautiful butterfly—the supersecret work was undertaken by a handful of Ghosn's most trusted Nissan top brass. None of them was Japanese, because Ghosn feared leaks would trigger a firestorm of protest.

The team members included key people who would later figure prominently in Ghosn's downfall, including his accused co-conspirator Greg Kelly and Hari Nada, the Malaysian-British plea-bargaining Nissan executive who headed the CEO-chairman's office and allegedly helped blow the whistle on years of alleged misconduct. McKinsey and Company was brought in as a management consultant; Goldman Sachs handled the banking end.

Caterpillar kicked off in the fall of 2012, more than two years before the Florange Crisis, and the team met again in early 2013 at the Alliance's official headquarters in the Netherlands, a Potemkin outpost with a skeleton staff established on neutral ground. Basing the Alliance entity, officially known as Renault-Nissan BV, in Holland carried the additional advantage of being able to shelter under the country's more relaxed corporate tax and reporting regulations.

"Ghosn met with us and gave us a brief of what he was looking for," said one of the project members. "Ghosn said, 'I want to meet you guys in January. We'll meet in Amsterdam where no one can see us meeting.' We all disappeared off the grid, and we met in the office. It was a privilege to be part of it. It was exciting and interesting and fascinating, putting together two mammoth companies into a single, merged entity."

As talks progressed, Renault executives were eventually brought in to nail down details.

They settled on a vision for a single entity, under a Dutch holding company, that would be traded under one ticker symbol, instead of separate stocks for Renault and Nissan. The new entity would be dual listed, jointly traded on the Paris and Tokyo stock exchanges, and perhaps have another listing in New York for deeper access to American capital markets. A key hurdle would be handling the French government's stake in Renault. Voices at both Renault and Nissan, even the non-Japanese executives, wanted the French state to sell down its holding and butt out.

Then, it fizzled. The finances and politics were deemed too complex and costly. A mutually beneficial share swap was undermined by uncooperative foreign exchange rates. Concerns reemerged about the expense and fallout of shuttering overlapping operations of the merged companies. Finally, there was significant doubt about winning support from the French and Japanese governments. Project Caterpillar was cocooned, and Ghosn instead pitched the convergence of functions, such as manufacturing, engineering, and human resources, under the umbrella of an Alliance-wide leader, across both companies as a compromise solution.

But even that rubbed people the wrong way, as cliques inside Nissan resented relinquishing or sharing control. To R&D teams, especially, it created overlap, redundancy, and lengthy squabbles about which technologies to pursue.

"The last several years of converging functions under Carlos Ghosn, the business was inefficient and even counterproductive to the Alliance," Saikawa said. "There was a lot of negative reaction to that forced convergence inside Nissan."

That should have been a red flag about the hurdles to further integration. But Ghosn never let the holding company idea die. In February 2018, three weeks before his sixty-fourth birthday, Renault renewed his contract for another four years.

This time, Ghosn's reappointment had strings attached. Renault's board handed him a delicate mandate: "Take decisive steps to make the Alliance irreversible."[16] Ghosn looked in his playbook and revived the old holding company plan. It was a move bound to inflame Nissan, and to the conspiracy minded, it was one that ultimately triggered the alleged plot to take him out after almost two decades at the helm.

Whatever the truth, in the minds of many Japanese at least, the word *irreversible* was clearly veiled code for one unacceptable objective: *merger*.

"At that time, Carlos Ghosn did not make it clear which way he would go," a top-level Nissan executive said.

The biggest collision yet was set in motion.

Those close to Ghosn say that, despite his best efforts to keep an uneasy peace and to balance colliding forces from continents half a world apart, even Ghosn believed the coming conflict was inevitable.

"He actually knew something like this was going to happen," said one top Alliance aide who worked with him in Paris. "He definitely knew the tightrope that he was walking on and talked to me about it fairly openly. At some point, he was going to have to make some very difficult trade-offs that would essentially please no one at either company."

8

THE FRENCH ARE DIFFERENT

AFTER A DECADE OF THE ALLIANCE, MEMORIES ABOUT how it all started (with one partner near collapse) were a bit hazy in Tokyo. There was no such difficulty in France. Both Renault and the French government wanted everyone to remember that they were the saviors of Nissan, and with a 43 percent shareholding they wanted the respect—and level of control—that they believed was their proper reward. "They believed that they had come in to rescue Nissan when no one else would. They kept asking, 'Where is the sense of gratitude?'" said one former Japanese official involved in discussions.

French pride would also allow them to say that the Nissan rescue was only the latest example of 150-plus years of French expertise helping out Japan. The first such ventures started in the 1860s as Japan was just opening its economy after centuries of near isolation. As Japan set its sights on rapid industrial expansion, foreign help was vital. In 1865, French companies provided an ironworks operation for the construction of modern warships that a Japanese navy would need (and would later use to devastating effect in the 1904–1905 war with Russia).

Another of the early successes was in the production of silk, for which there was eager demand from the salons of Europe. But as Japanese exports soared, quality plummeted, with unscrupulous mill owners pushing out as much volume as possible. The Japanese government response was one of the first examples of the industrial planning that would become a symbol of Japan in the period after World War II. Japanese authorities approached the French, who agreed to help create the state-supported Tomioka Silk Mill in 1872, using technology and expert advisers from France. The project was a huge success, helping to restore Japan's position in the market.[1] The facility would stay in operation for more than one hundred years until 1987.

The silk joint venture also showed the common ground for the two countries in the form of active government involvement in private enterprise. Whether under socialist or more business-friendly governments, the French government has played an active role in industry, going back to Louis XIV in the second half of the seventeenth century, when the minister of finance created a framework to regulate commerce. State intervention has continued ever since, despite some problems along the way. The government missed some key disruptive technologies: It invested in upgrading its canal network just as railroads became dominant, and it created a subsidy for sailing ships when steamships were taking over on the high seas.

After the Great Depression of the 1930s and the devastation of World War II, France created a new and powerful planning body, known simply as the Commissariat du Plan (Planning Commission). The commission put through a series of long-term economic plans in which the government was active in the outright management of many companies.[2] By 1970, the state was estimated to have direct control over five hundred industrial and commercial companies, with a minority stake in six hundred others. The government involvement was far greater than in any other Western country. The state controlled the monopolies in tobacco, coal mining, railroads, and radio/television and owned at least one major brand in oil, shipping, banking, advertising, and, of course, automobiles.

Government involvement—or interference, depending on your viewpoint—is taken for granted in France. "The question of nationalizations is not the emotional, philosophical issue in France that it would be in the United States . . . In past centuries, so much of France's wealth belonged to the state that private industry was forced to rely heavily on state patronage and accept state direction," the US Central Intelligence Agency said in a 1982 report that was declassified in 2008.[3] This government involvement has continued long after other nations had largely abandoned the idea. One of Margaret Thatcher's hallmarks in transforming the British economy when she came to power in 1979 was to cut loose many state-owned companies that were seen to be core to the nation's identity, including British Airways, British Telecom, and British Steel. Similarly, Japan broke up the massive Japan National Railways in 1987 and sold off its controlling stake in NTT, the national phone company, over a twenty-year period (although it has retained a 34 percent share).

France was swimming against the tide. In 1982, President François Mitterrand launched a comprehensive nationalization program of full or partial state ownership in hundreds of companies, including electronics and telecommunications group CGE, banking icon Rothschild, and aircraft manufacturer Dassault. It made France the most heavily state-dependent economy in Western Europe, representing 23 percent of the country's workforce.[4] The moves would be partly reversed starting in the late 1980s by Jacques Chirac, with further privatizations by subsequent governments. Despite this, even in the pro-business Macron era, the state retained shareholdings in many large companies that were viewed as strategic, and the idea of at least temporary nationalization was revived in the COVID-19 pandemic in 2020 to protect France's biggest companies.

. . .

In the case of Renault, the French government's interventions were in many ways a root cause of the turmoil that would lead to Ghosn's downfall and poison Alliance relations even after his ouster.

The corporate history of Renault is a typical one for major French companies. Régie Nationale des Usines Renault was formally nationalized by Charles de Gaulle in 1945 after the company and its family owners were caught up in accusations of wartime collaboration with the Nazis. With the move, the country's largest automaker became a government department, and it remains to this day a "national asset" with government bureaucrats still heavily involved in its affairs.

Renault has been big enough to retain some autonomy, ignoring postwar plans from government bureaucrats to restrict its range of models or even get out of auto production completely.

Unlike Nissan, it also sought global deals. In 1979, Renault took a stake in American Motors Corp., which in about five years it netted a $1 billion loss and new debt equal to half its sales. Given that the company employed ninety-eight thousand at the time, the government needed to mount a rescue plan. A tie-up with Volvo helped save on costs, but a planned merger that would have bailed out Renault was blocked by the Swedish company's shareholders.

The government then decided that privatization was the best solution, which took place in 1994 under the leadership of Louis Schweitzer, the suave but self-effacing Renault CEO.

Although born in Switzerland, Schweitzer was the classic insider in the French establishment. His father was a Nazi concentration camp survivor who would go on to head the International Monetary Fund, while grand-uncle Albert Schweitzer was the famed theologian, missionary, and winner of the 1952 Nobel Peace Prize. Jean-Paul Sartre, the novelist and philosopher, was a cousin. Schweitzer spent the first part of his career in government, rising through the ranks to become the chief of staff to Prime Minister Laurent Fabius before being dispatched to Renault in 1986, becoming CEO in 1992.

This loaded pedigree was very helpful in pulling the levers of power, but Schweitzer wasn't considered a schemer. He gained a firmly solid reputation in the auto industry as an honest and thoughtful person.

He brought in Ghosn as an executive vice president in 1996. When Ghosn took over, he was building on changes that Schweitzer had put in place during the previous four years. As Ghosn turned around Renault and then took the reins at Nissan, a clearly pleased Schweitzer said in 2003 that up to that point the Alliance had ". . . delivered faster than I expected—and much more than anybody expected."

Ghosn would get much of the credit as "Le Cost Cutter" at Renault, but it was Schweitzer who had started the painful steps of plant closures.

In many ways, he made the Alliance possible, steering delicate negotiations with Nissan. He dealt with complex cultural situations with style, making clear that the alliance should be an equal partnership, thus allaying many of the fears within Nissan and the Japanese government. Just as important, he was able to win the support of the French government, without which the deal would founder.

Even as Ghosn led the turnaround, industry insiders recognized Schweitzer's guiding hand as crucial. It was Schweitzer, not Ghosn, who earned Executive of the Year honors from Automotive News in 2000, which wrote that "A great executive makes it possible for his subordinates to shine." Another observer wrote: "Schweitzer is a gentle prodder. His willingness to let Ghosn take so much credit is a great lesson in how to get things done."

With his Lebanese background and an early youth spent in Brazil, Ghosn was at the opposite end of the social spectrum. His success in school in Paris was attributed to his intelligence and hard work. Similarly, his rise at Michelin, where he started after completing university, was clearly based on merit and his ability to deliver results rather than having the right connections. Even when he joined Renault, he still felt he was something of an outsider. "People had warned me that I was taking a chance. Executives brought in from the outside haven't always done well at Renault," he wrote in his autobiography, *Shift*. "I'd never worked in Paris during the time I'd spent in France . . . So I was something of a black sheep."

Ghosn also didn't have Schweitzer's polish. While Schweitzer was lauded for letting others take credit, Ghosn wrote in his book that when he was asked to take control at Nissan, "I thought that if I were in Louis Schweitzer's place, I'd have chosen me, too."[5]

In 2005, Ghosn took over from Schweitzer as CEO of Renault. He became chairman in 2009, which meant he was now on his own running two global companies on two continents eight time zones apart, with a total workforce of more than 250,000.

However, he was also now without his mentor when handling the often prickly French government, which remained his biggest single shareholder through its 15 percent stake in Renault. Although Renault was no longer completely state owned, it was still a symbol of France.

With the government's long history of intervention in the corporate affairs of "national champions," it was no surprise that there would be epic clashes—and the one between Ghosn and Emmanuel Macron, French economy minister and later president, would be a doozy.

. . .

Born into a professional family with both parents doctors, Macron graduated from the top schools for budding policy makers (his master's thesis was on Machiavelli), and went into the civil service in 2004, working at the Finance Ministry. Four years in, he took a highly profitable career detour, buying out his government contract for €50,000 ($71,000) and taking a senior post with the storied banking group Rothschild & Co. As an investment banker, he worked on a number of high-profile deals, and in four years made himself rich. This is not a big problem in most countries, but in France, the elites have a mixed view of wealth. Prestige comes from your heritage, education, and position in society; it is not something that you can easily buy your way into. Although Macron has a reasonably good pedigree in this context, he still portrayed himself as being an outsider. He returned to the public sector in 2012, becoming deputy secretary-general at the presidential office in a powerful behind-the-scenes role working for François Hollande. He moved up quickly, becoming a fully-fledged minister in 2014 at the Ministry of Economy and Industry. His role included responsibility for Renault, and working with Ghosn.

By all accounts, the two headstrong, dynamic, and highly successful individuals behaved as one would expect: they disliked each other intensely.

The French approach was also fundamentally different from Japan's perspective. Whereas Japanese policymakers had largely put behind them the 1960s days of industrial policymaking, the French government in general, and Macron in particular, maintained that companies should help support government policies. "In the view of the French, Renault has a duty to the French government and to the French people," said one former Japanese official who was involved in Renault-Nissan discussions.

Macron did not understand why the Japanese government would not negotiate directly on a government-to-government level, instead largely insisting that Alliance affairs were up to the two companies. The most damaging clash came in the Florange Crisis of 2015. Macron, perhaps channeling the work on Machiavelli he'd done in college, opportunistically saw the chance to strengthen the state's grip on Renault, and by extension Nissan, by using the law to double the government's voting stake in Renault. From the French government viewpoint, Renault had invested $5 billion in Nissan, taking on a considerable risk of losing it all if the carmaker could not be salvaged. Since the gamble had paid off (it was, after all, no sure thing at the start), it was time for Renault and France to receive their due, both in terms of financial profits and in ensuring that the Alliance would help preserve as many French jobs as possible. "From their perspective, they believed that Japan should accept that Nissan was no longer a Japanese company," said the Japanese official.

Observers also said that the lightning fast decision to increase its voting power in Renault was typical of Macron.

According to a former colleague, Macron "would always go in with both guns blazing," and the Florange play qualifies as that. It was considered bold and ill-conceived, taken without a proper understanding of the potential implications, which later proved to be real, serious, and long-running. "It was like a red flag to a bull," said one former Renault executive of the move. "All of a sudden, Nissan rediscovered that the French state is a very important actor in Renault. And that was a key source of worry for Japan," said another.

In pushing back in his attempt to steer a middle ground, Ghosn made few friends on the French side in the process, in part because of how he approached the negotiations. It wasn't like Schweitzer. "Ghosn had the absolutely insufferable conviction that he was above dealing with ministers," said a former French cabinet minister at the time. "So he'd only ever consider talking to a prime minister, which I doubt endeared him much to Macron, who was also rarely unaware of his own significance."[6]

Macron's bull-in-a-china-shop approach caused such a backlash that it precipitated the strategic retreat some eight months later that set a limit on how Renault could vote its shares in Nissan, particularly in the selection of the board and CEO. The Japanese company in turn agreed that it would not try to buy up more shares in Renault to launch a counterstrike.[7] Just as the original proposal had shocked the Japan side, the compromise was blasted as a severe loss to Renault—and France. It was a "failure of oversight," in the words of a Paris shareholder advisory firm.[8]

Some observers said that Macron had rushed through the compromise deal without much thought because he was on his way to form a new political party that would surprisingly result in his election as French president in 2017. "I was happy that I intervened, because I felt that Ghosn had gone too far in the 'Nipponization' of the group," Macron would later say.[9] From the French point of view, Macron's message was clear: Ghosn, the former whiz kid, was no longer to be trusted.

Tensions were high enough at the time that a June 2018 trip to Paris by Japan's minister of economy, trade, and industry Hiroshige Seko to promote Osaka's bid to host the 2025 World Expo turned into an emergency meeting about Renault and Nissan with the French Finance Ministry. The Japanese delegation, which was prepping for some Expo-oriented marketing, had to corral an auto expert to join the delegation at the last minute. "They were very eager to have talks at the government level," one METI official said on background. "We still had different views, although we were better able to understand each other," he said of the meeting. The differences over what the two governments should do remained, however, adding to the overall confusion about who was in charge of what.

. . .

Even as Ghosn saw himself as trying to hold things together, the French side saw conspiracies, with Ghosn's compensation again the lightning rod. In 2016, questions about his salary at Renault were being asked in the French Parliament. While his base pay and various bonuses for 2015 totaled a modest €3.01 million ($3.43 million), there was a hefty €4.18 million ($4.77 million) in performance-linked deferred payments and stock on top of that. In addition, Ghosn was also raking in $9 million from Nissan. (One of the charges against him in Japan in 2018 would be that he was annually hiding another $10 million to $12 million that he was scheming to get paid after he retired).

This was enough to upset French sensibilities. The situation worsened when the board went ahead with the payments, even after the shareholders, led by the French government, voted against the compensation plan at the April 2016 annual meeting. Macron, economy minister at the time, lashed out at what he said was Renault's "dysfunctional governance" after the board overturned the shareholder decision.[10] People close to Ghosn would later say that his attempts to avoid public scrutiny of his salary at Nissan were due in part to worries that an angry France, and the French government in particular, would take their revenge by cutting him loose from his role at the helm of Renault.

Skeptics at Renault came to believe that a money-seeking Ghosn was now concentrating his attentions back in Yokohama, since he saw Nissan as a softer touch to further boost his salary. Whereas Renault's board included outside directors from both its unions and the French government, Nissan's board was much more compliant. Some Renault executives complained that Ghosn was spending less and less time in Paris, and some feared he'd "gone native" and become primarily a Nissan man with too many Alliance issues decided by Nissan. As one Renault executive saw it: "The Alliance was managed on the basis of Japanese corporate culture, which was then exported to Renault."

. . .

Ghosn's outsider status and perceived refusal to toe the French line would come back to haunt him when he saw how the French government reacted to his arrest and imprisonment. Macron had studiously ignored requests for help from Ghosn and his wife, Carole. Some months after Ghosn's lockup, Macron tried to look more sympathetic. "I told [Japanese prime minister] Abe several times that the conditions of Carlos Ghosn's detention and questioning did not appear to be satisfactory to me," the president told reporters. But Ghosn thought that France should do much more than just lecture Japan on the state of its prisons. Speaking in Lebanon after his escape, he commented, "I wanted there to be more support.

A French political figure told me, 'If I were President, I would have taken you out within 24 hours . . .' But they abandoned me."[11]

At first, French public opinion appeared to be on Ghosn's side. "Initially, it was extremely strong on the conspiracy theory, meaning that the Japanese side organized a coup to get rid of Ghosn and to get rid of the French. That was extremely dominant at the beginning of the story," said one senior French executive.

But as the case against Ghosn unfolded (helped by leaks of damaging information by Japanese prosecutors), French public opinion shifted. An initial wait-and-see attitude over their one-time national hero turned negative for a number of reasons. One, Ghosn was still something of an outsider. "French and Japanese cultures are very different but Ghosn is far from both cultures," said one former Renault executive. Second, the sense that Ghosn saw the Alliance as a personal fiefdom grated against French sensibilities. As one US lawyer active in France put it: "In France, it's fine to have money, you just shouldn't make it obvious." Ghosn did little to help his cause by subsequent actions. Even as he sat in Beirut, a fugitive from Japan and unwelcome in France, he filed a lawsuit to recover his Renault annual pension plus performance related shares in Renault.[12] The issue was based on a technicality of whether he had voluntarily resigned from Renault or had been terminated, but the optics were far from positive.

. . .

The most flagrant issue for many French critics was a controversy over two lavish parties at the French symbol of excess, Louis XIV's Palace of Versailles. The affair blew up in 2019 with allegations that he had misused company money for a 2014 party to celebrate the fifteenth year of the Alliance, and that, in 2016, he had the company pay €50,000 ($55,000) toward the cost of a birthday party for his wife, Carole. The timing of the disclosure was convenient for the anti-Ghosn forces, and as the public mood turned nasty, both events became the subjects of an investigation by French prosecutors.

While the amounts of money were small change in the universe of alleged wrongdoing by Ghosn, the level of conspicuous consumption was clear to see. Guests in ball gowns and black tie were pampered by staff and entertainers in lavish period gowns and men's court suits. The 2014 event featured a sit-down dinner for 160 guests, few of whom actually came from the Alliance. The evening was capped by a massive fireworks display. A later audit done for Renault claimed the event cost €600,000 ($797,000), paid by the joint venture company in Holland, Renault Nissan BV. The figure is disputed by the Ghosn people, but it is clear that this was a pricey event, as can be seen in the slick video that Ghosn had made and which found its way onto YouTube when the scandal broke.

If Ghosn had any worries that this corporate largesse might be seen as improper, he certainly did not show it (hence the video). Even though it was meant to be a corporate celebration, the video shows no branding of any kind for the Alliance companies, and one invited guest said that the Alliance appeared an afterthought in the festivities.[13]

Ghosn and his wife were clearly pleased at how it went and returned for a similar soiree in 2016 for her birthday. This time, Ghosn paid the bill himself, with one potential caveat. Although the price tag was not disclosed, a person close to Ghosn said the total cost was around €325,000 ($359,700) (which would represent one-third of his annual base pay from Renault). The dispute was over the €50,000 ($55,340) facility charge payable to the museum. The Versailles people, saying they believed it was another corporate event, put it against the free night allowance that Renault had on the books because of a €2.3 million ($2.55 million) corporate donation to help with renovations. Ghosn's spokespeople said that the "comping" of the facility fee was not noticed amid all the charges (at that price, it might be easy to miss) and said they offered to repay. In any event, Renault was not actually out of pocket for the amount, a factor glossed over in the numerous media accounts, both in France and internationally. No matter; the PR damage was done.

In all, the French auditors hired by Renault said in 2019 that they found €11 million ($12.3 million) in questionable spending from 2009 to 2018.[14] To detractors, it was yet more evidence of wrongdoing by Ghosn, adding to the image that he was dipping into the company purse for his own use. But making a practical determination of whether they have a point is actually quite difficult. When Ghosn, or any CEO, jets around in the corporate plane, is he on business or pleasure? When in Davos, is he there on his own ticket? Should he pay for the food while on the plane? Can a spouse travel for free? If not, how much should they pay? All of this varies by company and by country and ends up as a judgment call. In reality, such corporate largesse is commonplace. It only becomes a point of controversy when a scandal erupts, at which time everyone is *shocked* to see what has been going on.

The French government was also to play a central, if inadvertent, role in the Ghosn affair through the 2018 agreement to keep him at Renault for another four years. With the condition that he explore ways to make the Alliance "irreversible," the nationalist wing at Nissan saw the threat of a French takeover as something that had to be countered, even as the Renault side maintained lingering suspicions that Ghosn was now playing for team Nissan. If it can be said that a balanced approach to a problem leaves no one happy, Ghosn was a model of even-handedness.

· · ·

With or without Ghosn, the French government remained keen on staying actively involved in Renault's affairs. In 2019, Fiat Chrysler (FCA Group) proposed a grand merger, a massive combination of largely second-tier brands in which Nissan would hold just 7.5 percent of the entire group shareholding. The deal was strongly backed by Renault's new CEO, Jean-Dominique Senard, who had been under pressure from the government to more strongly cement the Alliance. While Japanese government officials were, at least on paper, talking about how private-sector companies like Nissan and Renault should be left to their own devices to work things out, there was no such reticence in Paris. After all, wasn't Renault a national asset?

In the end, the French government got cold feet on moving forward too quickly and FCA yanked the deal at the last minute, leaving Senard in the lurch. Macron was by this time president and had left the negotiating to finance minister and close ally Bruno Le Maire, who said that he wanted more time to get Nissan on board. This was a somewhat unusual show of concern for the feelings back in Tokyo. He then went even further, undercutting Senard by trying to mollify Nissan with comments that the government may be willing to lower its stake in Renault, and even raised the idea that Renault might willingly cut its holding in its Japanese partner. French media reported that this infuriated Senard, who expected to be "backed up from the highest level of government." This was taken to mean President Macron. He sought an urgent meeting with the president, but Macron's calendar was apparently full. By this time, Macron had the issues of France, the future of the European Union, and Donald Trump to deal with.

While the French government believed that a merger would be the logical conclusion to the "French rescue" of Nissan, Alliance architect Schweitzer had long before seen the myriad potential problems it would cause. In creating the Alliance concept in 1999, he had specifically ruled out the idea of creating a new entity. "This is not a merger. People are not trying to build a common culture or common whatever," he said in an interview as the Alliance took shape. "Creating a common culture is time-consuming." The Alliance's multitude of corporate-culture issues would later demonstrate the value of this warning.

The French government meddling in the Renault-Nissan relationship over the years demonstrated the pitfalls of an industrial policy. The heavy-handed use of the Florange law, a creation that was itself a political convenience to rescue an ailing steel mill, and the various maneuverings by Macron and his lieutenants showed that politicians, even those with business savvy, can be drawn into a retrograde set of policies. In an era when auto factory workers are being replaced by the software engineers who program the factory robots, the push for more blue-collar jobs at any cost was the logical successor to the notion of subsidizing sailing ships as steam power took over the world, or investing in canals in the era of the railroad.

9

THE CASE IS BUILT

ON NOVEMBER 19, 2018, RIGHT WHEN PROSECUTORS were setting their trap for Ghosn at Tokyo's Haneda airport, his number two, a poker-faced Hiroto Saikawa, convened the regular monthly operations committee on the top floor of Nissan's world headquarters. After ticking off the routine agenda items with his four top lieutenants, Saikawa suddenly veered from business as usual.

"He said, 'Okay, let's make a break,'" recalled one executive who was at the meeting. "Saikawa called all the executive committee members into a meeting room by his office one floor down. He called us to give us the news before it broke in the press."

The impromptu klatch encompassed a wider group, including the heads of each business unit, from sales and marketing to manufacturing and engineering. They sat in stunned silence as Saikawa delivered the unbelievable news that Ghosn was being arrested.

"There was not too much discussion or reaction. They were shocked with nothing to say," one executive at the gathering recalled of his counterparts. "The first information the company could give was not too much."

But soon, the entire executive floor erupted into mayhem as prosecutors raided the place, seizing files, records, and other data. In a scene straight from a TV police drama, agents combed through Nissan's headquarters, packing boxes full of potential evidence. They especially zeroed in on the finance division, the secretary pool, and of course, Ghosn's office. One executive called it "complete chaos."

Later that evening, Saikawa—whose surname translates literally as "west river" in English—delivered the news to the rest of the world in a snap news conference. But executives said there was a marked elevation in his anger and outrage by then. At the earlier meeting with executives, Saikawa had been measured, almost apologetic, expressing concern about Ghosn's situation and not rushing to judgment about the charges.

"The first time he told us about the arrest, he made it look like it was a surprise, like he was supersad. I don't think he even mentioned he knew the reason. Just that Ghosn had been arrested, and he didn't know why," one executive said. "Then, he threw his boss under the bus. When I saw the press conference, it was a very different attitude. I was shocked."

Nissan's public relations department was caught flat-footed by the arrest. It had no prior notice. In preparing the company's initial press release, a heated internal debate broke out about striking the right tenor. An initial draft of the statement dripped with indignation, emphasizing Nissan's "shock" at the arrest. The final version was toned down to less bombastic boilerplate about cooperating with prosecutors and apologizing to shareholders.

Saikawa nonetheless came out swinging at the evening's main event. Striding out before the hundreds of journalists, he plunked down alone at a small table with a hastily printed paper name sheet taped to the front. Saikawa didn't even bother to bow in contrition, a ritual of any Japanese executive called upon to deliver a mea culpa for a corporate scandal. With cameras rolling for the world to witness, he then blasted his one-time mentor with a searing condemnation about financial misconduct and executive overreach.

"We must eliminate the negative aspects of Mr. Ghosn's regime. There are things that must be corrected, like the overconcentration of power in one individual, which resulted in distortion," Saikawa said. "It's very difficult to express this in words. Beyond being sorry, I feel big disappointment and frustration, and despair, and indignation or resentment."

By Japanese standards, it was an unapologetic, harsh repudiation of everything Ghosn.

"It was very, very, negative. We were like, 'Wow,'" recalled one top executive. "Nobody knew what happened to Mr. Ghosn in reality, at the time. How come he presented his boss this way? You don't assume that your boss is guilty up front. That was surprising."

. . .

At the press conference, Saikawa didn't dwell on the reasons for the arrest. The investigation was ongoing, and there was only so much Nissan could divulge, he said. For many days, the full scope of the prosecutor's suspicions was murky, with bits and pieces leaked to the Japanese media. When the initial grounds for arrest finally came to the surface, they left many scratching their head. The accusations centered on a seemingly tedious, technical matter of misreporting the company's official financial reports.

Prosecutors accused Ghosn, Greg Kelly, and Nissan—as a corporate entity—of failing to disclose more than $80 million of deferred income that was to be paid to Ghosn after retirement. The state maintained that all three had violated Japan's Financial Instruments and Exchange Act because this deferred compensation should have been disclosed in securities filings as an outstanding liability against the company's finances. Simply put, the company's investors and other stakeholders had a right to know but were never told.

But this was just the first of many allegations that would, in typical Japanese fashion, roll out over time. Tokyo prosecutors strung out their probe, piling on new allegations over the course of several weeks as Ghosn wallowed in jail. They did this in order to leverage the distinctly Japanese system of "rearrest," a practice that allows prosecutors to hold suspects for up to twenty-three days without formal charge while investigators continue their interrogation and fact finding. Each new tidbit digs up new leads. The Japanese call it "potato harvesting"—the domino effect of one witness or piece of evidence leading to another. Critics of the system call it "hostage justice" because it keeps people locked up as prosecutors pressure them to cave so as to escape detention. Japan has no preindictment bail system, meaning suspects are held until either they are indicted and become eligible for bail, their three-week detention period elapses, or prosecutors decide not to pursue the case.

Or until suspects are rearrested, when prosecutors can then reset the clock for up to another twenty-three days. The holding period is actually broken into three days and then two ten-day periods, in which prosecutors must get court approval to extend detention. But in practice, such approval is usually pro forma.

So, Ghosn's first arrest on November 19 started the first three-day holding. It was linked to suspicions of hiding about ¥4.9 billion ($44.38 million) of deferred compensation over five years, from Nissan's fiscal year 2010 through its fiscal year 2014. He was indicted of this charge on December 10, along with Kelly and Nissan, near the end of the first twenty-three-day jailing period.

He then would normally be eligible for bail, but that same day, prosecutors simultaneously "rearrested" Ghosn on a similar alleged undisclosed deferred compensation scheme, this one covering a new time frame (2016–2018). So, instead of qualifying for bail, Ghosn was hit with another twenty-three days in jail.

Over the eight years, prosecutors alleged, Ghosn and Kelly had masterminded unreported compensation totaling about ¥9.1 billion ($82.41 million). The deferred payout was far more than the ¥7.9 billion ($71.54 million) that Nissan had publicly reported as Ghosn's official compensation over the period. In fact, his total haul was more than double his declared compensation. Prosecutors later bumped up the total of postponed compensation to ¥9.3 billion ($84.22 million), from 2010 to 2018. They alleged this supposed scheme provided a convenient workaround for Ghosn, whose frustration with his compensation was an open secret over the years.

Prosecutors thought it was no coincidence the scheme started in calendar year 2010, when Japan's new rules required public disclosure of his income. Ghosn allegedly turned to the creative accounting to avoid the public scrutiny of reporting a supersize salary out of step with Japanese and French sensibilities. At the same time, it still allowed him to reap a package befitting his better-paid industry peers, in retirement. Under the prosecutor's narrative, Ghosn could have his cake and eat it too—he would be well paid but wouldn't let it show.

The size of Ghosn's total compensation was a closely guarded secret; few inside Nissan knew exactly how much he was pulling down. After Kelly's trial finally began in Tokyo in September 2020, Saikawa testified that, prior to the 2010 change in disclosure rules, Ghosn was believed to be making between ¥1.5 billion and ¥2.0 billion ($17 million and $22.8 million) a year. But after the rule change, Nissan disclosed annual remuneration at levels only around half that amount. Prosecutors say it was the gap that Ghosn hid and wanted paid back later.

An email purportedly from Kelly to his counterpart at Renault, dated April 2010, showed Ghosn's underlings busy at work trying to find ways to pay part of the CEO's compensation "without disclosing it publicly." But the key, according to the email, was finagling a "legal" means of doing so, and Kelly asked his counterpart to prepare a legal opinion answering his query: "What are the most likely legal implications?"

Later, during Kelly's trial, prosecutors painted a picture of Kelly and other Nissan executives spending considerable time and effort looking into a range of options to make up the shortfall, such as paying Ghosn extra through a Renault-Nissan joint venture, funneling funds through a nonconsolidated Nissan subsidiary or through another third company, selling him real estate or artwork on the cheap so he could sell it for a profit, and even providing Ghosn a loan that could later be forgiven. They also considered paying Ghosn in the form of an inflated pension, a noncompete agreement, and an "advisory fee" after he retired. Prosecutors say the money would flow through a system of "postponed compensation."[1]

· · ·

Rules for deferred income are notoriously complex in almost all countries as regulators and companies play a cat-and-mouse game over pinpointing reportable income. In Japan especially, the rules leave plenty of room for interpretation, and some observers began to argue that the case was anything but a slam dunk for prosecutors.

As December dragged on, public expectations mounted that some kind of bargain could be struck, that charges might be dropped, or that Ghosn would at least be indicted on the second accusation and released on bail. Some pundits wondered whether he might simply plead guilty and apologize—as so many suspects in Japan do—and get by with a suspended sentence. This outcome would allow him to avoid prison by serving out a probation period. But it would still be a considerable blow to the executive's lofty image and legacy. Instead, Ghosn dug in his heels. And prosecutors only tightened the screws.

In Japan, prosecutors deliver a near-perfect conviction rate, in large part because suspects so often confess during the duress of their initial jailing. This is the secret sauce in the country's "hostage justice" recipe.

But Ghosn showed no signs of folding.

"They thought, 'We're going to arrest the guy, we're going to shake the hell out of him, we're going to bombard him with bad media, and after two weeks, he will confess whatever we want.' That's what they bet would happen. Strike hard, get the confession, and then make a quick win," he said in an interview. "It didn't go this way. This was the first mistake."

For the initial week in jail, Ghosn sat silent and all but cut off as the world wondered what happened. His first public attempt to defend himself came a full nine days after his takedown. By then, Ghosn hired former Tokyo prosecutor Motonari Otsuru as a defense attorney. Otsuru issued the first formal denial to Bloomberg News on November 28 after meeting his new client.[2] Ghosn seemed to be finding some footing to fight back.

Then, almost out of nowhere, a third charge was leveled against Ghosn for a Japanese crime known as an aggravated breach of trust, this time for allegedly diverting Nissan company money for personal use. This rearrest came on December 21, more than a month into his detention, resetting the clock for another lengthy lockup with no chance of bail. This third arrest was much more serious than the first two. Unlike the previous charges, which revolved around money not yet disbursed, the December 21 arrest focused on funds Ghosn allegedly had already siphoned from Nissan to help him clear a personal financial pinch. This accusation was far more damning than alleging he skirted obscure financial filing rules, and it was something that easily stirred moral indignation among the Japanese public.

Neither Kelly nor Nissan was implicated in this third accusation. Prosecutors were clearly drilling down on Ghosn. Kelly himself was released on bail late Christmas Day 2018, after pleading for medical attention to address his neck problem. Kelly had been scheduled to undergo surgery in the United States for spinal stenosis when Nissan called him to Japan for "urgent business" in October. That call was actually the setup for Kelly's arrest. After more than a month in Tokyo's regimented detention center, Kelly's spinal condition only worsened. He finally received surgery after winning bail, in a Japanese hospital, but it came weeks behind the originally scheduled operation and left him with lingering numbness in his extremities. Kelly was required to remain in the country until his trial began, nearly two years later, on September 15, 2020.

The third accusation against Ghosn stemmed from personal investment losses related to swap contracts in 2008. This charge suggested that Ghosn's troubles started that year, because he had a foreign exchange swap contract with Japan's Shinsei Bank that was supposed to protect the value of his yen-based pay when converted into dollars. But with the start of the recession in 2008, the yen's sudden appreciation put that contract ¥1.85 billion ($16.6 million) underwater.

As Shinsei moved to close out the account and hand Ghosn a huge loss, he arranged to have the account transferred to Nissan as a form of collateral. Japan's regulatory body, the Securities and Exchange Surveillance Commission, flagged this as a potential conflict of interest and required Nissan to no longer hold the losses on Ghosn's behalf. In January 2009, a quarterly settlement came due on the contract, and Nissan nonetheless paid a small installment back to Shinsei. Ghosn allegedly reimbursed Nissan for this, meaning that the transactions were aboveboard so far.

But meanwhile, the cash-strapped CEO was still obliged to secure another source of collateral to replace Nissan, which was disqualified from holding the loss-making account for Ghosn by Japanese regulators. He allegedly found another backer in prominent Saudi businessman Khaled Al-Juffali, who is a part owner of a company with a 50 percent share in the Middle Eastern car distributor Nissan Gulf. Juffali is better known, however, as vice chairman of one of Saudi Arabia's largest conglomerates. He was a well-heeled financier and a board member of the Saudi Arabian Monetary Authority.[3] And he is also one of the dignitaries Ghosn would meet in his trips to the Davos economic summits. Juffali is believed to have offered his assets as collateral to underwrite a letter of credit that let Ghosn keep his swap contract at Shinsei. Nissan then got this burden off its books by reverting the contract back to the Japanese bank.

After that, Nissan made four payments to a subsidiary in the Middle East through a special "CEO Reserve" fund normally tapped for discretionary or emergency expenses. That subsidiary then allegedly transferred the funds to Juffali's company. Prosecutors claim this was payback for Juffali's help in resolving Ghosn's personal financial troubles. But Ghosn's lawyers and Juffali denied any quid pro quo. Nissan's transfers, they said, were legitimate business outlays to cover such things as marketing and incentive expenses.

In the Japanese media, this third charge became known as the "Saudi Route" of fund flows—in reference to the Saudi businessman linked to the transfers.

Nissan insiders said the company only began to gather documents related to this charge in November, the month of Ghosn's initial arrest. Prosecutors, able to search bank records and Ghosn's residence, picked it up from there and pieced together the final accusations. People at Nissan were not happy with the picture that emerged of Ghosn allegedly treating the company as his personal bank.

"Individuals don't borrow the creditworthiness of companies to support personal transactions. It's a conflict of interest," said one employee involved with Nissan's internal probe. "Second, getting the company to cover your losses, even if you pay the company back, is not appropriate. I couldn't get Nissan to do that for me. Finally, if it is established that these payments [to Juffali] were in return for the offer of collateral, and not for business, that means the company spent $14.7 million for no reason other than propping up Carlos Ghosn's personal foreign exchange swap contract. That is a loss of $14.7 million."

· · ·

On January 11, 2019, nearly two months after Ghosn's initial arrest, prosecutors finally indicted him on the Saudi Route breach of trust charge, and they also indicted Ghosn, Kelly, and Nissan on the second accusation of misreporting deferred compensation between 2016 and 2018. Ghosn was now indicted on three charges, and with no other arrests hanging over his head, he finally became eligible for bail.

Yet it would be nearly another two months before the court would approve his release as prosecutors and defense attorneys sparred over bail conditions. When Ghosn's release was finally approved March 5, bail was set at a reported record amount of ¥1 billion ($8.9 million). He paid it in cash.

After 108 days in lockup, Ghosn walked free from the monolithic cell block before a media circus of hundreds of reporters—held at bay behind a parking lot fence—as TV stations beamed the event live to screens throughout Japan. Expectations ran high that the man with a flair for showmanship might stage an impromptu press conference on the steps of the jailhouse. But what actually ensued made for an even wilder spectacle.

Ghosn emerged from detention dressed not in one of his trademark suits but in a workman's outfit, replete with a blue cap and fluorescent orange safety vest. A surgical mask concealed his face, and he was paraded out the front door by a phalanx of jailhouse guards all wearing their own facemasks to better befuddle the media. Ghosn was then packed into a Suzuki minivan outfitted with a work ladder on the roof. The disguise was meant to throw off any journalist eager to track Ghosn to the court-appointed residence where he would live while out on bail awaiting trial. But the smokescreen worked only long enough for a quick double take. By the time his vehicle left the front gate of the detention house, a pack of media-hired motorbikes and helicopters was in hot pursuit to chronicle his next moves across the capital city.[4]

Timed to his release from jail, the fallen auto titan issued a defiant statement calling his arrest a "terrible ordeal" and declared: "I am innocent and totally committed to vigorously defending myself in a fair trial against these meritless and unsubstantiated accusations."

Finally free on bail, Ghosn prepared to mount a defense and even opened a Twitter account to plead his case to the world. The banner photo for the verified @carlosghosn account depicted the downfallen executive in pensive profile overlooking a Japanese-style pavilion in a park. In early April, he posted his first tweet, promising to "tell the truth about what's happening" at an April 11 news conference.[5]

Little did he know, prosecutors weren't finished with him. And Ghosn's threat of a media offensive may have even fired their ire.

On the morning of April 4, the day after he sent that initial tweet pledging to hold court in public, authorities raided Ghosn's temporary residence in a Tokyo apartment building where he stayed with his wife, Carole. He was arrested for a fourth time and sent back to jail after less than a month out on bail. It shattered his plan for a press conference and saddled him with his fourth, most serious charge yet.

In the Saudi Route breach of trust charge, the third indictment against Ghosn, it was not entirely clear how much, if any, financial harm he supposedly inflicted on Nissan. His attempt to have Nissan shoulder his personal losses ultimately failed (though Nissan suspects the funds transferred to the Middle East in that case were in fact used as payback for Ghosn's personal financial favor). The new breach of trust accusation, however, claimed Ghosn had specifically diverted Nissan funds into his own pocket.

According to prosecutors, Ghosn approved payments of around $15 million from a Nissan subsidiary to a distributor between 2015 and 2018. The company, later identified as Oman-based Suhail Bahwan Automobiles, distributed Nissan vehicles in the region and was run by businessman Suhail Bahwan, another billionaire friend of Ghosn. The payments, again tapped from Ghosn's CEO Reserve fund, were earmarked as marketing expenses, but prosecutors alleged Ghosn received some $5 million of the disbursements as a kind of kickback. Some of that money supposedly was diverted into a US-based investment firm run by Ghosn's son, while some supposedly helped pay for his yacht, *Shachou*. Japanese media branded this fourth accusation as the "Omani Route."

Ghosn was indicted for this alleged scheme in a breach of trust charge on April 22, 2019, and released from jail following a twenty-two-day lockup, and after paying another ¥500 million ($5.4 million) bail. He now confronted a towering mountain of legal trouble and serious prison time, including up to fifteen years in a Japanese prison and a maximum fine of ¥120 million ($1.1 million) if found guilty on all four counts. And given Japan's near-perfect conviction rate, the odds seemed high he would be found guilty of *something*.

Ghosn categorically denied all charges and maintained his innocence. But even as he battled the official indictments from the prosecutor's office, a stream of seemingly endless accusations of other wrongdoing bubbled to the surface. These claims were not part of the criminal cases leveled by Japan's justice system; Ghosn wasn't even charged in these matters. Instead, they were part of a separate onslaught of assertion and innuendo leveled by Nissan. They centered on rampant misuse of company resources that, if true, was at least corrupt and unethical, if not outright illegal.

This parallel deluge of leaks began almost immediately after Ghosn's initial arrest.

Among the first accusations was that he misused a Nissan subsidiary to buy homes for himself in Rio de Janeiro and Beirut. A Netherlands-based company, called Zi-A Capital BV, had been set up in 2010 ostensibly as a venture capital fund to invest in up-and-coming technologies. Nissan investigators said they found that Zi-A was instead paying for real estate and had spent more than $22 million buying and renovating these company homes in Brazil and Lebanon for Ghosn. The pink-walled mansion in Beirut—so often shown in the media—is where Ghosn finally holed up after fleeing Japan, much to the aggravation of Nissan, which had paid for it and still claimed ownership rights.

Ghosn also was accused of having Nissan pay his older sister a consulting fee of $750,000 over more than a decade for no apparent work. "No one in Nissan, except a few particular persons, was aware of this fact," the company said, adding that "no deliverables" were found connected to the advisory fees. Ghosn's voluminous air travel also became a target. Nissan claimed Ghosn wrongly billed the company for $4.4 million worth of private travel for himself and his family on the corporate jet and chartered airplanes. Later, during Kelly's trial, among the expenses dragged out in court was one from 2016 detailing ¥3.4 million ($32,700) Ghosn allegedly billed the company for new suits.

Nissan also alleged Ghosn inappropriately took home about ¥140 million ($1.28 million) in stock appreciation rights through the manipulation of the exercise date to cash in at a higher price for a bigger payout.[6]

Ghosn's alleged wrongdoing soon spilled over from Nissan to the wider Alliance.

Nissan's internal investigators, for instance, uncovered alleged foul play at another Netherlands subsidiary with Mitsubishi, Nissan-Mitsubishi BV (NMBV). That 50-50 joint venture was supposedly created to reward employees at both companies who find synergies by giving them a share of the savings. But Nissan and Mitsubishi say they discovered Ghosn was using the entity to pay himself huge sums. He allegedly netted $8.9 million from a signing bonus and salary paid from NMBV without the knowledge or consultation of its other board members, Nissan's Saikawa and Mitsubishi CEO Osamu Masuko. Neither of those men, by the way, received any payments from NMBV.[7]

The companies said they dug up additional dubious dealings at Nissan's other Netherlands-based joint venture with Renault, Renault-Nissan BV (RNBV). Some €3.9 million ($4.5 million) of RNBV expenditures, for example, were deemed Ghosn's private expenses and unrelated to the business. The outlays covered an array of extravagant social engagements that painted an unflattering picture of an executive obsessed with living high at the company's expense.

They allegedly covered the 2014 party at France's Palace of Versailles, the entertainment of guests at the Carnival in Rio de Janeiro and at the Cannes Film Festival, gifts from Cartier in Paris, dinners at Marmottan Museum in Paris, and fees to Ghosn's personal attorney in Lebanon—despite the fact Nissan conducted little business in the country. RNBV was believed to have made another €2.37 million ($2.65 million) in donations on behalf of Ghosn, not the companies, to ten educational and nonprofit institutions, nine of which were in his ancestral homeland of Lebanon. Finally, Ghosn allegedly saddled RNBV with another €5.1 million ($5.71 million) for air flights that, the company alleged, were likely for the private use of him and his family.[8]

. . .

The lavish Versailles party was a particularly egregious episode gobbled up by international media, with guests filing through a formation of halberd-wielding soldiers in tricorn hats, then strolling the château's gilded chambers and delighting in string and harpsichord music, before tucking into a sumptuous meal at a candlelit table stretching the length of a hall.

The party at Versailles two years later to celebrate the birthday of his second wife, Carole, was a Marie Antoinette–themed soiree, replete with period actors in eighteenth-century costume and aristocratic wigs. It was so opulent it was featured in a *Town & Country* photo spread.[9] The palace events had become, in the public's eye, emblematic of the tone-deaf excesses of an executive left largely unchecked.

Ghosn's problems mounted with a probe by the US Securities and Exchange Commission (SEC) of the alleged deferred compensation. The commission charged that Ghosn, with Kelly's help, concealed some $140 million in undisclosed compensation and retirement benefits from 2009 to 2018.

Meanwhile in France, Renault said in early 2020 it would file a civil claim reserving the right to seek restitution from Ghosn for any alleged misappropriation of funds after French prosecutors began a preliminary investigation and referred the matter to a court. French tax authorities, in a separate probe, were also looking into transactions between Renault and its distributor in Oman and the French automaker's contracts with the Netherlands-based joint venture.[10]

Nissan, for its part, promised it would seek compensation for the millions of dollars it claimed Ghosn cost the company through his alleged criminal misconduct and other misuse of funds. And in February 2020, the carmaker made good on that threat by filing a civil suit in Japan against its former chairman for ¥10 billion ($91 million) in damages for his alleged "breach of fiduciary duty" and "misappropriation of Nissan's resources and assets."[11] That action came on the heels of an earlier civil complaint Nissan brought against Ghosn in the British Virgin Islands. In that lawsuit, Nissan claimed "unauthorized payments and transactions were processed through special purpose entities" and sought title to Ghosn's luxury yacht and other compensation.

As Ghosn later put it: "I'm being attacked from all sides."

. . .

Nissan claimed that Ghosn was able to orchestrate such a web of self-dealing, both of the illegal variety and the merely unseemly kind, because he had concentrated so much unchecked power in himself as chairman and CEO and an inner circle of enablers. No one could tell him no.

Within that crew, Nissan said, the top go-to man was Kelly, who in 2009 became the senior vice president controlling all matters at the office of the CEO, the Alliance CEO, the legal department, and global human resources. Whenever prickly questions landed on his desk—be they from the statutory auditors or the accounting department—Kelly quickly shut them down if they cut too close to Ghosn, Nissan said after Ghosn's arrest. Units under Kelly's control operated opaquely, "simply responding that it was a 'CEO matter.'" Meanwhile, a complex setup of shell companies blocked transparent oversight of subsidiaries, as with the firms in the Netherlands.[12]

Nissan later did an autopsy of the scandal, and in the resulting thirty-eight-page report to the Tokyo Stock Exchange, the company claimed that Ghosn—by leveraging his legacy of having saved Nissan from bankruptcy—had established a "personality cult" that made all his dealings "impenetrable territory." As a result, said Nissan, "the checks and balances function of certain administrative departments did not necessarily function effectively with respect to the problem concerning Mr. Ghosn's demands for his personal gain."[13] In other words, in a colossal failure of corporate governance, absolute power corrupted absolutely.

Ghosn (and Kelly) denied the whole lot of allegations. But amid this avalanche of accusation, Japanese sentiment flipped against the man long hailed as an adopted national hero. Even if Ghosn could beat the prosecutor's four indictments in a Japanese court of law, rehabilitating his reputation in the court of public opinion seemed all but impossible. The week after Ghosn's initial arrest, the *Nikkei* business daily, Japan's equivalent of the *Wall Street Journal*, argued in an editorial that Ghosn's achievement in creating the Alliance still deserved "high praise." But the opinion-leading newspaper then slammed the disgraced CEO for his more recent deeds.

"There is no question that the downfall of one of the auto industry's most powerful executives stemmed from his lack of respect for ethics and the law," the *Nikkei* wrote. "While Japanese executives have often committed corporate crimes to protect the reputation or fate of their companies . . . they rarely cross the red line out of sheer greed."[14]

10

MAKINGS OF A CONSPIRACY

IN JAPAN, GHOSN'S UNDOING SEEMED LIKE A STRAIGHT-forward case of greed and hubris. But half a world away in France—and in other corners of the international automotive industry—the arrest immediately triggered more sinister suspicions about a conspiracy to frame the foreigner. And as the pieces of that puzzle fell into place, a much different picture emerged.

News of Ghosn's arrest broke just before lunchtime in Paris, on a bright but chilly Monday. Renault was stunned. So was everyone in France. At Renault headquarters, executives groped in the dark for details, no matter how scant, about the prosecutor's charges and Nissan's accusations.

The man handed the unenviable task of filling in Renault's top brass was Philippe Klein, the senior French executive at Nissan and one of the original fix-it men Ghosn brought from Renault in 1999. He was also the executive who led Ghosn's first CEO office at Nissan, as a predecessor to Greg Kelly. A soft-spoken engineer and vintage car buff, Klein was the chief planning officer for Nissan at the time and the point person for devising the product lineups for Nissan, Infiniti, and Datsun.

Klein started his career at Renault as a powertrain engineer—arguably the nerdiest of car jobs—and bounced back and forth between the French carmaker and Nissan throughout his career. Having served as the top gatekeeper of the CEO Office, first at Nissan and then later at Renault, he was widely respected and trusted by both sides. Or, at least, he had been.

Back in Tokyo, Hiroto Saikawa ordered Klein to fly out immediately on a chartered private jet to be the Nissan messenger to France. But first, Klein had to make an important stop.

Even as Ghosn was being arrested that day in Tokyo, the French ambassador to Japan was hosting an embassy reception there. Among the dignitaries in attendance was Louis Schweitzer, the legendary Renault CEO who brokered the Nissan bailout in 1999 and picked Ghosn as his successor.

Klein had the delicate job of briefing them on what little he had learned from Saikawa.

It was an awkward discussion marked by shock and disbelief. But the real test awaited in Paris, where the blurry-eyed Klein touched down the next morning and rushed straight to Renault headquarters in Boulogne-Billancourt, in the capital city's western suburbs.

Klein's mission seemed straightforward: explain that Nissan had discovered significant wrongdoing by Ghosn and that his arrest should not impinge on the alliance with Renault. He was also tasked with urging Renault to start due diligence reviews of its own operations and of the Renault-Nissan BV entity in the Netherlands. Some details were still under wraps as prosecutors continued their investigation, he was instructed to say, but more would be shared in due course.

. . .

As Klein made the rounds of the seventh-floor executive suites, he was met with open suspicion. Foremost among the doubters was Thierry Bolloré, Ghosn's No. 2 at Renault. Like Ghosn, Bolloré started his career at tire maker Michelin. He then moved to auto parts giant Faurecia before joining Renault in 2012. Considered an aggressive custodian of Renault's controlling stake in Nissan, he was tapped as chief operating officer in February 2018, clenching pole position as Ghosn's heir apparent. Klein did not receive a warm reception.

"There was the perception that I was a kind of alien coming from another planet with a very strange message, or a pure traitor, or a stupid guy who was completely manipulated, or you've been in Japan too long," Klein recalled. "There was a lot of denial that this could even simply be possible. It was, 'This cannot be anything else but a plot from the Japanese.'"

In the back of Klein's mind, he was secretly wondering the same thing.

Lurking in the collective consciousness in Paris was a humiliating scandal that rocked Renault in 2011 and nearly took down Ghosn just seven years earlier. Renault had accused, falsely it turned out, and then fired three senior managers for supposedly selling corporate secrets about electric cars to foreign interests. Patrick Pelata, Renault's then COO and a revered product development guru long seen as CEO material, was forced to resign over the affair to shield his longtime friend and boss, Carlos Ghosn, from the political blowback. As a former schoolmate of Ghosn's at École Polytechnique, Pelata was one of only two people at Renault said to be on a first-name basis with Ghosn. (To everyone else at Renault and Nissan—even his top executives—he was always "Mr. Ghosn.") Was the takedown in Japan the beginning of another such misstep, only on a much larger scale?

Talk of a corporate conspiracy went viral almost as soon as Ghosn was arrested.

The initial charges—that he had hidden more than $80 million in postponed compensation—were dismissed by skeptics as a concocted ploy by Nissan, maybe in league with the Japanese government, to remove him from office. Why? Just nine months earlier, Renault said it would renew Ghosn's contract to lead the automaker for another four years, with one caveat. His mandate was to make Renault's alliance with Nissan "irreversible." Those were fighting words to some at Nissan.

What's more, the Florange Crisis from 2015, in which the French government secured double voting rights in Renault over the protests of Nissan, was still fresh in the memories of many in Yokohama. That showdown stoked long-standing suspicion in Japan about French intentions. Now, the conspiracists imagined a paranoid Japan consumed with the fear that the French government and Ghosn were positioning for an end game that might once and for all eradicate Nissan's independence and make it a subsidiary.

. . .

According to Nissan's and Saikawa's official narrative, Alliance relations and integration plans had nothing to do with Ghosn's arrest. To Nissan, it was a clear-cut case of misconduct. Saikawa, in a sit-down with Japan's *Shukan Bunshun* magazine months after the arrest, blasted his former mentor. "I wonder if Mr. Ghosn has ever had any love or sense of attachment to Nissan as a company. I wonder if Nissan was merely a tool for him and his family to enjoy a luxurious lifestyle," Saikawa said. "I seriously question if Mr. Ghosn has had any respect for Japanese people and Japanese society at all. If he had respect for Japan, he couldn't have committed such misconduct."[1]

But to the conspiracy minded, it seemed far more plausible that Nissan and Japanese authorities colluded to keep Nissan independent the best way they knew how—by taking out the only man holding the two companies together. It was only after the French government ordered Ghosn to bind them irreversibly that a key Nissan insider—as Nissan openly admits—first shared misgivings about Ghosn's alleged misdeeds. In this scenario, Ghosn wasn't guilty of any crime at all. He was collateral damage in a collision of nationalist instincts and the forces of globalism.[2] To Ghosn, this conspiracy storyline was a pillar of his defense.

"The only way you can explain it is that they wanted to not only eliminate me but destroy my legacy and completely reshuffle the power relationship between the three companies," Ghosn said in an interview for this book from Lebanon after fleeing Japan. "The Japanese came very quickly to the realization that, unfortunately, the biggest influence that Renault or the French would have on Nissan would be through me. So they said, 'Okay, if we get rid of him, it's over.' And that's exactly what happened."

In April 2019, he outlined it personally in a video communiqué released in lieu of the live press conference he hoped to host before a largely sympathetic audience at the Foreign Correspondents' Club of Japan. By the time the video was released, Ghosn had been thrown back in jail for a second time. His lawyers wisely prepared the seven-and-a-half-minute message in anticipation that he might be picked up and blocked from speaking.

"This is not about greed. This is not about dictatorship. This is about a plot. This is about conspiracy. This is about backstabbing," Ghosn said in the clip. "There was first a fear that the next step of the Alliance, in terms of convergence and in terms of moving toward a merger, would, in a certain way, threaten some people or eventually threaten the autonomy of Nissan."[3]

. . .

The seeds of conspiracy had been sown, by Ghosn's telling, when Emmanuel Macron became president of France in 2017 and stepped up the pressure for the "irreversible integration" of Renault and Nissan. Around January 2018, the French government informed the Japanese government it planned to fuse the management of both companies. According to Ghosn, he triggered a Japanese backlash by proposing a holding company structure for Renault and Nissan. He outlined the basics of his plan in an interview with *Automotive News* after escaping Japan. All three companies—Renault, Nissan, and Mitsubishi—would be combined under an umbrella entity, which would be based in a neutral territory, such as the Netherlands or Switzerland, and traded under one stock dual-listed in Paris and Tokyo, instead of separate tickers for Renault, Nissan, and Mitsubishi. Each carmaker would keep its own headquarters and own executive committees, but they would be overseen by the holding company's independent board. That board would have perhaps ten directors nominated from the boards of the carmakers.

Critically, Ghosn said the French government would sell its stake in Renault under his envisioned plan, and the companies would keep operational independence. What could possibly induce the French state to abandon its grip on one of the nation's industrial flagships wasn't entirely clear. And whether the three carmakers could work autonomously while trading under the same stock was a big question mark.

Ghosn floated the idea in early 2018 and immediately hit a wall of resistance in Japan, not only at Nissan but with the powerful Minister of

Economy, Trade, and Industry (METI), the guardian of Japan Inc. To Saikawa, a holding company was a merger gussied up with a fancier name. Some in the Tokyo government felt the same way. Publicly, METI maintained that the companies should decide their future direction between themselves. But internal Nissan emails from the period show that some Nissan executives felt the Japanese government was actually too aggressive in its opposition.

In April 2018, Hari Nada, then Nissan's senior vice president in charge of the chairman and CEO office, was locking horns with his counterpart at Renault about a merger proposal. Nada, an influential powerbroker appointed as Kelly's successor in the role, reported straight to Ghosn. In a leaked email to Ghosn updating on the status of talks, Nada dismissed Renault's merger proposal as simplistic. He also said it didn't account for the perspectives of Nissan's other shareholders. Nada wrote that Nissan's stance was thus: It preferred the status quo to a merger, but it actually preferred the dramatic step of rebalancing the crossholdings between Renault and Nissan over the status quo.

"I said that rebalancing involved Renault reducing its stake in Nissan (and Nissan increasing in Renault) so that both voted in each other plus, a restructuring of the contractual landscape so that neither party seeks control over the other plus, an exit of the French state plus finally, constructing a mechanism to preserve the benefits of the Alliance by ensuring a good succession to the current Alliance leadership," Nada wrote in the email to Ghosn. "Nissan would like to stay faithful to the principle of autonomous companies flexibly seeking win-win solutions."

Meanwhile METI, Japan's influential and watchful ministry for industry, began applying pressure in support of Nissan to the Agence des participations de l'État (APE), the French government's agency for managing state stakes in companies such as Renault and dozens of others. METI coordinated with Hitoshi Kawaguchi, then the senior vice president in charge of government affairs at Nissan. According to an email from Kawaguchi to Ghosn, Saikawa, and Nada, METI prepared in May 2018 a memorandum of understanding providing the French government "written proof of protection for Nissan's interest." Nissan, Kawaguchi added, had been asking "METI to stay behind us to support Nissan by trying to put a brake on French state/APE whenever necessary." He then attached a draft letter from METI to the French government.

METI's key message was that "Nissan is free to make its own decision" and that failure to respect that by the French side would damage the mutual trust of the carmakers that underpins the Alliance, which METI dubbed "the greatest symbol of successful Franco-Japanese industrial cooperation." METI then maintained that future discussions should focus on "essential elements." Primary among those was the trigger issue of "equality of shareholding cross-share structure," a topic anathema to the French. Even Kawaguchi thought this was over the top.

"The draft is going a little too far even in our view, when the French side is staying quiet," Kawaguchi wrote in the email to Ghosn and the others. "Though the support by the Japanese government is appreciated, it is a private company matter at the end of the day." Saikawa, in a reply, concurred, calling the hardball stance "somewhat disturbing" and saying a different approached was needed.

To Ghosn and his legal team, this mounting tension between France and Japan and between Nissan and Renault fueled a revolution to remove him.

· · ·

Yet, how the chairman's takedown actually unfolded is a matter of debate.

All sides seem to agree that Nissan's investigation into Ghosn began in early 2018 with a top-secret probe conducted by Kawaguchi, Nada, and Nissan's statutory auditor, Hidetoshi Imazu. The trio dug up more dirt. And they eventually looped in Toshiaki Ohnuma, then head of the Secretariat's Office, which handles matters relating to top executives, including compensation. Nissan's outside legal firm Latham & Watkins chipped in with legal advice and helped spearhead a worldwide audit of Nissan's affiliate companies. It is also clear that Imazu, instead of bringing the allegations to the Nissan board for consideration, as typically required of statutory auditors, took the unorthodox step of going first to the Tokyo District Public Prosecutors Office, igniting the firestorm.

Finally, no one contests the delicate matter of timing. Just as Kawaguchi and Nada were rooting out Ghosn's alleged misconduct, the two were simultaneously defending Nissan against his holding company idea.

Where narratives diverge is over motivations of these players.

. . .

Ghosn's attorneys maintain that this group of Nissan insiders trumped up wrongdoing as a pretext for ejecting Ghosn and derailing a merger. Kawaguchi and the others led a fishing expedition for any shred of misconduct and consulted with the Tokyo District Public Prosecutors Office on what might stick. The internal Nissan team also worked with a former vice minister from METI, Masakazu Toyoda, who became a director of the board in June 2018. All their efforts were laser focused on one outcome. The Ghosn camp maintained that around March 2018, Kawaguchi and Nissan's statutory auditor, Imazu, led a clandestine effort to dig up misconduct by Ghosn anywhere in the company. "Their aim was to prevent the integration of Nissan and Renault by finding Mr. Ghosn's 'improper acts' and ousting him from Nissan," Ghosn's lawyers wrote in an October 2019 court filing. "The purpose of this unjust and biased investigation was to restructure the relationship between Nissan and Renault (French government) by unseating Mr. Ghosn and preventing the 'integration' of the two companies."[4]

By Ghosn's account, the plotters and prosecutors essentially blackmailed Nada and Ohnuma into making witness statements and submitting evidence against Ghosn, in exchange for not facing their own criminal charges. Moreover, Ghosn maintained, Saikawa wrongly dodged arrest for some of the alleged misconduct. Saikawa, for instance, signed documents regarding Ghosn's postretirement compensation plans that involved consulting and noncompete agreements, as well as the annual securities reports that fell under scrutiny for allegedly being misstated. Ghosn's attorneys also claimed it was Saikawa, not Ghosn, who granted about half of the $15 million payment to Suhail Bahwan Automobiles under the Omani Route breach of trust charges. They noted that Saikawa was CEO at the time and, thus, in charge of the controversial

CEO Reserve from which the funds flowed.[5] To the defense team, the fact that Saikawa, an opponent of merger, evaded criminal charge was a glaring hypocrisy that showed prosecutors were boring down only on Ghosn as the main target. In this conspiracy, after all, it was important to leave Nissan in solid Japanese hands. To Ghosn's lawyers, this selective enforcement reflected rank racial discrimination; Japanese executives with dirty hands went free, while the foreigners were thrown in jail.

"In this case, there is no doubt that Mr. Ghosn has been discriminated against based on his race, nationality and/or social status," Ghosn's attorneys wrote in one court filing. Even within Nissan, an undercurrent of culture clash and racial divide pervaded the scandal, with non-Japanese employees finding it easier to buy into the conspiracy theory. One American Nissan engineer who, just before Ghosn's arrest, had relocated to Nissan's global technology center outside Yokohama put it plainly: "We pretty much think he got shafted."

Ghosn later compared his arrest with the Japanese surprise attack that catapulted the United States into World War II, saying that like the hapless Americans, he never saw it coming. "Did you notice what happened in Pearl Harbor?" Ghosn said.[6]

"There was frustration on the Japanese side, but I don't think anybody could imagine that they would react like this," he said. "There was no sign, there was no sign at all."

. . .

Others saw a slow-motion coup. From the early days of the Alliance, they say, Nissan and the Japanese always believed the foreign interlopers would eventually leave Japan, either by their own volition or with a push. General Motors had partnered with Suzuki and Subaru, only to abandon those stakes during the Great Recession. Ford eventually gave up its longtime grip on Mazda. Daimler bailed from its tie up with Mitsubishi. Renault's dabbling in Japan lasted longer than most, but its exit was bound to happen one day, that strain of thinking went.

At Renault, some even believed the Japanese had been quietly collecting *kompromat* on Ghosn for years, waiting for the day it might come in handy. If Renault wouldn't retreat on its own, there was always the "nuclear option" of blowing up the alliance that some Nissan executives pondered and even preferred.

"I'm not believing one second that this activity started because of the so-called news of the merger in 2016 or 2017 or 2018," said one longtime Ghosn lieutenant from Renault. "No, not at all. It was organized since the beginning. They saw that there was a threat, and they pushed on the red button. And that's easy to understand."

Add to this conspiracy theory the juicy tidbit that, in late 2018 just before his arrest, those close to Ghosn say he was planning a management shakeup at Nissan that would have benched Saikawa as CEO. Ghosn wasn't happy with the performance of Nissan, which had started to deteriorate. A top candidate for replacing Saikawa was José Muñoz, a Spanish executive responsible for record Nissan sales in North America who was then serving as the company's global chief performance officer. According to one account, Ghosn put it bluntly to Saikawa: he could back the holding company and retire with grace as Nissan's next chairman, or he would be summarily fired and replaced by Muñoz.

But the ax never fell on Saikawa. Instead, Ghosn landed in jail. In January 2019, Muñoz quit Nissan, and he later joined South Korean rival Hyundai Motor Co. as its global chief operating officer and CEO for North American operations. (Muñoz's exit was part of a wider exodus of non-Japanese executives from Nissan in the wake of Ghosn's arrest.) Ghosn later said he was pondering a management shuffle because Saikawa's performance was slipping, but he denied that Saikawa's firing was imminent in late 2018. Yet, to some in the Ghosn camp, it was only natural that Nissan's Japanese leadership would have wanted to thwart any eventual reshuffling of the top brass to preserve Japan's control at the top.

. . .

Nissan's official narrative was fuzzier. The company never publicly spelled out in great detail the steps leading to Ghosn's arrest. The investigation, it said, was spurred by a "whistle-blower" who initially remained unidentified, but later came to be understood as Nada. And through the end, Nissan maintained as its official stance that "The sole cause of this chain of events is the misconduct led by Ghosn and Kelly."

Like Ghosn's version, Nissan's telling begins with an internal investigation, but in this rendition, one initiated by Imazu. By the spring of 2018, it led to concerns about Zi-A Capital BV, the venture fund that was established to fuel startups but instead ended up paying for Ghosn's housing. Next, the internal investigators unearthed what they thought were illegal plans to conceal tens of millions of dollars of postponed remuneration.

According to this account, Nada and Ohnuma copped plea bargains with prosecutors because they had insider knowledge about the misconduct. In fact, they assert they helped facilitate the various deferred compensation schemes for several years over the 2010–2018 period. Both took advantage of a change to Japan's criminal code that introduced a Western-style plea-bargain procedure. It took effect in June 2018, making these Nissan employees among the first in the nation to shelter under the provision.[7]

Nada, especially, lurks in the background as one of the murkier figures in the entire Ghosn saga, partly because of his point-man role in negotiations with Renault and partly because of his role as a plea bargainer who admitted involvement in the alleged wrongdoing. An erudite Malaysian-born, British-trained attorney distinguished for having one of the poshest British accents of the many British employees working in Yokohama, Nada was a linchpin to the entire Ghosn takedown. But what made Nada turn on the boss he served faithfully for years as the trusted head of the CEO and chairman's office was one of the most puzzling questions of the whole Nissan scandal.

Nada, whose full name is Hemant Kumar Nadanasabapathy, joined Nissan in 1990, just two years after Ghosn's codefendant Greg Kelly joined in Tennessee. Like Kelly, he also leveraged a legal background to reach the top levels of the company. In 2014, he jumped from the position of head of legal affairs for Nissan in Europe to vice president in Japan for the office of the CEO with an expansive portfolio covering the Alliance office, legal department, organizational development, facility management, and global internal audit. Nada was fifty-four at the time of Ghosn's arrest.

Colleagues described Nada as a likeable, sociable, heavy smoker who is able to navigate the nonconfrontational approach of a Japanese company, building consensus outside meetings that paves the way for agreements. Nada was a key player in managing thorny intra-Alliance relations with Renault, and Nissan's nationalist old boys regarded him as a potent negotiator who fiercely defended the company's interests and autonomy.

In some accounts, Nada was painted as the real villain, scheming to eliminate Ghosn—either in a craven attempt to preserve his own position of influence from being diluted in a holding company or in a misguided, cold-blooded ambush to save Nissan from French rule. In others, he was described as an unwitting victim, thrust before prosecutors and forced to cooperate or face prison himself. Even Ghosn seemed somewhat baffled by Nada, writing in his book published after the scandal that Kawaguchi, Toyoda, and Imazu "put a gun to his head." They twisted Ohnuma's arm the same way, Ghosn contends.[8]

In a different narrative, Nada suddenly grew a conscience about facilitating so many financial transgressions over the years and decided to come clean under the new plea-bargain system. Nada saw that establishing a holding company structure opened a Pandora's box of new ways Ghosn could potentially milk the system. Whereas Renault, Nissan, and Mitsubishi—as publicly traded companies—were subject to strict discloser and auditing rules, they wouldn't necessarily be so transparent under a more nebulous holding company structure.

Even within the strictures of these public companies, that argument went, Ghosn still managed to play an elaborate shell game with paper companies to channel funds to himself. At a holding company, he might be unshackled to run wild through a looser corporate landscape with even more power as undisputed emperor and fewer people emboldened to act as a brake.

"The whistle-blower didn't want this kind of wrongdoing to grow," said one Nissan official. "If a merger were to happen, Ghosn would have taken advantage of the situation to take even more money from the companies. In a wider sense, it was about stopping him from ripping the companies off even more."

. . .

A more nuanced storyline came to light when Nada finally took the stand in Kelly's trial and offered his first public account of what happened. The picture that emerged was a portrait of an executive riven with conflict— someone who abused his position as the company's top legal officer but also wanted to make amends.

Yet some of the testimony also seemed to buttress Ghosn's conspiracy.

By Nada's telling, he was dragged into an existing probe of Ghosn's travel expenses in January 2018. That investigation was triggered by an internal whistle-blower the year before and was being led by company auditor Imazu. Kawaguchi reached out to Nada for his legal opinion on the matter. The inquiry eventually stalled because the suspected breach wasn't considered serious enough. But the matter got Nada thinking about a lot of other behavior he deemed dubious.

First, there was the use of Zi-A to pay for Ghosn's homes. Then, there was also the matter of the millions of dollars in suspected postponed compensation. Nada had a front-row seat to both issues. He helped set up Zi-A, and he worked for years on Ghosn's various retirement plans. In May 2018, Nada started spilling the beans to Imazu and Kawaguchi and urged them to consult outside lawyers, including Latham & Watkins. Zi-A ended up being another dead end; the prevailing opinion was that it didn't rise to an actionable offense. But the secretive Nissan team sank its teeth deep into the compensation question.

In court, Nada said the plan was to gather evidence against Ghosn, confront him at a board meeting, and compel him to resign. And if he didn't, the matter would be turned over to prosecutors. But things never got that far. Imazu first went to prosecutors to consult on the matter, supposedly without Nada's knowledge. And when Nada learned of this, it triggered warning bells because Nada himself had a hand in the alleged misconduct now under the microscope.

"I recognized prosecutors at least knew Nissan was involved," Nada testified. "I was concerned my own involvement would be misunderstood. . . . I was involved in carrying out many of the things Mr. Ghosn was under investigation for. My involvement could be mischaracterized."[9]

In July, an increasingly nervous Nada found his own lawyer to talk about plea bargains, conveniently snagging a high-powered attorney reputedly with close ties with then prime minister Shinzo Abe. In September, Nada made his first visit to the Tokyo Public Prosecutors Office, and on October 31, he clinched immunity under a plea deal. Nada managed to wiggle free from an inquest of his own making.

. . .

Yet, Nada's own testimony also showed that the impending merger with Renault loomed large in his mind, even as he plotted the legal strike against Ghosn. Back in mid-2018, he said, Ghosn was widely expected to retire the following year, finally bringing the tinderbox issue of the "irreversible" alliance to a head.

"I knew he was going to retire. I knew Mr. Ghosn was now talking about a merger. The merger is a consequence of Mr. Ghosn's retirement. I was sure the plan we had been talking about all along was now about to be executed," Nada said. "I felt the train was about to leave the station, and it had to be stopped."[10]

Nada's recounting of events was one of the first public confirmations from the Nissan side of what Ghosn was saying all along—that he wanted to merge the companies. And other documents aired in court highlighted Nissan's alarm at the prospect.

In February 2018, the same month Renault said it would renew Ghosn's mandate, Saikawa wrote an email to Nada warning that Ghosn "may be pushed or forced to promise some road map to make a merger in French context in return for the support of his mandate and compensation."[11] Also that month, Nada wrote his legal team flagging concerns that Renault planned to consolidate Nissan into its own balance sheet. "There may be a train running in Renault for Renault to fully consolidate Nissan," he advised. And in another email sent to Saikawa, just the day before Ghosn's arrest, Nada said Nissan should leverage the looming Ghosn scandal to force a rebalancing of its partnership with Renault.

"Nissan's position should be Mr. XXX's wrongdoing and removal as a representative director at Nissan is a fundamental change to the circumstances of the alliance, and a new governance for the alliance must be found," Nada wrote.

With the boss about to be arrested in a scandal of epic proportions, it seemed like an inopportune time to be obsessing over relations with Renault. The top brass at any other company might instead be crisis planning for the legal fallout and impending uproar among employees, suppliers, and customers.

Kawaguchi was fairly forthright in describing Nada, Imazu, and himself as likeminded—both in their opposition to Ghosn's merger idea and in their hunt for his alleged wrongdoing.

While testifying in the Kelly trial, the by-then retired government affairs chief said he lunched with Nada and Imazu two or three times a week in a private room in order to talk about the investigation. But Kawaguchi said the clique stayed hush-hush about their shared opposition to a merger. "It was an opinion that never got outside the circle in which it was discussed," he said. "They chose me as a person they could trust."

In Kawaguchi's view, Nissan needed more equal footing in the Alliance to make the partnership truly sustainable. And they saw Ghosn as a growing threat to this because of his sudden shift toward favoring integration. On the stand, Kawaguchi painted himself as a true Nissan patriot but Ghosn, a man wearing two hats as the leader of Renault and Nissan, as a conflicted chief executive.

"I worked for Nissan for more than forty years. I had a strong affection for the company and for protecting it," Kawaguchi said. "For Mr. Ghosn, it was different. He held two positions simultaneously."

Yet, Kawaguchi insisted under defense examination that the trio kept a clear line in their minds between the two issues: merger and misconduct. "We never fabricated any piece of evidence to substantiate this crime as a way to stop a merger," he averred.

Prosecutors apparently believed Kawaguchi's testimony was of so little value to their cause that they declined to ask him a single question, despite his role in the probe that triggered the arrest.

Buttressing Ghosn's argument that the investigation was a witch hunt was the fact that the trio's initial findings—suspicions about travel expenses and the Zi-A housing—led to nothing. Both by Nada's telling and by Imazu's, these issues evidently didn't rise to the level of criminality, and fizzled.

Imazu said he visited the Tokyo Public Prosecutors Office for the first time on June 16, 2018, some five months before Ghosn's arrest, to run their ideas up the flagpole. After hearing him out, prosecutors told Imazu that charges on those matters probably wouldn't stick. But prosecutors didn't completely dismiss his discoveries. Instead, they encouraged Imazu to keep digging.

As lead auditor, Imazu had the authority to launch such investigations. But the standard requirement is to report findings to the board of directors, other auditors, or the CEO. Imazu contends he didn't do that because prosecutors, fearing a leak, ordered him to keep things confidential.

In retrospect, it looked to critics like the trio of second-tier executives went rogue—secretly colluding to impose their own interpretation of Nissan's best interests while disregarding the board or the shareholders. In the Kelly trial, a defense lawyer asked Imazu, in light of the massive hit to Nissan's market value, whether he should have been more circumspect in running straight to prosecutors.

Said Imazu: "I did not think that way."

After meeting prosecutors, Imazu consulted with Kawaguchi and Nada about the visit and the request to keep investigating. On July 2, Latham & Watkins was hired to expand the internal probe.

The two major issues Imazu initially took to prosecutors apparently ended up having nothing to do with the indictments finally filed against Ghosn, namely those concerning deferred compensation and breach of trust; the so-called Saudi and Omani routes. To skeptics, this only underscored the sense it was all an elaborate fishing expedition.

At the same time, other documents presented in court indicated that the Nissan insiders were game-planning Ghosn's removal as early as May—around when Nada says he began working with Kawaguchi and Imazu. One chart commissioned by Nada envisioned different scenarios: What would happen if Renault let go of Ghosn, what if Ghosn himself resigned, and what if Nissan dumped Ghosn?

In one plan, Kawaguchi would be made Ghosn's successor as chairman of Mitsubishi.

Another document postulated an "actual conviction case" in which Ghosn is arrested. That scenario was predicated on uncovering "compelling evidence of material violation of laws/Code of Conduct" by Ghosn, though it didn't specify a particular breach. It uses code names, including "Charcoal" for Ghosn, "Red" for Renault, "Navy" for Nissan, and "Maroon" for Mitsubishi. The chart traces different routes to removing Ghosn, including one through a boardroom showdown and shareholder vote and another through conviction of a crime. Most paths end with Ghosn being removed, except the "worst-case scenario"—"Charcoal stays as Navy director."[12]

Was it pure happenstance the men orchestrating Ghosn's downfall were also battling against his merger? To more than a few, it was a little hard to swallow.

. . .

Nada's own misgivings may stretch back even further than 2018.

At the end of 2017, Nissan was being rocked by an entirely different scandal that was all but forgotten about after Ghosn's arrest. In that affair, Nissan was caught conducting faulty final inspections of cars at its plants in Japan for decades. In a humiliating blow, it was forced to recall more than 1.2 million vehicles, nearly every car it had made for sale in the home market over the previous three years.[13] And as part of the government-ordered redress, auditors scrutinized every nook of the company to root out misconduct. Whistle-blowers were encouraged to step forward, and compliance became paramount in internal company communications.

Nada, in his role as head of legal affairs and compliance, was suddenly thrust into the spotlight as the main cheerleader for cleaning house, an awkward position for someone who was allegedly bending the rules to help pay his boss. Nada lectured on the importance of corporate ethics in an internal video for rank-and-file employees. Viewed today, Nada's

2017 video oozes with eerie foreshadowing of the bigger crisis about to hit the company.

"Without compliance, I believe quite passionately, your organization will collapse," Nada sermonizes, wearing a blue suit, crisp white shirt, and red-striped necktie—along with his gold Nissan corporate lapel pin.

"It will either collapse dramatically in a single event, and we have seen that with companies who have not followed the law or who have got themselves into a terrible situation, where their stock market price will collapse, their leaders will go to prison, whatever," Nada continues. "And it can happen slowly, corrosively, over time . . . And that will lead down the line to the company falling apart."

Nada closes his message by urging those who encounter wrongdoing to step forward. Nissan introduced an anonymous whistle-blower system called "Speak Up"—although its progenitors probably envisioned it as a way to stop misdeeds like the assembly line shortcuts, not for taking down the chairman.

"You need a system where the bosses practice what they preach," Nada says straight-faced, without a hint of irony. "People need to know that if people break the rules, if things go wrong, there are consequences . . . Employees in the company need to be able to say, 'Something has gone wrong here.'"

· · ·

Saikawa, despite being CEO, ironically maintained that he was kept in the dark about the investigations until October—just a month before prosecutors sprung their trap on Ghosn. This was because, by this story-line, Nissan suspected he might be entangled in the wrongdoing as well.

Over the course of 2018, as the internal investigation whirred away behind the unwitting Saikawa's back, he was also stepping up the company's pushback to Ghosn's holding company plan. Saikawa's stance was clear: "The holding company is a way toward a full merger. There is no way to stop it. At the end of the day, if they end up with one board and two executive committees, it's the same as one company. So, a holding company that sustains independence is a kind of illusion." Saikawa was joined in the Nissan defense effort by Nada and Kawaguchi, who knew about the Ghosn probe but didn't let on to their boss.

Through the summer and fall of 2018, they worked with METI on preserving the Alliance and changing the balance of ownership and even had Ghosn meet chief cabinet secretary Yoshihide Suga to discuss Alliance relations. Suga relayed the prime minister's position, which perfectly echoed Saikawa's: Japan valued the alliance and wanted it preserved, but both companies must stay independent. Both wanted a "sustainable" Alliance, not an "irreversible" one.

Prosecutors eventually decided to clear Saikawa. And only in the final stretch of the investigation did Nada feel safe looping him in. In early October, Saikawa and Nada were traveling through Europe on an investor relations tour, when Nada took Saikawa aside in London. It was then, according to one recounting of events, that Nada first confided that Ghosn was in trouble. The statutory auditor would provide full details once they returned to Japan, he said. Saikawa purportedly turned to Nada and asked: "Is he going to be arrested?" Nada replied: "Probably, yes."

Later that month, Ghosn and Saikawa met discreetly to talk face-to-face about the future of the Alliance. But the only opening in Ghosn's schedule, in a location off the radar, was during a visit by him to Renault's assembly plant in Morocco. Saikawa flew there, knowing that prosecutors were already moving toward Ghosn's arrest back in Japan. Saikawa kept the appointment anyway, so as not to arouse suspicion. But he traveled with his bodyguard, partly fearful for his safety in case Ghosn had been tipped off. It was during this tête-à-tête, according to some accounts, that Ghosn made his ultimatum that Saikawa either back the holding company or pack his bags. The meeting ended with no breakthroughs in the standoff over the Alliance's structure.

It was the last time Saikawa saw Ghosn in person.

. . .

In the end, two competing narratives emerged over the buildup to Ghosn's arrest. In Ghosn's rendition, he is the victim of a corporate coup aimed at preventing Renault's takeover of Nissan. In Nissan's, he was simply the perpetrator of corporate crimes that unraveled when a whistle-blower came forward.

Yet not everything in these plotlines—coup or crime—adds up so neatly.

It is one thing to say Nissan and the Japan government wanted to prevent the carmaker from becoming an outright subsidiary of Renault. It was no secret where Japan stood on that matter; Nissan had been agitating for more independence for years. But it is a bigger leap to prove Japan Inc. framed Ghosn of a crime to do so.

And would a coup even work? Among executives on both sides of the Alliance, Ghosn was long among the most vociferous in defending the autonomy of the companies. A lopsided "merger of equals" of the kind that doomed DaimlerChrysler, Ghosn always insisted, was equally bound to fail if foisted upon his Franco-Japanese tie-up.

If Nissan wanted to take him out, the company was embarking on a big risk of miscalculation. Ghosn's successor—presumably Thierry Bolloré, a man constantly at odds with Saikawa—might be much less inclined toward Ghosn's balanced approach. In fact, overthrowing Ghosn might backfire and actually hasten a French takeover so feared by Nissan's old guard.

Moreover, it is completely possible to believe both storylines simultaneously: Nissan wanted to block Ghosn's proposed holding company, and Ghosn was in fact guilty of misconduct. Nissan's old guard may have seen a golden opportunity to leverage the newly uncovered wrongdoing to finally try forcing the Alliance rebalance they had wanted for so long.

Yet the timing sure seemed suspicious. After all these years—money started moving around in 2008, and Ghosn's alleged deferred compensation scheme dated back to 2010—why would his alleged misconduct suddenly surface as a flash point during this especially prickly showdown over the Alliance's future?

To Saikawa, there was a simple explanation. He stuck to the company line: "Timing-wise, it was pure coincidence."

11

JUSTICE
JAPAN STYLE

CARLOS GHOSN AND GREG KELLY WOULD NOT BE THE
only defendants in the Nissan affair. Japan's judicial system was also in
the dock, with the case bringing an uncomfortable spotlight on a legal
system that even the Japan Federation of Bar Associations has derided
as "hostage justice." It is a system where prosecutors wield much of the
power and acquittals are rare.

The judiciary, like the rest of the Japanese government, is based on
its constitution written in 1947 by a team of 24 US civilian and military
experts during the postwar occupation. It creates, at least on paper, an
American-style adversarial system in which the Public Prosecutors Office and defense lawyers argue before an impartial judge. But in a country that prides itself on consensus and conformity over conflict, the
reality is somewhat different.

Critics are quick to cite data showing a 99 percent conviction rate,
although the number is a bit skewed. It's more accurate to say that just 1
percent of the cases end in acquittal, whereas some others are adjourned
or otherwise end midtrial. Based on that, the conviction rate is actually nearer to 97 percent. For the small number who decide to fight the

charges, about five thousand in 2018, the acquittal rate at the end of a trial is 2.2 percent.[1]

That's not much consolation for defendants like Ghosn or his lieu-tenant Greg Kelly, but it's not that different than in the United States and other Western countries, where 90 percent of those accused of US federal crimes plead guilty, 8 percent of the cases are dismissed, and just 2 per-cent go to trial. At trial, almost everyone loses. Of 63,012 criminal cases in 2019, just 170 were found not guilty in a trial.[2] US state numbers tend to be lower since prosecutors generally accept more cases, but these still offer little solace for the accused. Data for California in 2013–2014 shows that 83 percent of those charged either plead guilty or are found guilty in a trial.[3]

Things were even worse in prewar Japan, when the country had an entirely different point of view on crime. "The Japanese concept of jus-tice . . . is rooted in regulating individual conduct according to norms that define the relationship of the individual to society. And these norms are defined by a history that predates Western legal concepts by thou-sands of years," Nobuhisa Ishizuka, a lecturer at Columbia Law School, said in an essay soon after Ghosn fled Japan.[4]

Japan's first attempt to create a "Western" style of justice was, like Ghosn, an import from France, with some elements later drawn from Germany. In the Meiji era from 1868, when Japan adopted a judicial sys-tem based on the Napoleonic Code of 1804, it replaced a patchwork of laws administered by local lords, typically with brutal results for any alleged wrongdoers. The change was part of Japan's drive to be a mod-ern nation, but was also based partly on practical necessity. Japan needed a legal structure that Western nations would accept so that it could rid itself of the humiliating doctrine of "extraterritoriality" under which for-eigners in Japan were not subject to domestic laws, giving them a kind of diplomatic immunity.

The provision had been forced on Japan by the United States, France, Britain, and other Western countries that had pushed Japan to open its ports to international trade. In theory, the laws of the perpetrator's home country were meant to apply. In practice, criminal actions by foreigners were largely ignored. Not surprisingly, this caused great ill will among the Japanese, who saw the foreigners as lawless invaders, which was not far from the truth. (China and other Asian countries had suffered under similar systems.)

The pretext from the Westerners was that since Japan had no legal code, it could not administer justice properly. Putting the French code in place changed that and extraterritorial provisions disappeared by the end of the nineteenth century.[5] The result was not exactly the adversarial system one expects in a courtroom today. The judge and prosecutor would sit together on the bench above everyone, looking down on the defendants and their lawyers.

This would ostensibly give way to the US justice system introduced in the 1947 constitution. But none of the previous systems ever went away entirely. Extraterritoriality hasn't even completely disappeared: US military personnel based in Japan (and in other countries) still have special legal privileges that remain a point of contention. Many of the current Japanese legal practices denounced by Ghosn have their roots in the French system, which, unlike the United States and United Kingdom, puts a greater burden of proof on defendants.

Although that has now changed with prosecutors and the defense equal, at least in terms of seating, some legal experts contend that Japan's system is "pseudo-adversarial" with a presumption of guilt, not innocence. "It is the accused who have to prove their innocence," Keiichi Muraoka, a professor of law at Hakuoh University and a former defense attorney, said in an interview for this book. He called the system extremely flawed. "Every day we struggle to achieve fair play in the court. We have a heavy burden to prove innocence; it is absolutely the reverse of what it is supposed to be."

Some experts contend that the entire goal of Japan's justice system is different than in the West. According to one European lawyer long active in Japan who spoke on background: "Western legal systems are based on trying to determine the truth; in Japan, the truth is not as important as harmony within society. Justice is here to restore peace."

. . .

Despite similar structures, there are a number of fundamental differences between the Japanese and US legal systems. One is in sheer manpower. There are forty-two thousand practicing attorneys in Japan, compared with 1.3 million in the United States. That means that there is one attorney for every 252 people in the United States, whereas the same attorney would need to spread himself out over 3,007 people in Japan. The gap reflects the fact that some legal functions are undertaken by other specialist groups in Japan, such as the handling of real estate transactions, and it reflects the cultural focus on consensus over discord. The gap is similar within the ranks of prosecutors. In Japan, there are approximately two thousand prosecutors nationwide. On a per capita basis, the US legion of thirty-three thousand state and federal prosecutors is six times larger.[6] Even with Japan's much lower crime rate, this differential in resources means heavy caseloads and long hours. It also helps to produce the long waits before cases go to trial. For Kelly, it was nearly two years from his November 2018 arrest until his trial began in September 2020.

There are also structural differences, which from the outset of the postwar system have tipped the scales against a defendant. There is no trial by jury, leaving the decision to convict up to judges who come from the same system and share the same sensibilities as the prosecutors. This was only partly remedied with the introduction in 2009 of "lay judges" who take part in some types of criminal cases and have shown a willingness to take a different line from the professionals.

Even more contentious is the fact that an acquittal can be appealed by the prosecution, whereas in most countries, including the United States, an acquittal ends all legal action against a defendant. Prosecutors make use of this on a regular basis, especially in high-profile cases, meaning that the virtually unlimited budget of the state can be used to overcome the limited means and endurance of a defendant. A study in 2010 found that prosecutors win 65.5 percent of their appeals, against just 10 percent by the defense.[7]

In terms of the mechanics of a case, there is a limited concept of "discovery" in which the prosecution's evidence is given to the defense team so that each side has access to the same evidence ahead of a trial. This would feature in the trial of Kelly, where thousands of pages of documents were given to the defense at the last minute, many others even after the trial was well underway, and some material was withheld completely. Such a step in the United States could easily result in an overturned verdict. But experts say that while this is also technically true in Japan, in practice, discovery is a long and drawn-out affair and depends on the defense knowing what to request. The ability to retrieve all court documents in the United States online was such a shock to Japanese reporters covering the Ghosn case that national broadcaster NHK did a long feature story on how it all works. The story noted that in Japan, only officially accredited reporters had been allowed to even take notes in a court hearing until a 1989 Supreme Court ruling.

Also, judges almost always defer to the prosecutors in key areas, such as in obtaining search warrants and issuing indictments, areas where it's much more difficult to get sign-off in the United States, an important check on prosecutorial power. A defendant also needs to be careful about what they write to their attorney in an email—the US concept of client-attorney privilege is largely absent.

But the most contentious point for many international legal experts is the refusal to allow defense attorneys to attend interrogations, a practice that flies in the face of accepted judicial practice in almost all Western countries. Defense attorneys are banned from such sessions, and critics charge that breaking down a suspect being held in custody through countless hours of interrogation is a common practice. Supporters of the Japanese system say that having a lawyer present for interrogations would be a major roadblock to getting the facts. According to Japan's Ministry of Justice, an advisory committee discussed the issue for three years and found that "if lawyers' attendance during interrogation were to be granted, it would make it difficult to discover the truth of the case due to the difficulty of obtaining sufficient statements from the suspects, which would significantly undermine the function of interrogation."

Long interrogations without an attorney were one of Ghosn's main complaints about his treatment. According to his lawyers, he was questioned for an average of seven hours daily, including on weekends and holidays. Prosecutors dispute those figures. They said that of Ghosn's 130 days in detention, he was questioned for only seventy of those days and never for more than four hours a day.[8] Former defense lawyer Muraoka figures Ghosn got off lightly. A Japanese suspect, he says, will often be questioned for up to ten hours daily. It is easy to see why confession is often considered the easy route out, especially since it is usually the only way to get out of custody on bail while the process grinds on.

With no lawyers present, there is also the chance for a prosecutor under pressure to chalk up wins to use intimidation to wear down the hapless defendant. Following a string of cases where confessions turned out to be completely untrue, the government in 2006 instituted recording of interrogation sessions, initially in limited cases. It didn't become mandatory for all interrogations until 2019.

Cultural issues also play into confessions. Having someone accused of a crime is a disgrace to a family in Japan. While the accused will almost certainly lose their job, close relatives will be similarly disgraced. A confession at least gets the matter out of the way and avoids a public trial that would create more negative publicity for all of those close to the defendant. In Japan, "the sins of the father" are indeed laid upon the children, as well as the rest of the family.

Some experts say that the shortage of prosecutors also plays a part in the reliance on confessions. Finding forensic evidence and the range of witnesses needed for a trial is much more time-consuming and costly than getting the defendant to sign their own guilty plea. While critics point to the fact that a suspect can be held for twenty-three days after they are detained, prosecutors see this actually as a very short window in which to get the necessary evidence for an indictment. In practice, if prosecutors cannot find enough evidence to indict in the twenty-three-day period, the case is dropped. "It's not a case of being hostage justice, it's how you conduct the investigation," one former prosecutor said in an interview for this book.

Seen from their own perspective, prosecutors work hard and are highly professional, with the single goal of making sure that only those guilty of a crime are prosecuted. One defense of Japan's seemingly unjust 97 to 99 percent conviction rate (depending on the calculation) is the fact that prosecutors only take on 37 percent of the cases brought to them, focusing on the ones that appear airtight.

This leads to an imbalance in the system where the proper execution of justice rests largely on the judgment of the prosecutors. As Ghosn himself observed in his dealings with the judicial system: "Prosecutors basically decide who is guilty or innocent, you don't need a judge and you don't need a defense."[9]

. . .

Part of this problem goes back to the very beginnings of an individual's career in the judicial system. After getting through law school and passing Japan's very strict bar exam, all future judges, prosecutors, and private attorneys enter the same one-year training program supervised by the Japanese Supreme Court.[10] They are by no means slouches. On average only 25 to 30 percent pass the bar exam. Before reforms in 2006, it was as low as 2 to 3 percent.

There they receive practical education on legal practices and are taught the principles of fairness. But as elsewhere in Japan, the system can take over. With everyone training together, the very people who should be on opposite sides of the scales of justice all end up working together and becoming instilled with the same viewpoints about the administration of justice.

It also means that judges, instead of coming from the ranks of experienced attorneys, almost always go straight from the Supreme Court training to the bench. They may therefore be younger than the prosecuting attorneys appearing before them in court, a potentially compromising situation in a country where seniority counts for almost everything.

One bureaucrat at the Ministry of Foreign Affairs found himself caught up in Japan's judicial quagmire. Masaru Sato was charged in a politically tinged case that was aimed primarily at a senior lawmaker who was convicted of bribery. Sato had stood by his own innocence but, along with the lawmaker, he was found guilty. He received a suspended thirty-month sentence, which did not seem overly harsh, until you realize that, since he never confessed, Sato had been held for the entire 513 days that it took for his case to be finalized. As a former government employee, he doesn't blame the people within the Justice Ministry. "The judges and prosecutors are good people; I don't have any grudges," he said in a 2020 symposium. "It's the system, it's a mechanism that has a way of crushing an entire person's life," he said.[11]

Ghosn also contended that the prosecutors were players in a broad conspiracy against him. He offered no concrete evidence, however, and at some levels the allegation appears unlikely. While they are seen as goal-driven and single-minded in their opinions, the prosecutors are also fiercely independent and are generally free of political influence. This was seen most clearly in the pursuit of Kakuei Tanaka, a former prime minister and political kingpin who had been charged in a 1976 bribery scandal involving aircraft maker Lockheed. Despite Tanaka's power within the ruling Liberal Democratic Party, prosecutors pursued the case and won a conviction.

Sato and other critics say that even though prosecutors abandon nearly two-thirds of the cases that come to them, the flip side is that in those cases that do go ahead, there is an incredible pressure to obtain a conviction. One former prosecutor said that if he were to lose just two cases, his career in the prosecutor's office would effectively be over. Under these pressures, it's understandable that prosecutors will be tempted to cut corners, especially when the judges, their former colleagues at the training center, are loath to call them out on such procedural issues.

In the worst cases, prosecutors may indulge in outright fraud. One such case shocked the entire justice system.

· · ·

In 2009, Atsuko Muraki, a senior bureaucrat at the Health, Labor and Welfare Ministry, was charged with using her authority to help a group fraudulently obtain the right to use discounted postage available only to charitable groups. The case was hardly an earth-shattering scandal, revolving around saving a few cents on mailings. But a misuse of authority, no matter how minor, was seen as a serious case, especially given the fact that she was a senior figure in the ministry.

The case was assigned to the Special Investigation Department of the Public Prosecutors Office in Osaka, in western Japan. This unit represents the elite within the prosecutor's office and deals with the most complex and potentially sensitive cases. (The Tokyo Special Investigation Unit was responsible for the Ghosn/Kelly case.)

Prosecutors had expected that, like most others in her situation, Muraki would quietly agree to plead guilty to what was a fairly mid-level offense. Like Ghosn, however, Muraki was in no mood to cop a plea. She strongly protested her innocence and, like Ghosn, she was put into solitary confinement, enduring a total of 164 days in detention. She later said that she had been heavily pressured to confess, with statements from her inquisitors that the charges weren't all that serious and that she probably would not do any prison time. In effect, the only way for her to get out of prison was to confess to a crime. She was unmoved. "Guilty is guilty, regardless of whether the sentence is suspended. The investigator's statement made me realize how completely out of touch the prosecutors were with the attitudes of ordinary people," she said in an interview years later.[12]

In her eventual trial, a key prosecution witness who had himself confessed to complicity while also implicating Muraki suddenly changed his testimony and said he had actually forged the document himself. In addition, some key dates in the evidence were found to be inconsistent. When challenged, the prosecutors claimed that they had already destroyed their notes of interviews so that the records could not be checked. The judge therefore threw out 34 of the 43 depositions presented by the prosecution, including 15 central to the case.[13] This was enough for Muraki to win an acquittal.

Amazingly, some members of the prosecution were unwilling to let the matter drop, saying that, in line with Japanese law, they should appeal the not-guilty verdict.[14] Cooler heads prevailed at the more senior levels of the prosecutor's office, however. This was just as well since another bombshell was on the way. The *Asahi Shimbun*, one of Japan's major newspapers, revealed that the lead prosecutor in the case had altered the dates on a floppy disk seized from the Health Ministry to make Muraki look guilty. The disk was never actually presented in evidence (its absence was noted by the defense since it contained key records) and the prosecutor claimed the alteration was a mistake.[15] Nevertheless, chaos ensued. The lead prosecutor soon found himself under arrest. Just for good measure, his two supervisors were also rounded up and charged with putting too much pressure on the prosecutor to win a conviction. They were each sentenced to eighteen months in prison, although (having pleaded guilty) their sentences were suspended. It's not known what they thought of their interrogations.

The scandal reverberated throughout the Justice Ministry. "This was a complete shock to me, I could never believe a prosecutor under any circumstances would do such a thing," one retired senior prosecutor said in a background interview. He was not alone. The nation's top prosecutor took responsibility for the debacle and resigned, even though he had only been in the job for six months and had no direct involvement in the case.

The ministry ordered a review in 2011, in which every prosecutor in the country was required to personally consider how they viewed their work to ensure this would never happen again. The ministry then took an unusual step of issuing a public report in which it laid down the standards that were to be expected by everyone working in the prosecution office.[16] "Obtaining conviction by any means in all cases is not our goal," it said. The elite special units were also opened up for broader scrutiny by officials outside their group and the videotaping of interrogation sessions was broadened. The national prosecutor's office issued a forty-page follow-up report three years later in which it detailed the reforms it had made and listed specific cases where taped confessions were seen as being coerced and therefore deemed as inadmissible.

For Muraki, there was a happy ending to her ordeal. Not only was she reinstated to her job, she was promoted four years later to the most senior level available to career bureaucrats, that of vice minister. After retiring, she was named as an outside director to the board of Itochu Corporation, one of Japan's biggest companies. But Muraki remains a vocal critic of the system. She and a relatively small band of legal experts echo Ghosn's own contentions, saying that reforms have not really eliminated the root problems.

. . .

Another complaint among the critics is that judges are overly cautious, not wanting to see their rulings reversed on appeal. This is not a theoretical problem. US scholars J. Mark Ramseyer and Eric B. Rasmusen examined two years of rulings among more than three hundred Japanese judges. They found that judges who convict rather than acquit get more promotions. It's even worse for judges whose decisions to acquit a defendant are overturned on appeal. In such cases, banishment to rural Japan is often the result. While this may be a pleasant change from overcrowded cities, it does little for one's career.[17]

A related problem is that judges face little oversight and therefore can have an inflated view of their ability to determine innocence or guilt. They will therefore sometimes ignore procedural points raised by the defense. "Japanese judges are very overconfident of their ability to find the truth. They are trained not to admit that they have made a mistake, even when there is a miscarriage of justice," says former defense lawyer Muraoka.

Another key player helping to keep the status quo is one of the very forces that should be exposing any miscarriage of justice: the news media. While reporters willing to challenge the system played key roles in Muraki's postage case, they are the minority. Most find it better just to go along with the system, which means writing stories on the carefully placed leaks from the prosecution.

Japan is hardly alone in this practice, which is used in high-profile cases everywhere to help sway public opinion. The system is quite simple. A prosecutor or police official will privately offer to provide an off-the-record "exclusive" story to a reporter assigned to cover the ministry or department. This will of course focus on the strong points in the prosecution case, helping to create the image that the defendant must be guilty.

Continuing to get this kind of exclusive access in the future will depend on whether the prosecutors are happy with the resulting story. In this cozy relationship, both sides benefit. Officials get their story out anonymously, helping to influence public opinion and demonstrate how they are doing a good job. The reporter gets high marks from their editors for being able to uncover exclusive news that the competition cannot match.

If a reporter refuses to play along, the officials can just go to another newspaper, and the uncooperative reporter will be seen as losing out to their rivals and likely be demoted. "You try to get on the good side of the prosecutors, especially as a young reporter. You get good information and while you know that you should write a balanced story, you can't talk to the defendant anyway," said one former senior reporter in explaining how it all works.[18]

This was put to good use during the Ghosn saga, with the media's stories turning generally more negative as more damaging information came out via leaks. "People have little sympathy now," one Japanese executive commented after Ghosn's flight. "They think it's his problem; he's a rich man and should handle it himself." Ghosn himself lashed out at the practice. "There have been a lot of lies in the story. A prosecutor does not care about the truth, he wants to win the case. He takes the case, he wants to win, and he doesn't care about the truth," he said in a March 2020 interview.[19]

. . .

These problems persist in part because the issue does not resonate with most Japanese people. With the nation's famously low crime rate, the average person will seldom have any experience with the criminal justice system, beyond asking for directions at the small police boxes dotted across every town and village. "Ordinary citizens probably don't think much about our criminal justice system," says former defendant Muraki. "I know I didn't. If I heard on the news that a suspect had been arrested in connection with a crime, I was just glad the perpetrator had been caught."[20]

For the average Japanese, and for foreigners who visit, it is hard to complain about the state of things. Most types of violent crime are practically nonexistent. (One exception is the rate of rape and domestic violence, where experts believe there is a worrying level of underreporting in what remains a male-dominated society.) For murder rates, a commonly used barometer since they are almost always reported, Japan competes with Singapore for the distinction of being the "world's safest country."

According to the United Nations Office on Drugs and Crime, there were 334 intentional homicides in Japan in 2018, or 0.26 per 100,000 people. In the United States, the comparable figure is 16,214, for a rate of 4.96 per 100,000. This makes the US murder rate nineteen times higher than Japan's.[21] The difference is even starker when it comes to gun violence. In the United States in 2017, there were 14,452 homicides using firearms, nearly forty per day, according to research by the University of Sydney.[22] In Japan, there were eight. For the year.[23]

The Justice Ministry seized upon this high level of safety in its defense of the system after Ghosn's departure. "Thanks to the persistent efforts made by Japan's police, judges, and prosecutors, and the Japanese public, Japan's crime rate is extremely low compared to other countries and it is fair to say that Japan is now the safest country in the world," Justice Minister Masako Mori said in a late-night news conference after Ghosn absconded. The average Japanese may beg to differ. They see Japan's safety in terms of how well they behave, not how well they are policed. A 2019 survey in the newspaper *Nikkei* found that only 43 percent found the police trustworthy. Public prosecutors did even worse at 39 percent.[24]

There is pressure for change, however, most notably from within Japan's legal system. The Japan Federation of Bar Associations, which represents all of Japan's forty-two thousand lawyers (and was the group to coin the phrase "hostage justice"), is leading the charge. The federation has been among the most vocal critics of Japan's justice system, with some success in helping to limit abusive interrogation of suspects through required taping of all sessions. But advocates say that they are largely ignored by the bureaucracy, where the real power sits. As elsewhere in Japan, change often comes from the *gaiatsu*, or foreign pressure, and in this regard the Ghosn case was to prove a lightning rod. Reflecting this, as international attention focused on the Greg Kelly trial, Justice Minister Mori appeared on a specially produced English-language webinar just before the trial began in September 2020. It was a rare event for a ministry that had long ignored the foreign media, including refusing to follow other ministries in offering English-language briefings to foreign reporters. In her remarks, she offered a potential concession, the possibility of allowing attorneys to be present during questioning of suspects. She said this was part of a review by a special judicial panel of experts. Only time would tell whether this was a genuine reform or just a stalling tactic to wait out the storm of foreign attention.

. . .

On balance, the system does appear to deliver justice in most cases, especially in the context of how Japanese society operates more broadly. As Mori pointed out, "Each nation's criminal justice system has its roots in its history and culture, being formulated and developed over a long period of time."

The risk is that to function properly, there must be goodwill on the part of all participants, in particular the prosecutors, who have by far the greatest power. Without the same level of checks and balances as elsewhere, prosecutorial wrongdoing can run unchecked. On the charge that the system needs to change, Mori inadvertently said at her news conference what many critics contend is the true state of Japan's judicial system. Ghosn, she said, should return to Japan to "prove his innocence."

The prosecution rests.

12

GHOSN FIGHTS BACK

ON JANUARY 8, 2019, A QUINTESSENTIAL JAPANESE winter morning with biting cold, electric-blue skies, buses with blacked-out windows rolled through the checkpoint of the Tokyo District Court, one after another. The fortress-like tower in the capital city's government-office district stands at the symbolic nexus of Japanese social authority. A block away is the moat-ringed Imperial Palace, seat of the Yamato Dynasty, the world's oldest unbroken monarchy dating back some 2,600 years. Next door is the country's original red-brick Justice Ministry building, a nineteenth-century edifice designed by German architects that embodies Japan's rushed, if somewhat reluctant, adoption of Western ways in its race to modernize.

Every weekday the buses haul in the accused—suspected rapists, murderers, thieves, and fraudsters—to fight their cases in the court. But on this day, the streets around the courthouse swarmed with reporters, photographers, and television crews, all craning for a glimpse of an especially famous defendant. After spending Christmas and New Year's in his frigid cell at the Tokyo Detention House across town, Carlos Ghosn would finally be making his first public appearance since the Shock.

Defendants in Ghosn's position are rarely afforded the kind of time before a judge that Ghosn would be getting this morning. Most of those accused just while away unseen in jail. But Ghosn's high-powered lawyer, himself a former prosecutor, knew a few tricks. He leveraged a seldom-used Japanese legal proviso that allows defendants to demand they hear directly from the court the reasons for their detention.

The brief public hearing was unlikely to change the course of Ghosn's trial, let alone get him out on bail—though his lawyers had repeatedly tried to spring him. To be sure, that morning's proceedings would be prompt, pro forma, and perfunctory. But the legal maneuvering on behalf of the ousted Alliance chairman, by then muzzled and nearly incommunicado for nearly two months, finally gave him a chance to tell his side of the story on a public stage with the world watching.

In addition to the hordes of journalists thronging the streets that morning, hundreds of housewives, part-time workers, college students, and the just plain curious were also waiting outside the courthouse, hoping to grab one of the few gallery seats to witness the historic hearing. Some 1,122 people entered the lottery for fourteen spots allotted to the public.[1] Some of the people waiting were tapped to enter the drawing on behalf of media outlets angling to increase their odds of having a reporter on the inside so they could one-up the pool report.

When Ghosn finally entered the Spartan courtroom, the ravages of his fifty-day lockup were evident to all. Gaunt and graying, he was visibly leaner after weeks on jail rations heavy on steamed rice and pickled vegetables. His cheeks were hollowed, his eyes sunken. And Ghosn's trademark jet-black hair was growing in half a shade lighter at the roots. Normally natty, he salvaged some of his former stature, courtesy of a dark blue business suit, but looked out of sorts without a necktie. Sealing the picture of his fall from grace, Ghosn was led into the chamber in handcuffs and roped around the waist. Instead of shoes, he had been forced to wear court-issued green plastic slippers, which seemed designed as much to demean defendants as to deter their escape. Observers could see Ghosn's toes twitching during the proceedings. Courtroom sketches plastered on the front pages of Japan's evening newspapers depicted a disheveled, withered man with a combative countenance.

. . .

Ghosn was afforded ten minutes to make a statement. He seized the opportunity with the efficiency and focus of a *Fortune* 500 executive making a boardroom pitch. With two guards in blue uniforms standing behind him, Ghosn professed his innocence and launched a point-by-point counterattack of the charges against him, addressing the court in a calm, controlled voice. It seemed, despite his worn-down appearance, his days in detention hardly dulled his old hyperrational self.

"I look forward to beginning the process of defending myself against the accusations that have been made against me," Ghosn told the court. "I have always acted with integrity and have never been accused of any wrongdoing in my several-decade professional career. I have been wrongly accused and unfairly detained based on meritless and unsubstantiated accusations."[2]

Regarding the first two allegations of hiding the more than $80 million in deferred compensation, Ghosn argued the actual amount was neither fixed nor disbursed. Thus, there was no violation of disclosure rules because there was no formalized postponed compensation to actually report. Plus, he maintained, prosecutors had shown no intent to violate the law.

"Contrary to the accusations made by the prosecutors, I never received any compensation from Nissan that was not disclosed, nor did I ever enter into any binding contract with Nissan to be paid a fixed amount that was not disclosed," he said, adding there was a simple way to gauge whether the money was material.

"The test is the 'death test': If I died today, could my heirs require Nissan to pay anything other than my retirement allowance? The answer is an unequivocal 'No.'"

Then, he went on to discuss the more serious first breach of trust charge—the so-called Saudi Route—in which he was accused of transferring his personal foreign exchange swap contract losses to Nissan, then having Nissan pay a Saudi business associate who helped him with collateral. Here, Ghosn admitted using Nissan as a source of temporary collateral. But he said the loss-making contracts were transferred back to him at no cost to Nissan. Ghosn's lawyer maintained that Nissan board minutes show company officials agreed to such arrangements for non-Japanese officers.

Ghosn maintained that the funds associated with the situation—the $14.7 million transferred from Nissan's CEO Reserve to a company owned by Saudi mogul Khaled Al-Juffali from 2009 to 2012—were not some kind of kickback, as alleged by prosecutors.[3] Ghosn's lawyer later conceded Juffali did extend a ¥3 billion ($27.7 million) letter of credit to help his client in 2009. But that, he said, was unrelated to the CEO Reserve outlays.

Ghosn said the Nissan funds compensated the Khaled Juffali Co. for helping the carmaker restructure distributors in the Middle East region and drum up regional financing. Juffali, Ghosn added, also worked as a go-between with Saudi Arabian officials, helping Nissan negotiate building a proposed auto assembly plant in the country as part of Saudi Arabia's push to diversify its oil-dependent economy. That factory never materialized, but Juffali did help Nissan win a license for a joint venture with his own company to sell Nissan vehicles in the kingdom.

In any event, his lawyers argued, the transfers from the CEO Reserve weren't signed off by Ghosn alone, as if from a personal slush fund. A number of executives also had to approve the disbursement, they said, including Greg Kelly, then head of the CEO Office, and Stephen Ma, who was the regional financial controller at the time but later became CFO of the entire company, after Ghosn left, in 2019.

Juffali backed Ghosn's defense in a statement saying he enabled Nissan to obtain a "significant" ownership position in that venture, known as Nissan Saudi Arabia.

"Clearly, Khaled Juffali Company has provided manifold, tangible services that continue to inure to the substantial benefit of Nissan Motor Co., Ltd. and Nissan Middle East," the statement said. "The $14.7 million in payments over four years from Nissan Motor Co., Ltd. were for legitimate business purposes in order to support and promote Nissan's business strategy in the Kingdom of Saudi Arabia and included reimbursement for business expenses."

Ghosn wrapped up his rebuttal with a naked appeal to Japanese sentimentality. He stressed how much he loved Nissan and how much he contributed to the nation's economy by saving one of its corporate icons from the scrap heap.

"I have dedicated two decades of my life to reviving Nissan and building the Alliance. I worked towards these goals day and night, on the earth and in the air, standing shoulder to shoulder with hardworking Nissan employees around the globe, to create value. The fruits of our labors have been extraordinary," he said, noting his oft-repeated talking point that the Renault-Nissan-Mitsubishi Alliance flourished to become the world's No. 1 auto group in 2017, producing more than ten million vehicles a year.

"We created, directly and indirectly, countless jobs in Japan and reestablished Nissan as a pillar of the Japanese economy," Ghosn said. "These accomplishments—secured alongside the peerless team of Nissan employees worldwide—are the greatest joy of my life, next to my family."[4]

Bilking Nissan was the furthest thing from his mind, Ghosn insisted. If he were indeed as money hungry as prosecutors were portraying, he averred, he would have had plenty of opportunities to jump ship for far more lucrative pay packages when Ford and GM came knocking on his door. At the hearing, he recounted how "four major companies" tried to lure him away from Nissan. He said he always turned them down out of loyalty to the Japanese carmaker. "Even though their proposals were very attractive, I could not in good conscience abandon Nissan while we were in the midst of our turnaround," Ghosn said. "Nissan is an iconic Japanese company that I care about deeply."[5]

. . .

The performance before the judge fronted a counterattack. It had taken nearly two months, but Ghosn finally could fight back, and he was aided by his lawyers and his wife, Carole.

During the January 8 hearing, the defense team didn't tackle the second breach of trust charge—the so-called Omani Route. The indictment for that charge came in April, three months after Ghosn's first court hearing.

But after that charge landed, Ghosn's legal team addressed the Omani Route allegations in a twofold attack. First, they argued, half of the $15 million in outlays flagged by prosecutors were actually approved by Hiroto Saikawa when he was CEO, not Ghosn. Furthermore, all of the funds were earmarked, with appropriate authorizations by relevant department heads and regional managers, all the way up to the global treasurer or CFO at headquarters, as incentives to stoke Suhail Bahwan Automobiles (SBA)'s market share and sales volume.

But more important, none of the funds transferred from Nissan to SBA ever found their way back, directly or indirectly, to Ghosn or his family, his lawyers said. Since the payments were made in Nissan's interest, not Ghosn's, their argument went, prosecutors had no grounds for pinning "financial damage" on Ghosn.

Later, Ghosn's defenders would question why Nissan continued to keep SBA on board as its regional distributor, even after Ghosn's indictment. If SBA had indeed been funneling kickbacks to Ghosn, wouldn't Nissan want to at least sever ties? Yet well into 2020, Nissan was still contracting SBA to sell its cars in the Middle East.

In early 2019, Ghosn's lawyers repeatedly requested bail and were repeatedly denied by the Tokyo court. At the detention center, he was granted a bigger space, along with a Western-style bed, instead of a Japanese futon mattress on the floor of a tiny cell. But until his third indictment three days after appearing before the judge, Ghosn's family members still couldn't visit, and even his own lawyers were granted only limited access.

It was while Ghosn was still locked up that his wife, Carole, opened another front in the fight to clear his name. Her burgeoning public relations campaign relentlessly pleaded his case to the international media and beyond, all the way to the United Nations, and aimed to indict the entire Japanese justice system. Her message was loud and clear, and one seldom raised so prominently on the global stage: Japan's system of "hostage justice" is an affront to human rights.

Carole lobbied Human Rights Watch to protest the "cruel and inhumane treatment" of the accused in Japan and press the Tokyo government to reform its "draconian system of pretrial detention and interrogation." The family then hired a high-profile human rights lawyer and former French ambassador, François Zimeray, to take the cause to the United

Nations Working Group on Arbitrary Detention. Carole embarked on a kind of shuttle diplomacy, leaving Japan to ask the French government to intervene, pressure the UN, and plead her husband's case in America.

She sat for interviews with nearly every major international media outlet, from broadcast to print, injecting her husband's saga into public discourse. In an opinion piece published in the *Washington Post*, Carole—who holds US and Lebanese citizenship—described, with palpable indignation, the April 4 predawn raid that led to Ghosn's fourth indictment on the so-called Omani Route. At the time, Ghosn was free on bail following his first three indictments and living with Carole in a cramped apartment near Tokyo's Shibuya nightlife and shopping district. But at 5:50 A.M., there was a forceful, foreboding knock on the door.

"More than a dozen Japanese prosecutors stood waiting on the other side. Then they stormed in. My heart plummeted," she wrote. Authorities seized her cell phone, laptop, passport, diary, and the letters she wrote her husband during his lockup, she said. "I was treated like a criminal even though I am not a suspect, and I have not been charged with anything. A female prosecutor even accompanied me and conducted a pat-down search each time I went to the bathroom. She stayed in the bathroom as I undressed and showered, handing me a towel when I stepped out . . . Prosecutors would not allow me to call my lawyer and tried to take me away for questioning, but I refused to go with them."[6]

Carole propagated the conspiracy theory of his arrest, writing, "What should have been settled in the Nissan boardroom has been turned into a criminal affair." And she concluded the *Washington Post* commentary by imploring then US president Donald Trump to take up Ghosn's case during an upcoming meeting at the White House with Japanese prime minister Shinzo Abe.

"Trade will be front and center," reasoned Carole. "It's hard to imagine that Trump would be indifferent to a Japanese government ministry interfering in the normal give-and-take of private business decisions by one of its automakers."

There was no indication Trump or Abe broached the matter. But Carole again urged Trump to make her husband a talking point at the 2019 Group of 20 summit of world leaders in Osaka. Most of these pleas—to

Trump, the French government, and the UN—initially went unanswered, but the campaign was a media-savvy gambit to marshal international opinion against Japan and Nissan. Japan has a long history of changing hidebound ways only under external influence. There is even a Japanese word for it: *gaiatsu*, which translates literally as "outside pressure."

The term dates back to US admiral Perry's forced opening of Japan for trade in 1854. The term again found prominence during the wave of Westernization that swept Japan after World War II, thanks to the US military occupation and its imposition of a new constitution. More recently, gaiatsu manifested itself in Japan's reluctant, last-minute decision to postpone the 2020 Tokyo Summer Olympics in the face of mounting international concern about convening the global sports cavalcade during the COVID-19 pandemic. Prime Minister Abe stubbornly insisted the games go on—until overseas Olympic committees, led by Canada and Australia, began canceling plans to attend. Only after international pressure forced the postponement did Japan grudgingly sound a serious alarm about the domestic spread of the virus and issue its own state of emergency like in other nations.

Typical of Carole's gaiatsu tactics were comments such as those in her 2019 interview with *Automotive News*. "Japan is one of the countries in the G7. They're not behaving like a G7 country," she said. "I see it more like China or Russia."

In pushing these buttons, Carole Ghosn stepped from the shadows and emerged as a potent, outspoken force in fighting for her man. It wasn't a natural role for her. She and Carlos were married only in 2016, following the finalization of Ghosn's 2012 divorce from his first wife, Rita. Also from Lebanon, Rita had met Carlos through a bridge-playing circle while she was studying pharmacology in Lyon, France. She accompanied Carlos from his 1985 assignment with Michelin in Brazil through his whirlwind ride to the top of Nissan and then Renault, hopscotching across four continents along the way. Both Carole and Rita are, like Ghosn, from the Lebanese Maronite Christian community. Ghosn and Rita—known to be homebodies during their early years in Japan—have three daughters—Caroline, Nadine, Maya—and a son, Anthony.[7] After the arrest, Ghosn's support network drew largely from those children and Carole.

To Ghosn, Carole was "my lioness."

She was born in Beirut in 1966 but spent most of her life in the United States. Carole attended both the American University of Beirut and New York University.[8] Comfortable in artsy, high-society circles, Carole was a player in the New York fashion scene and founded a company selling designer caftans, a kind of robe traditionally worn in the Middle East. Under her sway, Ghosn's worldview widened—she is said to have taught him how to ski in 2015, just as the executive was entering his sixties. Even before the crisis, Carole and Carlos were fiercely devoted to and protective of each other. With her long, wavy blond hair and pragmatic, forthright style, Carole was an effective, camera-friendly ambassador at a time when Ghosn could not speak. But she also became a lightning rod of controversy in her own right.

After Ghosn's arrest for the Omani Route allegations, for example, she was questioned by Japanese investigators over suspicions that some of that money was diverted to a company in the British Virgin Islands in which she had an ownership interest. Prosecutors believed it was through that company, called Beauty Yachts, that the Ghosn clan bought its luxury cruiser *Shachou*[9]—the big boat unabashedly named after the Japanese word for "company president." And the opulent 2016 Palace of Versailles soiree, hosted to celebrate Carole's fiftieth birthday, sparked more allegations of misused funds in France, while becoming fodder for snarky tittle-tattle.

· · ·

In addition to the claims of hostage justice, Ghosn's camp blasted Japan's handling of his case on numerous points which they said made it impossible for him to get a fair trial.

Among them was the assertion that Tokyo prosecutors had colluded with Nissan to investigate Ghosn, even though Nissan itself was a defendant in some of the allegations. Furthermore, Hari Nada, the former

Ghosn aide who headed Nissan's legal department only to turn on his boss as a plea bargainer, stayed in his post and continued leading Nissan's internal investigation into Ghosn's alleged wrongdoings. To critics of Nissan's investigation, this was an abject conflict of interest because Nada was implicated in some of the alleged misdeeds he was assumed to be investigating. In Western systems, by contrast, such plea bargainers usually recuse themselves or are sidelined. This dubious arrangement stirred controversy even within Nissan, especially among Nada's underlings who wanted Nissan's investigation and any claims against Ghosn to be beyond reproach.

One staffer, recalling a conversation with a top legal counsel under Nada, described morale as wretched: "He said, 'I'm a lawyer and I'm still reporting to a guy who is under plea bargain, when if it weren't for the plea bargain, he would be in the same situation as Ghosn. What does this say about me?'"

Nissan's external law firm, Latham & Watkins, meanwhile was tapped by Nada to help lead an independent investigation of Ghosn, even though the firm had previously been consulted on some of the very Ghosn compensation schemes now being chased by prosecutors. In all this, Nissan never sought to question either Ghosn or Kelly to at least get their side of the story.

Ghosn's defense team also accused Latham & Watkins of conducting illegal search and seizure of evidence. Its attorneys, they said, "stole" computers and hard disks with large amounts of Ghosn's personal information and correspondences with lawyers from an aide in Beirut. Tokyo prosecutors coordinated the swoop this way, with private citizens instead of investigators, so as to circumvent the normal warrant system, Ghosn's attorneys said.

Asked for comment on its work in the case, Latham & Watkins said it had no conflict of interest because its sole client was always Nissan, and that it had regularly discussed the engagement with the carmaker. "Latham disagrees with any suggestion that the internal investigation was biased, and notes that numerous independent agencies and law enforcement authorities from Japan and the United States conducted their own thorough and independent investigations and reached conclusions consistent with those of the internal investigation," the law firm said. It did not address the allegations from the Ghosn defense team.

Ghosn's team claimed Japanese prosecutors also illegally seized Carole Ghosn's possessions during the April 4 raid on the couple's cramped Tokyo apartment, the one where the officer stood outside Carole's shower with a towel. The search warrant then applied to only Carlos Ghosn's possessions, not hers, the lawyers said. But prosecutors confiscated her smartphone, computer, and passport, nonetheless. Carole Ghosn was later able to leave Japan because officers took only her Lebanese passport, not her US papers.

The litany of alleged overreach by prosecutors included accusations that authorities illegally leaked details of the case to the media and that they denied Ghosn's right to a speedy trial, as guaranteed by the Japanese constitution. Even as Ghosn prepared to jump bail and flee Japan at the end of 2019, more than a year after his arrest, there was still no official date for starting his trial.

Finally, Ghosn's attorneys accused Tokyo prosecutors and Nissan of conspiring to hide evidence. His lawyers said Nissan requested that prosecutors block access to six thousand pieces of email and other digital evidence.[10] In Japan, prosecutors are obliged to share all the evidence in hand only if ordered by a court.[11] But the accusation, again, sowed doubt about equal treatment.

"That remaining evidence is what prosecutors don't want us to see. So, we can assume that the evidence should be of benefit to us," one of Ghosn's lawyers said. "They are withholding evidence, so there is no telling what has been deleted."

. . .

The counterattack mounted by Carole and Ghosn's lawyers aimed to give Japan a black eye on the world stage. It painted the picture of a Japanese system paying lip service to its own rules while marching completely out of step with Western norms. Yet, in Japan, the unflinching prosecutors and court stood their ground, and the international reaction was more muffled grumbling than unified outcry.

Appeals to the French government never gathered great traction. Emmanuel Macron, who by then had ascended to the presidency, was no obvious ally. He and Ghosn had a topsy-turvy relationship dating back to the Florange debacle, when Macron humiliated Ghosn with his end-run to secure the French state's double voting rights in Renault. Macron also led the French government's push in 2015 to pressure Ghosn into taking a pay cut at Renault, amid criticism he was pulling down excessive compensation. By 2018, with "yellow vest" street protests still convulsing French cities in a crusade for economic reform, Macron's government was eager to avoid any move suggesting favoritism toward an elite, well-connected business leader. So, with an eye to the future, Paris washed its hands of Ghosn in an attempt to salvage the carmaker's teetering tie-up with Nissan.

Carole vented her disgust with Macron's disengagement in an interview with the *Journal du Dimanche*, a French weekly newspaper. "The silence from the Élysée Palace is deafening," she said. "I thought France was a country that defended the presumption of innocence. They've all forgotten everything Carlos did for France's economy and for Renault."[12]

Ghosn's saga also failed to animate America—at least in the way he hoped.

Even as Carole petitioned President Trump to champion her husband's cause, the US Securities and Exchange Commission (SEC)—the regulatory body overseeing stock trading and financial reports—was investigating whether Ghosn had also falsified US financial disclosures, as he was accused of doing in Japan. Just as Ghosn's defense strategy was beginning to coalesce, the US securities authority buttressed Japanese prosecutors' version of events when it alleged that he, with Greg Kelly's help, hid some $140 million in future payouts over nearly a decade through a scheme of misleading disclosures, backdated documents, cherry-picked foreign exchange rates, under-the-table contracts, and a host of bookkeeping tricks. By the SEC's reckoning, Ghosn schemed to conceal more than $90 million in compensation and then changed the calculation of his pension to plump it by an additional $50 million. The SEC charged Ghosn and Nissan, as a corporate entity, with violating the antifraud provisions of securities laws and charged Kelly with aiding and abetting them.

"Simply put, Nissan's disclosures about Ghosn's compensation were false," the codirector of the SEC's Enforcement Division said in a September 2019 statement outlining the findings. "Through these disclosures, Nissan advanced Ghosn and Kelly's deceptions and misled investors, including US investors."

The SEC's version of events sounded familiar. Ghosn wanted the handsome compensation of his highly paid industry peers, but he didn't want the unseemly spectacle of justifying it before a disapproving public in Japan and France.

"Ghosn became concerned about criticism that might result in the Japanese and French media if his total compensation became publicly known," the SEC said in its complaint. "To avoid public criticism, Ghosn and his Nissan subordinates took steps to conceal from public disclosure a substantial portion of Ghosn's compensation."[13]

Ghosn settled and paid a $1 million penalty, but he didn't admit to or deny the findings. As part of the settlement, Ghosn was barred from being an officer or director at a publicly traded US company for ten years. For an executive of his stature, that hit was likely a bigger blow than the fine. Still, his attorneys saw this as a small victory; they said the settlement cleared the air in the United States so the team could focus on Japan. But the SEC showdown spotlighted the fact that Japan was not alone in finding fault with Ghosn's compensation scheme. And in the court of public opinion, paying a $1 million penalty hardly looked like the play of an innocent man. The SEC case also foreshadowed the tough battle awaiting Ghosn in the Japanese courts. Tokyo prosecutors were publicly tight-lipped about their own findings and legal strategy. But the SEC case drew heavily on their evidence.

What the SEC case didn't explore, however, were the Saudi and Omani Routes, the two breach of trust charges framed purely as a Japanese affair. Tokyo prosecutors, citing the sensitivity of an ongoing legal case and the pending trial, demurred from spelling out details of these charges, just as they had in the deferred compensation case. The initial public disclosure of each indictment was encapsulated in a terse statement just a few paragraphs long. Meanwhile, the official media briefings in the basement of the Tokyo Public Prosecutors Office, right around the corner from the Tokyo District Court, were unilluminating exercises in no-comment Q&As. Details of any evidence against Ghosn would have to wait for trial, prosecutors insisted.

. . .

What emerged was a he-said, she-said collision of competing narratives.

In her interview with *Automotive News*, Carole Ghosn took a dim view of her husband's chances in the halls of Japanese justice. Completely clearing him would be a humiliating admission of the system's failures, especially in virtue of its vaunted conviction rate. Japan's legal institutions had already invested too much of their reputation in the case to let Carlos Ghosn slip through their fingers, she said.

"They're going to say, 'We did all this, and now he's innocent?' What's going to happen to their government or their judicial system?" she said. "Is it going to collapse? Is it going to change? Of course, to save face, they're going to have to find him guilty on something . . . The system is rigged."[14]

13

ALLIANCE UPHEAVAL

NISSAN AND ITS JAPANESE PARTNER MITSUBISHI MADE quick work of firing Ghosn as their chairman, both within a week of his arrest. Nissan's board voted unanimously to can Ghosn, tellingly with the approval of the two directors picked by Renault—including one Frenchman who was among the first thirty executives Ghosn brought with him to fix Nissan in 1999.

Yet even as Ghosn sat in jail, he kept his seat as a director at both companies. A board decision was enough to remove him as board chairman, but only a full shareholder vote could kick him off the board completely.

Nissan was in such a rush to wholly excise him from the company, it called an extraordinary shareholder meeting in April 2019 just to vote him off. The meeting promised to be explosive amid speculation that Ghosn, by then released on bail just days before his sixty-fifth birthday, might try to attend the conclave.

Even as an indicted criminal suspect, Ghosn remarkably still had the right to join the meeting, not only as a director but as one of the company's top individual shareholders. He owned 3.1 million shares of Nissan stock as of June 2017, the last time his holdings were detailed in the company's filings. Given Nissan's share price in early 2019, his sizeable stake was worth a cool $25.5 million.[1]

But no such drama would unfold because Ghosn was arrested yet again, on the fourth charge—the so-called Omani Route breach of trust—in the dawn raid on his Tokyo apartment just four days before the shareholders meeting.

Mom-and-pop Japanese investors lined up and down the street for a seat at the gathering. This time, it was held at the Grand Prince Hotel Shin Takanawa in Tokyo, a sprawling complex built on the former palace grounds of an Imperial family prince stripped of nobility status during the US occupation after World War II. During the meeting, seething investors booted Ghosn and Greg Kelly, the latter of whom had likewise kept his directorship following his arrest. But investors also blamed Hiroto Saikawa and Nissan management for allowing the alleged misdeeds to happen in the first place.

Mitsubishi waited until its regular shareholders' meeting two months later to cut Ghosn loose as a director, finally severing his last formal tie to Japan's auto industry.

Renault wasn't as quick. In the weeks immediately after Ghosn's initial arrest, its executives half a world away were reeling in shocked disbelief. They were loath to summarily dismiss their longtime chief without at least knowing more about the charges against him. Maneuvering under the assumption of innocent until proven guilty, it took Renault two months to remove him—and even then, the company did so reluctantly, through the face-saving maneuver of allowing—or more likely, forcing—Ghosn to resign.

. . .

Behind the scenes, the French and Japanese sides of the auto group were barely on speaking terms. Riven by distrust and infighting, the Alliance that Ghosn built over two decades seemed close to ripping apart without him. His ejection exposed conflicts that long simmered beneath the surface of the tie-up's tidy image as a rare cross-border success story. Speculation mounted that the Alliance might even collapse. Analysts began modeling different outlooks for the group's future, often including a breakup scenario.

"Would Renault and Nissan going their separate ways really be a terrible thing?" asked Max Warburton, a senior auto analyst at research brokerage AllianceBernstein, in a report. "The Alliance has never been fully functional and integrated. The real synergies between the companies are surprisingly modest. Renault could be profitable even without Nissan. There may be greater industrial logic for Renault to work with other partners. Perhaps the Alliance will be fine without Ghosn—his importance may be overstated. Or perhaps it will come apart at the seams—but it's possible that Renault could find an alternative way forward."

Concluded Warburton: "The importance of the Alliance has probably been exaggerated."

Market sentiment seemed to be that despite all the shared cost savings and cooperation on common vehicle platforms, further gains would be like squeezing blood from a stone. Especially now, with goodwill in short supply, prospects for collaboration seemed bleak.

Amid the upheaval, Nissan began jockeying for new leverage in the Alliance, agitating for a rebalancing of the cross-shareholdings and a greater say in Alliance affairs, starting with more influence over the appointment of its own directors.

And the damage went deeper than strained relations. Nissan executives were sucked into the round-the-clock distraction of tending to a badly bruised image, defending the company's actions, fighting with Renault, and overhauling corporate governance. Less attention was being focused on cars at a time when Nissan was in critical need of new product.

One of the first nameplates to take a hit was the trademark Nissan Leaf, the electric vehicle (EV) on which Ghosn staked the company's reputation as a technological trailblazer. By late 2018, Nissan had already introduced a second generation of the car, but a critical weakness was its lackluster driving range in an EV segment now crowded with new competitors. The public was clamoring for an extended-range version with a bigger battery that could drive longer distances. The long-awaited unveiling of that car, planned for the Los Angeles Auto Show, was scrubbed amid the chaos of the Ghosn scandal. Instead, it debuted months behind schedule under subdued fanfare, a missed opportunity.[2]

Meanwhile, amid the turbulence, Nissan executives were busy watching their own back, especially those dubbed "Ghosn Children," the executives who had been hired by him and promoted as part of his inner circle. Executives and managers at all levels, such as José Muñoz—the Spanish executive once believed likely to replace Saikawa—began bailing on Nissan. Some were pushed out of the company; others read the prevailing winds and jumped. Either way, the result was a massive brain drain of top talent.

By September 2019, some ten months after the arrest, the housecleaning had claimed no fewer than ten top executives—almost exclusively non-Japanese. The list included two global chiefs of Nissan Motor Co.'s Infiniti premium brand; the global head of sales; the global chief of human resources; the top designer at Infiniti; the global head of Alliance public relations; the executive who once led Ghosn's envisioned revival of Datsun as an entry-level brand for emerging markets; and the COO of Mitsubishi—a longtime Nissan executive who had risen through the ranks under Ghosn's watch.

"Have you seen rats who have not eaten? They are hungry. You know what happens among themselves? They eat each other," said one person close to the Nissan board. "That's exactly what happened, because people feared something was going to happen to them. We can't go name by name, because there were so many people."

The purge culminated in the September sacking of Saikawa. Never a popular figure within Nissan for his brusque management style, Saikawa was seen by many as the ultimate Ghosn Child. He was tripped up in his own misconduct scandal, a problem with his pay that only came to light in the post-Ghosn rounds of backstabbing and recriminations within Nissan. To his enemies, Saikawa was emblematic of the rot, having served as Ghosn's willing right-hand man so long.

Shareholders quickly soured on Nissan, and on Mitsubishi and Renault—and not only because the Alliance's future seemed shaky. Sales and profits began to plummet, first at Nissan, then across the Alliance, as the post-Ghosn malaise spread. The stock prices of all three companies plunged, and the Alliance teetered.

Nissan and Renault seemed poised for a colossal showdown over the future structure of the Alliance and who would control it, if it survived at all.

In late November 2018, just the week after Ghosn's arrest, top executives from Renault and Nissan met in person at the Alliance's Renault-Nissan BV (RNBV) headquarters in Amsterdam for a regularly scheduled meeting. Both sides tried to stick to business. But beneath the facade of civility, icy distrust chilled true dialogue. "It was pure shock for everybody," recalled one executive in attendance. Yet, the reasons for the shock differed. In Renault's camp, there was dismay over what they saw as a ruthless corporate coup. On Nissan's side, there was outrage over Ghosn's alleged crimes.

"You could see clearly different types of reactions within the companies. That difference in position only got worse over time," the executive said. "The more time that passed since Mr. Ghosn's arrest, the guys who were disappointed because he was arrested became more disappointed. And the guys who were disappointed because they believed the charges were true, they also became more disappointed."

In the weeks that followed, Nissan's biggest challenge was simply conveying to Renault the details of the allegations against Ghosn. Nissan wanted to deliver its full report directly to Renault's directors. But Renault's top brass, led by Thierry Bolloré, were fully convinced of a Nissan conspiracy. They wanted details via the more formal channel of the company's legal team. Nissan balked, asserting that they feared the complete report would be censored or never reach the full board, a body Nissan deemed more impartial.

Communication between the French and Japanese sides abruptly broke down.

"It moved from just meeting and talking with each other to letters, between the CEOs of Nissan and Renault and others," one Nissan executive recounted. "That kind of thing never happened in the past. It was getting extreme."

. . .

The Renault side, caught completely flatfooted, needed time to digest the arrest of its longtime leader. Bolloré and his inner circle were appalled by Nissan's aggressive, ruthlessly choreographed public relations blitz against Ghosn, from the very night of his arrest. Many at Renault feared Nissan, long resentful of the French company's control, was seizing the situation to sabotage the Alliance and finally make a break for independence.

"They had a massive propaganda plan. I could say PR plan, but it's beyond PR. It's propaganda," one Bolloré adviser said of Nissan. "We had not one idea what was going to happen. I have never seen that before when you have a compliance issue in a company, especially in the top management. Usually, you issue the shortest press release you can and try to preserve the reputation of the companies. All the choices of Nissan show they had a plan to hit not only Renault but also the Alliance."

An initial flash point was how to replace Ghosn as chairman at Nissan. Renault reserved the right to appoint top Nissan executives under the terms of the Alliance agreement. Now, however, Nissan leveraged the power vacuum to push back. Nissan executives said they wanted a bigger say in picking their next chairman. They also wanted to abolish the position of overarching Alliance chairman, a role Ghosn carved out for himself as the final arbiter at all three companies. Finally, Nissan wanted to wind down Renault-Nissan BV, the Netherlands-based joint venture that was gradually morphing into a prototype holding company of the kind Ghosn once imagined as the way to make the Alliance "irreversible." To Nissan, this was a Trojan horse for Renault control—it had final say on matters of Nissan's business and product plans, the company's lifeblood.

No doubt, Nissan was pressing new demands. The question was, Why now? Nissan executives argued that the rampant misconduct, at the hands of Renault-installed Ghosn, necessitated a rethink of business-as-usual. Citing Ghosn's alleged misdeeds as justification, they saw a chance to retune the Alliance to their liking. But seen from a more skeptical Renault perspective, and one held by many outside observers, Nissan's power play smelled more like the calculated final act of a cold-blooded coup that began with a fabricated takedown of Ghosn.

Was reworking or even disbanding the Alliance the real endgame?

Maybe. To hard-core traditionalists inside Nissan, going solo would have been perfectly fine.

. . .

Over the decades, foreign carmakers have bought small or even controlling stakes in several Japanese automakers. But as models of what might come next for Renault and Nissan, they weren't very promising. Most often, the overseas suitor gave up, and not always gracefully. From the 1970s through '90s, as Japanese brands ramped up their sales assault on Fortress America, beleaguered Detroit automakers decided, *If you can't beat them, buy them.* General Motors purchased sizable holdings in Suzuki, Subaru, and Isuzu. Ford took a controlling stake in Mazda. And in 2000, DaimlerChrysler—the German-American juggernaut itself grappling with internal division—bought control of Mitsubishi Motors, to create what it hoped would be a three-legged giant with bases in North America, Europe, and Asia.

Sometimes, the foreign players swooped in to help Japanese rivals who were struggling, as Ford did with Mazda. Sometimes, they bought a stake for a closer look under the hood at the Japanese way of making cars, which seemed to be taking over the world. But by the Great Recession, all these overseas partners were downsizing or dumping their holdings.

Mazda, which had grudgingly chafed under Ford's yoke since 1979, was elated in 2008, when Ford—then racing to avoid bankruptcy—chopped its controlling 33.4 percent stake in the Japanese carmaker to a minor 13 percent holding. Trumpeting Ford's retreat, a Mazda spokeswoman proclaimed, "Essentially what this means is that Mazda is a Japanese company again."[3] Mazda executive Takashi Yamanouchi, who went on to become Mazda's first post-Ford CEO, declared the US carmaker's move "a godsend."[4]

Mazda made a go of going solo. But that didn't last long. As one of Japan's smallest players, it fell victim to the same pressure facing everyone in the industry—the strain of huge investment in new technologies.

Profitability started to wane, and Mazda was looking for another protector. It found one in Toyota, which took a 5 percent stake in the Hiroshima-based company in 2017, bringing Mazda under the wing of Japan's No. 1 automaker.

The most acrimonious breakup undoubtedly came when Suzuki sued estranged partner Volkswagen to force the German automaker to sell back its 19.9 percent stake in Suzuki. VW bought into Suzuki in 2009 in a much-ballyhooed deal that filled the void left when GM divested from the Japanese carmaker. But within two years, Suzuki was bridling at what it said were VW's designs on an outright takeover. Chairman Osamu Suzuki, who had married into the company's founding family and took its name, demanded a "divorce" and blasted VW as a "ball and chain."

After nearly four years of legal wrangling in the International Court of Arbitration, the court ruled in Suzuki's favor in 2015. VW was forced to sell its shares, ending a dysfunctional alliance that failed to deliver a single joint project. Chairman Suzuki's reaction to the decision was telling: "I feel refreshed. It's like clearing a bone stuck in my throat."[5]

The track record of foreign automakers teaming with the Japanese was not good.

Yet decoupling Nissan from Renault would also be easier said than done. Two decades of steady integration had intertwined product planning, factory output, engineering, and crucially, purchasing of everything from steel and paper to spark plugs and fuel injectors. Leveraging their combined volume, they locked up nearly €100 billion ($109 billion) in joint purchases. Common platforms underpinned about 70 percent of all vehicles manufactured by Nissan and Renault. The two companies also shared about 75 percent of their engines and transmissions. Even if this integration had peaked with diminishing returns, teasing all that apart and divvying up the goods would guarantee years of negotiations and headaches.

Ford's protracted separation from Mazda foreshadowed the long, rocky road that might await a Renault-Nissan split. Ford began selling down its stake in 2008, but it didn't completely exit its Mazda holding until 2015. And even as late as 2020, the two companies were still nursing one last shared assembly plant in Thailand.

Breaking up is hard to do. So, in their official statements at least, Renault and Nissan remained steadfastly committed to sustaining the Alliance. And despite the roiled relations, a key breakthrough happened in late January 2019—when Ghosn finally was forced to resign as chairman and CEO of Renault. His trusted lieutenant Bolloré was appointed CEO. And, significantly, an outsider was brought in as chairman of Renault, in the hope of brokering a peace. Both sides took a step back from the lightning rod issue of "irreversible" integration and focused instead on bandaging the battered relationship that currently existed.

. . .

Renault's new chairman was Jean-Dominique Senard. Like Ghosn, Senard parachuted into Renault from Michelin—he was CEO of the tire maker when Renault approached him for the job. But in many ways, Senard was the anti-Ghosn.

A diplomat's son who traveled the world, Senard was the consummate establishment insider, in the vein of Alliance founder Louis Schweitzer. Already sixty-five when tapped by Renault, he was an elder statesman in French business circles, with deep connections to the government and a blue-blooded pedigree. Senard was tall, thin, and composed, cool, and deliberate—and French by birth. If anything, he seemed dull and dowdy. Ghosn, by contrast, was the intense, enterprising outsider. He oozed charisma and energy, but was shorter, born in Brazil with Middle Eastern roots. Ghosn spoke energetically, with generous gesticulation and always with an endless supply of data and detail at his tongue-tip. Senard was quieter and more economical in his word use. Whereas Ghosn might bowl over the Japanese, Senard seemed more soothing.

Senard immediately extended some olive branches. To start, he agreed not to seek the chairmanship of Nissan, suggesting instead a role as vice chairman. Saikawa had engaged in direct talks with Senard, sidestepping Bolloré and other top management at Renault, and was blunt in delivering Nissan's stance. Saikawa intimated to Senard that his insisting on the chairmanship would kick over a hornet's nest in Japan. Senard took the hint and acquiesced by settling on the No. 2 position. "When Mr. Senard came in, that was the time that we were able to come back to the normal debate, rather than the political conflict," Saikawa said.

Senard also agreed with Saikawa to put Renault-Nissan BV, the Netherlands-based joint venture, on ice as a forum for deciding Alliance affairs. And Senard agreed to a new, more balanced Alliance structure that he pledged would be based on consensus, not a Ghosn-style top-down approach. The new structure was not the radical overhaul Nissan might have wanted, but it was a step in that direction. Some at Renault also had reservations, believing Senard had sold out. But there was a new chairman calling the shots now.

On March 12, 2019, Senard and the CEOs of Renault, Nissan, and Mitsubishi took the stage at Nissan's global headquarters in Yokohama—the Japanese side's home turf—in a symbolic show of unity and proclaimed a "new start" to the Alliance. It was the first time the company heads had appeared together in public since Ghosn's arrest. Going forward, they said, decisions would be hammered out by a new four-member Alliance Operating Board, consisting of the three CEOs and Renault chairman Senard.

The new board would supersede other alliance bodies, such as the Netherlands joint ventures.

At the news conference announcing the breakthrough, Saikawa and Senard sat next to each other in the middle. Renault CEO Bolloré and Mitsubishi CEO Osamu Masuko flanked them, almost like outside observers. Saikawa, perpetually stern, steely and stressed in the months after Ghosn's arrest, now beamed with visible relief, cracking the occasional smile despite himself.

"For the alliance, this memorandum of understanding is a big new step," Saikawa said. "This is a true partnership on equal footing . . . It's a win, win, win approach based on consensus."[6]

The Alliance seemed back on track, for a short while anyway.

. . .

But within a month of the win-win-win new start, Senard incensed Nissan by trying to resurrect the mothballed merger proposal once championed by Ghosn. It was an idea that just wouldn't die on the Renault side, as the French government pressured Senard, just as it had with Ghosn, to build new scale and lock in control of Nissan. The talks didn't go far in the face of stiff Nissan resistance. But Senard's overture put Nissan on notice that despite the public showing in Japan, the underlying dynamics of the Alliance hadn't changed.

"He was in a way too hasty to make a good conclusion with which you could please the French government, specifically Macron," one Nissan executive involved in the negotiations said of Senard's gambit. "He wanted to do an honorable job for French society, which is to make the Alliance irreversible so that Renault could be safe forever and French employment can be saved."

The spurned Senard, still under pressure to score a blockbuster deal for Renault, then made another run for merger—but this time with Fiat Chrysler Automobiles (FCA). The latter company was formed in 2014, after Italian automaker Fiat swooped in to rescue the Chrysler Group following its 2009 bankruptcy during the Great Recession. Combining Renault and FCA seemed to be another holdover idea once considered by Ghosn. Later from Lebanon, Ghosn claimed that, before his arrest, he had been brokering an FCA merger and had expected to seal the deal with FCA chairman John Elkann in January 2019. Instead, Ghosn was jailed before it could happen. Ghosn's supposed maneuverings with FCA, for some reason, never emerged in the coup narrative as a reason for triggering Japanese blowback, and the issue fell by the wayside.

Senard's attempt to wrap up Ghosn's unfinished business broadsided Nissan, Japan, and the entire auto industry. When first rumors of a Renault-FCA tie-up surfaced, Saikawa said he was "not at all" aware of the talks.[7] But in late May 2019, FCA dropped the bombshell by publicly announcing a "transformational" $35 billion 50-50 merger proposal between the two European heavyweights. Nissan and Mitsubishi were mentioned only as footnotes, as a kind of supporting cast to the main protagonists.

FCA trumpeted the new megamaker as the world's No. 3 automaker with combined sales of 8.7 million vehicles, behind only Volkswagen and

Toyota. Stack that volume on top of the turnover at Nissan and Mitsubishi, it added, and global sales would eclipse fifteen million units, making it No. 1.

But the merger threatened to severely weaken Nissan's influence. The initial board of the new company, for example, would have eleven members, four each from Renault and FCA, but only one from Nissan.[8] Meanwhile, the Renault-FCA entity would keep its 43.4 percent stake and voting rights in Nissan, but Nissan's share in the new company would be diluted from 15 to only 7.5 percent.[9] Nissan was poised be the big loser in the deal, and worse yet for its management, Saikawa and his lieutenants were completely left out of the talks. It looked as if Renault was playing hardball with a Nissan it deemed increasingly difficult to manage. If Nissan didn't want to dance, Renault would simply find another partner.

Saikawa claimed he wasn't necessarily opposed to such a merger. In fact, the added scale could bring new cost savings for Nissan and Mitsubishi. In the US market, for example, Nissan could piggyback on Chrysler's successful line of Ram brand pickups and Jeep brand SUVs and crossovers, drawing from shared technology tool bins or using Nissan-badged versions of those tried-and-true products. But even as Saikawa said his company would not openly oppose the merger, he also set up roadblocks by insisting Nissan would abstain from voting in favor of it. Nissan, he said, needed more time to evaluate how exactly it would be impacted by the deal.

Then, barely a week after announcing the merger talks, Fiat Chrysler abruptly pulled the plug on the deal. The French government, eager to bolster its influence over the new entity, dragged its feet in approving the plan. One sticking point was an issue that had bedeviled relations between Renault and Nissan: jobs. Both FCA and Renault were saddled with production overcapacity; trimming the overlap was a top rationale for bringing the two together. But both sides balked at cutting jobs. At a Renault board meeting to discuss the merger, Nissan sat out the decision while representatives of the French state urged more time. The French state was also spooked by Nissan's resistance, and FCA grew wary of the downsides of teaming with Renault if Nissan wasn't fully on board.

The deal imploded, and FCA put the blame squarely on the French state—echoing similar complaints by Ghosn and Nissan over the years about French meddling. "It has become clear that the political conditions in France do not currently exist for such a combination to proceed successfully," FCA said in a statement that went on to thank Senard, Bolloré, Nissan, and Mitsubishi—but not the French government—for their "constructive engagement."

"You thought that people were onboard, but they were not even on the same boat," recalled one former senior Renault adviser.

· · ·

Senard's failed backroom dealing with FCA drew immediate backlash from Japan.

At Nissan's annual shareholders' meeting in June 2019, just three weeks after FCA broke off the Renault deal, furious investors assailed Senard for trying the end-run around Saikawa and blasted the incoming vice chairman of Nissan for not even owning shares in the Japanese carmaker. One attendee, channeling the palpable distrust in the room, said he feared a foreign takeover of Nissan and attacked the entire French nation as duplicitous.

"They are really sly," the shareholder said of the French. "Can you behave as a Nissan director and not just as the chairman of Renault? You would like to take advantage of the merger for Renault. That's obvious."[10]

A clearly shaken Senard poured forth an emotional riposte in English delivered to the 2,800 shareholders through a Japanese interpreter. He repeatedly implored shareholders to trust him. "The last thing that came in my mind was to be aggressive toward a company of which I am a director. I beg you to believe me on that," he said, conceding Nissan-Renault relations were in a "much worse state than I thought."

Senard defended the aborted FCA merger as ultimately benefiting all the Alliance partners, including Nissan. "You know who was very pleased after the announcement that this deal was stopped? All our competitors in the world," he said. "They understood that if this deal had gone through, it would have been a very, very strong feature for the alliance." Senard concluded: "There are no bad intentions at all."

But the damage was done. Trust in Renault's new boss melted away.

It didn't help that Senard was chauffeured away from the Nissan shareholders' meeting not in a Nissan-made vehicle but in an Alphard van, sold by archrival Toyota. And insult followed injury just four months later. With Renault and the Alliance in its rearview mirror, FCA announced it would merge instead with PSA Group, the maker of Peugeot and Citroën brand vehicles, and Renault's French archrival. FCA and PSA claimed their proposed 50-50 tie-up would create the world's fourth-biggest automaker—not No. 3 but plenty big enough to pressure the Alliance. The merged auto group was called Stellantis, a name rooted in the Latin verb *stello*, meaning "to brighten with stars."[11]

"Senard appeared to be a very reasonable, gentle businessperson," recalled one high-level Nissan executive involved with Renault relations. "In reality, he wasn't."

. . .

As the Alliance staggered on in limbo during its first year after Ghosn, Nissan's performance began to plunge, amid sliding sales, especially in the key US market. Nissan's operating profit dove 99 percent in the April–June quarter of 2019, and it fell another 70 percent in the July–September period. By the end of that fiscal year, on March 31, 2020, Nissan booked its first net loss in eleven years, the worst loss since Ghosn's first year at the company in 1999. By early 2020, Nissan's earnings were being throttled by the COVID-19 pandemic, as dealerships worldwide closed their doors and customers from Beijing to Los Angeles were forced to stay at home under lockdown. Looking ahead, Nissan forecast its worst-ever operating loss in the fiscal year ending March 31, 2021.

But the reality was Nissan's business was already in brisk decline before the pandemic. Operating profit margin stood at a robust 6.3 percent in March 2017, when Ghosn made Saikawa sole CEO. Three years later, Nissan was a money pit.

Investors reacted by racing to ditch their Nissan shares. From the beginning of 2019 until March 2020, the company's stock price shed 55 percent of its value.

The contagion soon spread to Renault and Mitsubishi. In 2017, while Renault was still under Ghosn's leadership, the French automaker posted record vehicle sales and operating profit.[12] But in 2019, the year he was dismissed, Renault recorded its first annual net loss in a decade.[13] By the spring of 2020, Renault's corporate bond rating was slashed to junk status. Mitsubishi, already mired in red ink before the pandemic hit, also booked a net loss for its full fiscal year through March 31, 2020, as operating profit caved 89 percent. Renault's share price plummeted 68 percent from the beginning of 2019 through the first quarter of 2020. Mitsubishi's sank 48 percent. It was an across-the-board reversal of fortunes.

To Ghosn, the Alliance needed someone just like him, a strong central figure to hold it all together. In a 2020 interview with *Automotive News* from his home in Lebanon, he called that the secret to his success: Being able to calm Alliance conflicts that constantly bubbled under the surface.

"Between 1999 and 2018, you never heard about any problem, because, obviously, I was the final decision maker, I installed a spirit of cooperation against the extremes. But we knew that the extremes were always there. They were always going to take advantage of any situation to have their opinion prevailing," Ghosn said. "They accused me of being a dictator, but frankly I was a decision-maker."

Many of his former lieutenants agreed, even after his arrest.

"Mr. Ghosn had a huge impact and influence in maintaining the Alliance because there were differences on business decisions between the companies, there were conflicts, and Mr. Ghosn is the one who, in the end, had to solve the conflicts and take a decision for the good of the Alliance," said one former high-level Nissan executive.

Ghosn wasn't shy about saying the Alliance was nothing without him and a vision.

"They thought that the guys after me would be able to run each company and the Alliance like nothing happened. But they were wrong, as the results have shown," Ghosn said in an interview for this book from Lebanon.

Still, others noted one of Ghosn's biggest failures, explosive allegations of rampant misconduct aside, was never cultivating a successor up to the task. One after another, heirs apparent vanished from the scene as Ghosn kept his grip on the auto group.

Patrick Pelata, Ghosn's No. 2 at Renault from 2008 to 2011, was once tipped as the chosen one. He was a well-liked product guru with a stellar record in leadership positions at Nissan and Renault. But he was forced to resign to shield Ghosn after the fake spy scandal at Renault, in which three employees were wrongly accused of handing secrets to the Chinese. Another contender with cross-company competence, Carlos Tavares, was pushed out as Renault's No. 2 when he confided in a news interview that he wanted to be CEO himself someday. He eventually was, at PSA Group, the French carmaker that outflanked Renault and hooked up with Fiat Chrysler. Meanwhile at Nissan, it once seemed chief planning officer Andy Palmer was being polished for the top post. But he also bolted, to become CEO of British sports car maker Aston Martin in 2014.

Even at age sixty-four, Ghosn showed no signs of leaving. That's when he signed on for another four years with Renault, through 2022. A whole generation of potential leaders felt frustrated that there was no road to the top for them.

"One of the things that was Ghosn's kryptonite over the years was his inability to successfully groom successors," said one former Alliance aide who worked closely with him. "It's not for lack of trying. It's because he's such a cult of personality."

As the Alliance wobbled without him, Ghosn seemed to relish in sniping at its troubles from the sidelines. He derided the group's new consensus-based approach as "Santa Claus management." He called Nissan's downward spiral "sickening." And he mocked Senard's botched attempt to broker a megamerger with FCA.

"The Alliance missed the unmissable, which is Fiat Chrysler," Ghosn said. "How can you miss that huge opportunity to become the dominant player in the industry?

"They said they want to turn the Ghosn page. Well, they have been very successful," he continued. "They turned the Ghosn page because there is no more growth. There is no more increase of profit. There is no more strategic initiative. There are no more initiatives, and there is no more Alliance."[14]

14

FOREIGN ENTANGLEMENTS

DESPITE ITS RISE AS A GLOBAL INDUSTRIAL POWER, Japan, like George Washington, has maintained a skeptical view of foreign entanglements. Much of the country's postwar economic strength was built on being able to do business internationally, but that is not the same as being able to work with foreign partners. Japan's export model meant that while electronics, industrial goods, and especially automobiles were sent around the world, control rested firmly with headquarters back home. Foreign countries represented market opportunities, not potential partners. "At the end of the day, you can have a Japanese company with a global presence, but you cannot have a truly globalized Japanese company," remarked one senior Japanese economic policy maker discussing the Nissan story.

With inflexible corporate cultures and exacting rules on how things should be done, Japanese companies have found it difficult to team up with other companies, either abroad or at home. In some ways, the fact that the Renault-Nissan-Mitsubishi Alliance remains in place is a tribute to what Ghosn and executives from the companies were able to achieve amid the numerous and expensive disasters that Japanese corporations have faced in trying to team up.

It's not (only) a case of Japanese nationalism. Corporate cultures in Japan are rigid within themselves. US and European companies will often go through ownership changes and new strategic directions, while employees need to be able to adapt to the ways of a new company whenever they change jobs. Although the situation in Japan is becoming more fluid, this type of upheaval remains the exception. Corporations largely continue as they were and most workers remain at their chosen employer for their entire career. For company and worker, there is therefore little knowledge of differing corporate models, whether at home or abroad. A Nissan executive would likely have just as many problems moving to Toyota as from Nissan to GM. Few have tried.

Another challenge for the Alliance was its model of equal partners. Looking globally, such "mergers of equals" are some of the most difficult to manage and some experts contend they do not really exist. "Marked differences often quickly emerge and make it clear there is no such thing as true equality between distinct organizations," wrote Mitch Berlin of the consulting firm Ernst & Young in a 2017 report. "And as two work feverishly to become one, divergent perceptions, strengths, and weaknesses manifest at every turn."[1] Such woes are difficult enough in one language and culture, while the Renault-Nissan Alliance was trying to operate across national boundaries, an eight-hour time zone difference, and three languages: French, Japanese, and the inevitable use of English as a compromise that would prove to please no one.

· · ·

Japan's first attempts at large-scale international tie-ups came through a big push in overseas investments in the 1980s, when huge profits and rising asset valuations at home gave Japanese companies the financial clout to look abroad. The results of these early forays into global empire building were not encouraging, with some failures becoming the stuff of Japanese corporate folklore. Among the most symbolic was Mitsubishi Estate's 1989 purchase of the company controlling New York's Rockefeller Center. (Confusingly, many companies bear the Mitsubishi name as part of their shared corporate history, although today they operate independently.)[2] The $1.4 billion price[3] for the iconic office complex in the center of Manhattan was based on internal calculations that office rents in the market would triple. This may have looked reasonable from the bubble atmosphere in Tokyo, where real estate was riding an unprecedented boom (that would itself famously crash in the next year, 1990). But for anyone familiar with New York's more volatile market, it was an unrealistic premise.

The reality was even worse than could be foreseen. Instead of rising, the New York office market went into one of its worst postwar slumps, and by 1995, Rockefeller Center was estimated to be worth half of its 1989 value. With Tokyo's market by this time suffering from an even steeper fall (Tokyo real estate would eventually decline an unprecedented 80 percent from its peak), Mitsubishi Estate wanted out at any cost and defaulted on the property's mortgage, effectively handing one of America's most prestigious properties back to the lenders. Mitsubishi's humiliating retreat was not a total catastrophe for the company, which would thrive in the coming years as it carefully nurtured its high-end properties in the more familiar territory of central Tokyo. It also managed to hold on to two of the more valuable office buildings in Rockefeller Center that would rebound in value, although not for many years.

In a similar bid for a trophy property, Japanese golf course developer Minoru Isutani purchased the famed Pebble Beach golf resort in Monterey, California, in September 1990 for $841 million, despite analyst forecasts that the property was worth around $600 million. With the purchase coming soon after the Rockefeller Center deal, there was the specter of rich Japanese taking over America, able to ignore the price tag due to their expanding wealth. This anti-Japanese mood hit its peak around this time as auto imports threatened the future of the Detroit Big Three.

In fact, Isutani was heavily in debt and after his plan to make Pebble Beach a members-only affair was rejected, he sold it just two years later at a 40 percent loss. (The new buyer was actually another Japanese group that was more careful in its stewardship of the property and was able to sell to a group of US investors in 1999 at a profit.)

Sony Corp. also struggled with its 1989 purchase of Columbia Pictures, one of the most famous of Hollywood's studios, for $3.4 billion, only to write off $2.7 billion of its value in 1995, an 80 percent loss. Harold L. Vogel, a longtime Wall Street media analyst, said at the time, "They were hoping for a cash cow and instead they got some money-losing operations. It's the understatement of the last five years to say this is not what they expected."

These are just the most notorious flops of the era. There were many more. An analysis by Japan's Nomura Research Co. in 1994 calculated that Japanese investors had lost $320 billion on their investments in the United States in just a decade, largely in the bond market as the dollar lost value against the yen.[4]

The reasons for this dismal track record were multifaceted. As seen in the Mitsubishi and Sony deals, there was a lack of understanding about what they were getting into. Mitsubishi Estate didn't understand the market; Sony didn't get the volatile world of movies. This is compounded by language issues. Generally, few senior executives in Japan have a solid grasp of English, especially in more conservative old-line companies. This creates a much higher hurdle for making an informed decision since few will be able to pore through the voluminous financial analysis that is available to English speakers. That in turn often means that those who are the English speakers in the group will have an outsize say. They are being pushed in turn by financial advisers who stand to make large fees if a deal goes through but earn little to nothing if the client walks away from a bad deal.

. . .

After a decade of bad deals, Japanese corporations exited the global stage in the late 1990s, partly because they had plenty of problems back home. They would return, however, in the early aughts after managing to clean up their balance sheets and build up large cash reserves. As one top-level Japanese executive said in an interview: "It didn't matter if we wanted to be international or not. With a shrinking domestic economy, we had no choice." They went shopping again. From 2005 to 2019, the total value of overseas investments by Japanese firms rose nearly fivefold. The United States was a major beneficiary of this trend. By 2019, Japan was the largest overseas investor in the United States at a total of $645 billion, a rise of 168 percent from ten years before.[5]

One problem remained, a belief among overseas bankers that Japanese companies were a soft touch and would be willing to overpay. With fees usually based on the value of a deal, this was to the benefit of practically everyone involved in the deal (except of course the shareholders of the Japanese buyers). Some more flops followed: In 2015, Japan Post Holdings, the national postal company that is also Japan's biggest bank and insurance group, spent $5.1 billion to buy Toll Holdings, a leading logistics delivery company in Australia. Within two years, it had to write off $3.6 billion.[6] Toshiba Corp. paid $5.4 billion for US nuclear reactor–maker Westinghouse Electric Co. in 2006, failing to adequately understand the scale of mismanagement in two big projects that would push the venerable US firm into bankruptcy protection in 2017.[7]

Although these money-losing deals showed that Japanese firms were often naïve, the new wave of buying did produce some notable success stories. One especially successful foray was the lightning fast action by Mitsubishi UFJ Financial Group (MUFG), Japan's largest and most profitable bank group, at the height of the global financial crisis in 2008 to buy a stake in US investment bank Morgan Stanley. As Lehman Brothers was spiraling into bankruptcy, the largest in US history, Morgan Stanley was desperately looking for a savior, with bankers from China's sovereign wealth fund CIC busily doing due diligence for a potential deal. MUFG's sudden interest was met with skepticism at the highest levels. According to Andrew Ross Sorkin in his book[8] on the crisis, when Morgan Stanley CEO John Mack told US treasury secretary Henry M. Paulson that talks were under way, Paulson replied acidly, "Come on. You and I know the Japanese. They are not going to do that. They'll never move that quickly."

They did, and ten years later, their initial $9 billion investment for 9.9 percent of Morgan Stanley was worth an estimated $24 billion, not to mention a regular flow of dividends, estimated to be worth another $4 billion.[9] (The deal also involved what is believed to be the largest check ever written. Such was the panic at the time that Morgan Stanley wanted the money immediately to help forestall a run on its stock. But due to a bank holiday, interbank transfers that would normally be used to move billions were not available. So, MUFG duly drew up a $9 billion check that was hand-delivered to Morgan Stanley in New York. That in itself raises the question of who or what, except for a Japanese bank, would keep $9 billion handy for a rainy day.)

But it's Japan's automakers who have had the biggest long-term success in the US market, with large-scale investments in "green field" sites around the country. This serves to show that large plants with big up-front spending and thousands of jobs can help to overcome cultural barriers. The first Japanese auto plant in the United States was Honda's, which opened in Marysville, Ohio, in 1982. Most, however, are located in lower-cost nonunion states, avoiding the bruising conflicts the US automakers have had with the United Auto Workers union. Nissan took the plunge in 1983 with its plant in Smyrna, Tennessee, the largest auto plant in North America.

Although Ghosn's later push for an ever-increasing market share in the North American market had become a key point of friction, he was by no means alone in seeing the United States as vital to success.

Toyota first began US manufacturing in a joint venture with General Motors at the NUMMI plant in Fremont, California, gaining valuable insights in how they could eventually get American workers to think and act like their counterparts in Japan. The work force at the GM factory was considered one of the worst in the industry, with high absenteeism, chronic labor issues, and low-quality output.

This did not deter Toyota. It sent workers all the way to Japan to provide them with the proper training/indoctrination. This would be an eye-opening experience. The plant became a model of success, one that would be replicated as proof that US workers could be instilled with the same work ethic as Japanese workers if they are managed properly.

It was an important milestone, showing the Japanese carmakers that they could produce overseas without sacrificing the attention to quality that set them apart. It also helped to ease—although not eliminate—US-Japan trade friction. The controversial invasion of Japanese autos would start to be replaced by the much sought-after invasion of Japanese investment. The NUMMI plant would continue to be historic. The two companies decided to shut it down in 2009, but it found new life as a manufacturing facility for Tesla.

Japan's attention on the "long game" was also clearly evident. When the Honda plant was still under construction, Shoichiro Irimajiri, president of Honda of America Manufacturing, made the unusual admission that the forthcoming plant was expected to lose money. But he said that he would go ahead anyway. "There is no explanation for that decision other than our commitment to our corporate philosophy, which told us that to serve the American market we must commit our resources to manufacturing in America."[10]

It was an affirmation of the Japanese corporate vision and an admission that few American CEOs could get away with. And like much of Japanese corporate strategy, it was part of a bigger plan. By 2019, direct employment by Japanese automakers in the United States totaled 93,600, with another 250,000 employed in related businesses such as suppliers. In all, industry figures show that direct investment since 1982 totaled $51 billion.[11] All of this created 24 manufacturing plants, 45 research and development design facilities, and 39 distribution centers across 28 states. It was a success story for all involved and played a key role in cementing the Japanese presence in the market.

But the awards for Japan's best and worst overseas investments do not come from the auto industry. They both go to one person, the flamboyant technology entrepreneur Masayoshi Son. Born in southern Japan to Korean parents, Son spent $20 million in early 2000 to invest in the then-fledgling Chinese internet shopping site Alibaba. By 2020, even after selling off part of the initial 34 percent stake, his holdings were worth an estimated $150 billion, a return of somewhere around 749,900 percent. This singular success has enabled Son to cover a multitude of other sins, most notably WeWork, the once high-flying shared workspace company. Son had invested $13.5 billion, only to write off $6.6 billion in its value in April 2020.[12] "I was foolish," he said of the investment after the writedown.[13] That's still small beer for Son, however. In the collapse of tech company shares in the dot-com bubble of 2000, he is calculated to have lost $70 billion. Not surprisingly, he takes the Japanese concept of a long-term perspective to a new height: His main company, the mobile phone operator SoftBank, has a three-hundred-year strategic plan. And he remains one of Japan's richest people.

. . .

The problems facing Japanese firms overseas pale in comparison to the hurdles facing a Renault that wants to invest in Japan. On paper, there are rich opportunities for foreign companies seeking to come into this well-established, secure, and potentially quite profitable market. While the economy grows at a modest 1 to 2 percent rate (a number that was once the laggard among major economies but one that the Western world can now identify with), there are hundreds of profitable companies sitting on valuable intellectual property and large cash holdings that would make a takeover remarkably inexpensive. In addition, with near zero interest rates, it can all be done with "other people's money." This was not enough to entice foreign capital, however. The total value of foreign investment into Japan totaled $205 billion by 2018. That left it in twenty-third position globally, just behind Poland. The United States was the world leader with $7.43 trillion pouring in from overseas.[14]

Foreigners in Japan complain of numerous issues, but most of the disconnect comes down to one basic difference. Whereas free-market capitalism rewards those who buy at the lowest price and sell at the highest, the Japanese viewpoint is different. In this perspective (which is by no means universal in Japanese commerce) it is better to make a reasonable profit and build long-term relationships. After all, you may need your business partner's help at some time in the future. In this cooperative world, the idea of a "hostile" takeover is an alien concept.

Still, given the potential to buy Japanese companies at a fraction of their potential value, a few hearty souls gave it a try.

One of the first, and most controversial, was Texas "oilman" (in pre-gender-awareness shorthand) T. Boone Pickens, who brought his Wild West style to Japan in 1989, becoming the largest shareholder in headlight maker Koito Manufacturing., a supplier to Toyota. Pickens controlled a 26 percent stake that he said cost him $1 billion. He took on the company, demanding seats on the board and changes in the company's operations to improve profitability. Pickens charged that Koito was actually subservient to Toyota as its major customer and that the automaker used what are known as "monopsony" powers (the inverse of a monopoly) to force Koito to deliver its products at the lowest possible price.

Koito charged that Pickens was after none of this. All he wanted, they said, was "greenmail," in which a corporate raider would loudly demand change and then quietly sell back their shares at a profit in order to go away. The saga became a major element in the US-Japan trade dispute, with members of Congress all too happy to take Pickens's side against a perceived Japanese monolith. This was when US politicians, business leaders, and labor unions all started to coalesce around the idea of a "Japan threat," presaging the US-China trade conflict some thirty years later.

Two years after he arrived, Pickens just as loudly declared that he was giving up, writing an op-ed piece in the *Washington Post* in which he made the reasonable point that Japan's keiretsu structure of interlocking companies created a cartel that kept corporations happy while consumers paid inflated prices. Pickens termed it "virtually feudal control over vast networks of suppliers and workers."[15] It was indeed one of the reasons that Japanese consumers paid among the highest prices in the world. (They have been steadily declining since 1990 as competition became more of a reality, not just a formality.)

In the end, Pickens did little to help the cause of opening up Japan. While Koito was not willing to play the US game, it certainly knew the rules, hiring a high-powered US PR firm to help present its case in the approved American fashion. The Texan, however, seemed a bit short on his own due diligence. While he said he purchased the shares from a disgruntled Japanese investor looking for change, it soon emerged that the shares were owned by one of Japan's richest men, with vast real estate holdings in Hawaii and elsewhere, and somewhat murky business connections. As this emerged, Japanese public opinion turned more clearly against Pickens. The Japanese partner would end up under arrest ten years later for allegedly helping some of Japan's top-tier "Yakuza" organized crime bosses in fraudulent financial deals.[16]

Even the more sophisticated arrival of British telecoms group Vodafone in 1999 proved no more successful than the Pickens raid. Vodafone was at that time the world's largest mobile phone operator, with experience in more than twenty markets around the world. The fast-growing Japan wireless market was dominated at the time by NTT DoCoMo, a spin-off from the national telephone monopoly Nippon Telegraph and Telephone Corp. Despite NTT's home-court advantage as one of Japan's largest corporations, Vodafone confidently predicted that it would "become a major national participant in Japan's rapidly expanding wireless market."[17]

The reality was different. Its J-Phone brand had technical disadvantages in the bandwidth space it had been given, yet another sign of how long-term relationships with politicians were paying off for the incumbent. Vodafone headquarters also had an outsize notion of how much money could be made in Japan and how long it would take.

A former Vodafone executive was quoted as saying that while London was pressing for higher profits, it was sending in "culturally insensitive" expat executives who had little knowledge of the market, another classic mistake. "Japanese managers and engineers were aware of the company's problems but were discouraged from saying anything and chose to keep silent," he said, according to a US embassy report that was later disclosed in a data leak.[18] Vodafone threw in the towel in 2006, selling the Japan operation to Son's SoftBank and taking a loss of $8.6 billion.[19]

· · ·

This unfortunately is not an uncommon story whenever foreign bosses and Japanese midlevel staff are brought together, where even routine meetings run into language issues and cultural differences about the expectations. In some cases, Japanese managers will plan their own strategy, disregarding the ideas of the foreigners. One foreign executive dispatched to work on a joint venture with a Japanese company in the 1990s told the story of heading into the office soon after his arrival on a Saturday, only to see the entire Japan management team holding a meeting. Asked what they were doing, he was told they were plotting the venture's strategy. Pointing out that had been done with both sides together during the week, the reply was that "this is the one that we'll really be following."

Building good business relations in Japan was always known for being difficult and time-consuming. Now, the potential reward was not seen as worth the effort and for big international investors, Japan was off the radar. While global mergers were rising, money coming into Japan remained minuscule in relation to the size of the economy. From 2005 to 2012, annual inbound direct investment totaled 0.17 percent of GDP. The level in the United States was ten times higher and for the developed economies in the Organisation for Economic Co-operation and Development (OECD) nations as a whole, it was twenty times Japan's number.[20] A rising yen (even as the economy languished) also served to hinder investment as valuations looked even less attractive.

The situation would not change in any meaningful way until 2012, when Shinzo Abe became prime minister for a second time, promising to restore Japan's economy to its former glory. He embarked on his "Abenomics" economic program. The main "arrow" (as he liked to call them) entailed record-high asset purchases by Japan's central bank, the Bank of Japan (BOJ). By 2018, the BOJ's assets would be equal to the annual economic output (GDP) of the entire nation. It owned almost half of all Japanese government bonds and was the largest investor in the markets for exchange traded funds (ETFs) and real estate trusts.

When Abe came to power, stocks were 50 percent lower than their 2007 peak five years before, just prior to the global financial crisis. Bargains could be found almost anywhere, with many of Japan's strongest blue chip companies selling for less than the breakup value of the assets they owned. At the same time, cross-shareholdings had declined, putting more of the shares in the hands of investors more interested in returns than in the long-standing ties of the keiretsu. Coupled with improving corporate governance and a newfound sense of respect for shareholder return, the market was again seen as a great opportunity, especially for the well-heeled private equity titans from abroad. This time, instead of the cowboy style of T. Boone Pickens, the tailored suits of Blackstone Group, KKR, and Elliott Management came calling.

They got off to a rocky start. With a reputation for stripping down the companies they buy to earn a quick profit, the foreign funds were dubbed *hagetaka*, the Japanese word for "vultures."[21] The early efforts produced some high-profile battles. New York–based Steel Partners failed in its long battle with Sapporo,[22] one of Japan's big brewers, to get a change in management, selling out in 2010.[23] Cerberus Capital Management similarly lost out in its bid to get the hotel, railroad giant, and property group Seibu to restructure its operations in 2015.[24] A low point for the US group came when it had tentatively suggested that Seibu close down a money-losing rail line that ran through a scenic area north of Tokyo. Seizing its chance, Seibu enlisted the support of small town mayors up and down the train line to talk about the catastrophic impact of a closure.[25] Cerberus was inundated with days of negative headlines.

But the foreigners did learn their lessons, moving away from high-profile battles to more discreet backroom discussions in the Japanese tradition. The US hedge fund ValueAct Capital worked with the previously scandal-hit medical equipment group Olympus in 2019,[26] winning seats on the board and helping with a business transformation that sent shares sharply higher. It didn't hurt that by this time, a majority of the Olympus board was from outside the company with a greater concern for the shareholders and less worried about internal sacred cows.

Elliott made headway in persuading Masayoshi Son and his SoftBank group to sell part of its own vast shareholdings to buy back shares and pay back debt in March 2020.[27] That prompted the shares to jump 55 percent in just a week, handing Elliott a tidy paper profit. Pickens would have been proud.

All of this contributed to a flood of new money from overseas, looking for new bargains. This was aided by the fact that central banks around the world were now following the lead of the Bank of Japan and pumping money into their own economies, pushing bond yields in most major markets to zero or even below.

. . .

Just as the party got going, however, establishment Japan appeared to get cold feet. In early 2020, the government abruptly tightened the rules on foreign purchases of companies deemed to be in strategic industries. Under the new regulations, any purchases of over 1 percent in a company deemed strategic would be subject to prescreening,[28] and the government's definition cut a pretty broad swath. It identified twelve broad sectors, including defense, aircraft, railways, technology, and telecommunications (pharmaceutical and medical equipment companies were added during the COVID-19 pandemic). In all, 14 percent of Japan's listed companies were covered by the new rules.

In taking the new, restrictive measures, the government appeared to have its eye mainly on any attempts of a dawn raid by increasingly wealthy Chinese companies. At the same time, the move no doubt made some entrenched boards breathe a little easier since it would reduce the chance of meddling by potentially pesky foreigners. And, yes, Nissan (along with the other big automakers) is on the list.

15

WE SEE ISSUES

HOW COULD CARLOS GHOSN, ONE OF THE WORLD'S most visible and respected executives, allegedly bilk Nissan Motor Co., one of the world's most visible and respected companies, for so many years without being exposed? Where was the corporate auditing, the board oversight, the compliance safety net? As soon as the charges against Ghosn were made public, these questions were asked, and they baffled observers.

After Ghosn's arrest, one of Hiroto Saikawa's top priorities was to address the question of just how it could have happened. He created what Nissan positioned as a special independent committee of directors and respected business figures to root out the rot and propose a better corporate governance structure that would prevent a repeat.

It was an awkward role for Saikawa, a Nissan lifer who rode Ghosn's coattails to the very top of the company, and whose signatures were on several of the documents at the heart of the allegations against Ghosn. Saikawa was often a polarizing figure—among Japanese and non-Japanese alike. He dismissed his detractors as backward cranks and old guard nationalists bent on breaking up the Alliance. Saikawa's supporters saw him as a task-oriented pragmatist; his lack of sentimentality made him a clear-eyed, effective business leader. His critics, for their part, considered his leadership style cold, stubborn, and arrogant.

He was saddled with the added baggage of being the prototype Ghosn Child. Even during the dueling with Renault over the years, Saikawa's underlings weren't always sure where he stood on the question of a merger.

To many inside Nissan, Saikawa was part of the problem, not the solution.

"In the morning he would be very aggressively protecting Nissan, and in the evening, he would say we can't fight against Renault," one former Nissan executive from the nationalist camp said of him. "From the beginning to the end, Saikawa never clarified himself. That was one of the reasons why we couldn't trust Saikawa."

Yet as Saikawa was still CEO, he envisioned a road to redemption through fixing the corporate governance problems that bedeviled Nissan. He would inject transparency and accountability, fortify oversight, revive the company's tumbling profits, and reset shattered relations with Renault. In short, Saikawa, already nearing retirement by early 2019, at age sixty-five, would save Nissan from its biggest crisis in twenty years. He would then hand over Nissan to a next-generation CEO and sail into a golden sunset.

Or at least that was Saikawa's plan.

. . .

Nissan's governance task force came back with its report on the Ghosn scandal in March 2019. The committee painted a scathing picture of Ghosn as a tyrant who ruled over a dysfunctional Nissan as his personal fiefdom. It exposed what it said were nebulous subsidiaries, forged documents, and shrewdly siloed business units controlled by trusted enforcers. It outlined how Ghosn allegedly maneuvered with few checks or balances in a world of rubber-stamp board meetings and lapdog auditors.

The report, compiled over the course of several months—but without interviews of Ghosn or Kelly—said Ghosn lacked "ethics as a manager" and maintained that the "root cause of the misconduct was the concentration of all authority in Mr. Ghosn."[1]

Until June 2018, when Nissan finally appointed its first independent outside directors, board meetings averaged less than twenty minutes long, it claimed. Ghosn disliked entertaining questions or other people's opinions, and he was prone to sidelining "fastidious" auditors, the report found. Subsidiaries such as Nissan-Mitsubishi BV (NMBV), the Netherlands-based subsidiary between Nissan and Mitsubishi, or Zi-A Capital BV, the startup seeder that actually paid for Ghosn's housing, operated as black boxes whose inner workings were hidden to outsiders. The CEO Reserve, the source of the suspect fund flows—the so-called Saudi and Omani Routes—to the Middle East, was opaque at best, it said, even though Ghosn said it required multiple sign-offs and was not a personal checking account.

"Mr. Ghosn was in a way deified within Nissan as a savior who had redeemed Nissan from collapse, and his activities were deemed impenetrable territory within the company," the thirty-two-page report said. Its conclusion: Nissan suffered from a "corporate culture in which no one can make any objections to Mr. Ghosn."

The committee recommended a complete revamp of Nissan's corporate structure to improve transparency and oversight. Among the suggestions was abolishing the contentious CEO Reserve fund and creating a position of a non-executive chairman. The board of directors would still have a chairman, but the person would be a director in charge of running the meetings, not wielding sway over wider operations in the company, as Ghosn had.

"At Nissan, one person had doubled as the head of management and the head of the supervisory body. But we have concluded that such a structure led to the wrongdoing," a governance task force cochair said at the time. "Nissan's chairman used to wear two hats, but we recommend that this should be abolished and the head of company management should be CEO and the head of the supervisory body be the board chair. These two roles should be separated."[2]

The report also recommended that a reconstituted board should consist of a majority of outside, independent directors, also something new. At the time, Nissan had nine directors, but only three were considered "outside," and one of those was a former Renault executive. Nissan got its first truly independent directors only in June 2018, just months before Ghosn's arrest. But one was a professional race car driver and the other was Masakazu Toyoda, a veteran of the Ministry of Economy, Trade and

Industry (METI). Both were initially dismissed as toothless Ghosn puppets, though they later emerged as some of his harshest critics.

If Ghosn had been expecting Toyoda to be a self-effacing former bureaucrat who was happy to pick up some director's fees in his retirement, he may have sorely miscalculated.

The former METI official had been the key player in many high-profile wrangles, going head-to-head with his Washington counterparts in the highly contentious US-Japan trade disputes of the 1980s and '90s, many of which revolved around Japanese auto exports. He was directing international policy planning a decade before Ghosn even landed in Japan.

Known for his un-Japanese bluntness, Toyoda rose to vice minister, the most senior rank open to nonpolitical appointees. "Anyone who worked with Toyoda knows that once he grabs onto an issue, he will not let go," one former colleague said.

In retrospect, Ghosn realized too late that he may have gotten more than he bargained for, saying in his 2020 book[3] he saw Toyoda as a key tactician in the conspiracy against him and that his postretirement job at Nissan was little more than an espionage mission on behalf of the ministry. Within the group of alleged plotters, Ghosn wrote, "Toyoda was undoubtedly the brain."

. . .

At the time, Nissan's board included statutory auditors. Theoretically, the lead statutory auditor can be the most powerful person in the company, wielding the authority to demand answers and insight on any inquiry. But in practice, the position is normally the preserve of loyal company insiders who are appointed as a kind of reward for their service. With so much vested in the company's old-boy network, these auditors rarely have the temerity to rock the boat with their longtime colleagues. In Nissan's case, Hidetoshi Imazu was named statutory auditor in 2014 after serving as a director since 2007. The veteran engineer joined way back in 1972; he was sixty-nine when the Ghosn scandal broke.

Not surprisingly, Nissan's task force found that the statutory auditor system failed to flag wrongdoing earlier, partly because it lacked true autonomy. So the task force recommended a new structure of separate committees handling corporate auditing, executive nominations, and executive compensation. These committees should also be dominated by independent, outside directors. Nissan had no outside committee selecting top executives or scrutinizing their pay. Such decisions, the task force found, were funneled through Ghosn, who even had latitude over his own remuneration. Conventional wisdom now dictated that system be torn down.

Even in Japan, the generous leeway allowed Ghosn in deciding executive pay, including his own, was out of step with convention, said Ben Garton, research manager for the Board Director Training Institute of Japan, which advises on corporate governance and compliance at Japanese companies. What really stood out was the gap between Ghosn's pay and that awarded his lieutenants.

"It's extraordinarily rare to see one person getting so much more than everyone else. And that's the situation that can happen if you leave it to one person," Garton said. "That in particular made Carlos Ghosn anathema. That was what really ended up pushing people's buttons."

During the trial of Greg Kelly, Ghosn's alleged enabler, testimony from one of the plea bargainers recounted how Ghosn had a habit of crossing out his own pay figures on salary spreadsheets and adjusting them upward or downward, seemingly on a whim.

"Mr. Ghosn was deciding all executive compensation. He was the only one making the decisions, and that's a fact," Nissan independent director Keiko Ihara—the professional race car driver turned board member bigwig—told *Automotive News* after Ghosn's arrest. "As a listed company, this is what's irregular."

. . .

The lack of a compensation committee, in particular, stood in stark contrast to the setups at many of the US companies Ghosn liked to benchmark his own pay package against. Following stricter US compliance guidelines, for example, General Motors, the company at which Ghosn once said he could make much more money, has an executive compensation committee and devotes more than thirty pages of its annual proxy reports to detailing its executive remuneration plans. Even Renault had a compensation committee, which exercised tight control over pay—especially the CEO's. Ghosn's fixed-compensation was capped at just €1 million ($1.18 million) in his final year, though variable compensation add-ons pushed his total package much higher. The French government, as Renault's biggest shareholder, was careful to avoid any impression that a state-backed enterprise was enriching corporate fat cats.

Nissan's governance task force turned an uncomfortable spotlight on the culture clash between Japan's traditional top-down style of corporate governance and the more transparent Western style it now recommended adopting. And it triggered a showdown over which way to go, as an energized Saikawa pledged to push through the reforms.

Experts in corporate compliance said changes were a long time coming, but that Nissan was hardly alone in grappling with the poor governance. All of Japan Inc., with its clubby keiretsu-driven cross-holdings, inward emphasis on executive control, and ambivalence toward shareholder rights, has long been at odds with US and European ways.

Executives from Renault, in particular, long looked askance at Nissan's standards, with some saying it was a system ripe for misuse and exploitation. Lax or ambiguous guidelines from such Japanese bodies as the Tokyo Stock Exchange created more weak links.

One Renault finance officer recounted how former Nissan president Yoshikazu Hanawa and former Renault CEO Louis Schweitzer, the two men who engineered the initial partnership between the two companies back in 1999, took the stage together during a media event at New York's Waldorf Astoria Hotel. A Japanese analyst there asked Hanawa for details on the consolidated net financial indebtedness of Nissan.

"He couldn't answer the question; Schweitzer had to answer it for him," said the former Renault executive, who worked at both companies under Ghosn. "He had no clue because the Tokyo Stock Exchange did not require consolidated accounts. They required parent company–only accounts. It was very loose from a numbers point of view, and it was then also very loose from a corporate governance point of view, because you had no independent auditors, or independent outside directors. And there was no third-party oversight.

"I was in the finance department when I arrived at Nissan, and I was just absolutely appalled at the state of their really antiquated systems," the executive said. "It was a completely different universe. Japan was very, very loose, in terms of controls."

Japanese regulators did finally recommend—in the early 2000s—that companies switch to the international three-committee governance setup in a bid to align the country with global standards and stoke foreign investment in Japan. In the United States, for example, the multi-committee system is a requirement of stock exchange listing rules, and committee members must all be independent.[4]

But as often happens in Japan, change was slow to take hold.

By 2020, a mere 65 of the 2,125 companies listed on the First Section of the Tokyo Stock Exchange had adopted the international committee structure that Nissan was poised to adopt under the task force's recommendation, according to data from the Board Director Training Institute of Japan. For their part, Nissan and Alliance partner Mitsubishi were among those that switched to three committees, but only after being stained by the stigma of the Ghosn scandal.

"It's the only structure that ensures proper compliance within the corporate governance code," Zuhair Khan, a corporate governance watcher and managing director at the Swiss bank Union Bancaire Privée in Tokyo, said of the three-committee approach. He added that it is the gold standard in the United States, where many companies have even adopted a fourth so-called risk committee to prepare for the unexpected, anything from market shocks to corporate fraud. "Nissan, in essence, has been forced to adopt it."

. . .

To much fanfare in the country, Japan also introduced a new corporate governance code in 2015 that required companies to carry at least two independent directors, in a bid to improve oversight and transparency. In the United States and Europe, independent directors are valued as autonomous third-party checks on the performance of the executives running the company and as guardians of shareholder interests. Japan Inc., however, was predisposed to giving the executives in charge of daily operations a freer hand—they were, after all, the experts fully immersed in the nitty-gritty of the business.

Japan also puts more faith in company founders—and their families—for having the incentive, if not the raw talent and know-how, to do what's right for their companies in the long run. Masayoshi Son, the founder of Japanese mobile phone and technology company SoftBank, the first purveyor of the Apple iPhone in Japan, keeps his hand on the wheel after nearly four decades. Tadashi Yanai founded the company that became Japan's answer to the US casual clothes chain the Gap. Even after turning seventy, Yanai still reported to work at 6:30 A.M. every day, directly calling the shots at Fast Retailing and its hip, ubiquitous UNIQLO stores, as chairman, president, and CEO. Shareholders are in no hurry to show him the door.

Japan's auto industry also has its share of family affairs. Osamu Suzuki famously married into the company's namesake family, adopted the surname, assumed the helm, and handed control to his own son, continuing the Suzuki dynasty. And Akio Toyoda, grandson of Toyota Motor's founder, was anointed president of Japan's biggest automaker in 2009. Akio's father, uncle, and even his grandfather's cousin all preceded him with their own terms as president. The Toyoda family managed to keep this outsized influence over the company for decades, even though Akio and his father are believed to own less than 1 percent of its stock in recent years.[5] Akio's own son has entered the company, fueling speculation about the next generation.

But Prime Minister Shinzo Abe, trying to reboot Japan's moribund economy in the 2010s through a policy initiative dubbed "Abenomics," decided a dose of international accountability might help jumpstart corporate performance. Among the reforms, regulators also called for slashing the cross-shareholdings that had long tied Japanese companies together in elaborate, sometimes inefficient, keiretsu groups. One key initiative was the new rule requiring more independent directors on Japanese boards.

Almost overnight, it sparked a cottage industry of non-Japanese businesspeople in Japan peddling their services as a way for companies to imbue boards with international perspective and diversity. Female directors were especially prized, under another Abe initiative, called "Womenomics," to bolster female participation in the workforce.

Toyota broke the mold by appointing its most diverse board to date in 2018, a group of directors that included one Japanese woman and two non-Japanese. One of the non-Japanese directors was the accomplished British wheelchair basketball athlete Philip Craven, who was a former president of the International Paralympic Committee. Toyota explained the choice of Craven as supporting the company's sponsorship of the 2020 Tokyo Olympics and its bid to promote "Mobility for All" through the development of self-driving vehicles.[6]

Japanese companies cast far and wide for new directors, sometimes into the pool of candidates with not-so-obvious management credentials. A Japanese noodle restaurant chain appointed a female Japanese television anchor. Japanese electronics giant Fujitsu added Japan's first female astronaut. Nissan's selection of race car driver Keiko Ihara was outside the box, though she proved a steely leader in the wake of the Ghosn scandal as an outspoken voice for change.[7] Critics chided that the new trend was mere window dressing and that seeking diversity for diversity's sake added little to qualified, well-informed corporate oversight.

. . .

Still, corporate Japan found board diversity easier to swallow than many of the other governance reforms being trotted out. In 2010, only 13 percent of companies listed on the First Section of the Tokyo Stock Exchange had two or more outside directors. In 2015, after the reform, 48 percent had them. By 2019, more than 90 percent did.[8] The new code was also credited with pushing Nissan to name its first independent directors. But Nissan did so only in 2018, three years after the new measures took effect.

Shareholder activists called Japan's reforms a step in the right direction, toward more accountable, US-style corporate governance. But the new rules also lacked teeth. If a Japanese company didn't appoint independent directors, for instance, it was merely required to explain its decision in its filings.

A classic example of Japan's aptitude for adapting without real change.

Meanwhile, in the United States, most big, publicly traded companies had boards in which the independent directors comprised the *majority* of seats, and had since landmark accounting scandals toppled telecom company WorldCom and energy giant Enron in the early 2000s. In Japan, even with Abenomics rules in effect, fewer than 100 of the top 1,800 traded companies have a majority of independent directors, estimates Aki Matsumoto, a corporate governance expert and executive director of Metrical Inc. in Tokyo.

At the same time, Matsumoto says that some 90 percent of Japanese companies are still led by an executive who simultaneously holds the positions of CEO and chairman, the toxic combination cited as a primary failure at Nissan because of the potential conflicts of interest and over-concentration of power. He estimates that in the United States, some 60 percent of board chairs are also CEOs, and the ratio falls even further in Europe, where it's customary for chairpersons to come from outside.

In Matsumoto's assessment of corporate governance, no Japanese automaker gets an A grade. Toyota, Honda, and Isuzu score highest with Bs; Nissan, despite having the highest ratio of independent directors among its Japanese rivals, gets a B–.

Even after Nissan's reforms, critics still poked at lingering weaknesses, saying that some independent directors lacked proper business qualifications and training, or were stretched thin in their responsibilities because of positions at other companies. The newly appointed American independent director Jenifer Rogers, for example, was concurrently a director at three other companies, including Kawasaki Heavy Industries and the trading house Mitsui & Co.

. . .

With the governance reform task force recommendations in hand and Abenomics reforms taking hold, Saikawa championed a sweeping overhaul of Nissan's corporate governance at the annual shareholders' meeting in June 2019. The proposed changes came straight from the committee report. The vote, a major step in Saikawa's plan to rehabilitate the embattled company before retiring, was scheduled shortly after Nissan upended Fiat Chrysler Automobiles (FCA)'s proposed merger with Renault by abstaining from backing the deal. It looked like smooth sailing. But Renault had other plans. The French carmaker, still stinging from its failed FCA overture, hit back at Nissan by saying it would in turn abstain from backing Saikawa's reforms, just two weeks before the shareholder's meeting. Nissan was infuriated.

On the surface, it looked like petty tit-for-tat. But the crux, again, was Renault's representation at Nissan, this time on the three new governing committees. Renault wanted guaranteed seats on the new bodies, which were designed to be filled and chaired by independent directors, so as to be free from of managerial influence. The demand threatened to derail a signature Saikawa achievement. But through some last-minute wrangling, the sides compromised. Renault leaders Senard and Bolloré were allowed seats on two Nissan committees—Senard on nomination, Bolloré on audit.[9]

With the path finally cleared, shareholders passed the sweeping reforms.

Saikawa, as controversial as he was in some corners, was also kept on as CEO—for the time being at least—and said he would take a 50 percent pay cut to atone for the Ghosn scandal. He celebrated the vote as an important "personal" victory in making things right at Nissan and then turned his eye to the next challenge: succession.

"I am reaching a big milestone personally in terms of fulfilling my responsibility," Saikawa said at the 2019 shareholders' meeting where investors approved his overhaul. "We need to think about the future of the company and succession plan, preparation for that, and be ready for the next step . . . In order to fulfill my remaining responsibilities, I would like to focus on and prepare the successors."[10]

Over the course of the summer of 2019, Saikawa also focused on reviving Nissan's collapsing business and rehabilitating rattled relations with Renault. His goal was to wrap up those loose strings by late 2019 or early 2020 and hand off to a successor by the end of the fiscal year finishing

March 31, 2020. He wanted the new nomination committee to come up with a list of candidates in September.

"I had a lot of homework to do," Saikawa recalled.

. . .

First came reviving Nissan's business. Saikawa had proclaimed that Nissan's performance had hit "rock bottom" after the company reported a 45 percent slide in quarterly operating profit in early 2019, but it hadn't. Nissan still had a long way to fall. In the following quarter, operating profit plunged an amazing 99 percent. Taking a page from Ghosn's cost-cutter playbook, Saikawa announced a plan to slash 12,500 jobs worldwide to restore operating profit margin from a meager 2.7 percent to 6 percent by March 2023.[11] He planned to shutter "loss-making overseas factories" to reel in bloated production capacity. At the time, Nissan was using only 69 percent of its worldwide factory firepower; the unused capacity simply racked up red ink. The goal was to boost factory utilization to a more respectable 86 percent.

Meanwhile, Saikawa secretly reengaged Senard to negotiate the future direction of the Alliance. Talks included reviving the failed merger with Fiat Chrysler Automobiles (Alliance leaders were still unaware that FCA had diverted its gaze to Renault's rival, PSA Group). Saikawa would demand details about how a renewed merger push would affect Nissan. He also explored rebalancing the cross-shareholdings between Renault and Nissan. One idea was selling down Renault's stake in Nissan to under 30 percent, possibly as low as 5 to 10 percent, a level deemed healthy under the Japanese government's new guidelines. In Saikawa's view, as long as the stake was below an effective 33 percent, the threshold for exercising control over a Japanese company, it would suffice. A friendly shareholder would ideally step in to buy that stake from Renault. If there were any rebalancing, Saikawa wanted to settle it quickly, before turning the focus to FCA.

. . .

Unknown to Saikawa as he was exploring all this, finding common ground with Renault would be the least of his hurdles. Inside Nissan, a faction of old-guard executives was maneuvering against him, the man they still considered the ultimate Ghosn Child. And ironically, they found their ammunition against Saikawa in the Ghosn misconduct report Saikawa himself commissioned.

After the task force's governance report was submitted, Nissan's own internal team continued investigating alleged misconduct. And it got a big tip-off on some juicy affairs when Greg Kelly, the American director and Ghosn lieutenant who was arrested with Ghosn, agreed to speak with Japan's *Bungei Shunju* news magazine. In a bombshell interview, Kelly alleged that Saikawa improperly manipulated a stock price-linked bonus system at Nissan to boost his payout by more than $400,000.

Nissan's internal team investigated, and Kelly was right. Through the falsification of the exercise date of the so-called share appreciation rights, a kind of stock option also known as SARs, to appear a week earlier than the actual exercise date, Saikawa was able to net an additional ¥47 million ($446,000). What's more, the internal investigation's findings were leaked to Japanese journalists before they were formally reported to Nissan's board, piling pressure on Saikawa to step down.

By the September 9, 2019, board meeting in which the internal investigative committee's findings were formally reported, Nissan's outside directors had had enough. They forced Saikawa to resign and announced he would step down as CEO within two weeks. Saikawa said he found that "a bit early" and tried to negotiate staying on longer—maybe several more months—until a successor could be named. But the board didn't yield, saying it was better to make a clean, fast break, drolly adding "We see issues around Mr. Saikawa."[12] They aimed to name a new CEO by the end of October. There would be no ride into the sunset for Saikawa.

Many following the saga now thought Saikawa was no better than Ghosn. But there were some differences. For starters, Saikawa was not accused of criminal action, as Ghosn had been. The misuse of share appreciation rights, the task force said, didn't violate the law, simply the company's own ethics policy. Thus, it was argued, there was no need to prosecute him. (Nissan ditched the use of SARs as part of its corporate governance reform. But in 2020, it brought back another stock-based incentive plan christened "restricted stock units.")[13]

Moreover, Saikawa wasn't alone in gaming the system this way. According to the task force, Ghosn had done the same thing, raking in ¥140 million ($1.3 million) in excess of what he should have received—an amount nearly triple Saikawa's stock award. Kelly also supposedly benefited from backdated share appreciation rights—to the tune of ¥7 million ($65,000). Two former directors and four other current or former executive officers also rigged their own stock payouts.

That list of others who improperly received overpayments, according to people familiar with the details, included plea bargainer Hari Nada. He supposedly derived a benefit approaching $300,000. But Nada, befitting his persona as the ultimate survivor, miraculously kept his job after being deemed not senior enough to warrant public sanction. That move only crystalized the view, among critics, that Nissan still faced huge compliance issues.

In the end, no one faced prosecution for these infractions. In any case, Saikawa agreed to pay it all back, which, in his eyes at least, was more than what Ghosn or Kelly did.

Saikawa was snared by his own misconduct. But inside Nissan, resentment and resistance had been building against him since Ghosn's arrest. Many lost faith in his leadership as Nissan's sales and profits spiraled down. Some top brass were peeved by the revelation that Saikawa had gone behind their back for clandestine negotiations with Senard about FCA. And others simply thought he should have stepped down at the beginning of the Ghosn scandal, to take responsibility for being the tainted chairman's loyal enforcer for so long.

In the end, even employees were becoming disillusioned with the company.

"You don't see a plan at Nissan. You just see a lot of bad behavior," said one former executive who eventually left amid the tumult. "If you can't trust people on corporate governance, how can you trust them to build the car you're going to put your family in? Do you really want to take a gamble with your family? Or are you just going to be done with it and buy a Volvo?"

. . .

The leadership upheaval reinforced the image of a rudderless Nissan. And it saddled the company with the weighty decision of picking a new CEO at a time when executives needed to be focused on turning its business around. Nissan's already razor-thin operating profit plunged another 70 percent in the July–September quarter of 2019. The beleaguered company had somehow managed to crash through Saikawa's "rock bottom." Being leaderless also complicated any meaningful breakthroughs in the relationship with Renault.

And besides, Renault was having its own problems in the C-suite.

In October 2020, perhaps sensing an opening with Saikawa's removal, Renault CEO and longtime Ghosn loyalist Thierry Bolloré renewed his questioning about the possible conflicts of interest in having Nada and the law firm Latham & Watkins conduct Nissan's internal investigation of the Ghosn affair. Nada, after all, had been implicated in the alleged wrongdoing, and the law firm advised Nissan in the past on the various compensation schemes under scrutiny. Latham & Watkins declined to comment, citing client confidentiality, but stood by its position that there was no conflict of interest in its work with Nissan or bias in its investigation.

. . .

Bolloré wrote a ten-page letter dated October 8 to the Nissan board, rattling off a long list of questions about the propriety of Nissan's investigation. "In particular, considering Mr. Nada's personal involvement in the Ghosn-related executive misconduct and the widely reported fact that he has entered into a plea bargain with the JPPO [Japan Public Prosecutors Office], who decided that he was qualified to become or remain a member of the Nissan Compliance Office?" Bolloré asked. "How is it possible that Mr. Nada continues to hold a senior corporate officer position within Nissan?" Bolloré added that he received an anonymous letter from a Nissan whistle-blower just the month before reporting "concerns about ongoing 'fraud and misconduct'" on the part of Nada and fellow plea bargainer Ohnuma.

Bolloré was hardly alone in raising red flags. Ravinder Passi, Nissan's then global general counsel and a direct report to Nada, also wrote the board raising concern about Nada's handling of the internal investigation. Passi was ignored and eventually transferred to Nissan's UK affiliate, an effective demotion. After Passi filed a labor complaint alleging whistle-blower retaliation, he was fired. Passi then made a second complaint against the company, where he had worked for some sixteen years, rising to one of its lead lawyers. Nada's 2017 video appeal for employees to speak up about misconduct seemed to have an asterisk when it came to impugning his own conduct.

Only at the Nissan board meeting held October 8, 2019, was Nada finally moved off legal affairs and made an "adviser." As head of Legal, it's perhaps not surprising he won a clean bill of health in the wide-ranging audit ordered by Nissan. "Nissan has found no evidence of inappropriate involvement by Nada in the internal investigation into executive misconduct led by former Chairman Carlos Ghosn and others," the company said in a press release announcing his job change. It added that Nada needed to focus on "forthcoming legal action," which presumably involved explaining to the Tokyo District Court just how he turned from rooting out corporate fraud to serving as a government witness.

It is doubtful Bolloré ever got satisfactory answers to any of his queries. Reports immediately began circulating that Senard intended to fire him.[14] And just three days after Bolloré wrote the Nissan board, he was summarily dismissed by Renault. Bolloré denounced his removal as a coup and called it "totally unexpected" and "stupefying."[15]

It marked an important moment in the Alliance's history. For better or worse, the house cleaning was nearly complete: Both Nissan and Renault were scrubbed of almost every Ghosn-era holdover.

"We started a very tough exercise, which was cleaning, removing a generation of people," said one person close to the Nissan board. "Some of them have left by themselves. Some of them, we had to remove. In

Saikawa's case, it was absolutely necessary. Bolloré too. He was support-ing Ghosn in a way that was supporting people who were implicated in the case. And he didn't realize it himself."

But not every holdover was gone.

Hitoshi Kawaguchi, the executive who served as Nissan's conduit to the Japanese government during the Ghosn probe, lingered on and retired to a hero's send-off in March 2020, with thank-you speeches in the headquarters' front driveway and a crowd of well-wishers. Imazu stepped down as statutory auditor in June 2019 and retired from Nissan in 2020 as well.

Ohnuma stayed on even longer. And so did Hari Nada, who somehow rode out each and every storm to emerge as one of the last men standing. Truth be told, Nissan needed both as key witnesses in the upcoming trial and could ill afford to cut them loose. Prosecutors and Nissan had more leverage if they were still on the payroll.

Still, the Alliance was in disarray and now run by interim leaders. Fiat Chrysler Automobiles merged with PSA Group, and Ghosn openly mocked his successors at Renault and Nissan for botching it.

With Bolloré out, Renault tapped CFO Clotilde Delbos as interim CEO. In mid-2020, former head of Volkswagen Group's SEAT brand Luca de Meo took over. Crucially, de Meo was paid €5 million ($5.6 million) in total compensation, much less than Ghosn's typical €7 million-plus ($7.9 million).[16]

Nissan moved more quickly. Within a month of Saikawa's ouster, it appointed as CEO Makoto Uchida, the head of Nissan's important China division. Uchida was not a Nissan lifer. He joined the company only in 2003, after working at the Japanese trading company Nissho Iwai Corp. He wasn't even widely known within his own company.

Uchida was seen as a compromise candidate, and his appointment was an outgrowth of lingering tensions with Renault. Nissan's old guard fa-vored Jun Seki, then a senior vice president for performance recovery, who was engineering Saikawa's turnaround plan. Another camp—led by Renault—supported Ashwani Gupta, a respected auto veteran from India who rose through the ranks at Datsun and Renault and was then the COO of Alliance partner Mitsubishi. Both had their detractors. Seki, a science and technology graduate from the National Defense Academy of Japan, was seen as a nationalist firebrand by some at Renault. And Gupta was deemed too close to Renault by many at Nissan. Moreover, although Gupta is fluent in Japanese, he was Indian, not a Japanese national. Some Nissan directors insisted that, after the Ghosn debacle, the next CEO must be native. Opposing sides settled on Uchida. But because he was only fifty-three and still inexperienced, Nissan couched his administration as head of a triumvirate. Uchida would be CEO, backed by Gupta as COO and Seki as vice COO.

The trio took office in December 2019, when Saikawa was supposed to be finalizing his triumphant turnaround and succession plan. The three men were left with a long list of leftover "homework" from Saikawa. Nissan's new leaders had to restore profitability, rekindle sales, rebuild trust in the company, and repair relations with Renault.

But before the end of that first month, Seki—apparently still stinging after being passed over—abruptly quit the company after thirty-three years there. Deciding he wanted be president of his own company after all, he jumped ship to Nidec Corp., a Japanese maker of electric motors for everything from robots and drones to refrigerators and washing machines. Seki's mission as Nidec's new leader was to expand into an auto industry priming for electric cars. Many at Nissan lamented his defection as another huge loss of talent and potent leadership.

. . .

At the Kelly trial, Toshiyuki Shiga, a Nissan COO and vice chairman under Ghosn, offered a simple explanation for what went wrong.

"To summarize, there was a failure of corporate governance at Nissan. Carlos Ghosn had changed gradually, and he wouldn't listen to other people," Shiga said. "But those who allowed that to happen share in the responsibility."

Yet through it all, Saikawa was proud and unapologetic.

He saw himself—not unlike how many saw Ghosn—as a victim of Nissan's Japanese old guard, the clique of traditionalists overly protective of their independence and afraid of cozying too close with foreign partners.

"There was still a mixed picture of the company, where you can see one group of people who are very modern, well-accustomed to a global management system, open to diversity, open to an alliance partner, while you also see another group who are not, who are still conservative and less open to newcomers," Saikawa said. "This was more of a problem for me. Some people believed let's go back to before, like in the 1990s, independent or Japanese-centric. These kind of things began popping up. I am a pro-Alliance guy. I wanted to internationalize."

To Saikawa, the removal of Ghosn only emboldened these conservative forces agitating for his termination as part of a scheme to re-Japanize the company. In that sense, Saikawa believed Ghosn damaged Nissan in two ways—first, through his alleged financial misconduct, and then again by shredding the fabric of international cooperation the Alliance had painstakingly tried to knit together over two decades.

Saikawa took the wheel in 2017 and drove head-on into an unprecedented crisis, never before seen in corporate Japan. Nissan was broadsided by the arrest of its onetime savior and longtime boss, Carlos Ghosn, then rocked by the near breakup of its Alliance with Renault, and finally throttled by the blistering collapse of the company's own profits and sales. Saikawa fought French pressure for an "irreversible" merger and then tried to clean up Nissan's moldering corporate governance. But in the end, he was drummed out of the company for ethical lapses exposed by a team he himself formed to find such misdoing. The new outside directors on the new corporate committees that Saikawa himself championed decided Nissan needed a fresh start without him.

To Ghosn, it rained down like divine justice. But Saikawa had few regrets.

"For Nissan, it was good that I was, at that time, in charge. Because it's not easy to properly handle this situation," Saikawa said of his wild ride as CEO before ending his forty-two-year career at Nissan. "I am proud of what I have done. It should be appreciated. Especially in the last year, I did a lot for Nissan. I myself believe I contributed a lot."[17]

16

SCANDALOUS AFFAIRS

JAPAN IS FAMOUS FOR ITS EXCEPTIONALLY LOW CRIME rate, sense of honesty, and high level of morality. In restaurants, there is little need to check the bill, possessions left out in public are never touched, and companies seldom worry about employee theft.

Individual honesty is the stuff of legend, but is also backed up by the data-happy Japanese bureaucracy. The Tokyo Metropolitan Police tracks every single lost item report (4.2 million items in 2019). According to figures from 2019, 153,000 mobile phones were handed in to the police that year, along with 372,000 wallets. Of those, 83 percent of the phones and 65 percent of the wallets got back to their owners. Even more astonishing is the fact that a total of $37 million was turned in to police (with $27 million getting back to the original owner).[1] This is in part a testament to the fact that older Japanese still prefer cash payments, even for business transactions.

While there is less relevant data for corporations, the Association of Certified Fraud Examiners says that in 2016–2017, it investigated 2,690 cases of occupational fraud globally involving companies or employees. Of those, 1,000 were in the United States, while Japan logged just 4.[2] Supporting the notion of strong corporate ethics in Japan, the prestigious

Dow Jones Sustainability World Index shows that Japanese companies rate highly in terms of their commitment to corporate responsibility and ethical behavior.[3]

So, why are there so many corporate scandals, even within some of Japan's biggest and most reputable corporations?

These crises have touched nearly every major industry and some have been serious enough to nearly bring down the company. Electronics group Toshiba was found to have inflated its stated profits over seven years in the wake of the global financial crisis of 2008–2009 to cover up problems. Kobe Steel, known for its advanced materials, was found to have altered quality tests. Other big names have also been found to falsify results, including Toray Industries, a leading maker of carbon fiber. In the financial sector, Long-Term Credit Bank of Japan and Yamaichi Securities Co. both shut down in the difficult business conditions of the post-Bubble 1990s when it was found they had hidden financial losses as the economy worsened.[4]

Even blue chip Toyota faced a scandal in 2009 with scary stories from US customers that its cars could suddenly accelerate for no reason. The focus was on an electronic gas pedal in the view that it had gone haywire (federal regulators said later that they could find little evidence that this had happened).[5] There was also a simpler explanation: the floor mats got in the way and pushed down the accelerator. Some later technical research suggested that the real cause was even more mundane: drivers pushed the gas pedal instead of the brake by mistake and as the car went forward, pushed even harder, thinking it would stop the car.[6]

From a corporate reputational point of view, the damage was done, however. The story tied into people's fears of computer-driven machines run amok. Toyota president Akio Toyoda went before a congressional committee (where he deeply apologized in the best Japanese tradition). The problem didn't stop there, however. A separate issue over a mechanical defect in some gas pedals emerged. As Toyota tried to cover it up, the US Department of Justice launched a massive probe, resulting in an acceptance by the company in 2014 that it had misled consumers.[7] Toyota paid out what was then a record $1.2 billion to settle the charges. US District Judge William Pauley said the case presented a "reprehensible picture of corporate misconduct."[8]

But the biggest global impact, and therefore arguably the biggest damage to the reputation of Japanese industry, came at Takata, a world leader in airbags. The company neglected internal warnings about the safety of its airbags, which could cause injuries from metal shards when activated. After an initial recall involving just four thousand vehicles in 2008, the numbers mounted over the years as more problems emerged.[9] By 2015, it had become the largest auto-related recall in history.

A key issue was that the company seemed unable to understand the full scope of the problem, with recalls continuing in waves as more issues came to light. In all, an estimated 100 million airbags were recalled, with the process still continuing into 2020. This was three years after Takata, facing massive potential lawsuits, filed for bankruptcy, with its assets sold to a Chinese competitor. The company had agreed in 2017 to pay $1 billion in US fines over the issue and three senior executives were indicted in federal court in Michigan on charges of knowingly covering up the problems. All were by then back in Japan with extradition prospects uncertain.[10]

Alliance partner Mitsubishi Motors is also no stranger to scandal. In 2016, the company was hit with a scandal over falsification of fuel economy standards. The disclosure of the false data, which went back twenty-five years, forced the resignation of the president and triggered a 35 percent fall in the share price. It was far from the first time that the company had been in trouble. In 2000, it had suffered serious reputational damage after admitting that it had for twenty years covered up a range of defects involving brakes, clutches, and fuel tanks. Other cover-ups were later found. As one news report noted at the time of the fuel scandal, "when it comes to the art of public mea culpas, few companies can top scandal-prone Mitsubishi Motors Corp."[11]

. . .

One of the reasons cited for these serial cover-ups and subsequent scandals is the narrow viewpoint of employees who live in the world of their lifetime employer. "The key issue is that lifetime employees live in a small society that has all the same types of people," remarked Kazuhiko Toyama, a Tokyo-based management consultant. "They care more about what is happening within a five-meter radius than common sense outside of it."[12]

One foreigner who knows this phenomenon well is Michael Woodford, former CEO of camera and medical equipment maker Olympus Corp. Like Ghosn, Woodford was a foreign CEO for a Japanese company immersed in a scandal, but rather than a participant in alleged wrongdoing, he was the whistle-blower. Woodford had risen through the ranks of Olympus in Japanese style, starting as a salesman in his native United Kingdom in 1981 and thirty years later catapulting in quick succession to be chief operating officer in April 2011 and then CEO just months later in October of that year. His new role was short-lived, however. Just two weeks after his appointment, he was ousted by a vote of the board. His removal came shortly after he had started to question hidden losses of $1.6 billion in speculative investments.

At the center of the scandal were outsized payments to offshore-based investment bankers who had worked on the company's $2 billion purchase of the British surgical products company Gyrus in 2008. Such fees are normally 1 to 2 percent of a deal's value, but in this case Olympus had paid a total of $687 million, one-third of the total purchase price. It later emerged that the payments, along with other questionable transactions, were a subterfuge. The money was being funneled offshore into secret Olympus accounts that had posted huge losses when the company had speculated in the global money markets in the 1980s and 1990s. Since they were offshore, the company did not need to publicly admit to the losses or subtract them from the company's overall earnings—that is, until the regulations were changed in the late 1990s.[13]

Woodford had started to question the Gyrus fees when he was head of European operations. Despite his pointed questions to senior management, he was soon promoted, to become corporate CEO in 2011. His appointment had itself been something of a mystery since he was relatively low on the corporate ladder, was based far from headquarters, and spoke limited Japanese.

According to Woodford, it became clear that his appointment was engineered by his predecessor Tsuyoshi Kikukawa, who intended to keep controlling the company from his new position as chairman. The foreigner Woodford was expected to play the role of an assenting junior and keep quiet about the financial fraud. This proved to be a major miscalculation on the part of Kikukawa, as Woodford continued to delve into the company's failed speculative investments. The chairman had only compounded his mistakes by persuading a compliant board to fire Woodford, who later called the meeting "an eight-minute corporate execution."[14]

The company tried to claim that Woodford was dismissed because of a difference in management styles. "Michael C. Woodford has largely diverted from the rest of the management team in regard to the management direction and method, and it is now causing problems for decision making by the management team," Olympus said in a press release a few days after his ouster.[15] This was certainly true since the company at that point seem convinced it could continue to engage in an illegal cover-up. In one bit of spite that would underscore the company's arrogance, the Olympus official charged with retrieving Woodford's company-issued items after the board vote told him he could take the bus to the airport to leave the country.

Woodford had his own ideas. He told his story to the *Financial Times* newspaper, and soon fled Japan over concerns for his safety given the potential criminal links in some of the transactions. His next stop was Britain's Serious Fraud Office, which agreed to take up the case, given the UK links via Gyrus. It was soon joined by the FBI and Japan's Financial Services Agency, which also launched their own investigations based on Woodford's evidence.

Olympus meanwhile staked out an unequivocal position, stating in no uncertain terms that everything was fine. It said that "the past acquisitions mentioned in the media were handled with the appropriate evaluation and procedures . . . These transactions were in no way improper and we are setting up an external panel of experts to examine and report on this acquisitions activity."[16] It is not clear if anyone responsible for all this saw the irony of announcing in the same breath that the transactions were completely legitimate and would also be investigated by an outside panel of experts.

At the same time, Olympus knew who was to blame for all the problems: "The disruption to business and loss of corporate value are truly regrettable and the company will consider taking legal action against him [Woodford] if this is deemed to be necessary." The company issued a series of questionable statements to justify the acquisitions, arguing that there was some sort of synergy between a manufacturer of containers for microwave ovens and the company's hospital equipment business (both are aimed at health, it implausibly argued). This finger-pointing and questionable PR did not fool investors. Even as the company said all was well, the share price plunged 81 percent in six weeks.

The independent report commissioned by the company, which emerged less than two months after Woodford's ouster, was no less scathing.[17] Filling 200 pages, it showed that Woodford had been right all along. A small group of executives at the very top had undertaken a series of highly speculative investments from the early 1980s. As markets went against them, the valuation losses piled up. At the same time, previously lax Japanese accounting rules were becoming stricter, making it more difficult to hide the growing deficits. The leadership group had used a group of somewhat shadowy investment bankers, who built a series of shell companies, mainly in the Cayman Islands.

"The core part of the management was rotten, and that contaminated other parts around it . . ." the panel concluded. It recommended that the board directors "who processed the problematic case [of firing Woodford] with a short 15-minute meeting should also be replaced at the appropriate timing." By this time Kikukawa and two other senior executives had already left the company and would soon be on their way to the Japanese courts, where they would eventually plead guilty to charges of abetting the crimes.

In the end, Olympus had to restate its earnings for a five-year period, resulting in a write-off totaling ¥123.25 billion ($1.58 billion).[18] The company pleaded guilty in the fraud and was fined ¥700 million ($7 million) in 2013, a relatively small penalty for a fraud of that scale. Kikukawa and the other executives involved were all given suspended sentences for fraud, with the judge noting that none of those responsible had actually gained personally. Kikukawa's good luck was due to run out, however. In 2017, he and seven other executives were found liable in a civil suit brought by Olympus. In a higher court judgment in 2019, Kikukawa and two others were ordered to pay a combined ¥59.4 billion ($543 million) related to the scandal.[19]

For Olympus as a company, there would be more tribulations ahead. In a US case in 2016, the company admitted to paying illegal kickbacks to help promote the sale of its endoscopes, agreeing to pay a penalty of $646 million.[20] The incident was another demonstration of the dangers of Japanese companies doing business overseas. Although such actions would technically be illegal in Japan, they are not treated as seriously as in the United States, and the company would not likely face such massive fines.

The company did eventually clean up its practices, however, and has emerged as a solid advocate of corporate governance, going well beyond the cursory measures to improve governance seen at Nissan under Ghosn and many other Japanese companies. A clear sign of this came in 2019 when the company abandoned the traditional Japanese tactic of opposing activist shareholders (who almost always come from overseas). Olympus agreed to give US hedge fund ValueAct Capital a seat on its board and launch a transformation program being promoted by the fund.[21] The decision to back the outsiders proved an immediate hit with investors, with the stock price rising 10 percent on the day of the announcement. For long-term investors, that made the company one of the best buys around. By the end of 2019, Olympus shares were up 1,369 percent from their 2011 low amid the scandal.

The seemingly reckless actions by the Olympus team could be understood, at least in terms of its broader goals. Having seen its core business face the new problems of a post-Bubble economic environment, it looked for a quick-fix solution rather than trying to take a scalpel to its core operations. This brought Kikukawa and his predecessors into the equivalent of get-rich-quick schemes, with the chances for big gains, as always, offset by the equal chances of huge losses.

They were, of course, abetted in all this by the investment bankers who at first proposed the deals with rosy scenarios of big profits and then continued to "help" by creating offshore funds to hide the problems.

Despite their central role, the most senior bankers were never brought to trial for any wrongdoing. One of the prime figures in the case, Hajime Sagawa, a former Nomura banker who later set up his own business in

New York and also lived in Boca Raton, Florida, did get caught up in the investigation by the US Securities and Exchange Commission (SEC). In settling the charges, the SEC barred him from the securities business for life (at the age of sixty-seven) but imposed no financial penalties. "In determining to accept the Offer, the Commission considered the cooperation Respondent afforded the Commission staff," the SEC said in its court filing.[22] It did not elaborate. A banker with Japan's Nomura Securities, who allegedly played a minor role and disputed the charges against him, was convicted along with two subordinates.

Olympus's accountants also avoided any sanctions in the case, despite a failure to uncover the problems that Woodford was able to expose. The independent report cleared the two firms, saying that "the masterminds of this case were hiding the illegal acts by artfully manipulating experts' opinions,"[23] a somewhat backhanded compliment to the apparent skill of those responsible for the scandal.

The Olympus scandal was also notable for the role played—or not played—by the Japanese media. The fraud first emerged via reports in a small Japanese investigative magazine called *Facta*, whose editor was a former editor at *Nikkei*, Japan's largest financial daily newspaper. As is often the case in Japan, mainstream media ignored the story, sticking to the company's line that it was all rumor and gossip. It was not until the *Financial Times* and other foreign media started their reporting that the *Nikkei* and other Japanese newspapers started to dig into the story. Gaiatsu pressure affects a wide range of institutions in Japan.

Although the Olympus affair was one of the highest-profile scandals in recent Japanese history, it was nothing compared to the Ghosn Shock. The two events share similar root causes, however. At both Olympus and Nissan, a powerful chairman was able to push through actions that should have been questioned by a truly independent board of directors. In the case of Olympus, a board ousted a newly appointed CEO with no questions asked on the instructions of an imperious chairman. In the case of Nissan, the board was similarly acquiescent, rubber-stamping Ghosn's requests without much of a look under the hood. In fact, one of Ghosn's primary defenses for the various changes in compensation rules and creation of offshore companies was that the board had approved everything.

Both scandals also demonstrated the PR risks of strong statements that could come back to haunt a company. When Olympus was confident it could get rid of Woodford, it felt free to declare that he was responsible for the company's problems and threatened legal action against him.[24] Similarly, Nissan's PR department made the implausibly bold statement in April 2019 that "The sole cause of this chain of events is the misconduct led by Ghosn and Kelly." Over the coming months, the company itself would plead guilty to charges over its filings to regulators, two senior executives would have to admit they entered into plea-bargain deals with prosecutors, and much of the top team, including then-president Saikawa, would be found to have used improperly dated share-linked incentives to increase their payouts. A good PR department would have counseled more caution in both cases.

But the Ghosn scandal also stands out from the others in one other aspect. In almost all of the corporate scandals that have befallen Japanese companies, the cause is usually a perceived need to cover up something that would damage the company. In none of the cases were those guilty of a cover-up accused of actions that benefited them personally. It was this aspect of the Ghosn affair that played a major role in turning public opinion against the man who had previously rescued one of their corporate titans.

Ironically, scandal had played a role in helping Ghosn to create the three-part Alliance. The Mitsubishi fuel economy crisis began when Nissan (which used Mitsubishi to build some of its cars) blew the whistle on its partner's mileage data falsification. After the scandal emerged in the media, Mitsubishi's shares quickly lost 35 percent of their value. That made it possible for Nissan to purchase a controlling 34 percent stake at a much lower cost, making Ghosn one of the world's top three auto executives in the process.

In the business world, every event—even a scandal—creates winners as well as losers.

17

SHATTERED LEGACY

JUST BEFORE 3:00 P.M. ON FRIDAY, MARCH 11, 2011, AS people across Japan were winding down work for the weekend, the country was ripped from its routine by a massive 9.0-magnitude earthquake. It was the strongest quake ever recorded in the seismically active island nation, a geologic cataclysm so convulsive it shifted parts of northern Japan thirteen feet closer to the United States, tilted Earth's axis, and may have even shortened the length of the day by a couple microseconds.[1]

The violent jolting soon precipitated even more serious worries.

The undersea temblor, centered just offshore from the northern city of Sendai, unleashed a tsunami towering to heights of 130 feet that obliterated everything in its path, far inland, for hundreds of miles up and down the Pacific coast. Worse still, the wall of water swamped Japan's Fukushima Daiichi Nuclear Power Plant, triggering meltdowns at three reactors that spewed radiation over swaths of the countryside.

The earthquake-tsunami-meltdown triple disaster killed more than nineteen thousand people.[2]

It also caused hundreds of billions of dollars of damage and splintered Japan's economic backbone. The calamity shattered the auto industry's intricately interwoven supply chain, throwing plants offline and throttling production for much of the rest of the year. Japan's automakers lost more than 1.5 million vehicles of output at the peak of the crisis.

And the shaking was felt clear across the world—underscoring the fragile, intertwined reality of today's globalized auto industry. Assembly plants in the United States and Europe run by such competitors as General Motors and PSA Group suspended or cut back production because they couldn't get key components from suppliers in Japan. Ford stopped taking orders for certain red and black vehicles because it couldn't get a specialized metallic paint pigment made only in Japan's quake zone. And a worldwide shortage of automotive microchips from Japan brought global auto output to a crawl for months. Carmakers everywhere were in a state of shock and scrambling to preserve their businesses.[3]

But ever-aggressive Carlos Ghosn wouldn't let a killer quake derail his expansion plans. Mere weeks after the tragedy, he was among the first CEOs to venture into the disaster area, despite radiation worries, and survey the damage at Nissan's Iwaki engine plant, where engines were thrown off the production line like toy building blocks and the factory floor sank by as much as four inches. He inspired workers to get it back online, and they did—remarkably by April 18.

Then in June, with "Fukushima" now a byword for the worst nuclear disaster since Chernobyl, relief workers still searching for bodies, and the nation's factories struggling to reboot, Ghosn took the stage to announce what would be his most ambitious business plan for Nissan since reviving the company a decade earlier. He called the six-year roadmap "Power 88," with the eights standing for the dual goals of 8 percent global market share and 8 percent operating profit margin. The plan even had a logo, in the form of wild, stylized brushwork calligraphy for the Chinese character *chou*, which means "challenge" in English.

"Challenge" was apt. The 8 percent market share goal alone, to be attained in six years by the end of March 2017, marked an ambitious leap from the 5.8 percent Nissan held at the time. In textbook Ghosn fashion, every target was quantified. Over the six years, Nissan would introduce fifty-one models and ninety new technologies. Nissan would grab 10 percent market share in the booming China market. The company's upscale Infiniti brand would take 10 percent of the global premium market. Nissan would cut costs by 5 percent each year. And crucially, the Nissan and Infiniti brands would attain a combined market share of 10 percent in the all-important US market, up from 8 percent. Given his forecast for over-all US market growth at the time, that objective implied an amazing 50 percent surge in US sales, to around 1.4 million vehicles from 908,000 in 2010.[4] "Fundamentally, we are optimistic," Ghosn would say of his plan.

Power 88 epitomized Ghosn's vision for the future of the auto industry. The key to success would be mammoth scale, new markets, and new technologies. His blueprint called for rapidly ramping up investment in emerging markets, such as India, Brazil, Mexico, Russia, China, and Southeast Asia, where expanding middle classes would be brimming with new customers racing to buy their first set of wheels. Ghosn expected the balance of Nissan's global business to flip—from 40 percent emerging markets and 60 percent mature markets in 2007 to 60 percent emerging markets in 2017.

In new technologies, Ghosn wanted Nissan and Renault to sell a combined 1.5 million electric vehicles. Nissan and Renault would offer as many as seven new electric vehicles (EVs) in addition to the Leaf, including a luxury all-electric from Infiniti. Later, Ghosn would add autonomous vehicles to his lofty to-do list.

To get there, Nissan would embark on a sweeping building blitz of factories and new assembly lines in China, India, Brazil, Mexico, and Indonesia. Nissan would also revive defunct Datsun as a low-cost entry brand to help it break into new markets. And Nissan would throw into overdrive investment into electric cars in Ghosn's bid to steal an early lead on rivals in this nascent, but costly, technology.

Simply put, Nissan would ascend to the top tier of global automakers—being a true frontrunner in emerging markets, developed markets, the premium segment, and in such new technologies as electric and self-driving cars. And Nissan would pull Renault to the top with it.

"Some may question whether we can achieve all of it," Ghosn said, asserting that his leadership would plow a path to success. "But I stand committed—as I did in 1999, in 2008 and in March 2011 when the earth-quake decimated some of our prized facilities—that we can deliver all the results."[5]

Power 88's audacious vision for expansion—especially against the backdrop of the natural disaster that still crippled the country—stood in bold contrast to the strategy then being pursued by archrival Toyota. In addition to grappling with its own earthquake trauma, Toyota was still reeling from a double whammy of financial losses and unprecedented recalls to fix faulty cars. Akio Toyoda, the scion of the founding family, took over as president in 2009 after the company had slumped to its first full-year operating loss in seventy years. In 2010, Toyota was further humiliated and thrown into crisis after being forced to recall millions of vehicles worldwide to address claims its cars would suddenly accelerate on their own, sometimes with fatal consequences. Toyoda was grilled about the safety of his company's cars during a US Congress committee hearing and made a personal pledge to improve quality. "I am the grandson of the founder, and all the Toyota vehicles bear my name," Toyoda told lawmakers in Washington, DC. "For me, when the cars are damaged, it is as though I am as well."[6]

Toyota's new boss said there was a clear explanation for Toyota's woes. His predecessors had embarked on a hubris-fueled quest to boost global market share to 15 percent. Toyota indeed became the world's biggest automaker, but at a terrible price. Its explosive international growth stressed Toyota's human resources. Its factories swelled with bloated overcapacity, its engineers let quality slide, and the company lost its customer focus. Overstretched, Toyota became vulnerable to economic downturns and was duly hammered when the financial crisis finally hit. It wasn't long before Toyoda was calling for an "intentional pause" on growth. He postponed factory investments for three years, renounced numerical targets, and preached going back to basics. Toyota's fall from grace would prove a prophetic cautionary tale for Nissan, which was stepping on the gas even as its top adversary slammed on the brakes.

. . .

Nissan ended up missing most of the Power 88 goals by the target date of March 2017. But the real reckoning came after Ghosn's arrest, when the scrutiny of his time at Nissan spread far beyond his alleged financial improprieties. When Nissan's stock price plunged, along with its sales and profits, his critics, including the company's new leaders, thought they knew the root cause: Ghosn's relentless worldwide expansion blitz, as exemplified by Power 88. To them, his push for ever-greater volume put Nissan on a collision course with crisis that continued long after he left. Nissan's sagging performance was proof of his folly, they said, and it upended Ghosn's legacy as an industry oracle and empire builder.

Suddenly, in the eyes of many, what Ghosn had really done over the years was stack a house of cards. Now, it was all falling apart.

Hiroto Saikawa was among the first to openly question Ghosn's business strategies. But the chorus was joined by Saikawa's successor, CEO Makoto Uchida, as well as by Renault chairman Jean-Dominique Senard, Renault's interim-CEO Clotilde Delbos, and even Mitsubishi chairman Osamu Masuko. All of them moved beyond faulting Ghosn's alleged ethical lapses to targeting his strategy. According to the new conventional wisdom, years of rampant expansion under Ghosn had dangerously overstretched all three companies, and massive restructuring was urgently needed to avoid collapse.

"By trying to hit over-ambitious goals, we caused a rapid decline in our performance. We have to set objectives that are challenging but achievable and understandable," Uchida said in his first news conference after taking office.

"We must admit our mistakes and correct course," said the new Nissan chief, who graduated with a degree in theology before joining Nissan during the Ghosn era.[7]

In early 2020, Uchida unveiled a new revival plan that would unravel Power 88. He would slash Nissan's global annual production capacity from the 7.2 million–vehicle level built up by Ghosn down to 5.4 million vehicles a year, a level much closer to actual sales.

Mitsubishi provided another stunning repudiation of Ghosn's growth push. Ghosn was appointed chairman of Mitsubishi in 2016 and immediately sent it into a multipronged push to scale up in the world's biggest markets, including Europe, the United States, and China. With Ghosn now gone, Mitsubishi abruptly abandoned any pretense to global conquest. Instead, it announced its own restructuring plan that narrowed

Mitsubishi's focus primarily on Southeast Asia, the brand's small, yet stalwart, sales stronghold. Mitsubishi's Masuko christened the new business strategy "Small but Beautiful."

"Instead of rushing to pursue expansion, I am convinced that pursuing a good balance between investment and healthy growth is the best option," Masuko said of his company's realignment. "We have redefined a future direction in which we will pursue strong profitability in spite of being a small player."[8]

Renault's new management also disowned Ghosn's growth obsession. Ghosn had wanted the French carmaker to turn out five million vehicles in 2022, a lofty jump from just under four million sold in 2018, Ghosn's last full year at the helm. When Renault slumped to a net loss in 2019, acting CEO Delbos proposed chopping 14,600 jobs and more than €2 billion ($2.24 billion) in costs over three years. Renault's global production capacity would drop by half a million vehicles by 2024. "We structured ourselves, including the way we work and the way we function, for an ambition that we never achieved," Delbos conceded.[9]

When full-time CEO Luca de Meo took the helm of Renault in mid-2020, he said more drastic surgery was probably needed. In an internal memo seen by Reuters, he said Renault should model its turnaround after that of French archrival PSA Group. Such a declaration might be especially galling for Ghosn. PSA Group was then headed by Carlos Tavares, the onetime Ghosn understudy who was forced out of Renault by the boss. Tavares was now a celebrated turnaround artist in his own right, after resuscitating PSA. De Meo said he would take difficult and necessary decisions to reboot Renault. "I would describe it as a revolution," de Meo wrote. "This revolution, which must be pushed forward by all the men and women of the company, I'm calling it a 'Renaulution.'"[10]

. . .

Undoubtedly, Nissan's performance promptly plunged after Saikawa took the helm as sole CEO in 2017. But the reality is Nissan's decline started earlier, during calmer times when Ghosn was still the unchallenged top dog. And the softening started in the critical US market. North America was long Nissan's biggest and most profitable cash cow—its assembly plant in Smyrna, Tennessee, is the country's biggest auto factory, with capacity to make 640,000 vehicles a year. But the American money machine ran into problems as Ghosn pushed his lieutenants to achieve the 10 percent US market share under Power 88.

To hit that mark, Nissan began selling cars at deep discounts. That strategy does indeed goose share numbers in the short term, but it's a ticking time bomb for long-term profitability. Cars sold with cash on the hood have lower resale value when owners go to trade them in or sell. Lower resale values, in turn, erode the value of the new cars being sold in two ways. First, people are reluctant to pay more for a new car that quickly loses its worth. Second, would-be buyers are asked to pony up bigger down payments because they are getting less for their trade-ins. It eventually becomes a self-destructive cycle. Nissan found it difficult to command higher prices for new cars because customers were conditioned to expect spiffs, industry lingo for discounts. And thanks to all the investment being channeled into emerging markets and new technologies such as electric vehicles, Nissan had less money to devote to new vehicles for existing markets, such as the US. Its lineup grew long in the tooth, and that made its offerings all the more unappealing. The GT-R sports car, for instance, was introduced by Ghosn in 2007 as an eye-catching brand-builder. But by 2020, one of the company's most visible nameplates—fondly nicknamed Godzilla by its worldwide fan base for its fire-breathing performance—had yet to receive a full redesign. As a result, even more discounting was needed to attract eyeballs to Nissan's aging portfolio.

US dealers, meanwhile, were being prodded to sell more cars through a program called stair-step incentives. The programs pay dealers a rebate for each car sold if the dealer reaches a certain threshold of the monthly sales target set by the automaker, known in industry parlance as "the factory." For example, dealers might get $200 per car if they reach 90 percent of the factory's monthly sales quota, and $500 if they meet 100 percent of the target. The incentives are called stair steps because the rewards increase with each step toward the target figure being dangled before them by the factory. The carrot incentivizes dealers to sell as many cars as they can, to get cash back on each sale. And the promise of getting $500 per car, instead of $200, means dealers will do almost anything to seal those final sales.[11]

But stair steps also have a self-defeating dark side. As the end of the month approaches, dealers inevitably start scrambling to meet their factory quotas. And to sell more cars, they often resort to rolling out desperate discounts to lure customers away from rivals, even those selling the same brand cars. On the surface, this seems like a textbook case of free-market capitalism in action. But the cutthroat competition induces what dealers and automakers both acknowledge is "unhealthy" behavior.[12]

For starters, stair-step incentives trigger a race to the bottom in pricing, as Nissan dealers in adjacent towns, or even in the same town, try to outdo one another on deals. This saddles the brand with a "bargain-basement" image and torpedoes resale value. Harried dealers, in a scrape to meet their quotas, are known to sell cars at a loss or even buy their own inventory. In the latter case, they turn around and sell these essentially brand-new cars as marked-down used vehicles, accelerating the downward spiral of diminishing brand appeal.

It might sound like a shopper's paradise, where customers have their pick from a parade of best buys. But in the long run, buyers also feel burned when they go for trade-ins and learn their Nissan Altima sedan, bought in a fire sale, is worth much less than the comparable Toyota Camry that wasn't propped up with giveaway cash. Customers also get peeved when they see that the Altima they purchased last month thanks to a $1,000 carrot is now being flogged with a $2,000 offer. It undercuts trust in local dealerships and in the brand. And when those Nissan buyers are ready for their next purchase, they are less likely to put Nissan on the top of their shopping list.

Stair steps are not unique to Nissan, but in the United States, under Power 88, Nissan was especially shameless in exploiting the cash splash.

Nissan also had a bad habit of padding its books with so-called fleet sales. Anyone who rented a car at an airport during that era was bound to have noticed a parking lot packed with more than its share of Nissan-badged vehicles on standby. Selling cars to commercial customers, such as Hertz, Enterprise, or Avis, is a crutch automakers use to boost sales when consumers aren't buying. But these sales are less profitable than pure retail transactions, and they also carry the added liability of undermining brand value. Few retail customers truly aspire to buy, as their personal car, the econobox they rented during that business trip to Las Vegas. Fleet sales can taint an entire brand. They were long the domain of struggling Detroit players. Such companies as Honda and Subaru, by contrast, religiously shun fleets and were routinely feted as the most profitable and most admired brands.

. . .

Such was the fix Nissan found itself in under Power 88. Just as US dealers felt pressured to meet their factory quotas, Nissan's top management team felt squeezed to deliver the 10 percent US market share for Nissan and Infiniti decreed by Ghosn. The man eventually charged with achieving this target was José Muñoz, the Spanish executive who was rumored to be next in line for the top post after Saikawa, but who left the company after Ghosn's arrest. Muñoz took over as chairman of North America at the beginning of 2014 and later rose to chief performance office in charge of realizing the boss's vision for the entire world.

Former Nissan dealer Steve Kalafer said Nissan's aggressive discounting and relentless drive for volume under Ghosn drove him to drop the brand for good.

"They'd do anything to sell another car," said Kalafer, chairman and CEO of Flemington Car & Truck Country, a family of franchises in Flemington, New Jersey, that sells a diverse spread of brands from Ford and Chevrolet to Volkswagen, Porsche, and Jeep. "In the last several years, it was really a Ponzi scheme. Let's report a profit today, worry about how it will unravel later, reporting increased profits on cars that truly weren't really sold, because they were still on deferred payment plans. And this was the megalomania of Ghosn and the people who followed him right to the edge."

Kalafer began selling Nissan vehicles in 1980. But after Muñoz outlined Ghosn's push for US market share in a dealer meeting, Kalafer said he saw the writing on the wall and bailed on the brand in 2016. "I left the meeting, got into an Uber, went to my franchise attorney, and said, 'I want to sell the Nissan franchise,'" he recounted.

"All they did was increase the money they paid. It didn't make the car worth any more money," Kalafer said of the incentives. "This is not going to end well. This is the beginning of the destruction of the value of the franchise, and any dealer that remains will be in jeopardy . . . I was watching a train wreck in slow motion, screaming."

As the Power 88 deadline approached on March 31, 2017, Nissan's business was beginning to groan under the strain of it. Ghosn failed to achieve either of the 8s—neither the 8 percent global market share nor the 8 percent core operating profit. In fact, Nissan achieved hardly any of the plan's ambitious objectives.

Muñoz did briefly deliver 10 percent US market share, just under the wire, in February and March 2017. And for the full year of 2017, Nissan and Infiniti teamed to sell a record 1.59 million vehicles in the United States for a consolidated share of 9.2 percent. Nissan's total US sales had climbed an amazing 50 percent from 1.04 million vehicles in 2011. Nailing the US market was an important achievement because the United States accounted for 28 percent of Nissan's global sales.

But the company paid a hefty price to get there. In Ghosn's last quarter as Nissan's CEO by himself, the carmaker's net income declined 16 percent and its operating profit slid 19 percent. During that July–September 2016 period, overall profit was hammered because Nissan spent a monumental $375 million on discounts and incentives to lure US buyers and chase market share. Regional operating profit in North America tumbled and US volume declined, despite Nissan's frantic efforts to prop up sales with deals.[13]

In retrospect, even Ghosn's executives realized things were starting to unravel.

"The writing was on the wall as early as 2017," said a former Renault executive who worked closely with Ghosn for more than a decade. "Both companies were slipping already, in terms of their financial performance, their brand strength, their technology. How did they do it? They bought market share, they bought fleets, they bought rentals, they bought all sorts of bad business, and their profitability started slipping. They chased volume in many of the emerging markets without having the appropriate base of profitability. And so, it's very surprising, he [Ghosn] ends up doing what he would criticize in other manufacturers."

When Saikawa took the reins in 2017, Nissan was reeling from the spiff spending. In an abrupt 180-degree shift, Ghosn's longtime enforcer swore off aggressive growth. "We are not going to raise numerical objectives to stretch ourselves," Saikawa announced, to the shock of industry watchers. "The theme now is steady growth and maintaining a certain level of profitability." His new strategy was as stunning for its repudiation of Ghosn as it was for swearing off the sauce of incentives that had become part and parcel of Nissan's business.[14]

But what makes incentives even more insidious is that they can't just be taken away. Saikawa cut back too hard and too fast on Americans' addiction to the cash outlays. Customers didn't want to shell out for Nissan vehicles they were accustomed to buying at a bargain. That's what the Nissan brand had become to American consumers, *a bargain brand*. Going cold turkey had the unintended consequence of triggering an even more rapid slump in US sales. Nissan's profits began to fall off the cliff. Truth be told, a mass-market brand like Nissan needed to maintain a certain level of high volume, but balance is key.

All of the course corrections would combine to unravel Ghosn's reputation as a miracle worker and management superstar. Ghosn may have been a great turnaround artist, but critics—and even former allies—were suddenly saying he took his eye off the road. Grand scale and perpetual growth were irresistible ideas in the wake of Nissan's initial turnaround, but now company leaders were literally saying they were the wrong goals: *Small is beautiful. Steady growth. Good balance. Challenging but achievable and understandable.*

As Ghosn talked about cobbling Renault, Nissan, and Mitsubishi into the world's biggest auto group, one of the world's smallest was running circles around them in terms of profitability. Japan's Subaru was barely selling one million vehicles a year worldwide—just one-tenth the Alliance's total at its height. Yet, Subaru routinely delivered double-digit operating profit margins, peaking as high as 18 percent in 2016—a level unthinkable to most players in an auto sector where 6 percent is considered healthy. Subaru was the darling of investors and the envy of the industry. Nissan, by contrast, wrapped Power 88 with an operating profit margin of 6.3 percent, on global sales of 5.6 million vehicles.

Missing Power 88's signature targets hardly fazed Ghosn. In late 2017, with Alliance global sales cresting ten million vehicles, Ghosn announced an even higher target: Renault, Nissan, and Mitsubishi would sell fourteen million vehicles annually in 2022. In retrospect, Saikawa scoffed at the target: "We just went for volume . . . It was a very risky and dangerous objective."

. . .

In shifting its strategy away from Ghosn's, the Alliance was falling back in line with other automakers' strategies to be a little bit more like Subaru, as that approach came into vogue.

General Motors, for example, was once the prototype for the Alliance, a behemoth and the world's biggest automaker for nearly eighty years. It was toppled by arrogance, bureaucracy, and complacency, and suffered a humiliating bankruptcy. So, the post–Chapter 11 GM decided it wouldn't sell all vehicles in all segments in all markets. It scaled back or quit selling cars altogether in Western Europe, Russia, India, Thailand, Africa, and Australia. It was, in some ways, small but beautiful. The lean, mean GM began booking relatively steady profits, despite the global downsizing.

Strategies for grandiose world-spanning auto empires fell out of favor in some corners, especially as emerging markets failed to deliver the rampant growth envisioned at the start of Power 88. The globalization championed during the Ghosn era was put on the back foot by trade conflict, Brexit, tension between the United States and China, the fragmentation of automotive regulation, and increasingly regionalized customer tastes. In Japan, for example, customers increasingly demanded pint-size minicars, with 660 cc, three-cylinder engines no bigger than those in some motorcycles. Such cars would never succeed in America, just as America's bestselling vehicle—the gargantuan Ford F-Series full-size pickup, replete with its offering of a 5.0-liter V8 power plant—would be a near impossible sell in Japan.

Even Ghosn's dismantling of the Nissan keiretsu system didn't seem so wise in the rearview mirror. Over the years, Toyota served as an enlightening counterexample. Instead of casting off its far-flung army of suppliers—together known as the Toyota Group—Japan's biggest automaker actually found strength in greater cooperation and circled ranks. Toyota worked even more closely with longtime group partners, such as Denso Corp. and Aisin Seiki Co., to push ahead in electrification and autonomous driving. As Nissan focused on nickel-and-diming parts makers to save money, its reputation as a business partner among suppliers plunged to the bottom of the industry—below Honda, General Motors, and Ford. Toyota, by contrast, stayed consistently at the top, for nearly a decade, as the carmaker suppliers most wanted to work with, according to a closely watched Supplier Working Relations Index published annually.[15]

Nissan needed to change with the times. In 2020, the leaders of Renault, Nissan, and Mitsubishi declared a new "leader-follower" strategy to divide the world into markets, each spearheaded by the partner strongest in that region. Under the model, Renault quit China, leaving it to Nissan. Nissan pulled back in Southeast Asia, handing control there to Mitsubishi, and it downsized in Europe, letting Renault take the lead in its backyard. Nissan would steer the United States and Japan.

"At Nissan, we wanted to do everything everywhere. We can't afford everything, everywhere," COO Ashwani Gupta told *Automotive News.* "We are going from globalization to regionalization. All this leads to less and less economies of scale, but investment costs are going through the roof. Many of our competitors are leaving markets, leaving segments and so on, which means Nissan also has to prioritize and focus."

Saikawa remained convinced Ghosn's dogged drumbeat for growth set the stage for decline. Saikawa said he regretted not stepping in sooner to pump the brakes, and he saluted the three-year "intentional pause" implemented at rival Toyota by its president, Akio Toyoda. Toyota's global sales volume crab-walked for a while after Toyoda put growth on hold. But Japan's biggest automaker laid solid foundations for robust long-term profitability during the pause by shoring up human capital, investing in product and reinforcing brand value.

"I remember the words of Akio Toyoda," Saikawa mused in a 2019 interview with *Automotive News* shortly after being forced to resign as CEO. "And if I had convinced Carlos Ghosn in a more explicit manner, starting maybe even from 2016, then our targets for performance could have been much, much milder. Maybe in the current situation, that is the biggest regret."[16]

. . .

All the while, Ghosn watched from Lebanon as Power 88 unraveled and Nissan atrophied. He heard the recriminations of those leading the companies he brought together and ran for nearly two decades. To Ghosn, it was bad enough being pinned for crimes he says were never committed. But it was nearly as sinister to smear his legacy as business leader, something never questioned until he was drummed out of the industry.

To be sure, Ghosn always cautioned against expanding at any cost. In unveiling Power 88, he pledged that the goal was *sustainable* growth, insisting: "The way we're going to reach it is as important as the objective itself."[17] A former top executive who worked in Ghosn's inner circle at Nissan insists Ghosn never "talked exclusively about just 'give me the volume.'" Instead, the executive said Ghosn would talk about profit to his performance and finance people and about volume to his salespeople, setting up a tension for his underlings to work out. "It was a tension for us to manage, in terms of, Okay, how can we do this together?"

Ghosn was outraged at being blamed for Nissan's reversal of fortunes. He bristled at any suggestion his vision for growth and investment set up any company, especially Nissan, for a fall. After all, Ghosn hadn't been CEO of Nissan since 2017. And the year he handed over the reins, Nissan and Renault each posted record annual net incomes. Only after that, he notes, did things really fall apart.

In any event, even though Nissan missed most of the Power 88 targets, Nissan at the end of the plan was still further along than at the beginning by many measures. Power 88 wasn't the complete flop his detractors claimed it was. It gave Nissan a head start in the nascent fields of electric and autonomous cars. And among its other successes was prioritizing early expansion in China, a decision that made Nissan one of the top players in the world's biggest market. As China rebounded quickly from the COVID-19 pandemic, having deep roots there was a key lifeline for a company struggling everywhere else.

"Attributing the difficulty of the company to the fact that I was pushing, or I was very ambitious? It's ridiculous," Ghosn said in an interview with *Automotive News* from Lebanon. "My ambition for the company and my engagement with the company were the basis of the revival of the company."[18]

To Ghosn, all the second-guessing about his corporate strategy smacked of ungrateful blame-gaming to cover the missteps of his successors, especially Saikawa.

"He showed all his talent, and you know where this talent went. He was fired from the company; he presided over the decline," Ghosn said of Saikawa. "And it is very sad for me to see now, in 2020, nobody is taking responsibility . . . it's a tough industry, where you need vision at the top. And all of that disappears when you have politics, explanations, excuses. So, the company collapses. With this kind of mindset, the results are predictable. And this is exactly what you're seeing today."

18

JAIL JAPAN STYLE

WHILE GHOSN MAY HAVE BEEN WORRIED ABOUT THE future of Nissan and the Alliance he had built, he had more immediate concerns in 2019. He had spent 130 days in a Japanese jail and was facing up to fifteen years in prison. It was a prospect that few would relish. While Japan's prisons are typically clean, orderly, and safe, the system is designed to ensure total obedience. Names are replaced with numbers, access to information from outside is tightly controlled, and there are strict rules on when you must sit, stand, or lie down.

The detention centers that hold suspects awaiting trial play a pivotal role in the system dubbed "hostage justice." They send a clear message to each inmate daily: Confess and you can be free; fight the charges and we will keep you locked up. For almost all who enter a detention center, it's a compelling argument.

Like most other countries, confessions and guilty pleas are the grease that keeps the wheels of justice moving in Japan. Even given the country's low crime rate, there is no way two thousand prosecutors nationwide could deal with all the cases in front of them if they needed to prove guilt through gathering enough evidence to present in court. Nor are there enough judges or courtrooms for the hearings that would be needed. The confession is therefore the shortcut for both the system and the accused.

. . .

In most cases, an initial arrest by the police will result in the suspect being sent to cramped cells in the basement of the local station while prosecutors decide whether to pursue the case. Small rooms hold anywhere from three to six people, with just enough room for the Japanese-style futon put on the floor at night. There is almost no contact with the outside world except for a shared daily newspaper and one radio news show daily. Exercise is at the discretion of the guards, who see the request as an intrusion on their day.

For those arrested in Tokyo, there is a daily shuttle to the Justice Ministry building on a broad leafy street home to the governing bureaucracy. Suspects don't see that, though, since the windows of their transport vans are blacked out. The first sight the detainee does see is the basement of the ministry building. Once there, groups of twelve sit together in a windowless and cramped concrete room for up to ten hours at a time. There is no heat in the winter nor air-conditioning in the hot Tokyo summers. They are forbidden from speaking or looking around. There they wait for their time with the prosecutor. While in custody, they can only call an attorney, or if they're a foreigner like Ghosn, their national embassy. Calls to family and friends are forbidden.

If after three days the matter isn't settled, the prosecutors must seek permission from a judge to hold the suspect for another ten days. According to the Justice Ministry, this happens "only if an independent judge finds that there is probable cause to suspect that the person has committed a crime and there is a risk of concealing or destroying evidence of crime or fleeing from justice."

That bar is set pretty low. According to the ministry's figures, judges approved 94.8 percent of all requests from the prosecutors for a suspect to be locked up while they investigated the case. For those accused, that is actually a marked improvement from 2006, when judges approved 99.6 percent of the prosecution's requests.[1]

For those cases, the next stop is a detention center. For Ghosn, this was the Tokyo Detention House in the nondescript Kosuge neighborhood in the northeast of the city. The twelve-story monolith can hold three thousand inmates but typically has many fewer. It also shows few outward signs of its function. There are no bars on the windows, no barbed wire, and no guard towers. A simple perimeter fence and a few police out front give it the feeling of a high-security data center. Since Ghosn, like other high-profile defendants, was arrested directly by the prosecutors, he was taken straight to Kosuge.

The facility is technically not a prison. It holds inmates still awaiting trial or appeals, along with those on death row (who technically are not serving prison terms; they are awaiting execution). It has been the temporary home for some of Japan's most notable accused felons. These include former prime minister Kakuei Tanaka, who despite his political muscle was still detained ahead of his trial and later conviction in the Lockheed bribery scandal of 1976. Prior to Ghosn, Paul McCartney was among the most famous foreign detainees in Tokyo (although not at Kosuge). He was held for ten days on a marijuana charge in 1980 when visiting for a concert tour. (Confined with others in the cell, he reportedly sang "Yesterday" at the request of a rather intimidating fellow inmate.)[2]

Kosuge is also a part of one of the most controversial aspects of Japan's justice system, the use of the death penalty. It is one of the seven detention centers around the country where capital punishment takes place. Doomsday cult leader Shoko Asahara was executed there over his role in a 1995 sarin gas attack on the Tokyo subway, in which thirteen people died and thousands fell ill, a senseless act that shocked the nation and the world.

The continued use of the death penalty in itself has brought international criticism since most advanced countries have ended the practice (the United States is the other main exception). In addition, the way it is administered in Japan adds what appears to be an unnecessary level of cruelty: Those sentenced to death are not told in advance when the execution may take place. Many prisoners sit on death row for years awaiting the final decision by the justice minister for the execution to go ahead. The prisoner is informed only on the morning of the execution, so that many wake up every morning for years without knowing whether it will be their last.

One convicted murderer spent nearly fifty years on death row before DNA tests years later put his case in doubt.[3] (Despite this, the government continued to push the case, and it was still in the courts in 2020.) Family members are given even less information. They are not informed until after the execution has taken place. Death is by high-tech hanging. A set of three buttons mounted on the wall of an adjacent room activates the opening of the floor beneath the noose-bound inmate. Each is pushed by a different official so that no one will know if they were responsible for sending the inmate to their death.

. . .

Scott McIntyre, an Australian journalist, knows the Tokyo Detention House well and talked of his experience. He was arrested in 2019 for trespassing when he entered the apartment building where his Japanese parents-in-law resided. His goal was to see his two children, who had been taken away by his wife who sought a divorce. Trespassing is a misdemeanor, but local police knew McIntyre since he had often gone to them demanding that they do more to check on the welfare of his children.

His case shines a light on another area of Japanese justice that falls under scrutiny: child custody. Japan does not allow joint custody and the critics say courts generally follow the legal premise that possession is nine-tenths of the law. Therefore a parent who holds the children will in most cases be given custody, a situation that only serves to encourage disputes and, in some much-publicized cases, abduction. Most of the notorious custody cases involve one foreign spouse, but the issue exists in domestic marriages as well.

McIntyre says he wasn't trying to abduct his children, just see them, but he suspects his previous efforts to speak with them, and the fact he had reached out to the police before to determine if his kids were safe, are what led to his arrest on misdemeanor trespassing charges. When first detained, McIntyre refused to go along. He insisted that he was innocent (after going through the lobby door of the building he went into the complex only briefly and never tried to enter the apartment). In his battle to get access to his children, the charges against him were a price he was willing to pay.

Fighting his case led to forty-five days in confinement, including twenty-five at Kosuge. By his description, life there was more martinet than sinister, more military boarding school than Rikers Island, the infamous New York City jail complex. The facility is clean, corruption-free, and safe from violence, at least inmate to inmate. At the same time, there are myriad rules, many of which appear intended only to grind someone down, and verbal abuse by guards is common. From the time they are processed, detainees never use their own name; instead, they are given a number, which must be shouted out at various times, such as when receiving food. Inmates are given two sets of green uniforms, a toothbrush, toothpaste, soap, and a small towel. The cells include traditional tatami, a Japanese woven flooring. Cells holding six inmates are a fairly cramped 250-square-foot space, allowing just enough room for the futon cushions to be laid out at night. You are not allowed to exercise in the cell, though there is a recreation session on the roof except on weekends, holidays, or rainy days. For those not doing some type of prison labor, most of the day is spent in the cell, where you must sit cross-legged on the floor on a small cushion in front of a low table. There are no chairs. Sitting against the wall is banned and you cannot lie down, except at nap time (during which you have to lie down, no choice). The prison says this is so guards can see whether someone is ill or has attempted suicide, which unsurprisingly is a major concern. The lights are dimmed somewhat at night but are never turned off for sleeping. For those who have some money, a prison account can be created to buy a range of goods from the prison store. These include snack foods, stationery supplies, newspapers, and magazines. Detainees can wear their own clothes and personal clothing is washed—up to two items twice weekly. When being moved to the communal baths or the roof, or while in an elevator, detainees must avoid all eye contact and face the wall. Visitors are allowed during weekdays, but all conversations and correspondence, all of which is monitored by prison staff, must be in Japanese (either by the participants or through an interpreter), making detention even more difficult for foreigners.

Like most others, McIntyre saw that this could go on endlessly and took the same road as the 93 percent of those accused—he switched his plea to guilty and after a short trial was given a suspended sentence, meaning that he would not have to serve prison time as long as he avoided any new legal problems.

. . .

Ghosn's time at Kosuge was in solitary confinement or what could be called a private room, depending on your viewpoint. While this provided more privacy, it further reduced his human contact. It was an obviously distant reality from the life of one of the world's most powerful executives. Roughly eight by ten feet, the room has a toilet, sink, and a low desk to use while sitting on the floor Japanese style. As in the common rooms, bedding consists of a futon mattress. The room is unheated, though fan units provide heat/air-conditioning in the corridors. Ghosn said he was refused permission to have pens and paper despite their not being specifically banned by the Justice Ministry rules. A watch also was not allowed, making it difficult to gauge time passing. He also complained about the prison diet of rice, soup, and a perfunctory serving of fish or meat, as evidenced by his gaunt appearance in court after fifty days of confinement.

Ghosn was allowed visitors, but sessions were very limited. Conversations needed to be translated so that guards would know what was being said. Under pressure about the conditions, officials later allowed him to finally have a bed mattress and some other household items to the extent that, when he left, a separate van was needed to cart away the various goods.

Even with those privileges, this is not an easy time. Ghosn's second and third arrests allowed prosecutors to prolong his confinement, and the fourth and final case against him sent him back to Kosuge for twenty-two days after he had gained his freedom. It was, Ghosn and critics of the system say, just part of the process to wear one down. In all, he spent 130 days at Kosuge.

This was shorter than for some others who refuse to confess. One white-collar defendant in the Michael Woodford Olympus fraud case, former Nomura Securities banker Nobumasa Yokoo, spent 966 days, more than two and a half years, in detention before his trial began.[4] He protested his innocence but was found guilty of helping in the company's fraud. The Olympus executives at the heart of the scandal each spent no more than forty days in detention. The difference? They confessed. "The approach is simple, confess and everything will be fine," said one Western lawyer who has handled criminal cases in Japan. The long confinement would not have been lost on Ghosn, who foresaw that prosecutors would drag their feet to put him under increasing pressure. As one former Japanese prosecutor who is now a critic of the system put it: "When prosecutors have a weak case, they will stall as much as possible."

Japan is not alone in lengthy pretrial detentions, which studies show have been on the rise in many countries. Although Ghosn had at one point said he would willingly go to France for trial, pretrial detention for serious crime can run more than two years there.[5] In the United States, the average terms vary widely but can be as high as 150 to 200 days for some types of crime, and that excludes those denied bail for serious offenses.[6] The biggest difference from Japan is that pretrial detention in other countries is almost always associated with violent crimes, along with people who cannot afford bail. In the West, detention becomes as much an economic issue as much as a judicial one. Ghosn would have been unlikely to face a Kosuge-like experience in Europe or North America.

. . .

With international scrutiny growing, Ghosn's lawyers repeatedly filed motions for his release on bail and, against all the odds, were successful, winning a court order for release 108 days after he was first put behind bars. The release was opposed by the prosecutors who argued that he could destroy evidence. Stopping the destruction of evidence is one of the few accepted reasons for pretrial detention under United Nations standards. Using detention to get a suspect to confess is not.

Ghosn was free, at least partly and as it would turn out, not for very long. Among the conditions from the court, he had to agree to have surveillance cameras outside his residence so the authorities would know who came and went. He also had to switch to one of the old-fashioned flip phones without internet access. Phone records also had to be submitted to the court. For any web access, Ghosn had to go to his lawyer's office.

History might have been much different if the court had accepted one of Ghosn's own proposals: to wear an electronic anklet that would allow authorities to keep track of his location at all times, a common way in other countries to monitor suspects on parole. Japanese authorities said they had no such systems in place. It was a fateful decision. If the idea had been accepted, Ghosn's eventual disappearing act would have been much more difficult to pull off.

Less than a month after his release, the authorities again raided his apartment on the new charges and took him back to Kosuge for a twenty-two-day stint, again upping the pressure to confess. Ghosn's people noted that the new arrest came just as he was about to give a news conference. Legal experts say that the prosecutors most likely kept this final trap in the form of the fourth and most serious charge ready to spring whenever they needed it. Later testimony in the trial of Greg Kelly would show that the probe was initially focused on potentially more serious fraud allegations, not the more technical salary issues. The final arrest appears to have exhausted the prosecutor's plays for a confession, and the tactics came under increasingly intense international scrutiny. With pressure growing and despite prosecutors' objections, Ghosn was again, against the odds, given bail by the judge. But this time, there were even more stringent conditions. The one he most loudly protested was that he could not see his wife, Carole.

To Australian journalist McIntyre, Ghosn's experience was hardly unique. "You are intimidated, humiliated, and exhausted into acquiescing into what they want you to say. You are told directly, 'Say what we want you to say and we'll look at you kindly.' What kind of justice is this?

"Ghosn thought he was being treated differently. That's not the case. He was being treated exactly like every Japanese prisoner and that makes it doubly concerning because what that means is there are so many people being brutalized by this system every day. The Japanese are too scared to complain and the only ones who are talking about it are the foreigners. I want to add my voice to this on behalf of the Japanese victims."

Ghosn and McIntyre are not alone in their criticism. French president Macron, who had generally refused to interfere in the Ghosn case, was quoted as saying to Japanese prime minister Abe at one point that it appeared the detention was "too long and too hard."

And Ghosn gained an important ally when a United Nations subcommittee issued a strong condemnation of Japan's actions. In a November 2020 report, the UN Human Rights Council's Working Group on Arbitrary Detention said that the repeated arrests and detention of Ghosn were "an extrajudicial abuse of process that can have no legal basis under international law." It also criticized his long interrogations and limited time with his attorneys. The independent group of experts said Japan should investigate the events and take "appropriate measures" against those responsible. Adding to this unlikely scenario, it suggested that Ghosn should get compensation and other reparations. The report also makes numerous references to the fact that the judges who had denied bail said that Ghosn might try to tamper with evidence, but did not say that they considered him a "flight risk." This was a delicate way to work around the fact that under UN standards, it is permissible to detain those who are at risk of flight, which in retrospect was certainly true for Ghosn.

Japanese officials strongly pushed back on the report's findings. The Foreign Ministry issued a statement defending the system, which it said was properly administered. The statement also pointed out the inconsistency in the report's statements about Ghosn as a flight risk and testily pointed out that the report did not represent an official statement by the UN.

While the report largely covered issues that have been previously raised by international groups, it provided Ghosn and others with a handy weapon to keep up a campaign of pressure on the government.

. . .

Government officials say that the lack of complaints from Japanese inmates speaks for itself. Unlike other countries, there has not been a prison uprising in Japan in the entire postwar period. Therefore, they argue, things must be going well, despite the international criticism. Outside groups, such as Human Rights Watch, are not convinced.[7] In its report on Japan's prison system, the group says that silence is a key part of the judicial system, both in terms of silence from the authorities over what takes place and the fact that talking or loud noise from prisoners is often punished. "A careful look at the Japanese prison system strongly suggests that the lack of serious prison disturbances may be related to the draconian discipline and the fear among prisoners and not necessarily the general contentment of the Japanese prison population," it says in a 1995 report. "Order is achieved at a very high cost: the cost of violating fundamental human rights and failing to observe international standards the country has ratified."

This international pressure has made the Japanese authorities defensive, if nothing else. After the negative publicity of the Ghosn case, Kosuge gave special tours to the media, showing neat and tidy rooms with newspapers and bags of potato chips carefully laid out on the communal table as if in a hotel room. Floors were polished to a bright shine and the walls had no scuff marks.

To show that it is a good member of the community, Kosuge also has its own form of the summer festivals[8] that are popular for neighborhoods throughout Japan. The gates to the grounds are opened up and the public can tour the facility. Visitors can also sample "Prison Curry" (which is apparently not actually available to inmates). Wooden cutouts provide a chance for children to have their pictures taken as prison guards (inmate cutouts are not available). There are also prison-made goods from around Japan, including shoes and handbags. There is also live music, including traditional Japanese drum ensembles. Inmates are not invited.

In the end, the circumstances around Ghosn's escape hardened views on both sides of the debate over the fairness of Japan's detention system. For those demanding reforms, Ghosn's decision to flee was at least understandable. They saw that the odds were stacked against him and they knew of the nearly endless pressure the state can put on a suspect.

For conservatives, it demonstrated exactly why detention is necessary and the risks of a greater use of bail. "This case raises the extremely serious issue of whether it's all right to continue the trend toward bail leniency," former prosecutor Yasuyuki Takai told NHK television.[9] "The legal profession and lawmakers need to quickly consider new legal measures or a system to prevent such escapes." The ever-logical Ghosn had already offered them an answer: ankle bracelets.

19

GREAT ESCAPE

JAM-PACKED JAPAN, A COUNTRY ALWAYS TIGHT FOR space, has a long history of land reclamation. And Kansai International Airport, the main air hub for the western metropolis of Osaka, is one of those projects, an artificial island sitting like an unsinkable aircraft carrier in Osaka Bay. A causeway connects the airport to the mainland, and just across Sky Gate Bridge R from the airport stands the towering Star Gate Hotel, billed as one of the tallest hotels in Japan—an ocean view from every room. A couple of hours before midnight on December 29, 2019, an American named Michael Taylor and an associate passed under the lobby's massive corkscrew-shaped chandelier to check out of Room 4609. The two men, in a rush to catch an important flight, then decamped from the hotel, wheeling out two oversized black boxes with aluminum trim, handles, and reinforced corners—the kind used to transport clunky but delicate audio equipment.[1] Their next stop was the private air terminal back across the bridge.

The men had landed in Japan only that morning, on a long-haul charter flight from Dubai. Upon arrival, they told Japanese immigration officials at Kansai that they were musicians. Should anyone ask, they even had a cover story of visiting Osaka to perform in the concert that evening by famed violinist Taro Hakase.[2] Now, a mere thirteen hours after their charter jet landed, Taylor and his companion had their cargo rolled back onto the jet still waiting for them, then boarded.

Taylor's looks might have signaled something was amiss. The burly fifty-nine-year-old exuded an air more military than musical, with his square jaw, buzz cut, and chiseled face. And there might have been another red flag: Taylor had earlier tried to "tip" one of the women working at the gate with a thick wad of Japanese yen worth about $10,000, bound with an elastic hair band. He had wanted to expedite their departure, on the premise they were running late.[3] She initially accepted it so as not to offend. But after conferring with coworkers about the unusual largess, she duly handed over the money to her supervisor to give back, ever mindful of propriety and noting that tipping isn't customary in their service-oriented nation. The foreign travelers proceeded on their way, and at 11:10 P.M., their plane finally lifted off into a partly cloudy night bound for Istanbul, Turkey.[4]

Only after they were wheels up did the surprise stowaway emerge.

As the plane hurtled westward with the night, Taylor went to check on the trunks. Back in the cargo hold, as Taylor later recounted to Vanity Fair, he was greeted by a gleeful Carlos Ghosn, perched cross-legged and carefree atop the equipment case. Ghosn had somehow done the unthinkable. Earlier that very day, in the course of mere hours, the indicted auto titan managed to slip off the radar in Tokyo, race halfway across the country, and have himself packed into a big box, then smuggled aboard the private jet now spiriting him out of the country. The audacious gambit would have him in his ancestral homeland of Lebanon before the new year.[5]

. . .

Unsuspecting Japan was at the time busy readying itself for the extended three-day New Year holiday break, opening a Year of the Rat in which Ghosn would finally stand trial. But on December 31, he stunned the nation, and the world, by announcing he was no longer dutifully abiding by his bail conditions in Japan but was seven time zones away in Beirut. Ghosn forfeited some $14 million in bail bond money, but he was finally beyond the clutches of Japanese justice: Japan has extradition treaties with only two countries, South Korea and the United States, and Lebanon doesn't extradite its own citizens.

Ghosn didn't waste a minute in rubbing Japan's nose in his great escape. His staggering first statement reverberated like a victim's proclamation of resistance:

"I am now in Lebanon and will no longer be held hostage by a rigged Japanese justice system where guilt is presumed, discrimination is rampant, and basic human rights are denied, in flagrant disregard of Japan's legal obligations under international law and treaties it is bound to uphold. I have not fled justice—I have escaped injustice and political persecution. I can now finally communicate freely with the media, and look forward to starting next week."

With Ghosn free to speak his mind after months fettered by restrictive bail conditions, he channeled renewed vitriol as the saga exploded anew on the world stage.

Japanese officials scrambled to respond, initially paralyzed by the holiday during which the country virtually shuts down for the first three days of January. When it finally reacted, Japan's Justice Ministry seemed as flabbergasted as the rest of the world by how Ghosn had managed to pull it off. It was a humiliating slap in the face to Japan.

Even his own Japanese attorneys seemed flummoxed by the vanishing act.

"I don't know how he left Japan. But I suspect that things like this wouldn't have been possible unless a huge organization was involved," said one of his lawyers, Junichiro Hironaka, at an impromptu media scrum after the news broke. Hironaka swore the defense team had nothing to do with the escape, insisting Ghosn "betrayed" them by bolting.

But he still sympathized with his client. "I can understand why Mr. Ghosn thinks the way he does. I believe there must have been a number of things unacceptable to him, ranging from the way he was detained to how the prosecutors gathered evidence, the way he was allowed to talk with his wife to the way the evidence has been disclosed," Hironaka said. "As a matter of course, he has violated bail conditions, and that is inexcusable. What he did is in violation of Japan's judicial system. That is not good. But that said, understanding why he had to resort to such an unlawful act is another matter."

Most in Japan were less forgiving, now viewing Ghosn as not just an indicted suspect, but an international fugitive. They saw his getaway as damning proof he was guilty all along. That he knew he couldn't beat the rap because the charges were true.

. . .

As drastic as it was, Ghosn's decision to abscond was in some ways an inevitable outcome of a long-coming collision between Japan's unbending justice system and an uncompromising über-executive used to getting his way. And it set in motion a cascade of intensifying conflicts.

Japan's red-faced Justice Ministry, determined to salvage some semblance of success, slapped Ghosn with an Interpol Red Notice, an official request for other countries to arrest him. That meant he could be picked up in transit at any airport and sent back to Japan to stand trial. Japan had effectively trapped him in Lebanon. Ghosn, a stratospheric executive who used to crisscross the globe with a portfolio of different passports, was now a man on the lam living in one of the world's smallest countries. Initially he holed up in the pink-walled mansion Nissan once bought for him to live in—with money channeled through a subsidiary originally envisioned as seeding new technology startups.

Prosecutors next turned the screws on Ghosn's wife, Carole, issuing an arrest warrant that accused her of giving false testimony to a Japanese court the previous April.[6] They followed that with a fresh warrant on Ghosn for allegedly breaking Japan's immigration laws when he snuck through Kansai Airport without getting his passport stamped. Prosecutors also announced related warrants for Taylor and his accused accomplices: his son Peter Taylor and George-Antoine Zayek, the partner who allegedly helped slip the black boxes through the airport.[7]

The companies Ghosn once led seized on his escape to dial up pressure as well. Nissan filed a ¥10 billion ($91 million) lawsuit against Ghosn in Yokohama District Court, for damages it claims he inflicted on the company.[8] French prosecutors accelerated their own investigation into suspected fund misappropriation by Ghosn at Renault. Renault in turn filed a petition reserving the right to seek its own damages from the ousted chairman.[9] The French investigation extended beyond the opulent parties Ghosn hosted at the Palace of Versailles to probe travel spending and financial transactions between Renault and an auto dealership in Oman.[10] Meanwhile in the United States, two public pension plans initiated a class action suit, on behalf of investors, against Ghosn—as well as Nissan, Kelly, Saikawa, and two other former executives—claiming damages for hundreds of millions of dollars lost when their Nissan stock tanked in the wake of Ghosn's arrest.

Ghosn also counterpunched. His international legal team, spearheaded by French human rights lawyer François Zimeray, pledged to unleash a "massive" onslaught of its own countersuits against the parties that allegedly reduced Ghosn to this lowly state of indicted executive on the run.[11] Ghosn sued Renault for some €250,000 ($278,000) of unpaid retirement benefits and later launched a bid to collect a supplemental pension worth €774,774 ($861,550) a year, plus shares valued at more than $10 million.[12] Separately, Ghosn filed a €15 million euro ($16.4 million) suit in the Netherlands, claiming wrongful dismissal as chairman of Nissan-Mitsubishi BV, their Dutch-based joint venture.[13] And his lawyer in Japan was considering a countersuit against Nissan's civil complaint there.

In early 2020, it appeared Ghosn would never actually face a Japanese judge to answer the charges against him. Yet the legal morass engulfing him, Nissan, and Renault somehow only deepened.

· · ·

In an interview from Lebanon, Ghosn conceded it would take years to clear all the cases. "With everything that's happened, I will never be fully vindicated. There is huge damage done already. To me, to my family, to my name," he said. "Let's be very realistic. I'm not going to restore what has been taken from me, but I can at least present an alternative explanation."

In some sense, confining Ghosn to Lebanon might have helped the Alliance. Nissan and Japan were conveniently spared months, if not years, of a trial and appeals that would have provided Ghosn an international soapbox to espouse his conspiracy theory and rail against the country's courts. Ghosn, growing older in full public view as the trial ground on, could have become a sympathetic figure and a potent lightning rod for international criticism of Japan's justice system. True, prosecutors would never get a chance to prove their charges and lay out evidence in court. But Nissan and Japan would still avoid some potentially cringeworthy court testimony while keeping the runaway Ghosn grounded in Beirut, and tarred with the presumption of guilt.

On the other hand, his escape created plenty of headaches for Nissan, the Alliance, and Japan. With Ghosn gone rogue, he was free to snipe at them with impunity from a safe haven. He wrote a tell-all book to air his side of the story, presumably short on prosecutorial input. And to spin a good yarn, Ghosn even secured the help of Hollywood high roller Michael Ovitz, the cofounder of talent agency Creative Artists Agency and a former president of Walt Disney Co. A person from Ghosn's camp described Ovitz as a personal "friend," adding that he might help evaluate proposals from studios, producers, content companies, and television networks. If a courtroom diatribe could damage the reputations of Nissan and Japan, a Ghosn-saga Netflix docu-series along the lines of *Tiger King* could be potentially devastating.

Ghosn's first two weeks on the lam in Lebanon previewed his coming counterattack.

Mere days after landing in Beirut, he called a global press conference in the Lebanese capital, where he assailed his accusers. The invitation-only spectacle targeted about one hundred reporters from dozens of big news organizations, from the United States, Europe, the Middle East, and Brazil. Notably missing were Japanese journalists—particularly those from the flagship national broadcaster NHK. Thoroughly disaffected with Japanese media, Ghosn allowed only three hand-picked outfits from the country in the room. The rest, he reckoned, had already had their say.

"If you've been selected, in my opinion, it was the only people who try to be objective into the situation, and all the other people were being sourced through the prosecutor," Ghosn said at the bombshell January 8, 2020, briefing, held at a Lebanese press club venue overlooking the aqua-blue Mediterranean along the Beirut Corniche. "For fourteen months, they've been telling everything Nissan and the prosecutors are saying, every single thing, without any single sense of analysis, without a single sense of criticism. I'm not running from them, and I'm counting on you to carry the message."

The scene reflected the rough-and-ready tone of the host country, then already tipping into financial crisis. Lebanon, which stabilized starting in the 1990s after its fifteen-year civil war, was once again ex-periencing unrest. Mass street protests rocked the capital in late 2019, inflation began to soar, the local currency plunged, and Lebanon would soon be racked by shortages of such essentials as food and medicines. The road to Beirut–Rafic Hariri International Airport, which reportedly runs through neighborhoods dominated by the Hezbollah Shia Isla-mist political party and militant group, was lined for miles with ban-ners commemorating the recent martyrdom of Qasem Soleimani, the commander of Iran's Islamic Revolutionary Guard Corps. He was wiped out by a US drone airstrike just days before Ghosn's Beirut press gath-ering, stoking tensions across the entire Middle East. Later, in August 2020, a massive explosion of ammonium nitrate would obliterate Beirut's port district, kill more than 150 people, injure thousands, and thrust the entire country into deeper chaos. (The Beirut residence where Ghosn resided—and that Nissan claimed as its own—was not too far from the blast. There was minor damage to the home, but Ghosn was unscathed.) Lebanon seemed like a wild and woolly place for the fallen business titan to settle, but as the latest addition to Interpol's wanted list, Ghosn had little choice but to call it home.

At the press conference, journalists on the invitation roster were screened through a metal detector, as hundreds of unlucky, unchosen news people swarmed the parking lot, pressing against the gates trying to get in. When Ghosn entered the room flanked by buff bodyguards, he was finally in his element, the media maestro who effortlessly commands crowds and wields ninja-like rhetorical skills in getting news outlets to relay his views. Now he seemed more animated than ever as he basked in the limelight.

Ghosn had put on a paunch and a double chin since his first public appearance—gaunt and gray in Tokyo court exactly a year earlier, to the day. But he looked dapper in a dark suit, white shirt, and red tie; his still-gray hair now lent an air of savoir faire. Ghosn declared: "I am here to clear my name. These allegations are untrue, and I should never have been arrested in the first place." Throughout the performance, his spirited defense elicited spontaneous applause from the Middle East press corps in attendance. To many, they were welcoming home a hero, and they unabashedly dispensed with any pretense of impartiality.

Ghosn launched into an impassioned point-by-point rebuttal that evoked a CEO's slide show presentation. He even revealed Nissan company documents that he said proved his innocence, though the projections were far too small for anyone to read. With his wife, Carole, in the front row, Ghosn held court for two and a half hours. Reporters screamed questions over one another and jostled to yank the microphone away from rivals. Ghosn answered them in English, French, Arabic, and Portuguese. He cracked jokes, vented bile, and spiced his feisty fusillade with animated gesticulation, including his trademark frenetic finger-wagging.

Ghosn slammed Nissan and the "handful of unscrupulous, vindictive individuals" who allegedly conspired to frame him. He saved his fiercest invective for Japan's justice system. The decision to jump bail, he said, was a no-brainer: "I escaped because I had zero chance of a fair trial . . . You are going to die in Japan, or you are going to have to get out."[14]

. . .

Indeed, Ghosn's own defense lawyers never guaranteed they could clear him in court. Rather, with the studied circumspection befitting their legal trade, they simply maintained he had a strong case and that they would fight hard to free him. At the same time, they admitted the deck is stacked against any defendant in their country.

"'Will there be a fair trial?' He asked me this question over and again," defense lawyer Takashi Takano recounted in a blog post shortly after Ghosn bolted.

"Each time, I explained to him Japan's legal practices based on my own experiences. I also talked about a discrepancy between the reality and the articles of the Constitution as well as laws. Unfortunately, a fair trial can't be expected for a criminal defendant in this country. Judges are not independent judicial officers but rather part of the bureaucracy. Japanese media organizations are merely PR entities of the prosecutors," Takano wrote. "Given Japan's judicial system and the situation surrounding it he has seen for about this past one year, I can't entirely dismiss this flight as 'an outrageous act' or 'a betrayal' or 'a crime.'"[15]

Those who know Ghosn say this lack of certainty was his breaking point. As a hard-charging CEO, his requirements for subordinates were always clear. Making and keeping commitments was one of his keystone management principles. He gave targets, commands, or orders, and if you wavered on delivering, you were out.

"He will always ask, 'Can you do this, yes or no?'" said one longtime Nissan executive who worked closely with Ghosn for more than a decade. "If you say you are unsure, he will switch you out. He will only work with 'Yes, I can.' I think Ghosn lost confidence in his lawyers. He's like, 'I hired you to achieve this. Can you commit or not?' That's his way. He wanted to hear, even if it's not true, 'Yes, we will win.'"

If Ghosn was initially optimistic about his chances, he grew increasingly despondent and frustrated as 2019 dragged on, his lawyer Takano conceded. This was especially true regarding the bail condition banning contact with his wife.

Only in late November 2019, after repeated petitions by his lawyers, was Ghosn allowed to speak to Carole, for the first time in seven months. But they could only talk by video conference for one hour, under the watchful eye of his defense lawyer at the attorney's office. Talk of the legal case was forbidden. On Christmas Eve, just five days before he fled the country, Ghosn was permitted a second video meeting. According to defense lawyer Takano, they talked about their children, family, friends, and memories. She was already in Lebanon, perhaps awaiting a visitor. But if Carole knew about the impending escape, she didn't let on to his lawyers. Ghosn later insisted his wife and children weren't involved.

The next day, Christmas Day—which is not a public holiday in Japan, where Buddhism and the native Shinto religions hold sway—Ghosn was jolted at a pretrial hearing where he learned that the charges against him would be separated into two trials, with one not starting until April 2021. Trials would proceed glacially, with just three hearings every two weeks. Defense attorney Takano estimated the whole affair would drag on for at least five years.

"You have the first trial, the appeal, and then eventually Supreme Court," Ghosn, by then already sixty-five, told his handpicked cadre of journalists at the Beirut press conference. "Five years of trial. And after this a 99.4 percent conviction rate. I was seeing myself staying practically all my life in Japan . . . I couldn't see Carole, I couldn't talk to Carole . . . The judge was surprised that I wanted to see my wife. Maybe for a lot of people it would have been not a punishment to see their wife. But for me, it was. They put me on my knees."

About the only question Ghosn wouldn't touch at his press conference was the one everyone wanted answered: How did he escape?

Ghosn demurred, then and in subsequent interviews, saying he didn't want to jeopardize his liberators. "There have been many stories about how I escaped," he said cryptically. "We heard a lot of things which are contradictory." He later conceded he was assisted by "not a small network." But he kept mostly mum, saying loose lips "will cause danger to those who helped me."[16]

Exactly how he escaped was not entirely clear. Still, a picture of the operation gradually emerged through various sources. First, there was the footage from ubiquitous surveillance video cameras scattered around Japan to monitor street corners, train stations, public plazas, and building entrances. Taxi drive-recorders and testimony from witnesses also helped. Japanese prosecutors say they spliced snippets together to re-create Ghosn's cross-country getaway. Next, there were the lawsuits triggered by Ghosn's escape in which evidence was made public. In Turkey, for example, prosecutors indicted seven people involved with the private jet operator that flew Ghosn out of Osaka to Istanbul. Five were charged with migrant smuggling.[17]

In the United States, Michael Taylor, who was believed to have left the Star Gate Hotel with the box containing Ghosn, was fighting extradition to Japan along with his son, Peter Taylor. Five were wanted for allegedly abetting Ghosn's escape and were picked up in Massachusetts in May 2020.

It turned out Michael Taylor was not a musician at all. He was a former US Army Green Beret trained in high-altitude parachute jumps, hostage rescue, and when necessary, lethal hand-to-hand combat. After retiring from the military, Taylor rebranded himself as a kind of "fixer" for hire to anyone in a pinch, like kidnap victims or, as with Ghosn, individuals in legal hot water in a foreign land. Taylor had allegedly spent months and hundreds of thousands of dollars planning this mad dash.

. . .

The vanishing act begins at the cream-colored brick and plaster house where Ghosn stayed during his second release on bail. Ghosn's second bail abode was positively palatial, even by the standards of upper-class Japanese, for cramped central Tokyo. It was an expansive three-story home with a two-car garage in a leafy, upscale neighborhood, not far from the Tokyo American Club, a meeting place for the city's elite.

Initial surveillance video captured Ghosn leaving the home around 2:30 P.M. on December 29 with no luggage. Footage purportedly showing Ghosn, which was aired on Japanese television, depicted a figure dressed in black from head to toe, wearing a dark cap and sunglasses. It might appear, like on so many other occasions, that Ghosn had simply gone for a walk. He soon ducked into the nearby Grand Hyatt Hotel in the Roppongi nightlife district.

This was hardly remarkable. Despite being tailed by private investigators and living in a home under court-ordered video surveillance, Ghosn was free to roam. He was often spotted at Tokyo restaurants, in the park, or at the supermarket. He even had a membership at a gym, where he did stretching exercises—in retrospect, perhaps to limber up for his boxed getaway. A chauffeured Toyota Alphard van—the top choice of Japanese executives for its roomy rear cabin—would typically shuttle Ghosn about town. He once took a tourist trip to the ancient Japanese capital of Kyoto—three hours away by train, more than five by car—with one of his daughters. And he reportedly celebrated his sixty-fifth birthday at the swank Grand Hyatt, three days after his first bail.

This time, however, Ghosn didn't visit the landmark hotel for a fancy meal. Instead, he rode the elevator to the ninth floor, operating the lift with a copy of a room key presumably given to him beforehand. He then entered Room 933. Court documents chronicle every step of the escape, down to the minute. There, the filings show, he was met by Peter Taylor, who had checked in the day before and had Ghosn's luggage. It's not known precisely how he got the bags; media reports later said they were dropped off by one of Ghosn's daughters.[18] Japanese court filings said a Toyota Alphard van dropped off two suitcases to Peter Taylor in the parking area of the Grand Hyatt at 2:06 P.M.

Once up in the room, Ghosn then changed his clothes.

Meanwhile, Peter's father, Michael Taylor, and colleague George-Antoine Zayek had landed at Osaka's Kansai International Airport at 10:10 A.M. that same morning. They raced up to Tokyo on Japan's famed Shinkansen bullet train, which turns what would be a seven-hour car drive into a two-hour and twenty-four-minute zip across almost half the country.

They arrived at Room 933 at 3:24 P.M., and all four men left the hotel, this time loaded down with luggage. Son Peter Taylor went off on his own to catch a plane for China at Narita Airport outside Tokyo. Father Michael Taylor stuck with Ghosn and Zayek. They headed back to Osaka on the Shinkansen, arriving there under cover of night. As they zoomed westward, surveillance footage purportedly shows, Ghosn donned a surgical face mask. This provided a modicum of cover for him—one of the country's most recognizable foreigners—but it wouldn't raise eyebrows. Long before the COVID-19 pandemic, Japanese were already compulsively wearing masks to safeguard against the common cold, pollen, and pollution. In concealing his face, Ghosn blended right in. More security footage shows all three entering the Star Gate Hotel near Kansai International, where they checked into Room 4609. But although Ghosn goes in, he never comes out. Instead, Michael Taylor and Zayek are seen leaving with the big, black audio cases. Inside one of them was the bundled-up Carlos Ghosn.

Before final checkout, Taylor left the hotel to visit the airport around 9:00 P.M. That's when he offered the female attendant the "tip." He then went back to pick up Zayek, and the two returned to the airport in two black limousine taxis at around 10:20 P.M. The men and their cases made their way to the airport's wood-paneled "Premium Gate Tamayura" for elite passengers and their private jets.[19] There, they chatted up security with friendly banter. Officials were, perhaps, a little less rigorous than usual. It was late, and they had been dealing with the crush of travelers before New Year, Japan's biggest holiday. The female attendant had already been working since 9:00 that morning.

Taylor's cases were too big to pass through the regular X-ray machines—purposefully. Taylor seemed preoccupied with not screening the boxes, an airport worker later recalled, insisting that the X-rays could damage the sensitive magnets of the guitar "amplifiers" inside. The tired airport staff, per Taylor's risky calculation, just waved the men and their cargo through without a proper check.

A Japanese ground crew worker later stated in an affidavit that he noticed the bigger of the two black cases weighing substantially more when they packed it on the plane that night, compared with when they had unloaded it that morning. In the morning, two people were enough to hoist it. That evening, it required five, he said.

"Because the large box was so much heavier than it had been at the time of arrival, there was then an episode where the staff members joked, saying, 'Maybe there is a beautiful young lady in the box,'" he recounted. "So, when I watched the news report that said Carlos Ghosn had left Japan by hiding in a container box for acoustic equipment, a bell rang in my head."[20]

Ghosn probably heard, through airholes drilled in the bottom of the box, the casual banter with airport staffers preoccupied with the holiday bustle. It is likely he could tell when his box was through security and getting loaded onto the plane; certainly he would recognize the noise and steep incline of a jet's takeoff. By the time the chartered Bombardier Global Express, a business jet with a range of more than six thousand miles, landed in Istanbul some twelve hours later, the game was nearly complete. There, Ghosn transferred to another plane bound for Beirut.[21]

The Turkish charter service that operated the planes, MNG Jet Aerospace Inc., later filed a criminal complaint saying it was duped into unwittingly facilitating Ghosn's escape. An employee, it said, falsified records to exclude Ghosn's name from the flight documentation, without the knowledge or authorization of the company.[22] A copy of the contract presented in court quoted a price of $350,000 for the Kansai getaway.

Turkish authorities detained an MNG Jet executive and four pilots for alleged migrant smuggling, while two flight attendants were charged with failing to report a crime. At their trial, one MNG Jet manager said he was forced to cooperate because his family was threatened. When the plane finally landed in Istanbul, the manager said, he met Ghosn on the tarmac and learned the soon-to-be-famous fugitive pondered parlaying his getaway into big bucks.

"Carlos asked me how much the plane cost . . . and told me about Hollywood producers who want to make this escape a movie," the MNG Jet manager told the court.[23]

Even US prosecutors, while arguing that the Taylors should be extradited back to Japan, seemed impressed with the sheer audacity of the scheme.

"The plot to spirit Ghosn out of Japan was one of the most brazen and well-orchestrated escape acts in recent history, involving a dizzying array of hotel meetups, bullet train travel, fake personas, and the chartering of a private jet," they wrote in a court filing. "Ultimately, Ghosn was hidden in a large black box and whisked out of Japan in the private jet without detection by Japanese authorities."

It appeared to have been long in the planning. Japanese prosecutors alleged Peter Taylor, the son, then only twenty-six, traveled to Japan at least three times between July and December to strategize. Records of Ghosn's meetings, required to be kept under his bail terms, showed Ghosn even powwowed with Peter Taylor four times in his attorney's office. Ghosn's lawyers came under fire for this. But they professed ig-norance of Taylor's background and the purpose of the meetings. They denied that anyone from the legal team sat in.

Whether or not they knew, Ghosn's lawyers may still have opened some loopholes for his escape. Nissan had hired private detectives to track Ghosn's movements. It was a perpetual sore point for Ghosn, some-times driving him to the verge of paranoia. "We would be in a restaurant and he would say, 'See those guys at the table over there? They're follow-ing us,'" one acquaintance recalled. "And I would have to say, 'Carlos, that's impossible! We sat down after they did.'" Ghosn's lawyers peti-tioned to have the private investigators stand down. Eventually they did scale back, which opened windows of opportunity for an unmonitored Ghosn to slip out of sight.

Passport control emerged as another weak link.

Under the conditions of Ghosn's bail, he was required to surrender his passports so that he wouldn't flee the country. His lawyers were en-trusted to keep the travel documents under lock and key at their office. Three passports were secured this way.

The defense team, however, finagled a way for Ghosn to keep one of his French passports as a kind of ID card. The front page was visible through a transparent casing, which was secured with a dial lock to pre-vent Ghosn from using it at an airport. Only Ghosn's lawyers knew the combination. But defense attorney Junichiro Hironaka later admitted to NHK that the case was made of plastic and could be easily smashed open with a hammer. When Ghosn's plane landed in Lebanon, his name wasn't on the flight manifest. Yet, when he presented his French passport at immigration, officials readily welcomed him home.

. . .

Opening up about the escape in an interview from Lebanon, Ghosn said he breathed a sigh of relief only after finally stepping off that plane in Beirut. The first couple of days, he said, "I spent time with my wife be-cause I was not able to see her for eight months." He also downplayed suggestions the operation required complicated preparation.

"People think these kinds of things take months to plan. It's wrong," he said. "These kinds of things you may do very quickly. Renting a plane is not a big issue. It's a very limited number of people. The operation was risky, but pretty simple."

Ghosn also said he was prepared to go straight to prison had he been nabbed mid-getaway.

"This was the risk, but the opportunity was freedom and the ability to move and reestablish your reputation," Ghosn said. "I didn't run because I was guilty. I ran because I knew that there was no justice possible for me in Japan."

Japan now faced the vexing problem of how to get Ghosn back and save face.

Tokyo petitioned Lebanon to extradite the indicted fugitive, but Lebanon stonewalled. Media reports from the Middle East speculated that Japan might pressure the cash-strapped Lebanese government by withholding support for badly needed aid from the International Monetary Fund. Lebanon did confiscate Ghosn's passport after the Interpol notice went out, and grounded him from international travel.[24] Talk also circulated that Ghosn would stand trial in Lebanon on the Japanese charges. Ghosn was open to that—presumably because a Lebanese court would be more sympathetic.

No real progress was made on getting Ghosn back to Japan. The tug-of-war between Japan and Lebanon settled into a stalemate.

Tokyo also went after the Taylors and Zayek. US authorities apprehended the father-son duo in May 2020, in a quiet, leafy town in central Massachusetts.[25] Zayek managed to keep a lower profile; his whereabouts weren't initially known. Bank transfer evidence presented in the Taylors' extradition case alleged Ghosn wired some $860,000 to a company managed by Peter Taylor.[26] And another filing alleged Ghosn's son, Anthony, made additional payments, in cryptocurrency transfers through a platform called Coinbase from January to May 2020, totaling $500,000.[27]

The Taylors' estimated total haul topped $1.36 million. Michael Taylor, in his *Vanity Fair* interview, insisted Ghosn's breakout was a break-even operation. The money covered the planes and the extraction team. He himself, he claimed, made zilch.

As the Taylor father-son duo languished in an American jail awaiting what seemed like inevitable extradition to Japan to face charges of helping Ghosn escape, the irony hung heavy. They embarked to free a man from almost certain prison in Japan. But now they were the ones locked up and in jeopardy of being sent back. They had swapped places.

In March 2021, after exhausting their appeals, the Taylors were indeed finally handed over to Japanese authorities and sent back to Japan. They were jailed in the same detention facility that once held Ghosn and Kelly, and faced charges that carried penalties of up to three years in prison.[28]

A similar fate befell some employees of the Turkish charter service that flew Ghosn to freedom. An executive and two pilots were convicted of migrant smuggling in February 2021. They were each sentenced to four years and two months in prison, although they were expected not to serve because of time already spent locked up.[29]

. . .

The swirl of bombastic headlines again cast a harsh light on Japan's legal system and stoked international sympathy for Ghosn. And it highlighted the Japan-versus-the-West undertone of the entire saga. The zeitgeist was captured by an editorial in the *Wall Street Journal* that called Ghosn's odyssey a "fiasco from its dubious start." Its Editorial Board's main takeaway was clear: "It's hard to blame him for fleeing Japan after his ill-treatment."[30]

Back in Tokyo, Justice Minister Masako Mori—the top lawyer who was roundly criticized for saying Ghosn should return to "prove his innocence"—suddenly found herself doing damage control. In a frantic international PR campaign that included a letter of protest to the *Wall Street Journal* over its commentary, she defended Japan's system as fair and balanced.

But even Mori, an admitted onetime admirer of Ghosn, couldn't help conceding that the Ghosn case had eclipsed one man and taken on a life all its own.

"The Justice Minister doesn't comment on individual cases, but I thought this was no longer an individual case," Mori said in an interview with Bloomberg News. "Carlos Ghosn is a famous person, and he not only made excuses about his own case, but he attacked the whole Japanese justice system." As for fighting to bring Ghosn back, Mori spoke for many in the nation when she made this pledge: "I will never give up."[31]

20

THE FORGOTTEN MAN

IN OCTOBER 2018, GREG KELLY, FORMER HEAD OF Ghosn's CEO office and Nissan's only American board member, was at home with his wife in Brentwood, Tennessee. The couple had moved back to the Nashville area, just fifteen minutes away from Nissan's North American headquarters, after spending six years in Japan. Kelly had retired from Nissan in 2015 after twenty-seven years at the company, mainly handling HR and legal issues. Now sixty-two, he was enjoying a retirement that had followed a high-pressure career.

The phone rang and on the other end was Hari Nada, the man who now held the same role to Nissan CEO Hiroto Saikawa. Also on the call was Toshiaki Ohnuma, the head of Nissan's Secretariat's Office. Nada told Kelly that he was needed in Yokohama for an upcoming meeting of the board. Kelly demurred. Why couldn't the meetings be done by teleconference? Given the global nature of the Alliance, board rules specifically allowed online attendance. Also, Kelly was waiting to be told whether he would need surgery for spinal stenosis, a potentially serious nerve condition, and wanted to avoid a grueling eighteen-hour trip. Not only that, the Thanksgiving holiday was coming up. Over a series of calls and emails, Nada was insistent. Kelly needed to be there in person. To make it easier, he offered the rare luxury of a company-chartered jet (such flights can cost $200,000, although Nissan had a leasing contract with a charter company). And, Nada promised, Kelly would be home for the holiday.

What Kelly didn't know was that Nada and Ohnuma were now in the service of the Japanese government. They were about to become among the first people in Japan to make use of a newly introduced plea-bargain system. Nada was effectively luring his former colleague into a trap. Kelly's US lawyer James Wareham said later that Kelly "was lied to by a private actor who was acting under the direction of the state of Japan." Kelly's wife, Dee, had a simpler characterization. She called it an act of betrayal.

Nada later claimed at Kelly's trial that he did not know about the arrest plans but "speculated" that it could happen. But Nada had to ensure the right timing for Kelly's flight. Both Ghosn and Kelly had to be in Japan before the authorities could move in, otherwise the trap would be sprung minus one of the targets. In the end, all went according to plan. Kelly's flight from Nashville was arranged for the same day as Ghosn's flight from Beirut. The only small hitch was because of traffic, which delayed Kelly's arrival at the hotel. Authorities instead swooped down on his van while he was on the highway. At that point both men were in custody, facing the start of their long ordeals.

. . .

Besides Ghosn, Kelly was the only other individual defendant in the Nissan case. Unlike his boss, he was not accused of benefiting from any of the alleged schemes. But as a senior executive supervising the CEO's office, the Legal Department, Global Human Resources, and Internal Audit, he was central to almost everything that went on at the top of the company. In 2012, he was rewarded with a seat on the board.

Kelly's rise to such heights was something of an unlikely journey. He had no direct experience in either manufacturing or selling automobiles. Before moving to Tokyo, his work had been firmly centered in Middle America. He started his career with the law firm of Barnes & Thornburg, one of the biggest in the country with a broad practice area, and moved to Nissan in North America in 1988, joining as a staff attorney at the Smyrna, Tennessee, plant.

Working in his specialty of HR, Kelly was part of a team that had one primary focus at the time: defeating an attempt by the United Auto Workers (UAW) to unionize the plant's 2,400 workers. The stakes could not have been higher for either side, and Kelly would play a central, if behind-the-scenes role.

For the UAW, it was part of a dire need to break out of a long downward slide in membership, which had fallen more than 30 percent over the previous decade, as part of a broader assault on unions during the Reagan years. The expanding Japanese manufacturers were therefore an important source of potential new members. On the other side, Detroit's Big Three were cutting workers. They were losing market share to the upstart Japanese brands that now built cars in their own backyard—mainly in Southern states—at a lower cost and with higher perceived quality. To help fight back, the Big Three were pressuring the UAW to pitch in with concessions. The two sides were at war, ironically, because of a common source of their suffering: the Japanese carmakers.

The stakes for Nissan were also high. Like the other Japanese automakers, they had generally avoided union representation in their plants. Nissan's operations in Japan are fully unionized, but management knew that the UAW was a different animal than organized labor in Japan, which often accedes to management's terms in tough times and seldom blocks moves to increase productivity. It was no accident that most of the Japanese plants in the United States were scattered through the South. Virtually every US state maintains investment promotion offices in Japan, and the southern states have two major attractions that they regularly pitch to Japanese manufacturers. One is generally lower wages; the second, the fact that they are "right to work" states, meaning you cannot force a worker to join a union as a condition of employment. (Another unrelated selling point is the number of golf courses and year-round golfing weather, an important consideration for the golf-fanatic Japanese corporate set.) Nissan did not want to be the first Japanese company to let in a potentially disruptive influence like the UAW. It was a matter of cost and reputation.

It was as high profile and as hard fought as any political contest. The UAW cried foul over Nissan's techniques, which included video messages from management that the union was "strike happy" and that a vote to unionize would endanger current benefits. "We will spend whatever it takes to win," a company spokesman was quoted as saying about the campaign. A UAW spokesman characterized it as "the most vicious anti-union campaign of the decade."[1]

In the end, the vote wasn't even close. Workers rejected the UAW by a 2–1 margin. At one event where the results were announced, antiunion workers cheered and waved American flags, oddly, to demonstrate the victory of a Japanese company over a US labor union.[2] A few days later, workers brought in on an overtime shift arrived to an all-American barbecue with management cooking hamburgers for the workers. It was perfect corporate theater.

Workers at Nissan, while paid less than their counterparts in Detroit, shared a sense of comradery. Instead of shop stewards on the lookout for possible contract violations, teamwork and equality were encouraged. As one veteran auto writer covering the story put it: "Despite the physical toil of the assembly line, many workers here say it's the best job they have ever held. The company pays well and treats them fairly."

The UAW vowed that it would be back. And it was, waging more campaigns against Nissan and others, and losing them all. (The most recent defeat came in 2017 at the Nissan plant in Canton, Mississippi.)

Kelly became head of Human Resources at Smyrna a year after the first union vote, in 1990, and by 2005[3] was vice president for HR for all of North America. One of his key initiatives was to manage the large-scale recruitment needed to replace personnel in California not willing to move to the new North American headquarters near Nashville. In 2008, Kelly was offered the senior job in the CEO office at the Yokohama headquarters. He was a long way from home and a long way from his expertise in US labor law. He was soon in charge of the legal team, HR, and auditing, unusual roles for a foreigner. Even within multinational operations in Japan, HR and audit are typically headed by Japanese executives who have specialist knowledge, not to mention the ability to read the regulations in Japanese. But it was not uncommon within Nissan, where many senior executives were brought in by Ghosn from around the world.

In Japan, Kelly maintained the low profile that he had cultivated in the United States, even as he had risen to senior levels, but the central nature of his role was clear. Executives said that people knew that it was better to stay on Kelly's good side. He was described as hard-working, diligent, and cordial. Someone who might join in after-work drinks on occasion but who stayed in corporate mode nevertheless.

. . .

For Kelly's case, Nissan and the prosecutors told a simple story: Ghosn and Kelly had been a duo, riding roughshod over procedures and proper oversight to get what they wanted—in this case, under-the-table compensation for Ghosn. "The cause of this chain of events is the misconduct led by Mr. Ghosn and Mr. Kelly," Nissan said in a statement a month after their arrest. "During the internal investigation into this misconduct, the prosecutor's office began its own investigation and took action."[4] The statement sought to separate the company from the government probe, but that wasn't quite accurate. Nissan had offered full disclosure of all documents to the prosecutors, and it had arranged for Kelly to be brought back for arrest, sidestepping any need for an extradition request, which would have been much more time-consuming and potentially fraught. "We gave the prosecutors our full cooperation," said one Nissan executive.

Kelly hit back at the prosecutors and at Nissan. His wife, Dee, recorded a somber video appealing for Kelly's release from the Tokyo Detention House that also held Ghosn, saying that the jail conditions with a Japanese futon and even the lack of a proper pillow could make his spinal condition a permanent disability. She also made clear who was really at fault: "Greg has been wrongly accused as part of a power grab by several Nissan executives headed up by the current CEO, Saikawa," she said. Kelly also sought help from the US government, including the US ambassador to Japan, William Hagerty, who was himself from Tennessee and had previously worked on investment packages for Nissan on behalf of the state.

After five weeks in custody, Kelly managed to get bail, gaining his release on Christmas Day with bond set at $630,000.

Their pressure on the Japanese side continued. Interviews given by Kelly and his wife talked of the unfairness of the system. They noted that Dee Kelly had come back to Japan on a student visa studying Japanese to be able to remain with her husband for an extended period. Kelly also enlisted some congressional muscle, resulting in a March 2020 open letter from Sens. Roger Wicker of Mississippi and Lamar Alexander and Marsha Blackburn of Tennessee, both states with a heavy Nissan presence. The trio said that the issues raised by the Kelly case cut to the core of Japan's relationship with the United States. "If Americans and other non-Japanese executives question their ability to be treated fairly in Japan, then that most important bilateral relationship in the world is at risk."[5]

Kelly wasted no time landing his own blows. He used an interview with one of Japan's most widely read magazines to drop the news that Saikawa had received compensation from share-price linked certificates that were redated to increase the amount payable, the scandal that later forced Saikawa to step down. In a second article for the magazine, he framed his work as normal business affairs meant to retain a valuable asset and to keep Ghosn from going to a competitor.

. . .

With Ghosn in Lebanon, the Kelly trial was the only game in town. It began on September 15, 2020, the day of Kelly's sixty-fourth birthday. It also was a trial that neither side wanted to see take place.

For Kelly, there was of course the main hurdle of winning a case against the notoriously difficult odds for defendants in the Japanese legal system. And the stakes were high, up to 15 years in prison (which would be highly unlikely) plus a fine of ¥80 million ($764,500). Kelly also had to face his accusers without the man he hoped would serve as an important witness to corroborate his defense. "I was thinking that Mr. Ghosn's testimony would be a strong piece of evidence to prove my innocence. But Mr. Ghosn is gone," Kelly said in the magazine commentary. Still he did not blame Ghosn and said he appreciated the strong support from his former boss. Ghosn, from the sidelines, continued to press Kelly's case, saying the US government should do more to gain Kelly's release.

Adding to the difficulty was the technical nature of the alleged wrong-doing, set against the simplistic approach often taken by Japanese prosecutors in complex cases. The prosecutor's office and Japanese judges deal with the full range of criminal allegations. Few are specialists in any type of law, certainly not the intricacies of corporate accounting. In such cases, it is easy to assume that something must be wrong (otherwise why would the defendants be on trial?).

"For financial fraud cases, criminal trials have hardly ever contested whether the accounting treatment was appropriate or not," said Yuji Hosono, a former CPA who had been convicted in an accounting case he says was based on a lack of understanding. "The attorneys don't really know the accounting standards," he said. Like many others, Hosono said he pleaded guilty in the case because he couldn't afford to keep fighting the charges.

The case against Kelly was also bolstered by the findings of the US Securities and Exchange Commission (SEC), which has deep expertise in such issues. Based on information from the Japanese authorities, the SEC filed its own civil charges. All three defendants, Kelly, Ghosn, and Nissan, settled the charges and Kelly paid a $100,000 fine.[6] While the three did not admit or deny guilt in the case, as is standard practice, the SEC's characterizations would make it more difficult for Kelly to say he did nothing wrong.

On the other hand, the case was also precarious for the Japanese prosecution office, which had seen its image damaged by its own scandals in the past. For them, Ghosn was the main target; charges against Kelly would be a good way to get him to turn against his former boss. Like Ghosn, however, he dug in his heels, and without Ghosn, they had to move against Kelly alone.

From the outset, it was difficult to show a motive for Kelly. He was not a beneficiary in the case. Was he really loyal enough to Ghosn to purposely undertake a criminal action?

One issue raised by Kelly and Ghosn was why the allegations were sprung on them by prosecutors who had already locked them up. Why, they asked, weren't they raised through an administrative action by the financial regulators, similar to the filing of civil charges by the SEC? This is also the standard practice in Japan, where such matters normally go to the Financial Services Agency. The regulator can then impose fines, make "business improvement orders," and sanction firms or directors for improper supervision. By going straight to criminal proceedings, the state had to meet the much higher standard of showing an intent to defraud—it could no longer just be a misreading of the rules. Underpinning this difficulty is the fact that no individual in Japan has ever been charged with violating the law in question, the Financial Instruments and Exchange Act.

As also highlighted in the report from the UN Human Rights Council's working group, the Ghosn and Kelly case served as a concrete example to demonstrate the concern from human rights groups of hostage justice in Japan. Prosecutors were used to a system where charges are announced and guilty pleas follow. Now, the world was seeing how that particular sausage was made. Both foreign and domestic legal experts would be closely watching the Kelly trial proceedings to see whether the prosecutors had built a solid case and whether the judges had properly served as the unbiased adjudicators of justice. In short, whether Japan could suitably handle a complex financial case would be open to an international airing for the first time. It was no surprise that the chief judge selected for the Kelly trial was seen as one of the most accomplished and knowledgeable within the Tokyo District Court.

In the court of public opinion, the case against Kelly also served as a proxy for the escaped Ghosn. In fact, the charges against Kelly did not include the most serious allegations facing Ghosn, which are based on the more concrete issue of allegedly using company money for his personal benefit. But such details would be lost if Kelly were to win an acquittal. The general perception would be that if Ghosn had been there, he, too, would have gone free.

Finally, prosecutors had to worry that even a conviction could cause a problem at sentencing. For the $1.6 billion Olympus fraud case, considered one of the most serious in Japanese history, the two executives at the center of the case each received a suspended three-year sentence, avoiding any jail time. Kelly's case wasn't nearly as serious. Could the judges impose stiffer terms here? If they did, it would appear to be a case of unduly harsh sentencing of a foreigner. If he received a similar or lesser sentence, however, international public reaction could well be to ask what all the fuss was about.

. . .

As the trial dragged on through the winter of 2020–2021, the prosecution laid out its case in great detail. Much of the time was spent on the various ways that Ghosn, with Kelly's help, had allegedly maneuvered to get a secret deal for extra compensation, with the payoff to come after Ghosn retired. The goal was to find a way to get the money to Ghosn without a public announcement that would likely offend both Japanese and French sensibilities. A number of witnesses said that Ghosn was mainly worried that the French government would force Renault to fire him if the real numbers came to light.

One of the star witnesses for the state was plea bargainer Ohnuma, the former head of Nissan's Secretariat's Office who reported to Kelly and managed Ghosn's salary issues. In twenty-two days of questioning, Ohnuma spelled out how various plans were considered over a nine-year period. "There was unpaid remuneration, and we considered how to make payment while avoiding public disclosure," he told the court. Under the extensive questioning, the self-effacing Ohnuma looked uncomfortable, but in many ways he was the perfect prosecution witness. He said that even as he was working on these schemes, he knew that they were improper. "I know that I have done legally unacceptable things," he said, a concept that was no doubt drilled home by the helpful prosecutors when they had privately questioned him in 2018 and offered a plea-bargain deal.

In the end, he flipped without much ado, signing a statement at his first meeting with the prosecutors. He also had kind words for his former boss and offered the not particularly helpful observation (at least from Kelly's perspective) that Kelly was no more guilty than he was. Thanks, anyway.

Kelly based his defense on three basic points: (1) he had nothing to do with Ohnuma's private discussions with Ghosn; (2) he was discussing a postretirement package that would keep Ghosn away from the competition, with nothing even decided; and (3) he was looking at fully legal solutions in consultation with the lawyers.

"I was not involved in a criminal conspiracy. I believe that the actions I and others took to find a lawful way to retain Mr. Carlos Ghosn after he retired were in the best interests of Nissan," Kelly said in his opening statement. "This matter should have been resolved at Nissan," he added in a swipe at those who had run off to the prosecutors without ever asking Ghosn or Kelly any questions about what was going on. It later emerged that the board of the company and the CEO, Saikawa, were equally in the dark.

The existence of some kind of plan to pay back Ghosn could not easily be refuted. The government introduced two memorandums on Ghosn's official stationery as president and CEO detailing the total remuneration, and the fact that about half of the annual pay was "postponed remuneration." Written by Ghosn, the CEO, to Ghosn, the employee, in 2011 and 2013, they showed that this shortfall would be repaid after he retired, when disclosure would no longer be required. The letters, a demonstration that Ghosn had full authority to write his own paycheck, were countersigned by Ohnuma.

The problem for the state was to show how Kelly was connected to all this. Whereas Ohnuma had talked extensively about his meetings with Ghosn, he was less direct about Kelly's involvement. This played into Kelly's contention that he had no idea about any payback for Ghosn. He was working, he said, on a way to lock in the high-flying executive after retirement, something that was very much in the company's interests. Notably, Ohnuma was less than decisive about whether Kelly was familiar with the incriminating letters. He cited three or four meetings at which he said the issues were discussed, but he didn't have any emails or other written evidence, despite the matter going on for eight years.

Filling the gap fell to second star witness and legal department head Hari Nada, who clearly saw that it was time to pay for his own get-out-of-jail card as a plea bargainer.

Over eight days of testimony, Nada liberally sprinkled in the phrase "Greg Kelly told me to do this" or "Greg Kelly instructed me to do that." Despite Kelly's claims, Nada said, there was a direct link between the reduction in pay that Ghosn had accepted—at least publicly—and the plans for lucrative postretirement deals. His own extended testimony brought the phrase "haircut" into the Japanese judicial record, referring to Ghosn's acceptance of a pay cut. The legal issue would be whether it was a haircut or, in reality, a toupee to cover up the truth.

The Nada testimony also produced one of the best lines of the trial, in which he quoted Kelly as saying of Ghosn's various maneuverings on his compensation, "Pigs get fat. Hogs get slaughtered." (The interpreters didn't even try to tackle that one.)

It also emerged that, separate from the "Ghosn-to-Ghosn" salary letters, the ever-resourceful Ghosn had also negotiated three drafts of a postretirement gig that would be worth as much as $110 million. These were duly signed by Saikawa and (in two cases) by Kelly as representative directors and kept by Ghosn under lock and key, presumably as an insurance policy. The suggestion was that Ghosn had been practicing the trusted principle of divide and conquer. With two teams of people working on the problem, he was more likely to get what he wanted.

The presiding judge signaled on the first day of the trial how he was viewing the case. (Judges in Japan can make statements and ask questions of witnesses.) He said a key area of focus in determining guilt was whether Ghosn would be providing any services to Nissan in exchange for the proposed payments. This would be an important hurdle for the defense. Even though it is technically up to the prosecution to create the body of proof, defense lawyers in Japan say it is actually the other way around. Judges are often willing to ignore technical issues in reaching a verdict (especially to convict) and look to the intent.

One Japanese corporate attorney reviewing the case said that the Kelly team would need to demonstrate that any postretirement deal was reasonable. The final agreement negotiated by Kelly in 2015 provided Ghosn with a one-off payment of around $50 million upon retirement. In exchange, Ghosn would agree to never work for a competitor, but he didn't have to provide any services to Nissan. Persuading three Japanese judges that this was not a backroom deal and that it represented a prudent use of Nissan's money was a tough sell, even in relation to an auto-industry legend.

The defense argued that, in any case, none of the various plans had ever been finalized. If never agreed upon, the argument goes, how could they be reportable costs in the company's financial reports and therefore how could Kelly be guilty?

The defense spent considerable time in court attacking the key prosecution witnesses Nada and Ohnuma. "All we have to do is discredit the testimony of Hari Nada and Ohnuma. Once they enter a plea agreement, they have to stick to the statement before the prosecution," said lead attorney Yoichi Kitamura in an interview. "We are asking the judges to bear in mind this testimony is not trustworthy at all," he added.

Another area of focus was the fact that Nada, along with the internal auditor Imazu and the government relations head Kawaguchi had, by their own admission in court, formed a team to bring down Ghosn. The goal for the defense was clear: even if we lose this case, we have proven that Ghosn was the target of a boardroom coup and Kelly was collateral damage.

It was also clear that Ghosn, Kelly, and the two whistle-blowers were far from alone in knowing about the protracted discussions over Ghosn's pay. Aside from Saikawa, who had signed the three documents promising generous postretirement deals for Ghosn, former cochairman Itaru Koeda and former vice chairman Toshiyuki Shiga had been involved in negotiating various potential packages over the years.

This would leave the prosecution in the unenviable position of explaining why, out of all these people, only Kelly and Ghosn were charged. The two plea bargainers, Ohnuma and Nada, could be explained since their testimony was presumably necessary to provide the evidence. But what about all the others, including Saikawa? Deputy Chief Prosecutor Hiroshi Yamamoto tried to head off this issue. "We, the prosecutors, have indicted those deemed as being prosecutable based on the details and contents of the evidence," he said at a briefing soon after the trial opened.[7]

His reticence was understandable. "It is hard not to see this as a case of selective prosecution," said Stephen Givens, a veteran corporate lawyer in Tokyo who followed the trial. "Kelly persuasively claims that the decision not to report Ghosn's future compensation was vetted by internal and outside lawyers, and widely known within and outside the company. Nissan as an entity has pleaded guilty to misleading disclosure. By what measure is he 'more guilty' than dozens of others responsible for preparing and vetting Nissan's securities reports?" As one foreign attorney who had been involved in other parts of the case put it, "If Ghosn and Kelly are guilty, then everyone is guilty."

Also hanging over the trial was another troubling question: Are foreign executives in Japan safe from capricious criminal prosecution? This issue was first raised as Ghosn's detention dragged on and its harsh conditions were exposed. Remarkably, the case and Ghosn's escape from Japanese justice found the editorial pages of the *New York Times* and the *Wall Street Journal* in unlikely agreement. "The charges against Mr. Ghosn— and his against Japan's courts—deserve a closer look," the *Times* editorial board said in a piece that suggested that Japan was as much on trial as Ghosn.[8] As for the board members at the *Journal*, their mind was pretty much made up: "Barring new and persuasive evidence from Nissan or prosecutors, Mr. Ghosn should stand acquitted in the court of public opinion."[9]

"I don't think the treatment of Ghosn surprised many foreigners here," said one long-term foreign executive. At the same time, said another, "it has clearly put a chill on executives from abroad taking a senior job with a Japanese company. It's a much riskier proposition than it was a year ago."

Some experts believe that the beginning of a plea-bargain system may open the door for more white-collar investigations in Japan, which would only increase the chill on foreign executives. As seen in the Ghosn case, a key insider can easily provide detailed, highly valuable information that would otherwise require many hours of research in the resource-restrained prosecution office. This could therefore encourage prosecutors to seek out those who can be pressured into turning into government witnesses. "Although prosecutors are taking a cautious approach for now, it is clear that the 'carrot' of a plea bargain puts the authorities in a stronger position to acquire highly sensitive and potentially incriminating evidence . . ." said attorneys Takayuki Inoue and John Lane of the Japanese law firm Nagashima Ohno & Tsunematsu.[10]

Kelly's wife, Dee, poked at Japan's efforts to put a good spin on its appeal as an international center of business. "In fact, there are many international business people who have told me they will not be traveling to Japan because of what has happened to Greg," she warned in her video in which she pleaded for her husband's release on bail.

From Japan's perspective, the plight facing Kelly was in some ways a more serious image problem than the Ghosn case. The charges against Ghosn could be painted as a case of overarching greed by an arrogant CEO. "It shows you should be concerned about coming to Japan if you are a crook," commented one foreign lawyer who works in Japan. But many foreign executives could more easily sympathize with Kelly's situation as the subordinate trying to execute on someone else's mandates in a country where he could not fully understand the regulatory and legal situation and could not even read the relevant laws. The litany of potential risks was laid out in *Chief Executive Magazine* by Jeffrey Sonnenfeld, a professor at the Yale School of Management:[11]

> Setting aside the cinematic drama of Ghosn's escape, the saga of his legal perils are filled with worrisome trends for global executives. Amid a surge of nationalism around the world, trade battles over tariffs, taxes, forced tech transfer, intellectual property, data privacy, government subsidization, currency manipulation, labor conditions and sustainability goals are exploding.

Sen. Wicker of Mississippi, one of the three senators who came to Kelly's aid, was more direct: he took to the floor of the Senate in October 2020 to condemn the arrest and trial of Kelly. "This needless ordeal sends an unmistakable message to the American business community. If you do business in Japan, you had better watch your back. When it suits Japanese interests, they could set a trap for you."

This was very much the case for a young French entrepreneur in the realm of digital currencies. Mark Karpeles was the owner of the Mt. Gox bitcoin exchange, which at the time was one of the primary bitcoin marketplaces globally. He went to Japanese authorities in early 2014 to report that his company had been hacked. The loss was initially estimated at 850,000 bitcoins, a theft totaling around $457 million (at 2020 prices, the coins would be worth $7 billion). Working with the police for over a year produced results, with a suspect duly arrested—Karpeles. He was charged with embezzlement and mishandling of company data. He spent four months in a police cell and then was sent to the Tokyo Detention House, which would later hold Ghosn and Kelly, and was held there for seven months. He too felt the pressure to confess. "It starts right when you are arrested with the police telling you that a confession will make the whole process easier. They don't say for who," he said in an interview for this book.

As in any good mystery novel, Karpeles figured that the only way to beat the rap was to find the true culprit himself. Working with US authorities, he helped to track down a Russian hacker, who was arrested in Greece and later convicted in France. Karpeles was found not guilty of embezzlement but was still convicted of the lesser charge of mishandling company data. "The judge had to give something to the prosecution," he says of the verdict. Despite it all, Karpeles still chooses to live in Japan. "I did get very bad treatment in Japan but at the same time I find Japan easier to live in than France."

Another brush with Japanese law saw a Toyota auto executive make a hasty exit from the country. Julie Hamp, a US executive for the carmaker, was promoted to head global PR in 2015. Her troubles began soon after her arrival in Tokyo when a box of personal effects she had shipped from the United States was found to contain the opioid painkiller oxycodone, which is tightly controlled in Japan. Unlike others in similar circumstances, Hamp was never charged for what was called a minor infringement.[12] But that was not before she spent three weeks in custody. In the end, she lost her job (the company said she resigned) and went back to the United States.

Hamp's case was another example of how prosecutors use the media to shape the story. Even though investigations were supposed to be ongoing, Japanese news outlets were fed off-the-record comments from "investigative sources"[13] who said Hamp wanted the drug for a knee problem and claimed that a medical examination showed that she didn't actually need the drug for her condition.[14]

Whether the Kelly and Ghosn cases will make foreigners in Japan more nervous about their legal risks also comes down to a matter of degree. "If you're coming from Hong Kong, where you can now be easily extradited to the Communist Party–controlled courts in China, Japan is going to look pretty free compared with that," said one foreign executive.

It goes the other way too. Japanese executives have found themselves in legal peril in the United States often in relation to the US's much harsher view of such practices as price fixing and bribery. While technically illegal in Japan, these crimes are typically pursued with much less zeal. This can mean that Japanese executives can run afoul of US law simply by behaving in a way that's reasonably normal in their country. Such prosecutions are on the rise. By 2018, the Antitrust Division of the US Justice Department had prosecuted cases against forty-six auto parts companies, with charges against thirty-two executives, most of them Japanese. Among them were four Japanese executives working in Ohio and Kentucky for Tokyo-based auto parts supplier Yazaki Corp., who were sentenced to prison terms of fifteen months to two years for price-fixing and bid-rigging.

Still others have avoided prosecution in the United States but find themselves effectively stranded in Japan because of it, just as Ghosn is stuck in Lebanon. In the Takata defective airbag scandal, which resulted in at least 400 injuries and 27 deaths worldwide—the largest safety-related auto recall in history—the company agreed to pay $1 billion in fines, but the three executives charged with conspiracy and fraud have remained in Japan and avoided prosecution.[15]

In many of the high-profile auto industry cases, the accused employees have been supported by their companies and remained with the company on the premise that they "took the fall" for more senior executives. "In most cases, the Japanese are pretty lenient and want to take care of employees,"[16] said one defense attorney in Tokyo involved in bid-rigging cases. Kelly, now on his own in Japan, should be that lucky.

COURSE CORRECTION

BATTERED AND BRUISED, NISSAN LIMPED THROUGH 2020, the year Ghosn was supposed to finally stand trial in Tokyo and bring closure to one of the wildest corporate scandals ever. But Ghosn was gone, and instead of closure, Nissan was bracing for its biggest-ever annual operating loss. The Alliance hung in an uneasy truce with each company mired in its own problems.

Makoto Uchida, Nissan's fifty-four-year-old CEO, was untested in a global leadership role. He launched a restructuring plan to restore profitability centered on a wave of badly needed new vehicles that would either power Nissan out of its slump or become a massive money pit.

Uchida's revival plan ironically took a page from Ghosn's 1999 playbook, when Renault saved Nissan. Uchida's plan, like Ghosn's, cut costs and downsized factories. He also pegged his new roadmap to the long-awaited redesign of the storied Z sports car, a sweet piece of eye candy guaranteed to start fans salivating and generate buzz for the beleaguered brand.

Nissan's sleek, rear slung two-seat Z-Car has been a motorhead favorite since its debut in 1969. But Nissan had killed the car in the United States in the mid-1990s as it shifted focus to SUVs and crossovers. Ghosn saw brand-building bullion in the legendary Z, and he channeled its magic at the 1999 Tokyo Motor Show when he spotlighted the Z as a key model to revive. It was resurrected in 2002 as the 350Z. (In Japan, the car still kept its original, cringey name: Fairlady Z, a moniker picked by Nissan's then president Katsuji Kawamata, who had become enchanted with the Broadway musical *My Fair Lady* during a trip to the United States.)

By late 2020, however, Ghosn's Z-Car hadn't had a redesign in 12 years, as a cash-strapped Nissan diverted money into rapid expansion under Ghosn. Z fans began to doubt whether Nissan even had the wherewithal to keep the car alive.

Uchida did. He made the Z a centerpiece of what he dubbed "Nissan A to Z." The "A" stood for an all-new, all-electric crossover called the Ariya that Nissan had unveiled the previous summer. The "Z" stood for . . . you guessed it. At the unveiling, Uchida climbed from behind the wheel of a shimmering, lemon-yellow "Z Proto," a retro-styled prototype of the next-generation Z, and he confirmed it was on the way soon.

Car geeks around the world erupted with glee.

Unlike Ghosn, however, Uchida teased his Z car with a personal touch. Projected on a massive screen behind him was a snapshot of a younger, hipper Uchida, circa 1993, with the first car he ever bought: a gunmetal gray 300ZX, the Z car's venerated fourth generation. In the photo, Uchida strikes a macho pose with a shaggy '90s heavy-metal hairdo, acid-washed shirt, and gold chain. One hand on the steering wheel, he dangles the other out the driver's window with a self-satisfied smirk. "When you drive the Z," Uchida said at the unveiling, "you will feel it moving you and Nissan into the future."

The unspoken message was loud and clear. After decades with a slick-suited businessman at the helm, Nissan was now run by a car guy. It would get back to the basics of making automobiles. The Ghosn scandal was in the past, and Nissan was focused on a bright, new day.

But putting Ghosn in the rearview mirror wouldn't be so easy. Just a day before the Z Proto's reveal, Greg Kelly's trial had started. The proceedings would not only air more Nissan dirty laundry, they would remind Japan, and the world, of the myriad collisions that triggered the scandal in the first place and the many conflicts that still seemed far from being resolved. It cast a public spotlight, again, on the perilous path of the Alliance while rekindling questions about Japanese business culture and the integrity of the Japanese justice system. Not to mention the million-dollar question of whether Ghosn was really guilty and what we should think of his legacy now.

. . .

Among the collisions at the root of the scandal was the pressure cooker of industry upheaval that was an impetus for creating the Alliance in the first place, and then a reason for tightening the relationships over Ghosn's tenure. Amid spiraling costs for better fuel efficiency, and electric and autonomous cars, automakers needed ever-higher volumes to sustain themselves.

The fact that Renault, Nissan, and Mitsubishi stuck it out for so long, despite the distrust that plagued them before and after Ghosn's arrest, was proof of the need for scale. For all their wrangling and bickering, they knew that divided they would fall. As of 2020, even as a few companies began to think small and local in light of the overambitious growth goals of Ghosn's Power 88 plan, consolidation, as preached by Ghosn, seemed here to stay.

Some carmakers tried to defy the shift. Japanese low-volume players Subaru, Mazda, and Suzuki, for instance, remained nominally independent. But Japanese giant Toyota had bought stakes in all three. In essence, Toyota brought the country's small players into a loose alliance of its own, one that also included mini-car specialist Daihatsu and truck maker Hino. Toyota's consortium delivered group volume in 2019 topping 16 million vehicles a year—far more than the 10.7 million boasted by Ghosn's Alliance at its height.

In Europe, Volkswagen Group already built its own empire by assembling a sprawling constellation of brands that included Bentley, Bugatti, Lamborghini, SEAT, Škoda, Porsche, and truck makers Scania and MAN, in addition to the headline marques Volkswagen and Audi. Combined, the Volkswagen Group brands notched just under eleven million deliveries in 2019.[1] Meanwhile, France's PSA Group was busy merging with Italy's FCA to form another global behemoth, Stellantis. And in late 2020, Honda—left by itself among Japanese carmakers—decided even it was too small to go it alone. Honda formed an alliance in North America with General Motors to jointly develop vehicles to be sold by both companies.

This mass merging of brands was presaged by the Alliance two decades earlier, though most of these new partnerships differed in one key way from the Alliance. They mainly built scale within the comfortable confines of their home market. Toyota took on other Japanese companies. Volkswagen circled with Europeans. And the PSA-FCA accord brought together two next-door neighbors. Rarely did they successfully grapple with the gaping gulf in language, corporate culture, market coverage, and national politics that separated Renault and Nissan.

Once a visionary tie-up, the Alliance now seemed to be sputtering. In 2020, Renault and Nissan put full merger talks on hold to focus on their own problems. But the uneasy détente really just kicked the uncomfortable discussion down the road. The French government was still the most influential shareholder in Renault, which in turn was the top shareholder in Nissan. Emmanuel Macron, Ghosn's longtime bête noire and the chief agitator for an "irreversible alliance" was still president of France. The wider auto industry was still gravitating toward consolidation. And the Alliance still needed the meatier synergies that only a combined balance sheet could truly deliver.

Two years after Ghosn's arrest, none of those problematic dynamics had changed. And they seemed to set the scene for another Alliance showdown sometime in the future.

Nissan's CEO Uchida seemed to follow in Hiroto Saikawa's footsteps as a merger skeptic. Publicly, he touted the Alliance as a key tool for strengthening all three companies. But complete integration? Not so fast. Uchida, when asked in a late 2020 interview with *Automotive News* whether he opposed a merger, struck a diplomatic note: "I would say 'no opinion.' The only thing we are thinking about today is how to make sure we ourselves are at the right level. Have we had a merger before in the past twenty-one years? No." Nissan hadn't budged.

Could Ghosn's delicate auto group survive very long without its longtime leader? Or was the intercontinental, intercultural partnership simply a bridge too far in a world where, in reality, nationalist instincts still hold sway? The trials and tribulations of the Alliance would be an important case study for the entire industry as rising auto giants in China and India began venturing abroad with designs for their own cross-cultural car-making empires.

. . .

Ghosn's prophetic take on industry consolidation was coupled with his spot-on prediction of the technological trends that would necessitate it. His vision for a future of electrified and self-driving cars gradually became reality and was becoming conventional wisdom.

By late 2020, the shift to pluggable cars was kicked into overdrive by increasingly stringent emissions regulations. Nearly one hundred all-electric or plug-in hybrid models were under development and slated to debut by 2024.[2] Potent new entries, such as Volkswagen's battery-powered ID.4 crossover, packed impressive ranges up to 250 miles on a charge. Tesla was racking back-to-back profits.

In China, the world's biggest car market, the industry expected half of all new car sales to be electrified vehicles by 2035.[3] Volkswagen envisioned producing twenty-six million full electrics by 2030 and was investing a whopping €73 billion ($86 billion) to make it happen.[4] General Motors raced to make 40 percent of its US lineup electric by 2025.[5] Forecasters predicted that by 2032, as many as twenty million new electric vehicles (EVs) would be sold every year worldwide.[6]

Meanwhile, old players and newcomers alike were diving into newfangled driver-assist systems, which were becoming de rigueur for premium brands and spreading rapidly down-market into volume models. Internet giant Google's Waymo subsidiary was testing fully autonomous ride-hailing on US roads—with no human safety driver onboard to intervene in case of a computer glitch.

Nissan, despite all its woes, was actually well placed for this era of electrification and autonomy, largely because Ghosn had the foresight to start early on the technologies. A new common platform for next-generation electric vehicles underpinned the Ariya crossover EV. And unlike the debacle from a decade earlier, when the Nissan Leaf and Renault

Zoe electric vehicles shared almost no engineering, Renault and Nissan would use the same platform this time. In autonomous driving, Nissan was equipping its vehicles with ProPilot, a technology championed by Ghosn, which allowed a driver to sit back as their car cruised down the highway, passing cars, changing lanes, and negotiating interchanges all by itself.

Ghosn can rightly claim these as some of his top achievements.

. . .

Japan also owes much to Ghosn. He first engineered the rescue of Nissan and then put together a unique international alliance that, despite all the obituary notices in the financial media, remains in place two decades later. He broke down Japan's inefficient keiretsu system and challenged the country's moribund seniority-based career ladder with a merit system. As an outsider, he had the will and the ability to tear down barriers no Japanese executive could or would.

At the same time, all this success in the face of rapid industry change was, in some ways, central to the accusations of wrongdoing that eventually drummed him out of the business.

In Ghosn's mind, his achievements justified top-scale compensation that would make many in Japan and France recoil. If Ghosn wanted such exorbitant payouts, he couldn't let it show.

Plenty of Ghosn's top brass seemed to agree he deserved high dollar, both for his performance and to prevent him from defecting, if he decided to take his flirtations with GM, Ford, and others to the next level. A small army of Nissan executives spent considerable time and effort trying to concoct ways to pay Ghosn extra—prosecutors say double what was actually disclosed.

That is where things strayed from the unseemly into the illegal, according to the indictments. Not only should Nissan have disclosed that extra pay, they say, but Ghosn had strayed even further by lining his own pockets at the company's expense. The breach of trust allegations insinuated he was gaming the system from all directions. And on top of these criminal charges came Nissan's litany of accusations about misappropriated funds—from hundreds of thousands of dollars for his sister to inappropriate housing and travel expenses and donations made with company money in his name to Lebanese schools and nonprofit institutions.

The prosecutors office's screaming subtext to all of this was plain and simple: when Ghosn couldn't get paid what he wanted publicly, he took what he felt he deserved privately.

Ghosn, of course, had a different explanation. He says he was framed with trumped-up charges by a cabal of old-guard nationalists within Nissan and a Japanese government that wanted to torpedo the "irreversible" integration of Nissan and Renault. Spooked by French maneuvering during the Florange Crisis and headstrong in its position as the stronger of the two partners, Nissan would do anything it could to prevent that, including getting rid of the man who would initiate a merger. Despite the carefully choreographed appearance of Alliance amity, an appearance Ghosn himself helped convey, tensions between the French and Japanese sides of the partnership long ran deep and hot, and never went away.

There is also a third explanation, that these two storylines are not mutually exclusive. It is possible Ghosn was both a fraudster and a fall guy. When he was working miracles, Nissan executives may have been more than happy to turn a blind eye to dubious dealings. But when Ghosn became the potential vector for an irreversible French takeover, they may have known just where to dig. In at least one sense, there was a conspiracy. Nissan executives Nada, Imazu, and Kawaguchi—the top lawyer, auditor, and government relations head—admitted in court that they had worked secretly for months to uncover alleged misconduct by Ghosn and then hand their chairman over to prosecutors. But were they doing this to stop his wrongdoing, as they contend, or really to torpedo the merger they opposed?

. . .

More broadly, the ugly scandal that enveloped Ghosn and the Alliance highlighted collisions between France and Japan over the role of government in modern-day international commerce.

The French government made no secret of its goal to reap the full benefit of its high-risk investment twenty years earlier. As economy minister, Macron outmaneuvered Nissan during the Florange Crisis, only to retreat into a compromise later. He remained undeterred, however. As French president, he kept pressing the case for an irreversible alliance knowing that a standalone Renault would face an uncertain future in an industry set on scale.

The exact role played by the Japanese government was less clear, though Florange left a lasting mark. Officials at the Ministry of Economy, Trade, and Industry (METI) were clearly concerned about Nissan's future and by Ghosn's steps to cut investment in new models that was needed to stay competitive. They also felt they had to go to bat for Nissan in the face of undue pressure from Paris.

While the Japanese government publicly preached that the Alliance was a private-sector affair, it also made clear that it did not want Nissan to collapse on its watch. As COVID-19 devastated the industry, the government-owned Japan Bank for International Cooperation put up $2 billion to help Nissan sell cars in North America.

But whether the government played a "deep state" role as alleged by Ghosn remains one of the open questions in the saga. He has charged that Nissan board member Masakazu Toyoda, a retired senior METI official who was a director for less than five months before Ghosn's arrest, was the mastermind. Ghosn has been less precise about how the Japanese government, including the Public Prosecutors Office, allegedly took part in a conspiracy to bring him down. While Japanese prosecutors—as in the United States—are part of a political establishment, they are also fiercely independent and were still trying to restore an image hit by previous scandals. Therefore, they would be unlikely to do a favor for another part of the government, even if they were asked. If the case failed, they would be the ones who would take the blame for damaging the reputation of the judiciary and the country's international image. For the actual prosecutors involved, it would likely mean an end to their career ambitions.

. . .

In assessing Ghosn's innocence, it was often said that where there's smoke, there's fire. With all the accusations hurled against him, such thinking went, surely some of it must be true.

But final judgment on the key criminal matters partly hinges on what standard is applied. There is the legal standard of Japan. And there is the international standard of other countries, such as the United States or France, which themselves differ.

The question is especially complex in the gray-shaded world of white-collar crime. While international standards vary little over what constitutes murder, the rules for what's considered improper accounting, regulatory noncompliance, or unfair business practices vary widely. For example, some Japanese auto executives are still being sought in the United States on bid-rigging charges that date back as long as a decade.[7] To the consternation of US consumer groups, the executives deemed responsible in the Takata airbag scandal were safely in Japan when the charges were announced and were never brought to justice. From this perspective, Japan's protests over the fleeing of Carlos Ghosn seem paradoxical.

The Ghosn story also raises questions over what constitutes a proper business expense vs. a personal benefit. Much to the consternation of international companies, the IRS figures that a wide range of benefits for US executives overseas, such as company-paid apartments, meals, and tuition for children in international schools all represent taxable income. For most other countries—including Japan—such payments are largely tax-free. The French claim that Ghosn had personally benefited from €11 million ($12.3 million) of Renault's money could be debated endlessly, with the accountants and lawyers involved in the argument likely the only ones to come out ahead. What's okay in one place isn't in another; what's illegal here is a cost of doing business there.

The often-vague nature of laws and regulations also muddles the picture. Kelly's US lawyer complained that the statute on which Kelly was charged would be seen as hopelessly vague in a US court. (What's argued in Kelly's case can be seen as a proxy for what may have been argued in Ghosn's.) While this could be seen as legal maneuvering, he was not alone in raising the issue. Foreign business executives often complain that Japanese regulators seize on the vague wording of regulations to take capricious actions. In 1998, one US financial firm was publicly cited by Japanese regulators for a $51 error on a client's statement.[8] It was not lost on insiders at the firm that their company was at the time posing a competitive threat to Japan's brokerage firms.

There are also differences between administrative penalties and criminal charges. In the case of Ghosn and Kelly (and Nissan), the matter over the compensation reporting was settled in the United States by a civil suit filed by the Securities and Exchange Commission (SEC). This is the typical route for such infractions. Criminal action is typically based on a referral from the regulators and is saved for the more egregious violations since the burden of proof is higher. Lawyers in Japan noted that in the Ghosn-Kelly case, the matter appeared to go straight from the company to the criminal prosecutors, an unusual short-circuiting of the process. They also note that it was the first time that individuals have been charged with criminal wrongdoing over the required financial regulatory filing involved.

With his escape, Ghosn is unlikely to ever face a Japanese trial. This precludes the chance for either him or the government to demonstrate that they were right all along. But in reality, a trial verdict probably wouldn't have satisfied either side. When the accusations are as arcane as false financial statements or the improper use of currency swap derivative contracts, a ruling is likely to be just as abstruse. But defenders of Ghosn and Kelly tried as much to delegitimize Japan's justice system and the Nissan investigation, as to defend against the criminal charges themselves. The strategy was aimed at creating, in the eye of international opinion, a lingering cloud of doubt around the validity of any guilty verdict.

. . .

Individual and government motives aside, how did Nissan's corporate governance fail so badly? Some see it as a harbinger of governance issues for the vast majority of companies in Japan. Even as the government and regulators have imposed new standards to ensure better oversight, and companies like Nissan have taken their own steps to improve, the uptake on reforms has been slow. By 2019, the percentage of outside directors among all directors at companies listed on the Tokyo Stock Exchange had risen to 31.5 percent. In the United States, it was 85 percent.[9]

Nissan rolled out sweeping reforms after Ghosn's arrest, bringing its management more in line with Western norms for transparency and accountability. But these advances were arguably overshadowed by deep-rooted problems with Nissan's playbook in handling its internal Ghosn probe. In short, the company took the litigious and public route, rather than quietly dealing with its issues in-house. And the ethical framework of its misconduct probe left much to be desired.

As concerns about Ghosn came to the surface, for example, why didn't executives drag him into the boardroom and tell him that things had to change? They could have threatened criminal prosecution as a way to get restitution. Houses bought by Nissan but used by Ghosn could have been restricted to proper company business or sold. Corporate governance could have been tightened with more stringent outside checks and balances. Then, there were the mountains of questions surrounding the propriety of Hari Nada's internal investigation of the alleged misconduct.

Nissan contends that taking the allegations against Ghosn directly to the board would have been like driving into a brick wall, because he had absolute control. Few executives were brazen enough to openly challenge the boss over business decisions, let alone fraud accusations.

But this is a weak defense of the company and its directors (who have a responsibility to properly supervise the management of a company and none of whom—save Kelly—have faced any charges in the case). The authority Ghosn had over his own salary and that of his senior executives was one handed to him by the board. It was in itself a clear recipe for potential abuse and was representative of too many corporate boards in Japan that serve as little more than rubber stamps for a strong CEO. If Ghosn were truly gaming the system, then it could be argued that the board only had itself to blame. That is small consolation for the shareholders who allegedly saw company money squandered and undeniably saw the value of their holdings plummet because of the Ghosn affair.

A year after Ghosn's arrest, Nissan and Renault shareholders were each about 30 percent worse off. "Nissan's behavior was just shocking," said a US lawyer active in Japan. "You don't set up a sting operation with the police to arrest the architect of this great Alliance. If they were interested in maintaining the share price, they would not have acted the way they did."

There is also the question of how Nissan dealt with—or refused to deal with—Nada, the former Ghosn lieutenant who signed a plea bargain when it became clear he faced exposure in some of the crimes Ghosn was accused of. Despite his close involvement in a criminal matter, he not only kept his job but remained at the helm of Nissan's internal investigation into the alleged misconduct for months after Ghosn's arrest. By the end of 2020, he was one of the last key figures of the Ghosn scandal still in Nissan's employ. Nearly all others had quit, retired, been arrested, or were fired. To Nissan's critics, Nada's murky backroom dealings only epitomized the conflicts of interest that blew up any pretense of impartiality surrounding the company's motivations.

The involvement of Saikawa and other executives in improperly plumping their own incentive payouts or helping finagle Ghosn's compensation only showed how deeply the rot reached. And when prosecutors gave a pass to the Japanese players and zeroed in on the foreigners Ghosn and Kelly, there was criticism that the whole legal action had an air of hypocrisy, if not outright discrimination.

Nissan management also looked at its role as not only one of cooperating with the government's investigation, which would be the case in almost any jurisdiction, but also assisting it. To some critics, it was a questionable move. They contend that a company has an obligation to cooperate with authorities, not take over their work for them. In all, Nissan reportedly spent $200 million investigating the case and could only find two people supposedly guilty of wrongdoing.[10]

If Nissan and the Japanese government truly conspired against Ghosn to block a merger, did they foresee the cascade of unintended consequences that would ensue? In the tried-and-true manner of Japan's corporate culture and justice system, they no doubt expected that Ghosn would have quickly pleaded guilty, been handed a suspended sentence, and quietly bowed out of the industry. But he didn't do that. Did his unexpected resistance, and brazen escape, make an attempted coup spiral out of control, and focus the world's attention on something Japan would rather have kept in the shadows? Ghosn's decision not to play by Japan's rulebook triggered upheaval that will likely reverberate for years.

Nissan's governance failures were central to the saga, but there was almost no discussion of a more fundamental governance issue predating the scandal: as CEO of Nissan and Renault, Ghosn was required—by principle and by law—to represent the shareholders of two entirely separate corporations. In fact, Ghosn often spoke of the difficulties in trying to please his subordinates at both companies and representatives from two governments. But he also had an obligation to increase the value of both companies to the benefit of its owners—the shareholders. How was he meant to act in a situation that would benefit one at the expense of the other? For example, increasing output at a Renault plant while cutting back at a Nissan facility could mean that the CEO of Renault has done his job while the CEO of Nissan has not.

"The boards of directors were comfortable having Carlos Ghosn as the CEO of both companies in 2005," said a former Renault executive who worked closely with Ghosn. "And from that point on, it put him in a position of potential fiduciary conflict."

The way out of this conflict seemed to be the holding company Ghosn once envisioned as his final act: putting Renault and Nissan together under a common stock ticker beholden to the same pool of investors. This was never the intention of the Alliance's original architect, Louis Schweitzer, and it was not what Nissan wanted, either, but it certainly could have solved many governance problems.

. . .

The collision between the Japanese justice system and its critics was one of the more intense of the entire crisis. It's a battle that now commands international attention and is unlikely to end soon.

There have been key reforms over the years. Interrogations are now recorded to monitor intimidation; lay judges bring an outside perspective into the rarified judicial universe. Bail is now more common, rising to 30 percent of requests in 2018. (Although the Ghosn escape could prompt a backlash from judges who would want to avoid similar embarrassments in the future.)

Proponents of reform said Ghosn's ordeal underlined just how much remained to be done. Topping the list for them was to allow defense lawyers to be present at questioning. While this idea had been rejected in the past, Japan's Justice Ministry commissioned a team of experts in 2020, with the ministry offering an ever so slight policy shift, in classic Japanese fashion. A ministry representative member noted at a meeting that there was no official "ban" on defense lawyers from taking part, it merely left the decision to the individual prosecutors.

It's the smallest possible progress, taken under gaiatsu foreign pressure. It is too soon to know if it merely demonstrates Japan's unparalleled ability to adapt without really changing, by paying lip service to the idea now and quietly dropping it later. There is strong opposition within the Ministry to any change, and Justice Minister Masako Mori noted that "In Japan, interrogation often remains the sole means to extract statements from suspects."[11]

Any changes will likely come slowly, but the pressure is clearly on. The Japanese government could not be pleased to see US senator Roger Wicker on the Senate floor describe Kelly's treatment as "a scandal worthy of Vladimir Putin, not our allies in Japan."

The UN Working Group on Arbitrary Detention dealt another blow to the country's image, saying that Ghosn's repeated arrests represented "extrajudicial abuse." Perhaps Ghosn was right after all.

For Japan Inc., the question is simple, but crucial: will the treatment meted out to Ghosn and Kelly make foreign executives unwilling to take up assignments in the country? Both foreign attorneys and HR firms say that since the Ghosn affair, they have received many more questions from candidates about the risk of legal action against them if they move to Japan. The arrival of a European executive to become CEO of a Japanese chemicals company two years after Ghosn's arrest was noteworthy enough to garner international news coverage.[12]

For Japan's efforts to position itself as the right place for international business, the Ghosn headlines could not have come at a worse time. Tokyo has largely lost out to Hong Kong and Singapore as the Asia headquarters for multinational companies. Japan had hoped to use the increasing crackdown by the Chinese government in Hong Kong as a chance to grab back some of that business. "What Japan offers that Hong Kong doesn't is freedom," said a Japanese lawmaker trying to attract more foreigners.[13] Ghosn and Kelly would likely disagree.

. . .

Ghosn's biggest battle seemed to be in the court of public opinion.

His accusers painted him as a man out for himself and desperate to keep the size of his takings under the radar. Thanks to regular leaks by the prosecutors, this became the accepted truth for many in Japan. And many of those who worked closely with him, in France and Japan, echo the voluminous testimony from the Kelly trial and the findings of Nissan's probe in agreeing on a central theme—compensation was always a lightning rod issue when it came to Carlos Ghosn. Regardless of the truth behind the charges, Ghosn's official biography would always be tarnished by a shameful, nonerasable asterisk: he ended a legendary automotive career after being indicted four times and jumping bail to live as an international fugitive.

His escape, in the minds of many in Japan, is all the proof needed of his guilt. But without a trial, the Ghosn question may ultimately remain a he-said, she-said deadlock. A not-guilty verdict for Greg Kelly could be held up by Ghosn as vindication-by-proxy, though the court very well could have cleared Kelly while convicting Ghosn as the real culprit.

More important, the Kelly trial shed no light whatsoever on the two breach-of-trust charges leveled only against Ghosn, the so-called Saudi and Omani Routes for which Ghosn was accused of misusing Nissan assets for personal gain.

Some in Japan still say Ghosn should get the benefit of the doubt. "The current fuss is a tabloid scandal. What damage did Ghosn do to Japanese society?" asked one retired Japanese executive.

Some of Ghosn's harshest critics even remain steadfast admirers. One of the Nissan plea bargainers who testified at Kelly's trial couldn't help heaping at least some praise on his former boss. When pressed to describe Ghosn, Toshiaki Ohnuma confided he was always nervous around the chairman and afraid of giving him disagreeable news. But the soft-spoken Ohnuma still seemed caught under Ghosn's charismatic spell. "I thought he was an excellent business leader," Ohnuma conceded. "He rebuilt Nissan. As I worked near him, I saw that he was quick and undaunted in making decisions. He also gave clear instructions. He was willing to listen to people."

Greg Kelly, the longtime lieutenant Ghosn abandoned in Japan to face up to fifteen years in prison for allegedly feeding Ghosn's hunger for higher compensation, called his former boss an "extraordinary executive" and someone who deserved an ample reward.

Even Saikawa offered grudging admiration. "I was very impressed. And I'm still impressed," Saikawa said of those early years reviving the Japanese automaker. But it came with a caveat: "The second part of his management was not very good. We needed to correct a lot of things."

For many this was the reality, a tale of two Ghosns, both found in one man.

. . .

As this book neared completion, Ghosn sat for a video interview from Beirut to reflect on his wild ride and shattered legacy. Tanned and trim with a tight-cropped haircut and stylish sideburns (he seemed reconciled to his thinning gray hair and did nothing to hide it), he spoke from his study, where the shelving behind his desk brims with books, photos, and other mementos from his decades as a celebrated captain of industry, a bygone era when he would jet between four residences on three continents and mingle with the elite.

Ghosn blamed the Alliance's problems on government interference. The point of no return was the Florange Crisis, which—he says—triggered an overreaction by a paranoid Japanese government-industry confederacy. Such knee-jerk nationalism gradually found wider currency amid a worldwide resurgence in protectionism and trade tensions—as demonstrated by the US-China trade dispute or the United Kingdom's withdrawal from the European Union.

But Ghosn insists these are speed bumps; internationalization is here to stay.

"I have proven operationally you can do that," he said. "If there were no political intervention, if there was no interference from the French state on one side, and the Japanese state from the other in reaction, I've proven you can run mega companies like this, with components which are nationally based but an entity which is global. It not only worked, it flourished. I didn't do it for six months. I did it for nineteen years."

Ghosn fought to rehabilitate his image through two new books (including one coauthored by his wife, Carole), a planned miniseries documentary, and even through community outreach in his new home of Lebanon. In late 2020, he launched an executive business program at a university north of Beirut. His guest lecturers were to include Thierry Bolloré, the former No. 2 at Renault who was fired and then reemerged as CEO of Jaguar Land Rover, and José Muñoz, the erstwhile Saikawa rival who left Nissan to help lead Hyundai.

As Ghosn sat in Lebanon, pondering his past and plotting his future, he knew it would be a rocky road to redemption. "I have a lifelong battle to restore my reputation, but I have no choice other than to fight for my legacy and reestablish my name," he said.

He seethed about what he called cooked-up charges. And he bemoaned the lowly state of Nissan, asserting, "Nobody said, 'How are we going to preserve the brand, how are we going to preserve the shareholders, how are we going to preserve the employees, how are we going to preserve our image?'"

Ghosn also remained unbowed and unrepentant about any role he may have played in the chaos engulfing his auto empire. And he waxed triumphant about lifting the group to its short-lived zenith atop the global auto industry, ticking off many of his proudest moments.

"The first achievement, that nobody can take away from me, is turning around Nissan," Ghosn said. "Number two, without any doubt, is the fact I was able to manage three companies within the Alliance, two for many years and then the third one for a couple of years, without any hiccup.

"It took my arrest to stop it."

Despite the allegations of fraud spanning Japan, France, and the United States, Ghosn refuses to admit any wrongdoing or even bad business judgment. In his mind, he remains nothing less than the upstanding boardroom general people knew until he was hauled away to the Tokyo Detention House that November night in 2018. He never exploited the Alliance as his personal piggy bank, he maintains, and he definitely isn't to blame for its near collapse after his arrest.

In a moment of circumspect soul searching, the aging runaway even brooded over a world that might have been. Indeed, to Ghosn at least, there was only one way he could have averted the whole scandalous affair. Back in 2018, when Renault came calling on the then sixty-four-year-old Ghosn to renew his contract—couched in the infamous proviso to make Renault-Nissan an "irreversible" Alliance—Ghosn simply should have said, "No, thank you."

"It was a serious consideration," he contended.

"I was sixty-four years old, going for another four years. I had plenty of other interesting things to do in life," he said. "What would have stopped all this is just recusing myself from another mandate and retiring from all my positions. It would have meant putting my well-being and my family in front of my professional career. But I think it would have been a fair trade, knowing that, for everything I've done in my life, at a certain point, it's time to say you're just going to stop. And that would have been a good moment to stop."

Opting for this alternative ending seems an incredible assertion for one of the most driven and ambitious executives ever to steer an auto company—a man who changed the auto industry and helped reshape swaths of corporate Japan.

After all the lockups, lawsuits, ruined careers, international recriminations, broken-down business plans, and accused accomplices left behind to face justice without him—was that really his biggest regret?

"Yes," Ghosn insists. "Without any doubt."

Perhaps, only those who best understood Ghosn can really say whether he was a sentimental family man or a cold, calculating corporate executive, a visionary innovator or a self-absorbed autocrat. The unsuspecting victim of a boardroom coup or simply a C-suite swindler who betrayed the trust of his company, colleagues, and shareholders.

Or was he a complicated combination of all these things?

As Ghosn built a new life in Lebanon, still under the cloud of suspicion, fighting civil suits and grappling with a tainted legacy, he exchanged almost certain jail time in Japan for a more comfortable, if different kind of prison, in Beirut.

Yet, there can be no doubt that Ghosn rescued a company from almost certain collapse, built an auto empire spanning the globe, and became one of the most influential foreigners ever to set foot in Japan—from the day he arrived as a celebrated fix-it man, right up to his daredevil bail-jumping escape as an international fugitive twenty years later.

ACKNOWLEDGMENTS

Even though I was born and raised in metro Detroit and surrounded by the auto industry growing up, my family comes from the architecture and teaching fields, and I was anything but a car guy. Only after joining *Automotive News* did I realize just how privileged I am to be covering what, *I think* at least, is the world's most dynamic, intense, and complex industry—especially from Asia, where world heavyweights Japan and Korea are chock-full of brands that are global household names.

No consumer product is as beguiling as the car. Every time you leave your front door, it isn't long before you see them, in all shapes, sizes, and colors. They conjure a rich mix of emotion. Everyone has an ingrained "memory on wheels": That family vacation, a high school date, the daily commuter grind, even a tragic accident. Zoom out and the intricately interwoven global industry that makes those vehicles encompasses so much more: technology, trade, labor, design, manufacturing, politics, and big personalities galore. It's an endless sea to navigate and explore.

I wouldn't be in a position to dive into this exciting world if it weren't for the help and support of my exceptional colleagues at *Automotive News*, the most professional and dedicated reporters I have ever worked with. I must thank Publisher Jason Stein and Chief Editorial Director Dave Versical for their blessing in pursuing this book; Chief Content Officer Jamie Butters for his creative brainstorming; Editor Lindsay Chappell, as the resident Nissan veteran, for his wisdom and expert insight; and former editors James Treece and Rick Johnson, for not only serving as my mentors over the years, as my predecessors in Tokyo, but also for their critiques of our early manuscript. I also must not forget Tokyo News

Assistant Naoto Okamura, the team anchor and stalwart workhorse who relentlessly scrambled on the Ghosn story from that very first news blast. And, naturally, my colleague Peter Sigal, the Paris correspondent who kept *Automotive News* readers abreast of everything Renault. Extra thanks are due my Japanese teacher, Ayumi Sato, for all her years of seemingly masochistic dedication to my (forever flawed) understanding of the host country's language and her help with translation and research.

Although this book has no sanction or authorization from Nissan, Renault, or Carlos Ghosn, we must also express our deep gratitude to executives at both companies and to Ghosn himself for spending the time and effort to tell us their sides of the story. Due to the nature of our reporting, most of these executives, engineers, and many more employees of all other stripes spoke only on background, so we unfortunately cannot thank you all by name here. But you know who you are. Some of you I have worked with for a long time. Others are new acquaintances who, for the sake of adding insight to this work, took the risk of sharing with us for the first time. Thank you, all.

More broadly, I would be remiss in not conveying my sincerest appreciation for the cooperation of Nissan public affairs over the many years I have covered the company, beginning with my very first visit to the old Ginza headquarters in 2007. The men and women there exceled in their job by deepening my understanding of Nissan, and with me, they always performed with competence and polish. The short list of people past and present, includes Sadayuki Hamaguchi, Yuki Morimoto, Lavanya Wadgaonkar, Koji Okuda, Nicholas Maxfield, Dion Corbett, Azusa Momose, Christopher Keeffe, Jeff Kuhlman, Jonathan Adashek, Alan Buddendeck, Simon Sproule, Toshitake Inoshita, Mitsuru Yonekawa, Tak Ishikawa, Camille Lim, Dan Passe, Dan Sloan, Steven Silver, Ian Rowley, David Reuter, Nathalie Greve, Travis Parman, Wendy Orthman, Trevor Hale, Amanda Groty, and Roland Buerk. I apologize to the many more who go unnamed here.

Both William and I must also give a deep bow to our stellar editor Scott Berinato and the rest of the team at Harvard Business Review Press. They gambled on signing two untested authors, and their guiding hand made the long march to completing this book remarkably painless, efficient, and smooth for the two of us neophytes. Further thanks to Katherine Flynn and the Kneerim & Williams Agency.

Of course, the ultimate arigatou goes to my family. Without the encouragement and greenlight from my wife Yumiko, I would likely have demurred from attempting any book, let alone a complicated tale like this one. But she pushed me to do it. Likewise, I must express deep indebtedness to my daughters, Nozomi and Miyuki, who never grumbled about the countless lost evenings and weekends when their never-present father was glued to the keyboard in his "spider hole" workspace. Instead, they were pillars of unflinching, cheerful encouragement. And lastly, I would like to thank my parents, the late Karl Hans Greimel Sr. and Jill, as well as my brother Tim, who have always had my back and showered me with love and support.

I am sure there are many more I have neglected to thank here, but please know this work was the product of so many people. Each and every contribution was an important piece of the puzzle and meant more than I can express here in words.

—Hans Greimel, 2021

It has been an incredible year of reporting and writing, not least for the fact that this project took place during one of the worst pandemics ever to hit the world. We must doubly thank everyone who helped in so many ways when there were other thoughts on everyone's mind.

Many who have helped have asked to remain in the background, so I cannot properly thank them here. But I must note the great assistance of Keiko Ohara, who as an attorney admitted in both the United States and Japan has helped in explaining the legal complexities. In addition, Yuuichiro Nakajima and Harry Nakahara, who contributed their many insights into corporate Japan. And Scott McIntyre, the Australian journalist who was himself caught up in Japan's criminal justice system and recounted its flaws, no less severe for not being unique in the world.

Also of great assistance were Arthur Mitchell, one of the first foreign attorneys to help Japan as it looked internationally, and Steven Givens for his analysis of the Greg Kelly trial. Reed Stevenson was always a huge help in bouncing around themes and viewpoints in this complex story, while Yvonne Chang's endless intellectual curiosity in researching helped to uncover important elements for us. Yann Tessier, Jean Francois Minier, Laurence Frost, and Fatim Diallo offered vital insights into all things French. Former colleague Chang-Ran Kim and long-time friend Sadaaki Numata graciously agreed to reading the manuscript in its early form to help provide direction and feedback.

In looking over what we've produced, it would not have been possible without the front-line reporting work of so many former colleagues at Reuters and the *Wall Street Journal*, who have been the true first drafts of history in explaining Japan, its economy, and the political forces that shaped so much of what took place. I must especially note the impressive chronicling of the last three decades by Linda Sieg of Reuters, who remains the go-to expert on all things Japan.

In addition to all the names mentioned above, we must add our fact-checker Roni Greenwood at Girl Friday Productions, who took nothing for granted and helped us avoid embarrassment in more cases than we would like to ever admit. For any mistakes that slipped through, it is only because we hid them well, not for any lack of trying on her part.

And finally, to John Butman, whose eye for a great story started us down this road. He was a friend to us both for far too short a time.

—William Sposato, 2021

NOTES

CHAPTER 1. GHOSN SHOCK

1. Hans Greimel, "Ghosn on Why Renault-Nissan Really Needs 2 CEOs," *Automotive News*, January 10, 2016, https://www.autonews.com/article/20160110/BLOG06/160119977/ghosn-on-why-renault-nissan-really-needs-2-ceos.

2. Marcelo Rochabrun and Ritsuko Ando, "Art and Cash-Filled Rio Apartment the New Battleground for Nissan, Ghosn: Court Filing," Reuters, December 10, 2018, https://www.reuters.com/article/us-nissan-ghosn-exclusive-idUSKBN1O91P9.

3. Nick Lawrie and Felipe Munoz, "Global Car Sales up by 2.4% in 2017 Due to Soaring Demand in Europe, Asia-Pacific and Latin America," JATO, February 20, 2018, https://www.jato.com/global-car-sales-2-4-2017-due-soaring-demand-europe-asia-pacific-latin-america/.

4. Hans Greimel, "Was the Ghosn Sting Compliance or Coup d'État?" *Automotive News*, December 2, 2018, https://www.autonews.com/article/20181202/OEM02/181209978/was-the-ghosn-sting-compliance-or-coup-d-etat.

5. Opinions adopted by the Working Group on Arbitrary Detention at its eighty-eighth session, August 24–28, 2020, Human Rights Council Working Group on Arbitrary Detention, November 20, 2020, https://www.ohchr.org/Documents/Issues/Detention/Opinions/Session88/A_HRC_WGAD_2020_59_Advance_Edited_Version.pdf.

CHAPTER 2. ROCK STAR CEO

1. "Ghosn: 'We Don't Have a Choice,'" *Automotive News*, November 9, 1999, https://www.autonews.com/article/19991108/ANA/911080721/ghosn-we-don-t-have-a-choice.

2. Richard Johnson, "Three Heroes Emerge to Resucitate Nissan" [sic], *Automotive News*, November 22, 1999, https://www.autonews.com/article/19991122/ANA/911220783/three-heroes-emerge-to-resucitate-nissan.

3. Carlos Ghosn and Philippe Riès, *Shift: Inside Nissan's Historic Revival* (New York: Currency Doubleday, 2005).

4. Miki Shimogori, "Toyota Chief Sounds Alarm on Restructuring Spree," Reuters, May 13, 1999, Factiva, https://global.factiva.com/ha/default.aspx#./!?&_suid=161352354216406872577845336212/1999.

5. "Ghosn: 'We Don't Have a Choice.'"

6. Lindsay Chappell, "Carlos Ghosn," *Automotive News*, May 19, 2008, https://www.autonews.com/article/20080519/ANA03/805190330/carlos-ghosn.

7. "Bad Manners," *Automotive News*, July 1, 2000, https://www.autonews.com/article/20000701/SUB/7010704/bad-manners.

8. "Ghosn Sees Potential in Renault-Nissan Alliance," *Automotive News*, April 29, 2005, https://www.autonews.com/article/20050429/REG/504290705/ghosn-sees-potential-in-renault-nissan-alliance.

CHAPTER 3. JAPAN IS DIFFERENT

1. "The Davos Manifesto 2020," World Economic Forum, December 2, 2019, https://www.weforum.org/the-davos-manifesto.

2. "The Gift Locomotive That Charmed Samurai Japan," Nippon.com, August 5, 2017, https://www.nippon.com/en/nipponblog/m00123/the-gift-locomotive-that-charmed-samurai-japan.html.

3. Árni Breki Ríkarðsson, "Origins of the Zaibatsu Conglomerates: Japanese Zaibatsu Conglomerates in the Meiji Period 1868–1912," January 2020, https://skemman.is/bitstream/1946/34702/5/BA_Origin_of_the%20Zaibatsu_Conglomerates_%28Arni_Breki_Rikardsson_2020%29.pdf.

4. Nissan, "Company Development," nissan-global.com.

5. David A. C. Addicott, "The Rise and Fall of the Zaibatsu: Japan's Industrial and Economic Modernization," *Global Tides* 11, no. 5 (2017), http://digitalcommons.pepperdine.edu/globaltides/vol11/iss1/5.

6. Corporate profile, Mitsubishi Group, https://www.mitsubishi.com/en/profile/group/qa/.

7. Satoshi Hara, *Fall Seven Times, Get Up Eight: Aspects of Japanese Values* (London: Gilgamesh Publishing, 2020), 23, 25.

8. "Japanese Companies Must Comply or Explain," *Nikkei Asia*, July 21, 2015, https://asia.nikkei.com/Business/Markets/Stocks/Japanese-companies-must-comply-or-explain2.

9. Kazuaki Hagata, "Abenomics Improved Japan's Corporate Governance, but More Work Remains," *Japan Times*, September 12, 2020, https://www.japantimes.co.jp/news/2020/09/14/business/corporate-governance-abenomics-japan/.

10. Ezra F. Vogel, *Japan as Number One: Lessons for America* (Cambridge, MA: Harvard University Press, 1979), 70.

11. Donald W. Katzner and Mikhail J. Nikomarvo, "Exercises in Futility: Post-War Automobile-Trade Negotiations between Japan and the United States," 2005, Economics Department Working Paper Series, 52, https://scholarworks.umass.edu/econ_workingpaper/52.

12. Carlos Ghosn and Philippe Riès, *Le temps de la vérité: Carlos Ghosn parle* (Paris: Éditions Grasset & Fasquelle, 2020), 113–114.

CHAPTER 4. THE GLOBAL STANDARD

1. Luca Cifferi, "Why Ghosn Favors Separate CEOs for Renault and Nissan," January 10, 2014, https://www.autonews.com/article/20140110/COPY01/301109952/why-ghosn-favors-separate-ceos-for-renault-and-nissan.

2. Clay Chandler, Janet Guyon, Cait Murphy, and Richard Tomlinson, "Foreign Powers," *Fortune*, August 11, 2003, https://money.cnn.com/magazines/fortune/fortune_archive/2003/08/11/346836/index.htm.

3. World's Most Respected Companies survey, 2004, PricewaterhouseCoopers, https://www.globenewswire.com/news-release/2004/11/19/319007/67904/en/General

-Electric-is-the-World-s-Most-Respected-Company-According-to-Financial-Times
-PricewaterhouseCoopers-Survey.html.

4. The Reconstruction Agency (Japan), https://www.reconstruction.go.jp/english
/topics/GEJE/index.html; Bertel Schmitt, with Carlos Ghosn, "Down by the Waterfront,"
The Truth about Cars (blog), July 16, 2011, https://www.thetruthaboutcars.com/2011/07
/with-carlos-ghosn-down-by-the-waterfront/.

5. Reuters, "Car Maker Turnaround King Ghosn Now a Knight," January 9, 2007,
https://uk.reuters.com/article/autos-ghosn-knight/car-maker-turnaround-king-ghosn
-now-a-knight-idUKNOA42749020061024.

6. Miguel Rivas-Micoud, *The Ghosn Factor: 24 Lessons from the World's Most Dynamic CEO*
(New York: McGraw-Hill, 2006).

7. Jamie LeReau, "Kerkorian Proposal Surprises GM," *Automotive News*, July 3, 2006.
https://www.autonews.com/article/20060703/SUB/60630067/kerkorian-proposal
-surprises-gm.

8. Nick Bunkley, "Wanted Man: Jobs He Might Have Had," *Automotive News*,
February 27, 2017, https://www.autonews.com/article/20170227/OEM02/302279956/
wanted-man-jobs-he-might-have-had.

9. Bryce G. Hoffman, *American Icon: Alan Mulally and the Fight to Save Ford Motor Co.*
(New York: Crown Business, 2012).

10. TARP Programs, US Department of Treasury, January 8, 2015, https://www
.treasury.gov/initiatives/financial-stability/TARP-Programs/automotive-programs
/pages/default.aspx.

11. Steve Rattner, *Overhaul: An Insider's Account of the Obama Administration's Emergency
Rescue of the Auto Industry* (New York: Houghton Mifflin, 2010).

12. Matthew Campbell, "Inside the Takedown of Renault-Nissan Chairman Carlos
Ghosn," Bloomberg News, January 31, 2019, https://www.bloomberg.com/news
/features/2019-01-31/inside-the-takedown-of-renault-nissan-chairman-carlos-ghosn.

13. "Carlos Ghosn Voted World's Most Influential French Person by *Vanity Fair*,"
Groupe Renault, December 22, 2015, https://group.renault.com/en/news-on-air/news
/carlos-ghosn-voted-worlds-most-influential-french-person-by-vanity-fair/.

14. Sean McLain and Nick Kostov, "Nissan and Carlos Ghosn Spar over Yacht," *Wall
Street Journal*, August 23, 2019, https://www.wsj.com/articles/nissan-and-carlos-ghosn
-spar-over-yacht-11566603222.

15. The English translation of the "Yukashoken-Houkokusho" for the year ending
March 31, 2010, Nissan, March 31, 2019, https://www.nissan-global.com/EN/DOCUMENT
/PDF/FR/2009/fr2009.pdf.

16. Form 20-F, Annual Report Pursuant to Section 13 or 15(D) of the Securities
Exchange Act of 1934, Toyota Motor Corp., 2011.

17. Form 20-F, Annual Report Pursuant to Section 13 or 15(D) of the Securities
Exchange Act of 1934, Honda Motor Corp., 2010.

18. Katsuhiko Mizuno, *Courtyard Gardens of Kyoto's Merchant Houses*, trans. Lucy North
(New York: Kodansha International, 2006).

19. Bernie Woodall, "Ford Increases CEO's Pay 48 Percent to 26.5 Million," Reuters,
April 2, 2011, https://www.reuters.com/article/us-ford-mulally/ford-increases-ceos-pay
-48-percent-to-26-5-million-idUSTRE73072S20110401.

20. Bernie Woodall, "GM CEO Akerson Paid 2.53 Million in 2010 SEC Filing," Reuters,
April 22, 2011, https://www.reuters.com/article/us-gm-compensation/gm-ceo-akerson
-paid-2-53-million-in-2010-sec-filing-idUSTRE73K5SD20110421.

21. Form 10-K, Annual Report Pursuant to Section 13 or 15(D) of the Securities
Exchange Act of 1934, General Motors Corp., 2010.

22. English translation of the "Yukashoken-Houkokusho" for the year ending March 31, 2017, Nissan Motor Company.

23. Peter Sigal, "Why Ghosn's Renault Paycheck Depends on EV Sales," *Automotive News*, June 18, 2018, https://www.autonews.com/article/20180618/COPY01/306189967 /why-ghosn-s-renault-paycheck-depends-on-ev-sales.

24. English translation of the "Yukashoken-Houkokusho" for the year ending March 31, 2018, Mitsubishi Motors Corp.

CHAPTER 5. MEMORIES ARE SHORT

1. William Mallard, "Japan Economy Extends Record Fall," Reuters, December 4, 1998, https://global.factiva.com/ha/default.aspx#./!?&_suid=1613438727292041805060788499016.

2. Linda Sieg, "Japan's Economic Glass—Half Empty or Half Full?" Reuters, March 9, 1999, https://global.factiva.com/ha/default.aspx#./!?&_suid=.

3. Edmund Klamann, "Sony Chief Says Japan Economy Risks Collapse," Reuters, April 2, 1998, https://global.factiva.com/ha/default.aspx#./!?&_suid=16134388894290100276218 45358925.

4. Minutes of the Monetary Policy Meeting, February 12, 1999, Bank of Japan, released on March 17, 1999, https://www.boj.or.jp/en/mopo/mpmsche_minu/minu_1999/g990212 .htm/.

5. David P. Hamilton and Bill Spindle, "Yamaichi Securities Shuts Down in Japan's Biggest-Ever Failure," *Wall Street Journal,* updated November 24, 1997, https://www.wsj .com/articles/SB880310313773643500.

6. Linda Sieg, "Tough Times in Japan May Not Be Tough Enough," Reuters, January 29, 1999.

7. Masami Ito, "Apologizing in Japan: Sorry Seems to Be the Hardest Word," *Japan Times*, February 21, 2015, https://www.japantimes.co.jp/news/2015/02/21/national /social-issues/apologizing-japan-sorry-seems-hardest-word/.

8. Daryl Loo and Masumi Suga, "McDonald's Japan Posts ¥22 Billion Loss after Food Woes," *Japan Times*, February 5, 2015, https://www.japantimes.co.jp/news/2015/02/05 /business/corporate-business/mcdonalds-japan-posts-%C2%A522-billion-loss-food-woes/.

9. Suguru Kurimoto, Hiroyasu Oda, and Kento Hirashima, "McDonald's Lovin' It in Japan as Consumers Forget Scandals," *Nikkei Asia*, September 20, 2017, https://asia.nikkei .com/Business/McDonald-s-lovin-it-in-Japan-as-consumers-forget-scandals.

10. Igarashi Daisuke, "Takeda CEO Would Have Scrapped Shire Deal If Leaked," *Globe Asahi News*, August 5, 2019, https://globe.asahi.com/article/12596062.

11. Bob Murray, "The Best-Known Westerner in Japan," *Management Today*, September 1, 1997, updated August 31, 2010, https://www.managementtoday.co.uk/japan-best-known -westerner-japan/article/411100.

12. Valerie Reitman, "Japan Is Aghast as Foreigner Takes the Wheel at Mazda—Putting Wallace in Charge, Ford Shows It Is Taking Control," *Wall Street Journal*, April 15, 1996.

13. "International: Samsung Overtakes Sony in 2005 Interbrand Top 100 Ranking," Exchange4Media, August 8, 2019, https://www.exchange4media.com/marketing-news /internationalsamsung-overtakes-sony-in-2005-interbrand-top-100-ranking-17147.html.

14. Kunio Saijo, "Jeans, Music and Drastic Cuts: How Kaz Hirai Remade Sony," *Nikkei Asia*, June 19, 2019, https://asia.nikkei.com/Business/Companies/Jeans-music-and-drastic -cuts-How-Kaz-Hirai-remade-Sony.

15. "Jack Welch at General Electric: $417 Million," *Forbes*, January 19, 2012, https:// www.forbes.com/pictures/ehii45khf/jack-welch-at-general-electric-417-million/?sh=58ee 289453bd.

16. "CEO Staying Power," Korn Ferry, Winter 2017, https://www.kornferry.com/content/dam/kornferry/docs/article-migration/CEOStayingPower.Winter2017.pdf.

CHAPTER 6. PRESSURE COOKER

1. J. Snyder, "Ghosn's Mantra: Go Big or You'll Go Away," *Automotive News*, May 25, 2010, https://www.autonews.com/article/20100525/OEM01/100529890/ghosn-s-mantra-go-big-or-you-ll-go-away.

2. Nissan Motor Co., press release, January 27, 2011, https://global.nissannews.com/en/releases/110127-01-e?source=nng&lang=en-US.

3. Groupe Renault, press release, January 10, 2011, https://media.group.renault.com/global/en-gb/groupe-renault/media/pressreleases/25521/resultats-commerciaux-monde-20102.

4. T. Swanson, "Driving to 545 mpg: The History of Fuel Economy," Pew, April 20, 2011, https://www.pewtrusts.org/en/research-and-analysis/fact-sheets/2011/04/20/driving-to-545-mpg-the-history-of-fuel-economy.

5. Angela Greiling Keane (Bloomberg News), "U.S. Completes 54-5 mpg Fuel Economy Mandate for Light Vehicles," *Automotive News*, August 28, 2012, https://www.autonews.com/article/20120828/OEM11/120829909/u-s-completes-54-5-mpg-fuel-economy-mandate-for-light-vehicles.

6. Clifford Atiyeh, "U.S. Sets Final Fuel Economy, Emissions Standards for 2021–2026 Vehicles," *Car and Driver*, March 31, 2020, https://www.caranddriver.com/news/a31993900/us-final-fuel-economy-emissions-standards-2021-2026/.

7. L. Chappell, "Spiffs Will Slice Price of Nissan EV," *Automotive News*, April 19, 2010, https://www.autonews.com/article/20100419/RETAIL03/304199977/spiffs-will-slice-price-of-nissan-ev; Hans Greimel, "Ghosn Electric Cars Are Worth the Billions That Will Be Invested," *Automotive News*, August 10, 2009, https://www.autonews.com/article/20090810/GLOBAL02/308109870/ghosn-electric-cars-are-worth-the-billions-that-will-be-invested.

8. L. Chappell, "Even before Leaf Launch Nissan Plans Battery Growth," *Automotive News*, October 1, 2009, https://www.autonews.com/article/20091012/GLOBAL02/310129768/even-before-leaf-launch-nissan-plans-battery-growth.

9. J. Snyder, "Ghosn's Mantra."

10. Hans Greimel, "Nissan, Renault Go Modular: Big Savings, Tough Problems," *Automotive News*, October 28 , 2013, https://www.autonews.com/article/20131028/OEM03/310289967/nissan-renault-go-modular-big-savings-tough-problems.

11. Hans Greimel, "New Nissan Leaf Pitched as High-Tech Showcase with 150-Mile Range," *Automotive News*, September 5, 2017, https://www.autonews.com/article/20170905/OEM05/170909882/new-nissan-leaf-pitched-as-high-tech-showcase-with-150-mile-range.

12. "How to Use Your Vacation Time," Expedia, October 15, 2018, https://viewfinder.expedia.com/how-to-use-your-vacation-time/.

13. Sergio Marchionne, "Confessions of a Capital Junkie," *Automotive News*, April 29, 2015, https://www.autonews.com/assets/PDF/CA99316430.PDF.

14. D. Busvine, "Geely Chairman Becomes Daimler's Top Shareholder," *Automotive News Europe*, February 23, 2018, https://europe.autonews.com/article/20180223/COPY/302249999/geely-chairman-becomes-daimler-s-top-shareholder.

15. B. Lutz, "Kiss the Good Times Goodbye," *Automotive News*, November 5, 2017, https://www.autonews.com/article/20171105/INDUSTRY_REDESIGNED/171109944/bob-lutz-kiss-the-good-times-goodbye.

16. Marchionne, "Confessions of a Capital Junkie."

17. L. Chappell, "Ghosn Not Keen on Industry Mergers," *Automotive News*, January 19, 2016, https://www.autonews.com/article/20160118/OEM02/301189972/ghosn-not-keen-on -industry-mergers.

CHAPTER 7. COLLISION COURSE

1. "Fiscal Year 2000 Financial Results and Nissan Revival Plan in Review," Nissan Motor Co., March 31, 2001, https://www.nissan-global.com/EN/DOCUMENT/PDF /FINANCIAL/PRESEN/2000/fs_presen2000.pdf.

2. Annual Report Summary, Renault, 2000, https://group.renault.com/wp-content /uploads/2014/07/renault_-_2000_annual_report_summary.pdf.

3. Annual Report, Renault, 2005, https://group.renault.com/wp-content/uploads /2014/07/renault_-_2005_annual_report.pdf.

4. Kim Hill, Adam Cooper, and Debra Menk, "Contribution of the Automotive Industry to the Economies of All Fifty States and the United States," Center for Automotive Research, April 2010, https://www.cargroup.org/publication/contribution-of -the-automotive-industry-to-the-economies-of-all-fifty-state-and-the-united-states/.

5. "The Motor Industry of Japan 2019," Japan Automobile Manufacturers Association, 2019.

6. "The French Automotive Industry," Comité des Constructeurs Français d'Automobiles, 2019, https://ccfa.fr/wp-content/uploads/2019/09/ccfa-2019-en-web-v2.pdf.

7. Hans Greimel, "The Juggernaut That's Not Japan," *Automotive News*, April 1, 2013, https://www.autonews.com/article/20130401/OEM01/304019981/the-juggernaut-that-s -not-japan.

8. Hans Greimel, "Nissan's Curious Math for Japan Production Not So Reassuring," *Automotive News Europe*, August 17, 2011, https://europe.autonews.com/article/20110817 /BLOG15/308179880/nissan-s-curious-math-for-japan-production-not-so-reassuring.

9. Nick Gibbs, "Europe Plant Capacity Crisis to Extend to 2016," *Automotive News Europe*, June 21, 2013, https://europe.autonews.com/article/20130621/ANE/130629997 /europe-plant-capacity-crisis-to-extend-to-2016.

10. Bruce Gain, "Renault Will Build Next Nissan Micra in France," *Automotive News Europe*, April 26, 2013, https://europe.autonews.com/article/20130426/ANE/130429920 /renault-will-build-next-nissan-micra-in-france.

11. Reuters, "Renault Unions Seek Clarification on Flins Plant Cuts," *Automotive News Europe*, April 11, 2014, https://europe.autonews.com/article/20140411/ANE/140419973 /renault-unions-seek-clarification-on-flins-plant-cuts.

12. "Nissan Racing to Build Strategic Indian Plant," *Nikkei Business Daily*, February 3, 2010, http://t21.nikkei.co.jp/g3/s/SENGD015. do?keyBody=NDJEDBIS03HH426A0302 2010%5CNID%5Cc3a97a2b&transitionId=10699cf3e231226d9e59a1f497251e4300c8b &analysisPrevActionId=SENGD014&start=21&totalCnt=39&parentTransId=106996 f5a6908129d39c5d6a38a5163dd8480&cnt=20&sor.

13. Reuters, "France Backs Down on ArcelorMittal Nationalisation," France 24, January 12, 2012, https://www.france24.com/en/20121201-france-180-million-deal -arcelormittal-steelworks.

14. Reuters, "France Increases Renault Stake in Challenge to Ghosn," *Automotive News Europe*, April 8, 2018, https://europe.autonews.com/article/20150408/ANE/150409876 /france-increases-renault-stake-in-challenge-to-ghosn.

15. "Renault Board Approves Alliance Stability Covenant between Renault and Nissan," Groupe Renault, December 11, 2015, https://group.renault.com/wp-content /uploads/2015/12/renaultgroup_74374_global_en.pdf.

16. Laurence Frost, "Renault Board Asks Ghosn to Stay, Pursue Closer Nissan Integration," Reuters, February 15, 2018, https://www.reuters.com/article/us-renault -board-idUSKCN1FZ2KM.

CHAPTER 8. THE FRENCH ARE DIFFERENT

1. National Diet Library, Japan, https://www.ndl.go.jp/france/en/.

2. C. J. F. Brown, "Industrial Policy and Economic Planning in Japan and France," *National Institute Economic Review*, no. 93 (1980): 59–75, http://www.jstor.org/stable /23875311.

3. General CIA Records, Document Number (FOIA)/ESDN (CREST): CIA-RDP83- 00857R000100010005-6, Release Decision: RIPPUB, Original Classification: S, Creation Date: December 21, 2016, Sequence Number: 5, CIA-RDP83-00857R000100010005-6.pdf.

4. "France Begins $8 Billion Takeover of Private Industry and Banking," *New York Times*, February 15, 1982, https://www.nytimes.com/1982/02/15/world/france-begins-8 -billion-takeover-of-private-industry-and-banking.html.

5. Carlos Ghosn and Philippe Riès, *Shift: Inside Nissan's Historic Reversal* (New York: Crown Business, 2004), 59–60.

6. Laurence Frost and Michel Rose, "Seeds of Renault-Nissan Crisis Sown in Macron's 'Raid,'" Reuters, November 28, 2018, https://jp.reuters.com/article/us-nissan-ghosn -renault-macron-insight/seeds-of-renault-nissan-crisis-sown-in-macrons-raid-idUS KCN1NX1GK.

7. Laurence Frost and Gilles Guillaume, "Renault-Nissan's French Peace Deal Leaves Investors Underwhelmed," Reuters, December 12, 2015, https://www.reuters.com/article /us-renault-nissan/renault-nissans-french-peace-deal-leaves-investors-underwhelmed -idUSKBN0TU17R20151212.

8. Frost and Rose, "Seeds of Renault-Nissan Crisis."

9. "Macron Tells Abe He Is Worried About Carlos Ghosn's Time in Prison," *Japan Times*, January 28, 2019, https://www.japantimes.co.jp/news/2019/01/28/business/macron -tells-abe-worried-carlos-ghosns-time-prison/#.Xxv6dUBuLcs.

10. "Renault Board Maintains CEO Pay Deal Despite Shareholder Revolt," Reuters, April 30, 2016.

11. Full transcript of Al-Arabiya's interview with Carlos Ghosn, July 11, 2020, https:// english.alarabiya.net/en/amp/features/2020/07/11/Full-transcript-of-Al-Arabiya-s -exclusive-interview-with-Nissan-ex-boss-Carlos-Ghosn.

12. Agence France Presse, "Ousted Ghosn Seeks Retirement Benefit from Renault," January 14, 2020, Factiva, https://global.factiva.com/ha/default.aspx#./!?&_suid=16138 00912544057961264856987778.

13. *March 9th, 2014 Versailles—Carlos Ghosn Roi*, posted May 9, 2019, https://www .youtube.com/watch?v=X4Fz9ThQvH4.

14. Reuters News, "Renault's Board Triggers Process to Recover Ghosn's Suspect Expenses," June 5, 2019, https://www.reuters.com/article/us-renault-nissan-ghosn /renaults-board-triggers-process-to-recover-ghosns-suspect-expenses-idUSKCN1T52HR.

CHAPTER 9. THE CASE IS BUILT

1. Hans Greimel and Naoto Okamura, "Ex-Nissan Exec Kelly Takes Stand, Calls Ghosn 'Extraordinary Executive,'" *Automotive News*, September 15, 2020, https://www .autonews.com/automakers-suppliers/ex-nissan-exec-kelly-takes-stand-calls-ghosn -extraordinary-executive.

2. Kae Inoue, "Ghosn Denies He Passed Trading Losses to Nissan," *Automotive News*, November 28, 2019, https://www.autonews.com/article/20181128/COPY01/311289968/ghosn-denies-reports-he-passed-trading-losses-to-nissan.

3. Norihiko Shirouzu, "Nissan Sources Link Latest Ghosn Allegations to Khaled Al-Juffali, Vice Chairman of One of Saudi Arabia's Largest Conglomerates," *Japan Times*, December 27, 2018, https://www.japantimes.co.jp/news/2018/12/27/business/corporate-business/nissan-sources-link-latest-ghosn-allegations-khaled-al-juffali-vice-chairman-one-saudi-arabias-largest-conglomerates/.

4. Hans Greimel, "Ghosn Walks Free on Bail, Ready to Fight 'Meritless' Charges," *Automotive News*, May 4, 2019, https://www.autonews.com/executives/ghosn-walks-free-bail-ready-fight-meritless-charges.

5. Hans Greimel and Naoto Okamura, "Ghosn Takes to Twitter with Plans to 'Tell the Truth'—If He Avoids Another Arrest," *Automotive News*, April 3, 2019, https://www.autonews.com/automakers-suppliers/ghosn-takes-twitter-plans-tell-truth-if-he-avoids-another-arrest.

6. "Improvement Measures Status Report to Tokyo Stock Exchange," Nissan Motor Co., 2020, https://www.release.tdnet.info/inbs/ek/140120200116447351.pdf.

7. Hans Greimel, "Alliance Partners Turn Up Heat on Ghosn," *Automotive News*, January 29, 2019, https://www.autonews.com/executives/alliance-partners-turn-heat-ghosn.

8. "Improvement Measures Status Report."

9. Ania Nussbaum, "Ghosn Defends Use of Versailles for Wife's Birthday Party," *Automotive News*, January 9, 2020, https://www.autonews.com/executives/ghosn-defends-use-versailles-wifes-birthday-party.

10. Agence France-Presse, "Renault Files Civil Claim against Ghosn," February 24, 2020, https://www.rfi.fr/en/wires/20200224-renault-files-civil-claim-against-ghosn.

11. Hans Greimel, "Nissan Sues Ghosn in Japan for $91 Million," *Automotive News*, February 12, 2020, https://www.autonews.com/executives/nissan-sues-ghosn-japan-91-million.

12. "Improvement Measures Status Report."

13. "Improvement Measures Status Report."

14. "Greed Drove Nissan's Ghosn into a Trap," *Nikkei Asian Review*, November 29, 2018, https://asia.nikkei.com/Opinion/The-Nikkei-View/Greed-drove-Nissan-s-Ghosn-into-a-trap.

CHAPTER 10. MAKINGS OF A CONSPIRACY

1. Hans Greimel and Naoto Okamura, "Ghosn Lawyer Pokes at 'Peculiar' Case; UN Receives Claim of Human Rights Abuse," *Automotive News*, March 4, 2019, https://www.autonews.com/executives/ghosn-lawyer-pokes-peculiar-case-un-receives-claim-human-rights-abuse.

2. Hans Greimel, "Was the Ghosn Sting Compliance or a Coup d'État?" *Automotive News*, December 2, 2018, https://www.autonews.com/article/20181202/OEM02/181209978/was-the-ghosn-sting-compliance-or-coup-d-etat.

3. Hans Greimel, "Ghosn Slams 'Backstabbing' Nissan Leadership, 'Mediocre' Performance," *Automotive News*, April 9, 2019, https://www.autonews.com/automakers-suppliers/ghosn-slams-backstabbing-nissan-leadership-mediocre-performance.

4. H. Kawatsu, "Intended Claims Document, Defendant: Carlos Ghosn Bichara," Tokyo District Court, 17th Criminal Division Department, October 17, 2019, https://tokyotom.freecapitalists.org/2020/01/05/oct-17-2019-petition-filed-carlos-ghosns-lawyer

-dismissal-prosecution/comment-page-1/?unapproved=91932&moderation-hash=coe
346847dace821a9766bdf9017fe88#comment-91932.

5. Kawatsu, "Intended Claims Document."

6. Hans Greimel, "Ghosn Takes Case to International Court of Public Opinion," *Automotive News*, January 8, 2020, www.autonews.com/executives/ghosn-takes-case-international-court-public-opinion.

7. Takayuki Inoue, "New Plea Bargaining System in Practice," International Law Office, August 12, 2019, https://www.internationallawoffice.com/Newsletters/White-Collar-Crime/Japan/Nagashima-Ohno-Tsunematsu/New-plea-bargaining-system-in-practice.

8. Carlos Ghosn and Philippe Riès, *Le temps de la vérité: Carlos Ghosn parle* (Paris: Éditions Grasset & Fasquelle, epub 2020), 113.

9. Hans Greimel and Naoto Okamura, "Legal Fears Led Nissan Exec to Flip on Ghosn," *Automotive News*, January 31, 2021, https://www.autonews.com/legal-file/legal-fears-led-nissan-exec-flip-ghosn.

10. Hans Greimel, "Ghosn Trial Figure a Portrait of Conflict," *Automotive News*, February 14, 2021, https://www.autonews.com/executives/ghosn-trial-figure-portrait-conflict.

11. Greimel, "Ghosn Trial Figure a Portrait of Conflict."

12. Greimel, "Ghosn Trial Figure a Portrait of Conflict."

13. Hans Greimel and Naoto Okamura, "Inspection Scandal Fueled Dissatisfaction," *Automotive News*, November 24, 2018, https://www.autonews.com/article/20181124/OEM02/181129833/inspection-scandal-fueled-dissatisfaction.

CHAPTER 11. JUSTICE JAPAN STYLE

1. Supreme Court of Japan, "Chart 25—Breakdown of Primary Trials—Single Court Judge, Three-Court Judge, Confessions—All District and Summary Courts," 2018, https://www.courts.go.jp/app/files/toukei/625/010625.pdf.

2. Department of Justice, "United States Attorneys' Annual Statistical Report Fiscal Year 2019," https://www.justice.gov/usao/page/file/1285951/downloadtable2a.

3. Public Policy Institute of California, "California's Criminal Courts," October 2015, https://www.ppic.org/publication/californias-criminal-courts/.

4. Nobuhisa Ishizuka, "Why Is Carlos Ghosn Afraid of the Japanese Justice System?" *New York Times*, January 16, 2020, https://www.nytimes.com/2020/01/16/opinion/carlos-ghosn-japan.html.

5. "Extraterritoriality—Japan," Encyclopedia of American Foreign Relations, https://www.americanforeignrelations.com/E-N/Extraterritoriality-Japan.html.

6. Japan Federation of Bar Associations, "Basic Statistics (2019)," www.nichibenren.or.jp/document/statistics/fundamental_statistics2019.html.

7. Setsuko Kamiya, "National Double-Jeopardy Practice Scrutinized," *Japan Times*, December 4, 2012, https://www.japantimes.co.jp/news/2012/12/04/national/double-jeopardy-practice-scrutinized/#.Xww1HoBuLcs.

8. "Prosecutors Hit Back at Ghosn's '8 Hours of Questions' Claim," France 24, January 23, 2020, https://www.france24.com/en/20200123-japan-prosecutors-hit-back-at-ghosn-s-8-hours-of-questions-claim.

9. Carlos Ghosn, interview on Alternative Justice Seminar, April 24, 2020, https://www.youtube.com/watch?v=xkftr7CSYtk&feature=youtu.be/xkftr7CSYtk.

10. Supreme Court of Japan, "Training of Legal Apprentices," https://www.courts.go.jp/english/institute_01/institute/index.html#T1_1.

11. Alternative Justice Congress Day 1, "False Charge Mechanism in Accounting Fraud," April 22, 2020, https://www.youtube.com/watch?v=8aEgdMFEsYU&feature=youtu.be.

12. "Railroaded: One Woman's Battle Against Japan's 'Hostage Justice,'" Nippon.com, March 27, 2019.

13. The Editorial Board, "Examine Prosecution Process," *Japan Times*, October 23, 2010, https://www.japantimes.co.jp/opinion/2010/10/23/editorials/examine-prosecution-process/.

14. "Prosecutors Set to Abandon Appealing Acquittal of Bureaucrat over Postal Discount Scam," *Mainichi Daily News*, September 15, 2010, https://global.factiva.com/ha/default.aspx#./!?&_suid=161339257403302722496819583209.

15. "Maeda Confided in Bosses/Top Prosecutors Failed to Act on Evidence-Tampering Issue," *Daily Yomiuri*, September 23, 2010, https://global.factiva.com/ha/default.aspx#./!?&_suid=161339270647708559317864772398.

16. Public Prosecutors Office, "The Principles of Prosecution," September 28, 2011, http://www.kensatsu.go.jp/content/000128760.pdf.

17. J. Mark Ramseyer and Eric B. Rasmusen, "Why Is the Japanese Conviction Rate So High?" revision of July 12, 2000, http://www.rasmusen.org/published/Rasmusen-01.JLS.jpncon.pdf.

18. Atsushi Yamada, "Alternative Justice Congress Day 1: False Charge Mechanism in Accounting Fraud," Alternative Justice Seminar, April 24, 2020, https://www.youtube.com/watch?v=xkftr7CSYtk&feature=youtu.be/xkftr7CSYtk.

19. Carlos Ghosn, "Horie Takafumi Spoke to Carlos Ghosn in Lebanon," YouTube, March 6, 2020, https://www.youtube.com/watch?v=L8Y8FyJrgvI&feature=youtu.be; https://www.arabnews.jp/en/japan/article_12790.

20. "Railroaded," Nippon.com.

21. "Homicide Rate" (2018), United Nations Office on Drugs and Crime, https://dataunodc.un.org/content/data/homicide/homicide-rate.

22. Sydney School of Public Health, University of Sydney, "United States—Gun Facts, Figures and the Law" (2017), https://www.gunpolicy.org/firearms/region/united-states.

23. Mark Schreiber, "Dealing with Gun Issues in a Nation with Few Guns," *Japan Times*, March 2, 2019, https://www.japantimes.co.jp/news/2019/03/02/national/media-national/dealing-gun-issues-nation-guns/.

24. "Poll Shows the Self-Defense Force the Most-Trusted Organization," Nikkei, January 21, 2019, https://www.nikkei.com/article/DGXMZO40237230Q9A120C1905M00.

CHAPTER 12. GHOSN FIGHTS BACK

1. Kenji Tatsumi, "'Charismatic Businessman' Ghosn Looked Thinner in Court Appearance," *Mainichi*, January 8, 2018, https://mainichi.jp/english/articles/20190108/p2a/oom/ona/011000c.

2. Hans Greimel, "Ghosn's Statement in Tokyo Court," *Automotive News*, January 8, 2019, https://www.autonews.com/executives/ghosns-statement-tokyo-court.

3. Hans Greimel, "Gaunt, Graying Ghosn Protests His Innocence in Court,"*Automotive News Europe*, January 7, 2019, https://www.autonews.com/executives/gaunt-graying-ghosn-protests-his-innocence-court.

4. Greimel, "Ghosn's Statement in Tokyo Court."

5. Hans Griemel and Naoto Okamura, "Ghosn Focuses on Next Rescue: Himself," *Automotive News Europe*, January 13, 2019, https://www.autonews.com/executives/ghosn-focuses-next-rescue-himself.

6. Carole Ghosn, "My Husband, Carlos Ghosn, Is Innocent of It All," *Washington Post*, April 19, 2019, https://www.washingtonpost.com/opinions/global-opinions/my-husband -carlos-ghosn-is-innocent-of-it-all/2019/04/17/57ec43e6-6140-11e9-bfad-36a7eb36cb60_story .html.

7. Agence France-Presse, "Carole Ghosn: Carlos's Wife Puts Her Head Above Parapet," France 24, April 24, 2019, https://www.france24.com/en/20190424-carole-ghosn-carloss -wife-puts-head-above-parapet.

8. Nick Kostov and Sean McLain, "Carole Ghosn, in Defending Her Husband, Takes On Japan's Legal System," *Wall Street Journal*, January 21, 2020, https://www.wsj.com /articles/in-defending-her-husband-carole-ghosn-takes-on-japans-legal-system-11579617889.

9. Kyodo News, "Ghosn's Wife Questioned over Alleged Nissan Fund Misuse," *Nikkei Asian Review*, April 11, 2019, https://asia.nikkei.com/Business/Nissan-s-Ghosn-crisis /Ghosn-s-wife-questioned-over-alleged-Nissan-fund-misuse; Kyodo News, "Ghosn's Son and Daughter Questioned in US at Tokyo Prosecutor's Request," January 9, 2020, https:// english.kyodonews.net/news/2020/01/365bf7fc1089-ghosns-son-daughter-questioned-in -us-at-tokyo-prosecutors-request.html?phrase=East%20Japan%20Railway%20&words=.

10. Hans Greimel, "Ghosn Lawyers Ask Court to Dismiss Charges, Citing Violation of Rights," *Automotive News*, October 24, 2019, https://www.autonews.com/executives /ghosn-lawyers-ask-court-dismiss-charges-citing-violation-rights.

11. Naomi Tajitsu and Tim Kelly, "A Year after Arrest, Ghosn Seeks Trial Date, Access to Evidence," Reuters, November 19, 2019, https://www.reuters.com/article/us-nissan -ghosn/a-year-after-arrest-ghosn-seeks-trial-date-access-to-evidence-idUSKBN1XT150.

12. Gearoid Reidy and Chester Dawson, "Ghosn's Moment of Truth Arrives as Deposed CEO Faces the Press," Bloomberg Quint, January 8, 2020, https://www.bloombergquint .com/business/ghosn-s-moment-of-truth-arrives-as-deposed-ceo-faces-the-press.

13. *United States Securities and Exchange Commission, Plaintiff, v. Carlos Ghosn and Gregory L. Kelly*, 1:19-CV-08798 (United States District Court Southern District of New York, September 23, 2019).

14. Hans Greimel, "Ghosn Getting Fit for the Fight of His Life," *Automotive News*, October 7, 2019, https://www.autonews.com/executives/ghosn-getting-fit-fight-his-life.

CHAPTER 13. ALLIANCE UPHEAVAL

1. Hans Greimel, "With Ghosn Free on Bail, Japan Can't Look Away," *Automotive News*, March 11, 2019, https://www.autonews.com/executives/ghosn-free-bail-japan-cant-look -away.

2. Hans Greimel, "Collateral Damage in Tokyo," *Automotive News*, December 10, 2018, https://www.autonews.com/article/20181210/OEM02/181219968/collateral-damage-in-tokyo.

3. Hans Greimel, "Ford Reduces Mazda Stake to 13%, Raises $540 Million," *Automotive News*, November 18, 2008, https://www.autonews.com/article/20081118/COPY01/311189925 /ford-reduces-mazda-stake-to-13-raises-540-million.

4. Hans Greimel, "How Ford's Partnership with Mazda Unraveled," *Automotive News*, August 24, 2015, https://www.autonews.com/article/20150824/INDUSTRY_ON_TRIAL /308249993/how-ford-s-partnership-with-mazda-unraveled.

5. Hans Greimel, "Volkswagen Must Sell Shares in Suzuki, Court Decides," *Automotive News*, August 30, 2015, https://www.autonews.com/article/20150830/COPY01/308309996 /volkswagen-must-sell-shares-in-suzuki-court-decides.

6. Hans Greimel, "Renault, Nissan, Mitsubishi Defuse Tension and Outline 'New Start,'" *Automotive News*, March 12, 2019, https://www.autonews.com/automakers -suppliers/renault-nissan-mitsubishi-defuse-tension-and-outline-new-start.

7. Hans Greimel, "Renault-FCA Merger Plan Unleashes Fresh Uncertainties on Nissan," *Automotive News*, May 27, 2019, https://www.autonews.com/automakers-suppliers/renault-fca-merger-plan-unleashes-fresh-uncertainties-nissan.

8. Greimel, "Renault-FCA Merger Plan."

9. Luca Ciferri, "Nissan Big Loser If FCA and Renault Merge," *Automotive News Europe*, May 27, 2019, https://europe.autonews.com/blogs/nissan-big-loser-if-fca-and-renault-merge.

10. Hans Greimel, "Renault Chief Endures Nissan Shareholders' Fury," *Automotive News*, July 1, 2019, https://www.autonews.com/executives/renault-chief-endures-nissan-shareholders-fury.

11. PSA Group, press release, July 15, 2015, https://www.groupe-psa.com/en/newsroom/corporate-en/stellantis-le-nom-du-nouveau-groupe-qui-sera-issu-de-la-fusion-de-fca-et-groupe-psa/.

12. Laurence Frost, "Renault Posts Record Earnings, Strengthening Ghosn's Hand," *Automotive News Europe*, February 16, 2018, https://europe.autonews.com/article/20180216/ANE/180219792/renault-posts-record-earnings-strengthening-ghosn-s-hand.

13. Reuters, "Renault Plans $22 Billion 'No Taboos' Cost Cuts After First Loss in Decade," *Automotive News Europe*, February 14, 2020, https://europe.autonews.com/automakers/renault-plans-22-billion-no-taboos-cuts-after-first-loss-decade.

14. Hans Greimel, "Ghosn Regrets What Might Have Been," *Automotive News*, January 12, 2020, https://www.autonews.com/executives/ghosn-regrets-what-might-have-been.

CHAPTER 14. FOREIGN ENTANGLEMENTS

1. Mitch Berlin, "Why There's No Such Thing as a Merger of Equals," *Business Insider*, June 14, 2017, https://www.businessinsider.com/what-are-challenges-with-merger-of-equals-2017-6.

2. Braven Smillie, "Another Japanese Acquisition Gone Bad," Associated Press, May 12, 1995, https://apnews.com/article/75ee1bcd6ba0905a29a02174e0b68844.

3. Fred Hiatt, "Japanese to Buy 51% of Rockefeller Center," *Washington Post*, October 31, 1989, ttps://www.washingtonpost.com/archive/politics/1989/10/31/japanese-to-buy-51-of-rockefeller-center/d6cca3ff-9e5a-4593-b6f0-4f939f464624/.

4. Paul Farhi, "Sony's Surprise: It Says It Overpaid for Columbia," *Washington Post*, November 18, 1994, https://www.washingtonpost.com/archive/business/1994/11/18/sonys-surprise-it-says-it-overpaid-for-columbia/875f545d-2e92-42e1-9e54-207c429aa45c/.

5. Select USA, International Trade Administration, US Department of Commerce, "U.S. Foreign Investment (FDI) Stock, 2019," https://www.selectusa.gov/stock.

6. Kosaku Narioka, "Japan Post to Take $3.6 Billion Write-Down over Toll Holdings," *Wall Street Journal*, April 25, 2017, https://www.wsj.com/articles/japan-post-to-take-3-6-billion-write-down-over-toll-holdings-1493106614.

7. Tom Hals and Jessica DiNapoli, "Toshiba Reaches Deal to Help Resolve Westinghouse Bankruptcy, Rebuild Finances," Reuters, January 17, 2018, https://www.reuters.com/article/us-toshiba-accounting-westinghouse-bankr/toshiba-reaches-deal-to-help-resolve-westinghouse-bankruptcy-rebuild-finances-idUSKBN1F7028.

8. Andrew Ross Sorkin, *Too Big to Fail* (New York: Viking, 2009).

9. Quentin Webb, "Breaking Views—Morgan Stanley Has Paid Off Smartly for MUFG," Reuters, May 16, 2018, https://www.reuters.com/article/us-mufg-results-breakingviews-idUSKCN1IH08C.

10. John Holusha, "Japan's Made-in-America Cars," *New York Times*, March 31, 1985, https://www.nytimes.com/1985/03/31/business/japan-s-made-in-america-cars.html.

11. Japan Automobile Manufacturers Association, "JAMA in America, an Enduring Partnership," May 2019, https://www.jama.org/wp-content/uploads/2019/05/final-report -standard.pdf.

12. Sam Nussey, "SoftBank to Write Down WeWork by $6.6 Billion, Compounding Portfolio Misery," Reuters, April 20, 2020, https://www.reuters.com/article/us-softbank -group-results/softbank-to-write-down-wework-by-6-6-billion-compounding-portfolio -misery-idUSKBN22C011.

13. Lauren Feiner, "SoftBank Values WeWork at $2.9 Billion, Down from $47 Billion a Year Ago," CNBC, May 18, 2020. https://www.cnbc.com/2020/05/18/softbank-ceo-calls -wework-investment-foolish-valuation-falls-to-2point9-billion.html.

14. Organisation for Economic Co-operation and Development, International Direct Investment Statistics 2019, https://read.oecd-ilibrary.org/finance-and-investment/oecd -international-direct-investment-statistics-2019_g2g9fb42-en#page18.

15. T. Boone Pickens, "The Heck with Japanese Business," *Washington Post*, April 28, 1991, https://www.washingtonpost.com/archive/opinions/1991/04/28/the-heck-with -japanese-business/1330da7b-fa0b-416b-93d6-d88a02577d10/.

16. "National Mob Boss Held over Real Estate Fraud," *Japan Times*, May 21, 2001, https://www.japantimes.co.jp/news/2001/05/21/national/mob-boss-held-over-real-estate -fraud/#.Xr5VBoBuLcs.

17. "Vodafone Airtouch Increases Ownership in Japan," Regulatory News Service, press release, October 7, 1999, https://global.factiva.com/ha/default.aspx#./!?&_suid=1613 44056127401222673511927568.

18. Scoop.co.nz, "Cablegate: Why Did Vodafone Fail in Japan?" June 23, 2006, https:// www.scoop.co.nz/stories/WL0606/S01319/cablegate-why-did-vodafone-fail-in-japan .htm.

19. Cassell Bryan-Low, Andrew Morse, and Miho Inada, "Vodafone's Global Ambitions Got Hung Up in Japan," *Wall Street Journal*, March 18, 2006, https://www.wsj.com/articles /SB114264873803102084.

20. "Foreign Direct Investment, Net Inflows (% of GDP) 1981–2019," World Bank, https://data.worldbank.org/indicator/BX.KLT.DINV.WD.GD.ZS?end=2019&start=1981.

21. Kana Inagaki, "Japan Inc. Wakes Up to Investor Activism in Its Own Backyard," *Financial Times*, August 27, 2019, https://www.ft.com/content/03c0cafo-c8a4-11e9-a1f4 -366940iba76f.

22. Naoko Fujimura and Shunichi Ozasa, "Steel Partners Loses Vote to Oust Sapporo Directors," Bloomberg, March 30, 2010, https://www.bloomberg.com/news/articles/2010 -03-30/steel-partners-loses-vote-to-oust-sapporo-directors?sref=KRTu8A3f.

23. Naoko Fujimura, "Steel Partners Sells Entire Stake in Sapporo Holdings," Bloomberg, December 16, 2010, https://www.bloomberg.com/news/articles/2010-12-16 /lichtenstein-s-steel-partners-sells-its-entire-stake-in-sapporo-holdings?sref=KRTu8A3f.

24. Atsuko Fukase, "Cerberus Sells Big Chunk of Seibu Stake," *Wall Street Journal*, May 22, 2015, https://www.wsj.com/articles/cerberus-sells-830-million-chunk-of-seibu -stake-1432279872.

25. Kazuaki Nagata, "Saitama Urges Seibu to Keep Chichibu Line Open," *Japan Times*, March 27, 2013, https://www.japantimes.co.jp/news/2013/03/27/national/saitama-urges -seibu-to-keep-chichibu-line-open/.

26. Olympus Corp., press release, January 11, 2019, https://www.olympus-global.com /ir/data/announcement/2019/contents/ir00001.pdf.

27. Phred Dvorak, "SoftBank to Sell $41 Billion in Assets, Signaling End of Buying Spree," *Wall Street Journal*, March 23, 2020, https://www.wsj.com/articles/softbank-to-sell -41-billion-in-assets-plans-big-share-buyback-11584944934?mod=article_inline.

28. Kosuke Takami, "Japan Names 518 Companies Subject to Tighter Foreign Ownership Rules," *Nikkei Asia*, May 9, 2020, https://asia.nikkei.com/Business/Markets/Japan-names-518-companies-subject-to-tighter-foreign-ownership-rules.

CHAPTER 15. WE SEE ISSUES

1. Special Committee for Improving Governance Report, Nissan Motor Co., March 27, 2019, https://www.nissan-global.com/PDF/190327-01_179.pdf.

2. Hans Greimel, "Nissan Considers Sweeping Reforms in Wake of Ghosn Scandal," *Automotive News*, March 27, 2019, https://www.autonews.com/executives/nissan-considers-sweeping-reforms-wake-ghosn-scandal.

3. Ghosn Carlos and Philippe Riès, *Le Temps de la vérité: Carlos Ghosn parle* (Paris: Éditions Grasset & Fasquelle, epub 2020).

4. Corporate Governance Factbook, Organisation for Economic Co-operation and Development, 2019, www.oecd.org/corporate/corporate-governance-factbook.htm.

5. Hans Greimel, "At Toyota, 'It's Not That Easy' Being a Toyoda," *Automotive News*, June 7, 2019, https://europe.autonews.com/automakers/toyota-its-not-easy-being-toyoda.

6. Hans Greimel, "Toyota Names Most Diverse Board Yet," *Automotive News*, March 9, 2018, https://www.autonews.com/article/20180305/OEM02/180309712/toyota-names-most-diverse-board-yet.

7. K. Moriyasu, "Japan's New Corporate Governance Code Unlocks Opportunities," *Nikkei Asian Review*, June 11, 2015, https://asia.nikkei.com/Business/Japan-s-new-corporate-governance-code-unlocks-opportunities.

8. Masato Kanda, "Corporate Governance Reform in Japan Securities Summit," presentation, March 1, 2016, Japan Securities Dealers Association, http://www.jsda.or.jp/en/activities/international-events/jss2016/05MrKanda_presentation.pdf.

9. Natsuki Yamamoto and Togo Shiraishi, "Nissan's Ghosn Crisis: Renault Agrees to Support Nissan's Management Reform Plan," *Nikkei Asian Review*, June 21, 2019, https://asia.nikkei.com/Business/Nissan-s-Ghosn-crisis/Renault-agrees-to-support-Nissan-s-management-reform-plan.

10. Hans Greimel, "Saikawa Wins Reforms at Nissan, Signals Handover Power," *Automotive News*, June 25, 2019, https://www.autonews.com/automakers-suppliers/saikawa-wins-reforms-nissan-signals-handover-power.

11. Hans Greimel, "Nissan Will Cut 12,500 Jobs after Profit Plunges 99%," *Automotive News*, July 25, 2019, https://www.autonews.com/automakers-suppliers/nissan-will-cut-12500-jobs-after-profit-plunges-99.

12. Hans Greimel, "Help Wanted: An Inspiring CEO," *Automotive News*, September 16, 2019, https://www.autonews.com/executives/help-wanted-inspiring-ceo.

13. "Introduction of Stock-Based Compensation Plan," Nissan Motor Co., press release, August 20, 2020, https://global.nissannews.com/en/releases/release-5f786044eb466dfe0a86a13a52043a3a-200820-02-e.

14. Peter Sigal, "Renault May Replace CEO Bolloré, Reports Say," *Automotive News Europe*, October 8, 2019, https://europe.autonews.com/automakers/renault-may-replace-ceo-bollore-reports-say.

15. Peter Sigal, "Former Renault CEO Denounces Coup Against Him," *Automotive News Europe*, October 10, 2019, https://europe.autonews.com/automakers/former-renault-ceo-denounces-coup-against-him.

16. Peter Sigal, "Renault's New CEO Will Be Paid Less Than Ghosn," *Automotive News Europe*, June 23, 2020, https://europe.autonews.com/automakers/renaults-new-ceo-will-be-paid-less-ghosn.

17. Hans Greimel, "Nissan's Ousted Saikawa Unbowed," *Automotive News*, December 2, 2019, https://www.autonews.com/executives/nissans-ousted-saikawa-unbowed.

CHAPTER 16. SCANDALOUS AFFAIRS

1. National Police Agency, "Lost Property Handling Status," March 27, 2020, https://www.keishicho.metro.tokyo.jp/about_mpd/jokyo_tokei/kakushu/kaikei.html.

2. Report to the Nations, Association of Certified Fraud Examiners, 2018, https://www.acfe.com/report-to-the-nations/2018/Default.aspx.

3. Dow Jones Sustainability World Index, S&P Global, September 23, 2019, https://www.spglobal.com/esg/csa/static/docs/DJSI_Components_World.pdf.

4. "Corporate Scandals," *Japan Times*, https://www.japantimes.co.jp/tag/corporate-scandals/.

5. NHTSA, "U.S. Department of Transportation Releases Results from NHTSA-NASA Study of Unintended Acceleration in Toyota Vehicles," February 8, 2011, https://one.nhtsa.gov/About-NHTSA/Press-Releases/2011/U.S.-Department-of-Transportation-Releases-Results-from-NHTSA%E2%80%93NASA-Study-of-Unintended-Acceleration-in-Toyota-Vehicles.

6. Meagan Parrish, "The 2009 Toyota Accelerator Scandal That Wasn't What It Seemed," Manufacturing.net, August 11, 2016, https://www.manufacturing.net/automotive/blog/13110434/the-2009-toyota-accelerator-scandal-that-wasnt-what-it-seemed.

7. United States Department of Justice, "Justice Department Announces Criminal Charge Against Toyota Motor Corporation and Deferred Prosecution Agreement with $1.2 Billion Financial Penalty," March 19, 2014, https://www.justice.gov/opa/pr/justice-department-announces-criminal-charge-against-toyota-motor-corporation-and-deferred.

8. David Shepardson, "U.S. Asks Judge to Dismiss Toyota Acceleration Case as Monitoring Ends," Reuters, August 9, 2017, https://www.reuters.com/article/us-toyota-settlement-idUSKBN1AO1RK.

9. Hiroko Tabuchi and Christopher Jensen, "Now the Air Bags Are Faulty, Too," *New York Times*, June 23, 2014, https://www.nytimes.com/2014/06/24/business/international/honda-nissan-and-mazda-join-recall-over-faulty-air-bags.html?_r=0; *Automotive News*, "TIMELINE: Takata's Airbag Crisis Began in 2008," June 25, 2017, https://www.autonews.com/article/20170625/OEM10/170629833/timeline-takata-s-airbag-crisis-began-in-2008.

10. Steven Overly, "U.S. Indicts Three Takata Executives, Fines Company $1 Billion in Air-Bag Scandal," January 13, 2017, https://www.washingtonpost.com/news/innovations/wp/2017/01/13/u-s-indicts-three-takata-executives-in-faulty-airbag-scandal/.

11. Yuki Hagiwara and Matthew Campbell, "Mitsubishi Motors' Scandal Was an Accident Waiting to Happen," Bloomberg, May 18, 2016, https://www.bloomberg.com/news/articles/2016-05-18/mitsubishi-motors-scandal-was-an-accident-waiting-to-happen?sref=KRTu8A3f.

12. Hagiwara and Campbell, "Mitsubishi Motors' Scandal."

13. Dennis Elam, Marion Madrigal de Barrera, and Maura Jackson, "Olympus Imaging Fraud Scandal: A Case Study," *American Journal of Business Education*, January 18, 2016, https://clutejournals.com/index.php/AJBE/article/view/9577.

14. Max Nisen, "Michael Woodford Olympus Firing," *Business Insider*, November 27, 2012, https://www.businessinsider.com/michael-woodford-olympus-firing-2012-11.

15. Olympus Corp., "Olympus Corporation Resolved Dismissal of President Michael C. Woodford," press release, October 14, 2011, https://www.olympus-global.com/en/info/2011b/if111014corpe.html.

16. Cesar Bacani, "Olympus Scandal: Bye, Old Guard, Hello . . . Old Guard?" *CFO Innovation*, October 30, 2011, https://www.cfoinnovation.com/olympus-scandal-bye -old-guard-hello-old-guard.

17. Olympus Corp., "Investigation Report," December 6, 2011, https://www.olympus .co.jp/jp/info/2011b/if111206corpj_6.pdf; English summary report at https://www .olympus-global.com/ir/data/announcement/pdf/if111206corpe.pdf.

18. Juro Osawa and Kana Inagaki, "Olympus Results Reveal Cash Crunch," *Wall Street Journal*, December 15, 2011, https://www.wsj.com/articles/SB10001424052970203430404577 097473230925372.

19. "Former Olympus Execs Ordered to Pay Damages in Multibillion Yen Case," *Mainichi*, April 28, 2017, https://mainichi.jp/english/articles/20170428/p2a/00m/0na /003000c.

20. "Medical Equipment Company Will Pay $646 Million for Making Illegal Payments to Doctors and Hospitals," US Department of Justice, March 1, 2016, https://www.justice .gov/opa/pr/medical-equipment-company-will-pay-646-million-making-illegal-payments -doctors-and-hospitals.

21. Olympus Corp., "Notice Concerning Transformation Plan 'Transform Olympus' to Develop Itself as a Truly Global Medtech Company and Change in Representative Director," news release, January 11, 2019, https://www.olympus-global.com/ir/data /announcement/2019/contents/ir00001.pdf.

22. US Securities and Exchange Commission, "In the Matter of Hajime Sagawa, Respondent," February 27, 2015, https://www.sec.gov/litigation/admin/2015/33-9733.pdf.

23. Yoko Kubota and Nobuhiro Kubo, "Panel Clears Audit Firms of Olympus Scandal Blame," Reuters, January 16, 2012, https://www.reuters.com/article/us-olympus-auditors /panel-clears-audit-firms-of-olympus-scandal-blame-idUSTRE80G00620120117.

24. Olympus Corp., "Company Response to Media Reports," press release, October 19, 2011, https://www.olympus-global.com/ir/data/announcement/pdf/nr111019e.pdf.

CHAPTER 17. SHATTERED LEGACY

1. Kenneth Chang, "Quake Moves Japan Closer to U.S. and Alters Earth's Spin," *New York Times*, March 13, 2011, https://www.nytimes.com/2011/03/14/world/asia/14seismic .html.

2. The Reconstruction Agency (Japan), https://www.reconstruction.go.jp/english /topics/GEJE/index.html.

3. Hans Greimel, "Now: No Parts, Crippled Plants," *Automotive News*, March 28, 2011, https://www.autonews.com/article/20110328/OEM01/303289952/now-no-parts-crippled -plants.

4. Hans Greimel, "Ghosn Targets Big U.S. Sales Growth for Nissan," *Automotive News*, October 31, 2011, https://www.autonews.com/article/20111031/OEM01/310319857/ghosn -targets-big-u-s-sales-growth-for-nissan.

5. Carlos Ghosn, "Nissan Midterm Plan" (speech, Nissan Motor Co. media conference, Yokohama, Japan, June 27, 2011).

6. Hans Greimel, "Akio Toyoda Waves Family Flag, Heir Makes Crisis Personal Challenge, *Automotive News*, February 24, 2010, https://www.autonews.com/article /20100224/OEM02/100229940/akio-toyoda-waves-family-flag-heir-makes-crisis-personal -challenge.

7. Hans Greimel, "Ghosn to Nissan: Don't Blame Me for Your Struggles," *Automotive News*, March 9, 2020, https://www.autonews.com/executives/ghosn-nissan-dont-blame -me-your-struggles.

8. Hans Greimel and Naoto Okamura, "Mitsubishi Chief Says 3 Partners Are Stronger Than 1," *Automotive News*, June 24, 2019, https://www.autonews.com/executives /mitsubishi-chief-says-3-partners-are-stronger-1.

9. Peter Sigal, "Why Renault Is Thinking Small," *Automotive News Europe*, June 5, 2020, https://europe.autonews.com/blogs/why-renault-thinking-small.

10. Gilles Guillaume, "Renault CEO Warns Deeper Cost Cuts May Be Needed," *Automotive News*, September 9, 2020, https://www.autonews.com/automakers-suppliers /renault-ceo-warns-deeper-cost-cuts-may-be-needed.

11. John Sotos, "The Trouble with Stair Step Incentives," Sotos LLP, April 23, 2013, Lexology.com, https://www.lexology.com/library/detail.aspx?g=263d604d-62c1-4a79 -a8b5-045ce2aac9bd.

12. Jeremy Anwyl, "Stair-Step Programs, Good or Bad for Business?" Edmunds.com, June 26, 2012, https://www.edmunds.com/industry-center/analysis/stair-step-programs -good-or-bad-for-business.html.

13. Greimel, "Ghosn to Nissan."

14. Hans Greimel, "Nissan Softens Its Targets Through '22," *Automotive News*, November 13, 2017, https://www.autonews.com/article/20171113/RETAIL01/171119926 /nissan-softens-its-targets-through-22.

15. Plante Moran, "Toyota Sweeps Supplier Relations Ranking in Study; Is 'Most Preferred' Customer," Cision PR Newswire, June 22, 2020, https://www.prnewswire .com/news-releases/toyota-sweeps-supplier-relations-rankings-in-study-is-most-preferred -customer-301080323.html.

16. Hans Greimel, "Nissan's Ousted Saikawa Unbowed," *Automotive News*, December 2, 2019, https://www.autonews.com/executives/nissans-ousted-saikawa-unbowed.

17. Hans Greimel, "Nissan's Task: Grow and Solve Quality Issues," *Automotive News*, July 4, 2011, https://www.autonews.com/article/20110704/OEM01/307049978/nissan-s -task-grow-and-solve-quality-issues.

18. Greimel, "Ghosn to Nissan."

CHAPTER 18. JAIL JAPAN STYLE

1. National Police Agency, "Police Detention Administration in Japan," https://www .npa.go.jp/english/ryuchi/Detention_house-Eng_080416.pdf.

2. Bradley Calvin, "How Sir Paul McCartney Endured Prison and Other Hardships," Medium, August 4, 2019, https://medium.com/@thoughtmedley/how-sir-paul-mccartney -endured-prison-and-other-hardships-887db95b28fd.

3. Emiko Jozuka and Yoko Wakatsuki, "This Japanese Man Spent Almost Five Decades on Death Row. He Could Go Back," CNN, March 22, 2020, https://edition.cnn.com /2020/03/21/asia/japan-death-penalty-hakamada-hnk-intl/index.html.

4. Kana Inagaki and Robin Harding, "Fate of Olympus Financier Shines Light on Japanese Legal System," *Financial Times*, June 10, 2019, https://www.ft.com/content /382998a4-81f4-11e9-b592-5fe435b57a3b.

5. Local Expert Group (France), "Pre-Trial Detention in France," Fair Trials International, 7, June 13, 2013, https://www.fairtrials.org/wp-content/uploads/Fair _Trials_International_France_PTD_Communiqu%C3%A9_EN.pdf.

6. Patrick Liu, Ryan Nunn, and Jay Shambaugh, "The Economics of Bail and Pretrial Detention," Hamilton Project, 6, December 2018, https://www.hamiltonproject.org /assets/files/BailFineReform_EA_121818_6PM.pdf.

7. "Prison Conditions in Japan," Human Rights Watch Asia, March 1995, https://www .hrw.org/sites/default/files/reports/JAPAN953.PDF.

8. Johannes Schonherr, "Tokyo Detention House Prison Festival," Japan Visitor, https://www.japanvisitor.com/japanese-festivals/prison-festival.

9. Linda Sieg, Reuters, "Ghosn's Escape May See Japan Impose Stronger Bail Conditions on Defendants," *Japan Times*, January 1, 2020, https://www.japantimes.co.jp /news/2020/01/01/national/crime-legal/ghosn-escape-bail-conditions/#.XyeLwEBuLcs.

CHAPTER 19. GREAT ESCAPE

1. In the Matter of the Extradition of Michael L. Taylor, Case 4:20-mj-01069-DLC (US District Court for the District of Massachusetts, May 20, 2020).

2. In the Matter of the Extradition of Michael L. Taylor.

3. May Jeong, "How Carlos Ghosn Escaped Japan," *Vanity Fair*, July 23, 2020, https:// www.vanityfair.com/news/2020/07/how-carlos-ghosn-escaped-japan.

4. In the Matter of the Extradition of Michael L. Taylor.

5. David Gauthier-Villars, Mark Maremont, Sean McLain, and Nick Kostov, "Carlos Ghosn Sneaked Out of Japan in Box Used for Audio Gear," *Wall Street Journal*, January 3, 2020, https://www.wsj.com/articles/carlos-ghosn-sneaked-out-of-japan-in-box-used-for -audio-gear-11578077647.

6. Bloomberg, "Japan Seeks Interpol Red Notice, Ghosn's Wife Report Says," *Automotive News*, January 20, 2020, https://www.autonews.com/executives/japan -seeks-interpol-red-notice-ghosns-wife-report-says.

7. Hans Greimel and Naoto Okamura, "Tokyo Prosecutors Get Arrest Warrant for Ghosn, Alleged American Accomplices," *Automotive News*, January 30, 2020, https://www .autonews.com/executives/tokyo-prosecutors-get-arrest-warrant-ghosn-alleged-american -accomplices.

8. Hans Greimel, "Nissan Sues Ghosn in Japan for $91 Million," February 12, 2020, *Automotive News*, https://www.autonews.com/executives/nissan-sues-ghosn-japan -91-million.

9. Benoit Van Overstraeten, "Renault Reserves Right to Seek Damages Depending on Ghosn Probe," *Automotive News Europe*, February 25, 2020, https://europe.autonews.com /automakers/renault-reserves-right-seek-damages-depending-ghosn-probe.

10. Reuters, "French Prosecutors Step Up Ghosn Probe over Palace Party, Report Says," *Automotive News Europe*, February 20, 2020, https://europe.autonews.com/automakers /french-prosecutors-step-ghosn-probe-over-palace-party-report-says.

11. Hans Greimel, "Ghosn Legal Team Plans 'Massive' Offensive," *Automotive News*, January 13, 2020, https://www.autonews.com/executives/ghosn-legal-team-plans -massive-offensive.

12. "Ghosn Postpones Suit Seeking Retirement Pay from Renault," Radio France Internationale, February 21, 2020, https://www.rfi.fr/en/wires/20200221-ghosn-postpones -suit-seeking-retirement-pay-renault.

13. Reuters, "In Dutch Court, Ghosn Seeks Release of Internal Documents," February 10, 2020, https://jp.reuters.com/article/renault-nissan-ghosn/in-dutch-court-ghosn-seeks -release-of-internal-documents-idUSL8N2AA1WQ.

14. Hans Greimel, "Ghosn Details 'Plot' to Oust Him, Condemns Nissan Executives in Japan," *Automotive News*, January 8, 2020, https://www.autonews.com/executives /ghosn-details-plot-oust-him-condemns-nissan-executives-japan.

15. Takashi Takano, "Thinking about Criminal Trials: Takashi Takano@blog," Livedoor Blog, January 4, 2020, http://blog.livedoor.jp/plltakano/.

16. "Full Transcript of Al-Arabiya's Exclusive Interview with Nissan Ex-boss Carlos Ghosn," Al-Arabiya, July 11, 2020, https://english.alarabiya.net/en/amp

/features/2020/07/11/Full-transcript-of-Al-Arabiya-s-exclusive-interview-with-Nissan
-ex-boss-Carlos-Ghosn.

17. Ezgi Erkoyun, "Suspects in Ghosn's Escape Stand Trial in Turkey," July 3, 2020, *Automotive News Europe*, https://europe.autonews.com/automakers/suspects-ghosns -escape-stand-trial-turkey.

18. David Yaffe-Bellamy, "Ghosn Probe Finds Daughter Met with Accused Escape Accomplice," *Automotive News Europe*, July 17, 2020, https://europe.autonews.com /automakers/ghosn-probe-finds-daughter-met-accused-escape-accomplice.

19. In the Matter of the Extradition of Michael L. Taylor, 4:20-mj-01069-DLC, Exhibit J, Record of Statements, Testimony of Kayoko Tokunaga, United States District Court for the District of Massachusetts, August 7, 2020.

20. In the Matter of the Extradition of Michael L. Taylor, Exhibit K, Record of Statements, Testimony of Narikuni Kawada, (United States District Court for the District of Massachusetts), August 7, 2020, 4:20-mj-01069-DLC.

21. Ali Itani, "Was This Carlos Ghosn's Final Trip of 2019?," *Arab News Japan*, January 1, 2020, https://www.arabnews.jp/en/japan/article_7844/.

22. Phil LeBeau, Kathy Liu, and Meghan Reeder, "Carlos Ghosn's $350,000 Getaway Flight," CNBC, January 6, 2020, updated January 8, 2020, https://www.cnbc.com /2020/01/07/nissan-ex-chairman-carlos-ghosns-350000-getaway-flight.html#:~:text=This %20music%20equipment%20case%20found,the%20bottom%20of%20the%20case.

23. Ezgi Erkoyun, "Suspects in Ghosn's Escape Stand Trial in Turkey," *Automotive News Europe*, July 3, 2020, https://europe.autonews.com/automakers/suspects-ghosns-escape -stand-trial-turkey.

24. Eric Knecht and Laila Bassam, "Lebanon and Japan Have 40 Days to Agree on Ghosn's Fate," *Automotive News Europe*, January 24, 2020, https://europe.autonews.com /automakers/lebanon-and-japan-have-40-days-agree-ghosns-fate.

25. Nate Raymond and David Shepardson, "US Arrests 2 Men Wanted in Japan for Ghosn's Escape," *Automotive News*, May 20, 2020, https://www.autonews.com/executives /us-arrests-2-men-wanted-japan-ghosn-escape.

26. The Coinbase cryptocurrency is from "Exhibit B" in In the Matter of the Extradition of Michael L. Taylor, Case No. 20-mj-1069-DLC; In the Matter of the Extradition of Peter M. Taylor 2020, Case No. 20-mj-1070-DLC (United States District Court for the District of Massachusetts); the $860,000 wire transfer (actually $862,500) is from "Documents 1–4" of In the Matter of the Extradition of Michael L. Taylor; In the Matter of the Extradition of Peter M. Taylor 2020.

27. Janelle Lawrence and David Yaffe-Bellany, "Ghosn's Son Paid Accomplice, Suspect Prosecutors Say," *Automotive News*, July 23, 2020, https://www.autonews.com/executives /ghosns-son-paid-accomplice-suspect-prosecutors-say.

28. David Yaffe-Bellany (Bloomberg News), "Escape Artist Accused of Freeing Carlos Ghosn Can't Evade Reckoning in Japan," *Automotive News*, March 2, 2021, https://www .autonews.com/feature/escape-artist-accused-freeing-carlos-ghosn-cant-evade-reckoning -japan. River Davis (Bloomberg News), "Japan scores Rare Win with Extradition of Alleged Carlos Ghosn Accomplices," *Japan Times*, March 3, 2021, https://www.japantimes .co.jp/news/2021/03/03/national/crime-legal/ghosn-escape-extradition/.

29. Reuters, "Turkish Court Convicts Executive, Two Pilots in Ghosn Escape Trial," *Automotive News Europe*, February 24, 2021, https://europe.autonews.com/automakers /turkish-court-convicts-executive-two-pilots-ghosn-escape-trial.

30. Editorial Board, "The Carlos Ghosn Experience," *Wall Street Journal*, December 31, 2019, https://www.wsj.com/articles/the-carlos-ghosn-experience-11577826902?mod =article_inline.

31. Isabel Reynolds and Emi Nobuhiro, "Japan Justice Minister Vows She'll Never Give Up on Ghosn Trial," Bloomberg, February 12, 2020, https://www.bloomberg.com /news/articles/2020-02-11/japan-justice-minister-vows-she-ll-never-give-up-on-ghosn -trial.

CHAPTER 20. THE FORGOTTEN MAN

1. Richard Walker, "U.S. UAW Says Nissan Pressing Anti-Union Line," Reuters News, July 26, 1989, Factivahttps://global.factiva.com/ha/default.aspx#./!?&_suid=1613444591018 07543653814868068.

2. Harry Bernstein, "Defeat at Nissan a Setback, but Not Devastating to UAW," *Los Angeles Times*, August 8, 1989, Factiva, ttps://global.factiva.com/ha/default.aspx#./!?& _suid=16134447096470516185607678453.

3. Danielle Szatkowski, "Who Is Carlos Ghosn's Alleged Co-conspirator, Greg Kelly?" *Automotive News*, November 20, 2018, https://www.autonews.com/article/20181120 /OEM02/181129981/what-we-know-about-ghosn-s-alleged-american-co-conspirator-greg -kelly#:~:text=Greg%20Kelly%2C%2062%2C%20joined%20Nissan,created%20by%20 Chairman%20Carlos%20Ghosn.

4. Amy Chozick and Motoko Rich, "Carlos Ghosn and Nissan Board Member May Soon Leave Japanese Jail," *New York Times*, December 20, 2018, https://www.nytimes .com/2018/12/20/business/nissan-greg-kelly.html.

5. Sen. Roger Wicker, Sen. Lamar Alexander, and Sen. Marsha Blackburn, "Greg Kelly: U.S. Hostage of Japanese Justice," RealClearPolitics, March 10, 2020, https://www .realclearpolitics.com/articles/2020/03/10/greg_kelly_us_hostage_of_japanese_justice .html.

6. U.S. Securities and Exchange Commission, "SEC Charges Nissan, Former CEO, and Former Director with Fraudulently Concealing from Investors More Than $140 Million of Compensation and Retirement Benefits," press release, September 23, 2019, https://www .sec.gov/litigation/litreleases/2019/lr24606.htm.

7. Hans Greimel and Naoto Okamura, "Execs Sought Ways to Cloak Ghosn's Pay, Witness Says," *Automotive News*, October 18, 2020, https://www.autonews.com/executives /execs-sought-ways-cloak-ghosns-pay-witness-says.

8. The Editorial Board, "Carlos Ghosn, Victim or Villain?" *New York Times*, January 8, 2020, https://www.nytimes.com/2020/01/08/opinion/carlos-ghosn-escape-japan.html.

9. The Editorial Board, "Ghosn, Baby, Ghosn," *Wall Street Journal*, January 8, 2020, https://www.wsj.com/articles/ghosn-baby-ghosn-11578528745.

10. Takayuki Inoue and John Lane, "New Plea-Bargaining System in Practice," *International Law Office*, August 12, 2019, https://www.internationallawoffice.com /Newsletters/White-Collar-Crime/Japan/Nagashima-Ohno-Tsunematsu/New-plea -bargaining-system-in-practice.

11. Jeffrey Sonnenfeld, "Gone Ghosn: Caveats for Global Commerce," *Chief Executive*, January 2, 2020, https://chiefexecutive.net/gone-ghosn-caveats-for-global-commerce/.

12. Agence France-Presse, "Japan Not Prosecuting American Toyota Exec in Drug Case: Reports," *Industry Week*, July 7, 2015, https://www.industryweek.com/leadership /companies-executives/article/21965510/japan-wont-prosecute-us-toyota-exec-in-drug-case -reports#:~:text=The%20arrest%20of%20Toyota%27s%20most,was%20intercepted%20 at%20the%20airport.

13. Kyodo News, "US Toyota Exec 'Asked Father to Mail' Controlled Painkiller," *Japan Times*, June 25, 2015, https://www.japantimes.co.jp/news/2015/06/25/national/crime-legal /u-s-toyota-exec-asked-father-mail-controlled-painkiller/.

14. Kyodo News, "Arrested Toyota Exec Didn't Need Painkiller, Medical Checkup Finds," *Japan Times*, June 20, 2015, https://www.japantimes.co.jp/news/2015/06/20 /national/crime-legal/arrested-toyota-exec-didnt-need-painkiller-medical-checkup-finds/.

15. David Shephardson, "Ford Recall of 3 Million Vehicles to Cost $610 million," Reuters, *Automotive News*, Jan. 21, 2021, https://www.autonews.com/regulation-safety /ford-recall-3-million-vehicles-cost-610-million. Philip Nussel, "Japan Throws Stones at Ghosn from Glass House," *Automotive News*, January 11, 2020, https://www.autonews .com/commentary/japan-throws-stones-ghosn-glass-house.

16. Hans Greimel, "Confessions of a Price Fixer," *Automotive News*, November 16, 2014, https://www.autonews.com/article/20141116/OEM10/311179961/confessions-of-a-price -fixer.

CHAPTER 21. COURSE CORRECTION

1. "Volkswagen Group Records Higher Deliveries in 2019," Volkswagen Aktiengesellschaft, January 14, 2020, https://www.volkswagenag.com/en/news/2020 /01/volkswagen-group-records-higher-deliveries-in-2019.html.

2. "Here Are (Nearly) 100 EVs Headed to the U.S. through 2024," *Automotive News*, October 4, 2020, https://www.autonews.com/future-product/here-are-nearly-100-evs -headed-us-through-2024.

3. Reuters, "New-Energy Vehicles Make Major Inroads, Engineer Group Predicts," *Automotive News*, October 29, 2020, https://www.autonews.com/china/new-energy -vehicles-make-major-inroads-engineer-group-predicts.

4. "VW Increases Spending on Electric Self-Driving Cars," *Automotive News Europe*, November 13, 2020, https://europe.autonews.com/automakers/vw-increases-spending -electric-self-driving-cars.

5. H. Lutz, "GM Ups EV Spending, Says 40 U.S. Lineup Electric in 2025," *Automotive News*, November 19, 2020, https://www.autonews.com/future-product/gm-ups-ev -spending-says-40-us-lineup-electric-2025.

6. LMC Electrification Automotive Sector Impact Report, "Global Personal Vehicle Outlook* by xEV Technology Type," *LMC Automotive*, October 20, 2020, https://lmc-auto .com/wp-content/uploads/2020/10/LMC-ELECTRIFICATION-AUTOMOTIVE-SECTOR -IMPACT-REPORT-20TH-OCTOBER-2020.pdf?utm_source=LMC+Automotive&utm _campaign=b32b37c315-EMAIL_CAMPAIGN_2020_04_20_02_52_COPY_01&utm _medium=email&utm_term=0_ea028aeefa-b32b.

7. Philip Nussel, "Japan Throws Stones at Ghosn from Glass House," *Automotive News*, January 11, 2020, https://www.autonews.com/commentary/japan-throws-stones-ghosn -glass-house.

8. Jiji Press English News Service, "SESC Seeks Punishment against U.S. Brokerage Instinet," October 12, 1998, Factiva, https://global.factiva.com/ha/default.aspx#./!?& _suid=16138917913630340418748611461.

9. Saki Masuda, "Japan's Boards Evolve as Outside Directors Occupy 30% of Seats," *Nikkei*, October 2, 2019, https://asia.nikkei.com/Business/Business-trends/Japan-s-boards -evolve-as-outside-directors-occupy-30-of-seats.

10. Matthew Campbell, Kae Inoue, and Reed Stevenson, "With Carlos Ghosn Set to Bare All, Nissan Prepares Its Offensive," Bloomberg News, January 7, 2020, https://www .bloomberg.com/news/articles/2020-01-07/as-ghosn-prepares-to-bare-all-nissan-makes -plans-to-strike-back?sref=KRTu8A3f.

11. "On Japan's Criminal Justice," Japan Ministry of Justice Webinar, September 10, 2020.

12. Peter Landers, "Two Years After Ghosn's Arrest, Another Foreign CEO Takes a Chance on Japan," *Wall Street Journal*, October 23, 2020, https://www.wsj.com/articles/two-years-after-ghosns-arrest-another-foreign-ceo-takes-a-chance-on-japan-11603448884.

13. Isabel Reynolds and Emi Nobuhiro (Bloomberg News), "Japan Looks to Lure Hong Kong's Finance Workers Following Security Law," *Japan Times*, July 1, 2020. https://www.japantimes.co.jp/news/2020/07/01/business/japan-hong-kong-finance-workers/.

INDEX

ABOUT THE AUTHORS

HANS GREIMEL is an award-winning American business journalist who covers Japanese, Korean, and other Asian automakers from Tokyo as the Asia editor at *Automotive News*. Greimel has written about Nissan for more than a decade and interviewed Carlos Ghosn multiple times over that period. Greimel also flew to Beirut, Lebanon, in January 2020 to attend Ghosn's first press conference after his stunning escape from Japan. Greimel's coverage of the Ghosn scandal for *Automotive News* won the 2019 Folio Eddie Award in the category of Best Series of Articles. Greimel has reported from nineteen countries on four continents. Prior to joining *Automotive News*, Greimel was a foreign correspondent with the Associated Press, with postings in Japan, South Korea, and Germany. Greimel's prize-winning work includes his coverage of the arrest of Carlos Ghosn, the rise of China's auto industry, the leadership style of Toyota president Akio Toyoda, Toyota's unintended acceleration crisis, the 2011 earthquake-tsunami in Japan, and a groundbreaking exposé of rampant price fixing among Japanese auto parts suppliers. Greimel has been featured as a global automotive industry expert, both in English and Japanese, for international broadcasters, including the BBC, ABC, Bloomberg TV, TV Tokyo, Al Jazeera, and Reuters TV, as well as the Japanese networks NHK and TBS. Born near Detroit, Michigan, Greimel has a bachelor's degree in political science and philosophy from the University of Michigan and a master's degree in international affairs from Columbia University in New York.

WILLIAM SPOSATO is a Tokyo-based writer and commentator with more than twenty years of experience specializing in Japan's economy and foreign relations. He currently reports on Japan-related issues as a contributor to *Foreign Policy* magazine. Previously, he was deputy bureau chief, Tokyo, for Dow Jones/the *Wall Street Journal* and held a number of roles at the Reuters news agency over a sixteen-year career that included serving as the chief correspondent and bureau chief in New York and as the bureau chief and editor for Tokyo. He moved from Japan in 2002 to be editor for the countries of South Asia, based in Mumbai, India. Sposato also worked for five years as a radio producer, writer and editor for CBS News in New York. He began his career as a freelance writer and radio reporter in London. In addition to his work in journalism, Sposato spent five years as a partner at the Kreab/Gavin Anderson communications consultancy in Tokyo and continues to advise clients in Japan on issues related to communications training and the news media. In addition, he teaches on the media and society for Japanese universities, including Sophia University and the Tokyo University of Foreign Studies. He is a native of the New York area and a graduate of Stanford University, where he received a bachelor's degree in economics.